the **grand circle** tour

MICHAEL **ROYEA**

the **grand circle** tour

a travel and reference guide to the
american southwest and the **ancestral puebloans**

THE COUNTRYMAN PRESS
WOODSTOCK, VERMONT

Maps, photographs, and illustrations by the author unless otherwise noted.

Part 1 (pages xvi-1): Source: http://www.loc.gov/item/99446198
Indian Reservations west of the Mississippi River. Library of Congress, Geography and Map Division.

Part 2 (pages 394-395): Source: http://www.loc.gov/pictures/item/96514482
Navajo riders in Canyon de Chelly, c. 1904. Library of Congress, Prints & Photographs Division, Edward S. Curtis Collection, LC-USZ62-116676

Book design and composition by S. E. Livingston

The Grand Circle Tour
ISBN 978-1-58157-254-4

Published by The Countryman Press, P.O. Box 748, Woodstock, VT 05091
Distributed by W. W. Norton & Company, Inc., 500 Fifth Avenue, New York, NY 10110
Printed in the United States of America

10 9 8 7 6 5 4 3 2 1

Contents

Introduction

The American Southwest is a vast area stretching from Texas to California, but the Grand Circle Tour concentrates on the region inhabited by the Ancestral Puebloans: northwestern New Mexico, northern Arizona, southern Utah, and southwestern Colorado. This is often referred to as the Four Corners, the place at which the four states meet at a common point, or the Colorado Plateau Region (see Map 1).

This is one of the most spectacular regions in the world, with a great geological diversity in a relatively small area. Most sites are only a day's drive or less from the Four Corners. It is a marvel of geologic variety from the depths of the Grand Canyon, where the rocks are 2 billion years old, to badlands, mountain ranges, and a volcano that is less than a thousand years old.

And then there is the archaeology. One of the greatest civilizations north of Mexico lived and thrived in this region, a fact that is sometimes difficult to believe when one sees the landscape of today. The Ancestral Puebloans (Anasazi) have left their mark in even the most remote areas of the Southwest, from pueblos with only a few rooms to the massive complexes found at Chaco Canyon. Estimates of the number of sites range into the tens of thousands.

For more than one thousand years, the people inhabited the Colorado Plateau and made the desert bloom using their knowledge and skill, struggling in an environment that is marginal at best, unforgiving at worst. They built houses and towns, irrigation systems and roads, created ceramics and jewelry, celebrated their religion and observed the heavens, and, in general, led a peaceful existence until the forces of nature, and European contact, changed their world forever.

The Southwest is an archaeologist's and tourist's paradise, with so many sites that are easy to find and gain access to. Most can be visited by car. With a choice of sites from large to small, simple to complex, anyone can enjoy the experience of visiting these places and seeing the remains of this great civilization. However, this experience is enhanced by a better understanding of the past and knowledge of the present, which is where this guide comes in.

The first part is a guide to the various sites, archaeological, geological, and scenic, on the Grand Circle Tour, which encompasses the major, and many minor, places throughout the region and can be completed in two weeks. As the tour is in a circle, it may be started at any point and in either direction, and, if time is a factor, only a small section can be utilized, completing the tour over several trips.

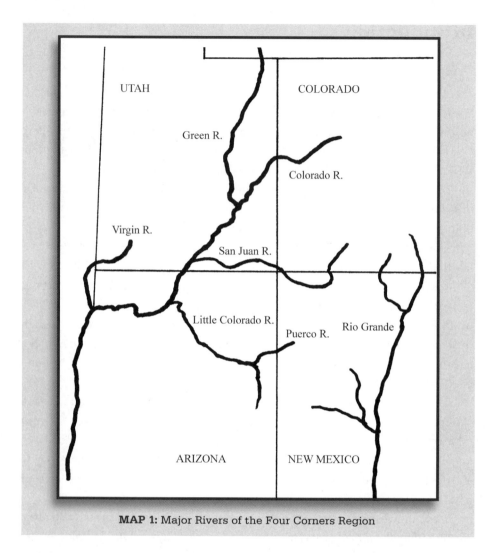

MAP 1: Major Rivers of the Four Corners Region

The second part is an overview of the history of Native American habitation in the region from around 10,000 B.C. to the present, as well as a quick reference guide that covers geology, housing, ceramics, and rock art, among other topics.

The Southwest is a wonderful place to visit but it can be difficult, as it is spread out, sparsely populated, with few roads in some areas and many sites that are not well known. Everyone has heard of the Grand Canyon, but how many know that there are hundreds of ancient sites on the South Rim of the Canyon, including one open to the public, or have heard of Edge of the Cedars in southeastern Utah, which contains one of the best collections of pottery in the Southwest, or Red Cliffs, an obscure Virgin pueblo? This guide will help you get the most out of any visit to this enchanting land, whether this is your first trip or one of many.

The term "Anasazi" has become controversial recently, thus I use the term "Ancestral Puebloan" because this version has come to be generally accepted by Native Americans and the Park Service. However, it is not the perfect replacement for the use of "Anasazi" because it too carries with it remnants of history—not least of which is the Spanish conquest of the Americas that was arguably more detrimental to those ancient peoples than what happened between tribes.

Most of the sites in the book are open all year, though a few are seasonal. The National Parks are generally open from dawn to dusk but monuments and state-run sites have varying hours of operation. Most facilities open by 8 AM in the summer and 9 AM in the winter. I give opening/closing times for most sites in the book but these are subject to change and should be considered general. It is best to check the websites or call if arriving early or late.

Quick Timeline Reference

PERIOD	YEARS
Paleo-Indian	10,000–5500 B.C.
Archaic	5500–100 B.C.
BM I	[no longer used]
BM II	100 B.C.–A.D. 500
BM III	A.D. 500–700
P I	A.D. 700–900
P II	A.D. 900–1100
P III	A.D. 1100–1300
P IV	A.D. 1300–1540
P V	A.D. 1540–present

Long House, west end, Wetherill Mesa, Mesa Verde

Using This Guide

The Grand Circle Tour is based upon a travel course for university students that I teach at Bishop's University in Quebec. The course focuses on Native American history, culture, and archaeological sites in the Southwest. The main tour takes two weeks, in which you will visit all of the major national parks in the region, six in total, as well as 16 archaeological sites (Mesa Verde is both a national park and an archaeological site). The tour begins in Albuquerque, New Mexico, and travels clockwise, which is how the guide is laid out; but, being a circle, it may be followed in either direction.

Main sites are numbered with directions to each one, what to see, and how to make the best use of your time. Included for each is a detailed guide, trails with a rating of the difficulty level, hints and precautions, as well as detailed maps for most sites. There are also suggestions for which towns are best to stay in to save mileage and time; however, I do not list specific motels or restaurants, as there are many listings to be found on the Internet or through a travel agent, or by contacting a Chamber of Commerce in the region. Another good source is the Grand Circle Association at www.grandcircle.org

TRAIL RATINGS

The purpose of a rating system for the trails is to give an idea of the ease or difficulty of each and takes into consideration the total distance, conditions of the trail, the time of year, and the elevation change.

Easy: These are generally flat with no hills or stairs, short in length, which is less than ½ hour to complete, round-trip, often paved, and sometimes wheelchair accessible.

Moderate: These trails are longer and/or contain some changes in elevation, but still should not be any problem for most people. Most of the trails on the tour are either easy or moderate.

Difficult: These trails are longer, usually requiring at least an hour or more, with several changes in elevation. They may also include rocky stretches and steep drop-offs along the trail edge.

Very difficult: There are not many trails in this category. These are long and/or steep and rocky and should not be attempted unless you are in good physical condition and used to hiking long distances.

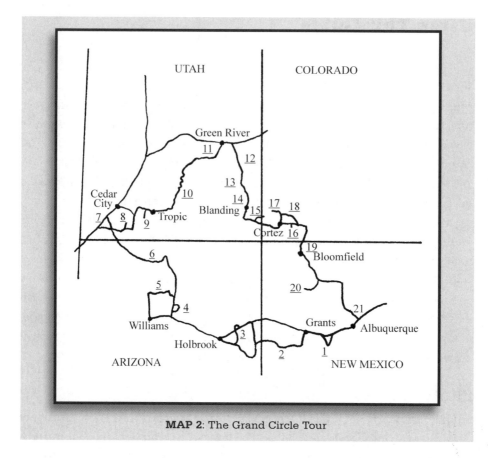

MAP 2: The Grand Circle Tour

THE GRAND CIRCLE TOUR

Part 1 of the tour is divided into 14 days. There are 21 numbered primary places to visit on the main tour, plus another 20 unnumbered places within the circle. The tour sites are listed in order (beginning from Albuquerque) with the numbered tour sites described first, followed by the other sites in the vicinity. You can follow the Grand Circle Tour or use this as a standard travel guide.

All the places are described in the guide, along with directions, what to see, and how to better appreciate each one. Some are small and can be seen in less than ½ hour, whereas others could be explored for days, though a maximum of one day is calculated for the tours offered in this guide. Map 1 (page viii) illustrates the four states and the major river systems, Map 2 shows the overall tour with the 21 numbered sites; Maps 3–6 (pages xiii–xiv) show the individual states and include highway numbers, the main sites, all the extra sites, and also some towns. The maps are not to scale nor do they show distances (most distances are given in the travel sections) or all the

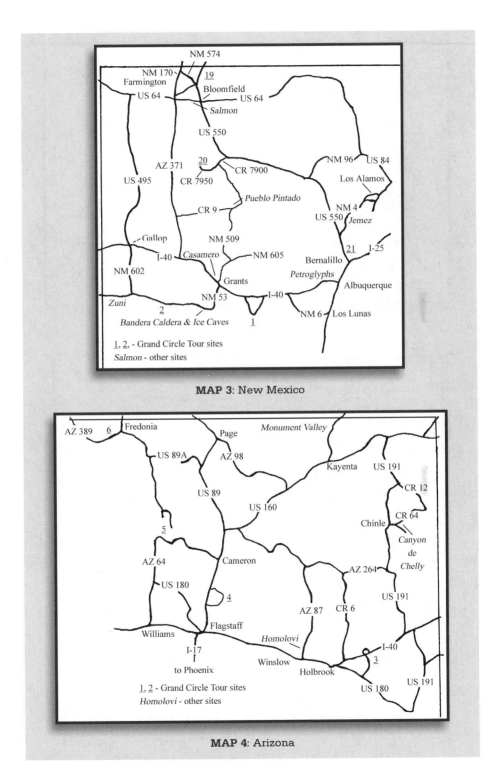

MAP 3: New Mexico

MAP 4: Arizona

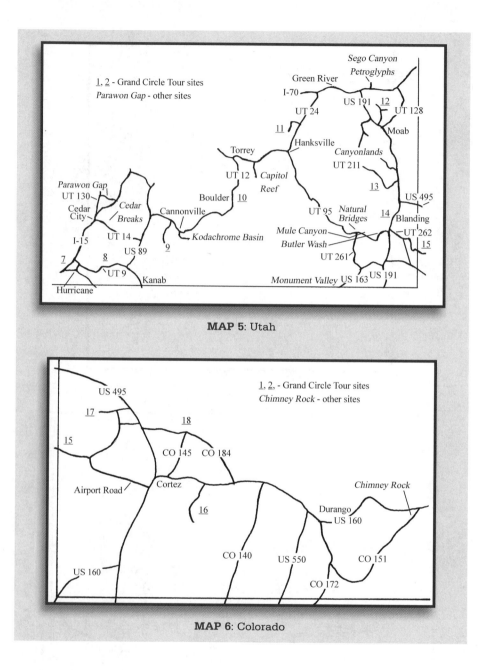

MAP 5: Utah

MAP 6: Colorado

roads, so it is recommended that you also use an atlas or state maps. **NOTE:** GPS can be unreliable in some of the desolate areas of the Colorado Plateau.

Part 2 contains a timeline for the Ancestral Puebloans, their history, several additional topics in alphabetical order, and a glossary of terms.

NOTE: The plans and maps are not to scale and the archaeological site plans do not show all rooms nor which areas are excavated or not. On all plans and maps, north is toward the top of the page unless otherwise indicated.

WEATHER

The Colorado Plateau contains a great variety geographically, but most is rated as the high desert and receives very little rain or snow during the year and is prone to long periods of drought. In the summer, from late May to early September, temperatures are commonly in the upper 90s (30s C) and even surpass 100°F (38°C) in some areas, with thunderstorms in July and August that can cause flash flooding. Winters, as much of the plateau is very high in elevation, can be cold and snowy; some areas are closed during this season, though most stay open year-round and are only closed during the occasional storm. It is best to check local road conditions before attempting some of the routes. Spring and fall are ideal times to travel in the Southwest, as the weather is usually milder, there is less chance for rain, and the sites are much less crowded. But even at these times, some of the roads in the higher passes may be closed, and a few sites do not open until the end of May.

The relative humidity remains low even if the temperature is cool so it is important to drink plenty of water and carry it with you at all times, even for a short hike. Dehydration is a common, and dangerous, condition that is easily avoided by simply drinking water throughout the day. Symptoms of dehydration include extreme thirst, leg cramps, nausea and/or dizziness, headache, disorientation, fainting, or coma. It can lead to death.

BE CONSIDERATE

When visiting archaeological sites, it is important to follow a few simple rules, which are in fact the law

- Never collect anything or move any objects, do not sit, stand, or crawl over walls.
- Do not touch rock art or deface it in any way.
- Report any violations to a ranger or staff member immediately.
- These sites are considered sacred ground so be respectful when visiting.
- Remember, the sites belong to us all and it is our duty to protect them.

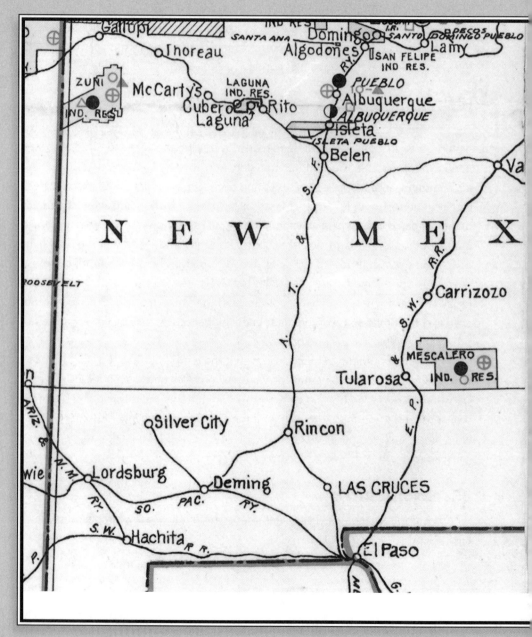

Office of Indian Affairs map of Indian Reservations West of the Mississippi, circa 1923.

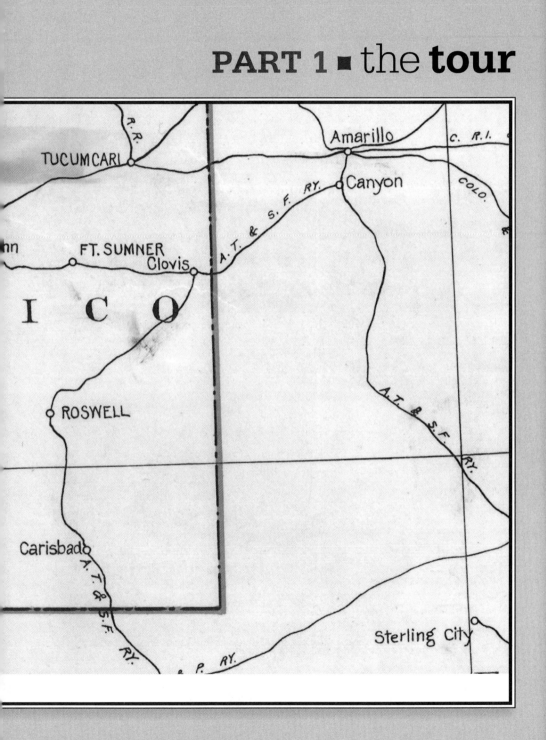

day 1

Acoma
New Mexico

The pueblo of Sky City, one of the
oldest continuously inhabited towns in
North America, sits on a high mesa on
the Acoma reservation and is private
land. It is not in the parks system,
either state or federal.

1. Acoma

GETTING THERE: From the Sunport (airport) in Albuquerque, follow I-25 North to I-40 West and proceed to exit 108 (60 miles [96 km]) for Acoma/Sky City, then continue south (a left turn at the end of the exit ramp) for 11 miles (18 km) to the visitors center. For an alternate route, that is more scenic and completely avoids driving through Albuquerque, head south on I-25 from the Sunport to exit 203 for NM 6 at Los Lunas and turn right at the red light. Follow NM 6 until it reaches I-40, then head west to exit 108. This route is about 10 miles (16 km) longer.

If you are driving on I-40 eastbound from Grants, take exit 102 and follow the signs for Sky City (to the south, or right) to the visitors center.

THINGS YOU NEED TO KNOW: Acoma or, as it is more commonly known, Sky City, is on the Acoma Pueblo Reservation and is controlled by the Acoma people. Photography is not allowed on the reservation (you will see signs next to the roads), except for Sky City, for which you must purchase a permit and attach a tag to your camera. The permit must be purchased at the visitors center before going onto the mesa. You can tour Sky City but only with an Acoma guide; again, the arrangements must be made at the visitors center. The tours are offered almost every day of the year and depart at different times, depending on the season. Winter hours are 9:30 AM to 5 PM; summer, 9 AM to 7 PM. Amenities include a museum, gift shop/bookstore, and restaurant in the visitors center. For more information, phone 800-747-0181 or visit www.acomaskycity.org. Call ahead for tour times.

TOURING ACOMA

After exiting from the freeway, you will drive past the casino and continue south through town and out into the desert. One of the first things that you come upon is the Enchanted Mesa on the left-hand side of the road, which rises up out of the surrounding flat desert. Just beyond this is the Sky City mesa, which is over 370 feet (112 m) high. At first it appears to be just another large hunk of rock protruding toward the sky, but as you draw nearer, the outlines of buildings begin to emerge, the same scene the Spanish observed over 400 years ago (see History of Acoma, page 6). The large building coming up on your right is the visitors center, where you must stop; you are not allowed to drive onto the mesa.

Inside, you buy the tickets for the guided tour and a permit for each camera. Call or check the website for prices. Small buses leave the parking lot with a guide on board, drive up the steep, winding road, and stop in a plaza near the church. The tour takes you into the church, San Estevan del Rey. No pictures are allowed inside the church or of the cemetery in front. You proceed around the village past many displays

San Estevan del Rey Mission, Sky City

of pottery and other artisan objects for sale. These are made by the Acoma people. Most of the time you may have an opportunity to talk to the artists or their family members. The guide gives you the history of the Pueblo and interesting insights into Pueblo culture. At the end of the tour, you have the option of riding the bus back to the visitors center or walking back by going down the original trail that was used before the construction of the road. This trail is not very long—it takes about 15 minutes—but the trip down from the mesa to the bottom is steep, slippery in places, and full of large rocks and high steps, so caution is recommended.

Around 30 people live in Sky City but most spend the night out of town, when Acoma has no electricity or running water. Visitors are not allowed to wander around the town without a guide nor enter any buildings unless invited. Gratuities are accepted by the guides.

From the visitors center you can return to I-40 the same way you came or turn right out of the parking lot and follow the signs back to the highway. At the T, if you turn left instead of right, which is the direction to I-40, you can follow an old road that goes under the freeway and on to Grants, but be aware that there are no signs along the way.

Once back on I-40, continue west to exit 85 for Grants, which has many motels and restaurants and is a good location to stay the first night. With the detour to Acoma it is about 100 miles (160 km) from the airport at Albuquerque to Grants.

HISTORY OF ACOMA

Acoma means "a place that always was" and tribal legend states that it has been inhabited from the beginning. Archaeological evidence shows that the mesa was occupied from at least A.D. 1200. Sky City is believed to be the oldest continually inhabited town in North America, though the inhabitants of Taos Pueblo make the same claim. Sky City is built on bedrock and there has not been much accumulation of debris over time, so this makes it more difficult for archaeologists to determine earlier dates. It probably was occupied well before A.D. 1000.

The ancestry of the Acoma peoples is unknown. Archaeologists think they migrated from Mesa Verde, though some evidence disputes this and places them here much earlier, as the people themselves believe. These stories claim that the Acoma welcomed migrating peoples to their lands, which would probably have been when Mesa Verde was abandoned in the late A.D. 1200s. The Acoma farmed in the valley below the mesa and along the nearby San Jose River, where they had set up irrigation for their crops. Along with the permanent settlements, they constructed farmhouses next to their fields where they would stay to tend the crops and protect them from animals and intruders. Many of these remains have been found.

First contact with the Spanish occurred in August, 1540, when Captain Hernando de Alvarado and Fray Juan de Padilla were sent east from Zuni by Don Francisco Vásquez de Coronado. Coronado was governor of a northern Mexican province and the first European to venture beyond Zuni to the east, where he remained for two years. He also organized and led a second expedition into the Southwest. They described Acoma as a fortress, an inaccessible stronghold atop the mesa with houses three and four stories high and with a large supply of corn and beans as well as many turkeys. The people were friendly and greeted the Spanish warmly, offering gifts and trading with them. Coronado marched past later that year and also found the Acoma hospitable. By 1542, Coronado returned to Mexico without having found the fabled Seven Cities of Gold.

In 1582, Antonio de Espejo, a wealthy Mexican, sponsored an expedition led by Fray Bernardino Beltran and Espejo recorded their encounter at Acoma. He estimated that the population was 6,000 and there were a cistern for water and a large amount of supplies on the mesa. The farmland around the mesa was well irrigated using a highly developed system that was an improvement on that used by the Spanish. The Acoma gave the party deerskins, corn, and turkeys and entertained the visitors with juggling and dancing.

In 1598, Juan de Oñate arrived at Acoma and read to the Native Americans the Act of Obedience and Homage, which proclaimed that they were now under the "protection" of the king of Spain. Oñate then continued west to Zuni and Hopi. This was during the end of October.

Captain Juan de Zaldivar and 30 men followed Oñate, arriving about a month later. They, too, were received in a friendly manner by the Acoma. At this point, no one knows just what happened or why, on December 4, the Acoma attacked the Spanish soldiers, killing Zaldivar and two other captains. The Spanish considered this a grievous breach of the agreement and on January 21, 1599, Vincente de Zaldivar, Juan's brother, arrived at Acoma and three times asked the Acoma to surrender, which they refused to do. That night the Spanish scaled the cliffs and a vicious battle followed that lasted three days. The Acoma surrendered on January 23 after more than 600 Native Americans had been killed, including women and children. Between 70 and 80 men were taken prisoner, along with 500 women and children, some of whom were imprisoned in kivas, then murdered and thrown off the cliff.

A trial was held at Santo Domingo Pueblo during the first week of February 1599. The Acoma were found guilty. The men over 25 years of age were sentenced to have one foot cut off and to 20 years of servitude in Mexico. Males aged 12 to 25 were given 20 years of servitude, as were females over the age of 12. The girls under 12 were given to Fray Alonso Martínez to distribute in the "kingdom" and do with them as he saw fit. The boys under 12 went to Vicente de Zaldivar for an unknown fate. The old men and women were confined to other pueblos.

Oñate was replaced in 1609 and recalled to Mexico, were he was put on trial for these atrocities and found guilty of hanging two Acoma without cause and for the slaughter that had been perpetrated by Vincente de Zaldivar. He was sentenced to perpetual banishment from New Mexico and exiled for four years from Mexico City and fined. Vicente de Zaldivar was also found guilty and was banished from New Mexico for eight years and from Mexico City for two years, and fined.

There was little contact between the Spanish and Acoma after this. Most settlement of the region occurred farther east, so the Acoma remained isolated, at least for a short period.

In 1629, Fray Juan Ramírez was assigned permanently to Acoma, where he assisted with the rebuilding of the pueblo and had the mission church of San Estevan constructed between 1629 and 1640. The church was 100 feet (30 m) long and 35 feet (10 m) high, with walls 9 feet (2.7 m) thick at the base. A retaining wall was built in front of the church around the edge of the mesa and filled with dirt to serve as a cemetery. All the materials, including the fill for the cemetery, had to be carried up to the top of the mesa on the backs of the Acoma, an estimated 20,000 tons (18,200 mt) of earth and water just for the church, which was constructed with adobe bricks, as was the rebuilding work on the village, rather than with the traditional stone. Approximately 168 men and women died building this church.

The Pueblo Revolt of 1680 was concentrated in the northern pueblos, which were too far away for the Acoma to join in the battle, but they did kill all the Spanish on the mesa. By 1692, Don Diego de Vargas had regained control over the pueblos, for the most part peacefully, and on November 3 of that year convinced the Acoma to relinquish. Resettlement began in 1693, but hostilities continued with some of the northern pueblos until 1695. During 1696, renewed enmity, again in the northern pueblos, caused some people to flee to Acoma. On August 13, Vargas attacked Sky City, capturing eight Acoma, who he offered to trade for the refugees from the other pueblos. The Acoma refused, so Vargas destroyed their fields and took their sheep, retreating after three days. The following year, the refugees left Acoma and founded Laguna Pueblo several miles to the northwest. Finally on July 6, 1699, Acoma and Zuni Pueblo made peace with the Spanish.

During the 18th century, Acoma was isolated from the other pueblos. Forced to give up land to resettle Navajo, the Acoma also suffered from severe droughts, raids by Apache, and smallpox. In 1768, the census of Acoma indicated a population of 1,114 residents, but by 1795 it was down to 860. Acoma and Laguna joined with the Spanish in 1774 on an expedition against the Navajo to try to prevent their excursions into Pueblo territory. The latter part of the century saw many raids by, and battles with, the Apache who were being driven out of their native territories. Despite all the strife, the Acoma were noted at this time for making the finest blankets in New Mexico from wool and cotton.

On September 16, 1821, Mexico became independent from Spain but this did not affect the Acoma or the other Pueblo, as the policies and laws remained unchanged.

A new era for the Pueblo began in 1846 with the United States taking over control of New Mexico from the Mexicans. The first surveyors were at Acoma on October 21, 1846. The Pueblo did not become part of the reservation system at this time, so they had no federal protection and were caught in the middle between white settlers' and other Native peoples' land claims of traditional Acoma territory.

New surveys in the 1870s pushed back the boundaries of Acoma and US land agents deliberately caused problems between Acoma and Laguna over disputed boundaries. In 1877, a patent for the Pueblo lands was signed into law by President Rutherford B. Hayes, but it was not accepted by the Acoma as they disputed the boundaries that had taken much of their rightful land. They continued to lobby for new surveys but were denied, even though some government officials knew the patent was unjust.

Kiva, Sky City

The 1890s brought drought and epidemics to Acoma. In the early 1900s, there was a great increase in agricultural production, thanks to a government program of bringing in farmers to assist the Pueblo with both crops and livestock. This continued until WWII, but was followed by a decline after the war. In 1913, Acoma became a reservation.

After the war, tourism increased for the Pueblo, bringing in much needed revenue; it also helped the pottery industry. Acoma pottery was produced mostly by the women, and still continues to be today. But even with these added sources of revenue, by 1967, 86 percent of the Acoma people had an annual income of less than $3,000 per year. This changed in 1982, when the government allowed high-stakes bingo parlors to operate on reservations, which would evolve into the casinos of today. This has greatly profited the Acoma, who have used the money to buy back some of their traditional lands. Today, they own over 400,000 acres (16,000 ha). The current population is around 6,000, with about 30 still living in Sky City.

day 2

El Morro
New Mexico

- National monument, established 1906
- 2 square miles (5 square km)
- Elevation at visitors center, 7,218 feet (2,380 m)

Petrified Forest
Arizona

- Originally designated a national monument in 1906, to prevent the removal of petrified wood
- Established as a national park on December 9, 1962
- 146 square miles (378 square km)
- Elevation ranges from 5,300 to 6,235 feet (1,600–1,900 m)

Nearby Sites

◎ Casamero Pueblo

◎ Bandera Crater and Ice Cave

◎ Zuni Pueblo

2. El Morro

GETTING THERE: From Grants, New Mexico, it is about 42 miles (67 km) to El Morro. Take exit 81 from I-40 at Grants and turn left onto NM 53, or you can drive through town and follow the signs for NM 53. Soon after leaving Grants you will be driving through evergreen forests and climbing over hills on switchbacks before leveling out onto grasslands. The site is on the left and is clearly marked. If you are coming from the west through Zuni, follow NM 53 to the site, or if you are arriving from Gallup, take NM 602 to NM 53. Turn left.

As soon as you turn onto the road to the site, there is a pullout on your right that is a good place to stop for a scenic view of El Morro. The light-colored cliffs on the right are Inscription Rock. A'ts'ina Ruins are on top of the mesa to the left, but not visible from your place of arrival. Continue on to the visitors center.

The cuesta of El Morro

THINGS YOU NEED TO KNOW: The park is open every day, except Christmas Day and New Year's Day, from 8:30 AM to 6 PM in the summer and 9 to 5 in the winter. Temperatures are very hot in the summer and can be cold in the winter. Expect thunderstorms in July and August. Sometimes the trail over the mesa is closed due to ice, snow, high winds, or lightning. Amenities include picnic tables and camping areas in the park and restrooms at the visitors center. There is an entrance fee. For more information, phone 505-783-4226; visit www.nps.gov/elmo; or write to Superintendent, El Morro National Monument, HC 61, Box 43, Ramah, NM 87321.

El Morro is a cuesta, a mesa that gradually rises at an angle and then drops off suddenly in a sheer cliff. The ruins of A'ts'ina are on the top of the mesa. This is a P IV site that had over 500 rooms built around a central plaza. A small section on the northeast

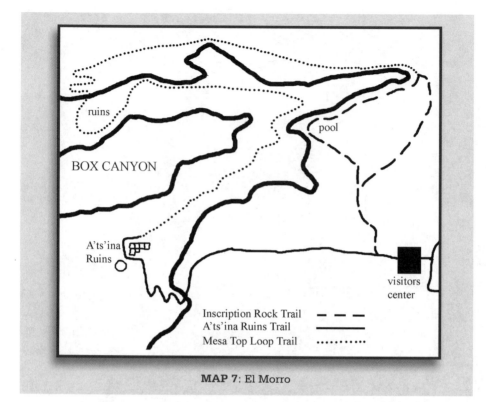

MAP 7: El Morro

has been excavated and stabilized and includes several rooms, a square kiva, and an adjacent large, round kiva. The pueblo was inhabited for about 60 years. At the bottom of the mesa is a natural catchment about 12 feet (3.6 m) deep that collects the rainwater that drains from the top and is the only reliable source of water for 30 miles (48 km) in either direction. This is the reason the Ancestral Puebloans lived here and it is also on the main trail from Acoma to Zuni.

The other story is Inscription Rock. The soft Zuni sandstone is ideal for carving and the proof of this can be seen around the base north of the waterhole. This rock is a living history of the Southwest and contains ancient petroglyphs and inscriptions by the Spanish, Mexicans, and Americans, with most of the postinvasion inscriptions dated. The soft nature of the sandstone makes it very easy to carve, which allowed for the intricate and beautiful inscriptions that line the walls of the mesa, some of which could be considered works of art.

There is a small museum in the visitors center.

TOURING EL MORRO

After paying your entrance fee at the visitors center, exit through the back doors to the trailhead. It is a good idea to get a copy of the trail guide, which the ranger will lend you or you may purchase, as this guide contains translations of most of the Spanish inscriptions. There are three options for visiting the site: (1) the loop trail to Inscription Rock; (2) the trail to the A'ts'ina ruins and back (which may be combined with the previous trail); or, (3) the mesa loop, which includes everything.

Inscription Rock Trail

This is an **easy** trail that is paved and has a slight incline and is wheelchair accessible with some assistance. Allow from 15 minutes to an hour, depending on how intensely you study the inscriptions. After exiting the visitors center, follow the trail to your right and then bear left at the Y. As you come over the small incline you will have a good view of the cliffs. The long streaks of dark desert varnish lead down to the pool. Continuing down the path you will find yourself beside the pool, an extraordinary sight in the middle of the desert.

The pool is about 12 feet (3.6 m) deep—notice the depth marker—and holds around 200,000 gallons (750,000 L) of water. It is believed to be fed by rain and snow melt from the mesa and not by springs, but remarkably remains full of water even after long periods of drought, so there is some speculation that there is another source for the water (so far, no one has been able to prove this). Some inscriptions are around the back of the pool, where there was at one time a sandbar. In 1942, a massive rock fall filled the pool, and during the removal of this debris, the sandbar was also taken out and the old dam reinforced.

The inscription by E. P. Long of Baltimore, Maryland

A petroglyph showing mountain sheep

The Zuni call this place A'ts'ina, the "place of the writings on the rock"; the Spanish, El Morro, the "headland"; and the Americans, "Inscription Rock." Today it is the only record of its kind that allows people to see an original "document" chronicling the history of this region from the Ancestral Puebloans through the Spanish, Mexican, and American occupations. From this point of the trail onward, the inscriptions give a firsthand account of those who lived here or simply passed by, though sometimes it is not easy to understand their meanings. I highlight only a few as follows.

Just after the pool, you will see some examples of the petroglyphs that were carved or pecked into the rock by the Ancestral Puebloans and are the most difficult to interpret. There are many "readings" of them (see Rock Art, page 447) but most of their meanings are unknown. You may have trouble seeing some of the inscriptions as the contrast is very low and, depending on the position of the sun, they are also extremely difficult to photograph. Following these petroglyphs is one of the most elegant examples of penmanship, the inscription by E. P. Long (photograph, previous page) who accompanied Lt. Edward F. Beale in 1857 (marker 4 in the El Morro guide-book). Beale was leading a caravan of camels across the Southwest to Los Angeles to test their effectiveness at long-distance desert travel. The camels had been imported from Egypt and Turkey and were trained in Camp Verde, Texas. They proved very effective, much better than horses or mules, but Camp Verde fell into the hands of the Confederates at the beginning of the Civil War and the Camel Corps ended. Next is an inscription in neat block letters, BECKINRIDGE, the name of the man in charge of the 25 camels in Beale's caravan (marker 5).

A bit farther along the trail (marker 9) is one of my favorite petroglyphs, four mountain sheep in a row. The ancient peoples depicted many different animals in their rock art, which may have had something to do with hunting rituals. Even though they were primarily farmers, wild meat always supplemented their diet. Following this is the earliest nonnative inscription (marker 10) by Don Juan de Oñate, who, on his return from traveling to the "South Sea" (the Gulf of California) carved the following:

> Pasó por aquí ei adelantodo don Juan de Oñate del descubrimiento de la mar del sur a 16 de abril de 1605.

> Here passed by the Governor-General Don Juan de Oñate, from the discovery of the Spanish Sea, the 16th of April, 1605.[1]

(For more about Oñate, see pages 7 and 416)

The first Americans at El Morro were Lt. James H. Simpson, of the US Army's Topographical Engineers, and an artist named Richard Kern in September 1849 (marker 21). They spent two days recording and drawing the inscriptions and were the first to realize the great importance of this site.

You are now at the end of the inscriptions and can either turn back, following the loop trail to the visitors center, and take the trail to the ruins on the mesa, option 2, or continue on this trail to the top of the mesa and then onto the ruins, option 3, the descriptions of which follow.

A'ts'ina Ruins

Follow the trail to your left after exiting the visitors center to go directly to the ruins on the mesa. This is a **moderate** trail that rises approximately 200 feet (60 m) with many steps carved into the rock. To the ruins and back will take about 45 minutes.

The trail winds through trees before it begins to ascend the mesa, growing steeper as it continues, but there are great views once you clear the treetops. Beware of the many cacti growing near the trail, and you may see a snake along the upper section. Finally you emerge from around a bend in the trail to the excavated section of A'ts'ina Ruins.

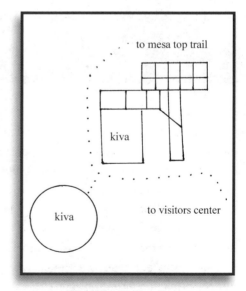

PLAN 1: A'ts'ina Ruins

1. Dan Murphy, *El Morro National Monument*, Tucson, AZ: Western National Parks Association, 2003), 6.

A'ts'ina ruins

Originally there were at least seven small villages scattered in the valley, but between A.D. 1275 and 1300, their occupants constructed this pueblo, abandoning the lower villages. The reason is not known but it may have been a much easier place to defend from attack. What you see was excavated and stabilized in the 1950s by Dick and Natalie Woodbury and is only a small portion of the entire pueblo. Bypass the ruins for a moment and walk over to the great kiva (the round one on your left). Past the kiva is the central plaza; the mounds on the left, right, and straight ahead are the remains of the entire pueblo. The plaza would have been completely surrounded by the pueblo with only one entrance from the outside. There would have been a double row of single-story rooms on the inside, then a double row of two-story rooms and another double row of rooms, in some sections two stories, and in others, three stories. There were no openings along the outside walls. The pueblo was built of stone with adobe mortar; some of the stones were from an earlier, but much smaller, pueblo that was in the same location. There were between 500 and 800 rooms altogether and it was built as a single unit.

Now walk over to the excavated rooms. The first room is a square kiva, which became much more common in the P IV period, the usual shape being round. This kiva still has the standard elements, including a hearth, deflecting stone, and ventilator shaft, the same as the round kiva behind you (see page 426). Several other rooms are visible, some of which were used for storage and others, for living areas, but most of them have an unknown function. You are standing on the second story looking down into what would have been the ground floor.

Several of the rooms had white plaster on the walls but the site was not protected after being excavated, so the plaster fell off and areas that were painted were not recorded or photographed. If you look carefully at the walls you will notice the chinking with small stones that is characteristic of Chacoan masonry (see page 430). Because, when the site was excavated, no photos were taken before restoration, we cannot be sure whether the chinking was original or that this is the way the archaeologists thought it should be restored. Speculation was used in a great many early restorations of ancient buildings.

In the early A.D. 1300s, the people left the pueblo moving to the west, where they formed six villages in the Zuni area. These were the pueblos and the people, the Zuni, that Coronado encountered when he first arrived in the Southwest (see page 415).

To return to the visitors center, follow the same trail back down the mesa.

Square Kiva

The Box Canyon

Mesa Loop Trail

This is a **moderate** to **difficult** trail, especially if the temperature is hot. It is a 2-mile (3.2 km) loop with a 200-foot (60 m) rise in elevation and some steep, rocky areas and sheer drop-offs once on the mesa. It will take about 1½ to 2 hours. Do not attempt if it is very windy or icy or there are any thunderstorms in the region. Sometimes the trail is closed, so inquire at the visitors center before heading out.

This trail continues from the end of the Inscription Rock Trail (see page 15) in a counterclockwise direction. You can also go up to the ruins first and walk in a clockwise direction, but I have found it easier to go up the mesa from this side and come down from the ruins.

The trail continues past the last inscriptions and meanders along the north side of the mesa, gradually climbing until you come to the switchbacks, where it becomes steep very quickly. When you finally emerge on the top, there is a mound on the left: a small pueblo that has not been excavated. As you walk past this mound you see the box canyon to your right; on the other side of this are A'ts'ina Ruins. The trail now turns out to the north edge of the mesa, allowing for some spectacular views. The trail is marked with small rock cairns and continues around the box canyon over the rocky surface of the mesa. In some places steps have been cut into the rock but these are modern, not ancient. The trail leads up a small slope to the ruins of A'ts'ina (see Plan 1, page 17; follow Trail 2 on Map 7, page 14, to return to the visitors center).

Back at the visitors center is a small museum, as well as a bookstore. This concludes the tour of El Morro.

GEOLOGY OF EL MORRO

The light-colored Zuni sandstone was formed from windblown sand dunes in the Jurassic period 170 million years ago. This sandstone is very soft and held together only by clay and not silica cement. It consists of very fine grains that are uniform in size, which indicates that they were windblown as opposed to deposited by water. The upper layer of darker rock is Dakota sandstone, which formed from streams and an ancient sea around 70 million years ago, during the Cretaceous period, and which is much harder than the Zuni sandstone; thus, it protects the softer sandstone from eroding too quickly.

After the formation of the Dakota sandstone, there were several uplifts of the area (see page 432), followed by much erosion. The valley surrounding El Morro was once at the same level as the mesa. This uplift also split the sandstone vertically, which allows water to seep into the cracks. When the water freezes and expands, the outward pressure shears off large slabs of stone, producing the perpendicular cliffs. The box canyon was formed by runoff from the top of the mesa, most of which is slanted toward the southwest.

3. Petrified Forest National Park

GETTING THERE: It is about 120 miles (190 km) from El Morro to the Petrified Forest. From El Morro, return to NM 53 and turn left. You will soon pass through the small town of Ramah, where food and gas are available as well as at the next town, Zuni Pueblo. Continue on NM 53 until you cross the Arizona border, where the highway number changes to AZ 61, until you come to US 191. Turn right (north) on US 191 to I-40 westbound. Take exit 311 to the north entrance of the park. If you are arriving from the west, exit at Holbrook onto US 180 toward St. Johns and turn left after about 20 miles (32 km), which brings you to the south entrance.

THINGS YOU NEED TO KNOW: The park is open every day except Christmas Day. The park road is open generally between 7 AM and 8 PM but exact hours vary according to date. Please check the website for park road hours on the date you plan to visit. There are only two picnic grounds and no campgrounds. There is an entrance fee. Temperatures are very hot in the summer and cool in winter, and it can be extremely windy in the spring. The road may be closed in the winter due to ice or snow. **NOTE:** Arizona remains on standard time year-round, so if you are traveling in late spring, summer, or early fall, the time will be one hour earlier than in New Mexico. For more information, phone 928-524-6228; visit www.nps.gov/pefo; or write to P.O. Box 2217, Petrified Forest, AZ 86028-2217.

The Petrified Forest is known mostly for the petrified wood found throughout this region, but there are also several ancient ruins and petroglyphs, as well as the Painted Desert. The Painted Desert is made up of mudstone, siltstone, claystone, and volcanic ash, which makes the rock soft and unstable. This unstable surface does not allow vegetation to gain a foothold on its slopes, resulting in the bare, multicolored landscape visible today.

This area formed around 220 million years ago. The petrified logs date to 200 million years ago and were deposited by floods and mudflows from mountains to the south. The trees were swept onto the plains and quickly covered with volcanic ash and mud that deprived the organic matter of air, preventing the growth of bacteria. The result was that the wood did not decay. Silica, a glass found in volcanic material, leached through the ground and attached itself to the organic matter, filling the cells over time with minerals that turned the wood to stone. The color is determined by the type of mineral that is present in the petrified logs.

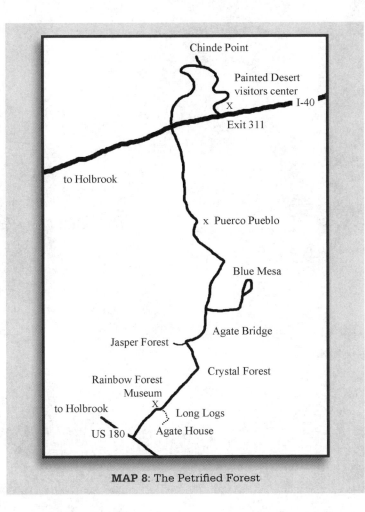

MAP 8: The Petrified Forest

From 220 to 200 million years ago, this area was a great flood plain where hundreds of species of plants thrived along with crocodile-like phytosaurs, large amphibians, small dinosaurs, fish, and insects. After this, the region was covered by deposits from the sea. A great uplift of the area 70 million years ago cracked and broke the logs into the pieces visible today. The coniferous trees that formed the logs are an extinct species known as *Araucarioxylon arizonicum* and were up to 9 feet (2.7 m) in diameter and 200 feet (60 m) tall. In many examples, the rings of the trees can be seen, each ring representing a year of growth.

TOURING THE PETRIFIED FOREST

Soon after exiting from the interstate you will come to the Painted Desert visitors center, whose amenities include a restaurant, gift shop, gas station, and post office, as

The Painted Desert from Chinde Point

well as restrooms. If you do not need any of these services, continue to the entrance gate just past the visitors center.

The first stop is Chinde Point, about 2 miles (3.2 km) past the gate. There are covered picnic tables at this stop, the only ones in the northern section of the park, and restrooms. Chinde Point also has a wonderful view of the Painted Desert, which begins just east of the park and continues almost as far west as Flagstaff.

After leaving Chinde Point, turn right (south) and you will pass four turnouts with views of the Painted Desert, all on the right. Lacey Point is the best. Continue south for about 5 miles (8 km) to the Puerco Pueblo turnoff, which will be on your left. The trail from the parking lot around the ruins is **easy** with little grade change and only a short distance to walk.

Puerco Pueblo

Archaic Indians lived in this region on a seasonal basis and carved points from the petrified wood. After A.D. 900, there was more rainfall and the first pueblos began to appear, along with agriculture. The Native Americans also traded arrow points with surrounding peoples. Puerco Pueblo is on a low mesa and was first occupied from A.D. 1100 to 1200. It was a small site used seasonally. The ruins visible today date from A.D. 1300 to 1380 (P IV), after which time the inhabitants burned the pueblo and left, never to return. The site consisted of 124 single-story rooms, three deep, built in a rectangle around a central plaza. The two inside rows of rooms were living spaces; the back, or outside, ones were used for storage. Entrance was only through the roof, as there were no doors in the exterior walls. The square kivas were probably an influence of the Mogollon, who lived to the south.

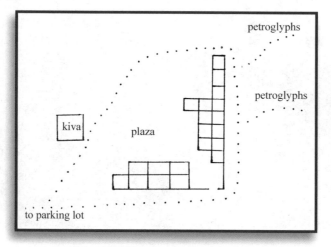

PLAN 2: Puerco Pueblo

Puerco Pueblo

Puerco pueblo

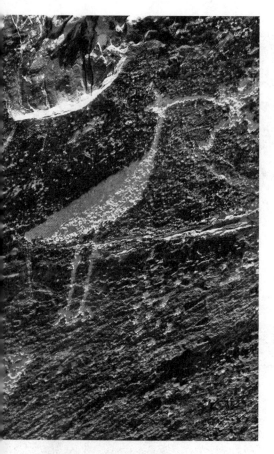

The stork petroglyph

As you follow the trail piles of rubble, unexcavated sections of the pueblo, appear on your left. There is a reconstructed square kiva on your left, as well as several unexcavated kivas that appear as depressions in the ground. The trail continues through the central plaza. The room blocks completely enclosed the plaza, the heart of the pueblo, a layout typical of the P IV period. Earlier pueblos had open plazas in front of the room blocks. The change seems to have been for defense (see page 412).You may walk around the many reconstructed rooms, which in one area are three wide.

There are many petroglyphs on the boulders along the edge of the site that have broken off and tumbled down from the low mesa. One spiral is crossed with a shaft of sunlight around the summer solstice in June and is believed to have been used by the Ancestral Puebloans for astronomical observations. There is also a unique image of a stork with a frog in its mouth. The petroglyphs, including the stork with the frog (above) are past the structures and down two short trails that have a few steps. There are restrooms beside the site.

From the Puerco Pueblo parking lot, turn left onto the road to continue south. The next area you travel through is called the Tepees for the cone-shaped mounds on either side of the road. The layers of blue, purple, and gray were formed by sedimentation from fast-running rivers and are known as bentonite clay. This clay swells when wet and then shrinks and cracks as it dries, a process that allows erosion, as can be seen in the formations. Because of this instability plants cannot gain a foothold, leaving the mounds barren. Areas such as these are known as badlands and can be found in many parts of the west. **CAUTION:** This stretch of road has few turnouts and the shoulders are narrow, so be aware of drivers stopped on the road to take pictures. Continue south to the Rainbow Forest Museum parking lot.

Agate House

The trail to the Agate House pueblo begins in the parking lot of the museum. Be careful, as the road and parking lot are practically one, with only painted lines dividing them. To reach Agate House, cross the road (to the side where the gift shop is) and follow the paved sidewalk over the dry wash and turn to your right along what used to be a road to the trailhead. It is ½ mile (0.8 km) to this point. The trail to Agate House is **easy**, with only a slight rise in elevation, but it is long, 2 miles (3.2 km) round-trip from the museum. Allow at least 1 hour. Beginning at the same point is the **LONG LOGS TRAIL**, which is about a ½-mile (0.8 km) loop, plus the 1-mile (1.6 km) round-trip from the museum, and has the largest concentration of petrified wood in the park.

Agate House is a P III pueblo. It has eight rooms and was reconstructed in 1934 using the original building material, petrified wood. This pueblo is unique for that fact but if you look around the small hill on which it was built, it is easy to understand why the ancients chose this material; there is nothing else. Puerco is on a low mesa of sandstone, so building material was readily available, but at Agate House there is no

Agate house

stone, or even clay with which to make adobe, so the ancient people made use of the next best thing: the petrified wood, which is abundant. Shimmering in the sun, the petrified wood structure looks wonderful, even if the original reason for using this material was practical rather than aesthetic. Agricultural fields would have surrounded the pueblo.

Return to the museum, where there is a collection of fossils, including some small dinosaurs, and also a bookstore. Directly behind the museum is the **GIANT LOGS TRAIL**, an **easy** ¼-mile

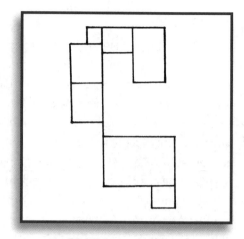

PLAN 3: Agate House

(0.4 km) trail that has a few steps. Along here are some of the largest examples of petrified wood in the park, including a few with the petrified bark still intact. You can see the individual growth rings on some examples if you look carefully.

Remember, it is strictly forbidden to collect any petrified wood in the park, no matter how small, and any infraction is punishable by fines and/or imprisonment. Examples may be purchased in the gift shops or at locations outside the park where it is legal to collect the material.

OTHER SITES IN THE PARK

There is wilderness hiking in the Painted Desert, along with several more viewpoints next to the road in the northern section. To your right as you travel south past Puerco Pueblo is the turnoff to **NEWSPAPER ROCK**, but the trail is closed, so you can only see the petroglyphs by using the spotting scopes installed at the lookout. If you do not have binoculars it is not very interesting. Past the Tepees on the left is the road to the **BLUE MESA**, a 3-mile (4.8 km) loop road that leads to a 1-mile (1.6 km) loop walking trail. This is a **moderate** trail with a steep incline at the beginning, followed by a level path that winds through the barren multicolor formations. It is a spectacular trail.

Farther on is the **JASPER FOREST**—more petrified wood—and the **CRYSTAL FOREST TRAIL**, which is **easy** and less than a mile and contains more examples of differently colored petrified wood. Plan on at least a full day if you want to visit all the stops and trails.

From the Rainbow Museum, continue south, through the southern gate, until you come to US 180. Turn right toward Holbrook, which is 20 miles (32 km) away and has many motels, restaurants, stores, and other amenities.

This concludes the second day of the Grand Circle Tour. The approximate timeline is: 1 hour from Grants to El Morro; 1½ to 2 hours at El Morro; 2 hours to Petrified Forest; 2 hours in the Petrified Forest; and ½ hour to Holbrook.

◎ OTHER SITES NEAR GRANTS OR ON THE ROAD TO HOLBROOK

If you have more time or are only exploring a smaller region, there are several other sites off the main tour in this region. Near Grants is Casamero Pueblo, and on NM 53 are the Bandera Crater and Ice Cave, as well as Zuni Pueblo, each described briefly as follows.

◎ Casamero Pueblo

This is referred to as a Chacoan outlier (see page 360) because of certain architectural designs that are found in buildings at Chaco Canyon, which lies about 50 miles (80 km) due north. To find the site from Grants, take I-40 west to exit 63, about 22 miles (35 km), turn right at the end of the exit ramp, and when you come to the T, turn right again onto old Route 66 and left on CR 19 north, the first road you come to. It is around 4 miles (6.4 km) to the site but the ruins are tricky to find. Soon after turning onto CR 19 you cross a set of railroad tracks and then pass an electrical plant on your left (beware of large trucks turning). After the entrance road to the plant you cross a second set of tracks, and 100 feet (30 m) beyond this, there is a gravel pullout on the left, with a tiny sign: This is the parking area for Casamero. An **easy** trail, 100 yards (90 m) long with a slight incline, leads to the ruins.

Casamero was excavated between 1966 and 1975 and stabilized in 1976 by the Bureau of Land Management. It was occupied from ca. A.D. 1000 to 1200 and consisted

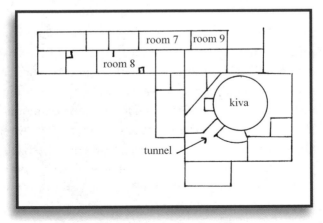

PLAN 4: Casamero Pueblo

Casamaro Pueblo, center, foreground

of 21 ground-floor rooms, 6 second-story rooms on the west side, and 1 kiva. It was built in an L shape with the open plaza facing south, a typical Puebloan layout. The stonework, referred to as banded masonry, uses large, flat stones placed in horizontal rows interspersed with smaller chinking stones. The builders used limestone and sandstone for the large building blocks, and limestone fragments and pot sherds for the chinking. Two hundred feet (60 m) to the southeast is an unexcavated great kiva about 70 feet (21 m) in diameter, indicated by a circular depression. This kiva signifies that there was a large population in the area. Many such sites have been found from the Basketmaker period to the Pueblo and Navajo. There were probably more people living in the area during the Native American occupation of Casamero than there are today.

As you walk up the path, the ruins come slowly into view. You are entering the site

from the southeast into the plaza, most likely the same way a visitor would have arrived when it was occupied by the Ancestral Puebloans. On your left, toward the west, are the living and storage rooms. Straight ahead is the kiva, built into the structure rather than separated from it. This is another Chacoan feature: constructing a round kiva in a square or rectangular room.

In the west section is a double row of rooms with a second story over the outside rooms. Room 7 (outside row, fourth from the south end) was used for refuse: The archaeologists found burnt corncobs, sweepings of ashes and charcoal, turkey eggshells, and the remains of a child. This last is not uncommon, as the Ancestral Puebloans buried their dead under room floors and in middens. The practice was not offensive to the deceased as they believed that everything came from Mother Earth and returned to her, be it humans, pottery, or the sweepings from the floor. Room 8,

Casamaro rooms 7 (right, foreground) and 9 (left, center)

the long room in the inside row, west side, was used for food storage. Again, this is typical of ancient pueblos, where the residents lived in the upper rooms and used the lower for storage.

Notice the masonry inside the kiva that is different from the rest of the structure, constructed of small limestone blocks with no chinking or large stones. On the southeast side of the kiva is a tunnel that entered from the adjacent room and was probably used in some ceremonies. It would have been dramatic for a priest/spirit to suddenly appear in the room among the participants during the ceremony. The tunnel, while not common to kivas, is found in several other places, including Chaco Canyon and Mesa Verde. There also would have been an entrance through the roof.

Although Casamero is a small site and not visited by many tourists, it is certainly worth the detour. It is also a very scenic spot with the red mesa to the west and a clear view in other directions.

CAUTION: You are permitted to roam freely through this site but do not climb on the walls or damage or remove any part of it. Remember, it is the visitors' responsibility to protect such sites as this, and in return it will remain open to the public.

◎ Bandera Crater And Ice Cave

This site is 25 miles (40 km) from Grants on NM 53 and also 25 miles (40 km) from El Morro. There are signs indicating the turnoff to the crater, which is on your left if you are coming from Grants. A short, narrow dirt road leads to the gift shop (trading post), where you pay a fee before heading out on the two trails, both of which begin at this point. It is open from March thru October, 9 AM to 4 PM. For information, visit www .icecaves.com.

One trail goes to the ice cave, and the other, to the crater. The former is **easy** except at the end, which consists of many steps down a well-worn stairway to the cave. This takes about 20 minutes. The trail to the crater is **moderate** with a steady though not steep incline and is over 1-mile (1.6 km) round-trip, so allow at least 45 minutes.

Bandera Caldera, from the end of the trail

The Ice Cave

Pick up the free brochure when you pay your admission fee, as this gives information on the numbered locations along the trails and is very helpful.

The Ice Cave is at the bottom of a collapsed lava tube, where the temperature never rises above 31°F (0.5°C), which keeps the ice from thawing. Early homesteaders used this and other smaller caves as refrigerators before electricity was available. The ice is 20 feet (6 m) thick and dates back 3,400 years. The green tint is Arctic algae.

You also pass some small ruins on this trail (marker 6), which consist of low walls made of lava rocks. There are many archaeological sites in this region but during the 1940s and 1950s, these sites were dug by locals and the artifacts sold. This is private land and the practice was, and in some areas still is, legal.

The trail to the crater is well worth the trip, as it winds around the side of the hill, giving the hiker outstanding views of the distant extinct volcanoes and the bizarre rock formations caused by the lava flows. At the end you are rewarded by a spectacular view across and into the crater.

CAUTION: Stay on the trails, as some of the areas are hollow underneath and dangerous to walk on, and, as well, the many nooks and crannies are inhabited by rattlesnakes.

◎ Zuni Pueblo

Driving west on NM 53 from El Morro to the Petrified Forest you pass through Zuni Pueblo, the largest of the 19 pueblos in New Mexico, with a population of around 10,500 and a territory exceeding 400,000 acres (162,000 h). Start at the visitors center, located on the east side of town on NM 53, to your right as you drive west. The center can provide you with information on visiting the pueblo, the restricted areas where tourists are not allowed, permits for taking photographs, and guided tours (reservations required). The A:shiwi A:wan Museum and Heritage Center is to the left at the four-way stop (driving west in the middle of town) and on the corner to your right, where the road curves to the right around a large building. It is set back from the street, so watch carefully as it is easy to bypass. The visitors center is open Monday through Saturday, 9 to 5:30 in the summer; Monday through Friday from 9 to 5:30 the rest of the year. There are restaurants, a B&B in Zuni, and nearby campgrounds.

Along the highway are many artisan shops, some of which are open to the public, and you will find jewelry, pottery, paintings, weavings, beadwork, Katsina dolls, and many other fine handcrafted objects made entirely by the local population. For more information, contact the visitors center (505-782-7238) or the governor's office (505-782-7000).

A History of Zuni

Zuni, or ancient Halona, may be the oldest pueblo, as evidence of pithouses dating to A.D. 700 has been discovered. Ten miles southwest of Zuni are the ruins of Hawikuh, one of six pueblos that the Spanish found when they arrived in the Southwest, and the first pueblo Coronado encountered in 1540 (see page 415). Coronado attacked Hawikuh and after a day's fighting, the Zuni abandoned the town to the Spanish but soon reoccupied it. The missionaries later built a church there that was burned down in 1680 during the revolt, in which Zuni participated, and was abandoned shortly afterward for good. Excavations were carried out in 1922 and 1923, and the site is dated to at least A.D. 1200. Today you may arrange to visit the site through the visitors center.

North of Zuni is the Village of the Great Kivas, named after two great kivas discovered there. There were 86 ground-floor rooms and 7 kin kivas. The site, which had been abandoned before the arrival of Coronado, was excavated in 1930 and dates from A.D. 1000 to 1150. It is possibly a Chacoan outlier (see page 360). It may be visited on a guided tour.

Agriculture was once the main economy for Zuni but now the arable land has been greatly reduced. The mainstay today for about 70 percent of the population is the arts. It is a wonderful place to spend some time browsing through the many shops and meeting the artists, who are exceedingly friendly.

day 3

Wupatki National Monument
Arizona

- Established as a national monument in 1924
- 55 square miles (143 square km)
- Elevation 4,900 feet (1,490 m) at the visitors center
- Consists of two separate parks, Wupatki and Sunset Crater

Nearby Sites

◎ Canyon de Chelly

◎ Homolovi Ruins State Park

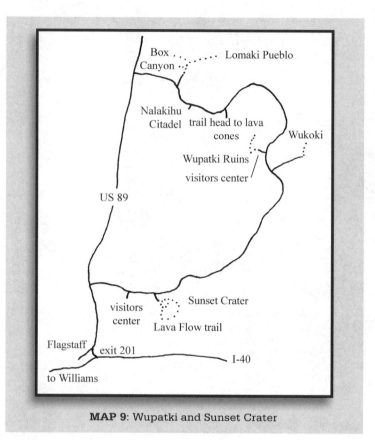

MAP 9: Wupatki and Sunset Crater

4. Wupatki National Monument

GETTING THERE: From Holbrook take I-40 West toward Flagstaff to exit 201 for US 89 north. Follow US 89 North for about 16 miles (26 km) to the turn for Wupatki/Sunset Crater (south entrance), which will be on your right. The visitors center for Sunset Crater is 2 miles (3.2 km) from US 89 and Wupatki is 18 miles (29 km) farther. The road is 35 miles (56 km) total and loops back onto US 89, 15 miles (24 km) north of the south entrance. If you are arriving from the north, it is around 20 miles (32 km) from Cameron to the turn for Wupatki, which is on the left. The entrances are well marked.

THINGS YOU NEED TO KNOW: Wupatki and Sunset Crater are open year-round, except on Christmas Day. There is a single entrance fee for both parks. The visitors center is open from 9 AM to 5 PM; the sites, from sunrise to sunset. In Sunset Crater, there are a few trails and pullouts; at Wupatki, there are six archaeological sites, all of which are close to the road with **easy** trails. The parks are separate but connected by a single road. There are no facilities except for restrooms and picnic grounds and a campground at Sunset Crater. For more information, phone 928-526-1157 or write to National Park Service, Flagstaff Areas, 6400 N Highway 89, Flagstaff, AZ, 86004. For more about Wupatki, visit www.nps.gov/wupa; for more about Sunset Crater, visit www.nps.gov/sucr.

This area had been sparsely populated before the eruption of the Sunset Crater Volcano in A.D. 1064 (see page 53), mostly by the Sinagua, who lived in scattered villages throughout the region and to the west. The ash from the eruption helped maintain moisture in the soil, and by the 1100s, the area was heavily populated by not only the Sinagua but also the Kayenta who lived to the east, the Mogollon from the southeast, and the Hohokam from the south. These sites, of which there are more than 2,000, are unique in that they have a cultural mix from the various groups whose territories all met in the Wupatki region.

The Ancestral Puebloan influence is seen in the walls, which are double coursed and made of cut sandstone held together with mud mortar. Kivas and Kayenta pottery have been found at the sites.

TOURING WUPATKI

The six archaeological sites to visit are (in order, driving from south to north): Wukoki, Wupatki, Citadel (a.k.a. Citadel Ruin), Nalakihu, Box Canyon and Lomaki.

Wukoki

As you enter from the south you first pass through pine forests and then the black lava lands of Sunset Crater Volcano National Monument (see page 53) emerging into the desert. Shortly after you pass the sign for Wupatki National Monument, there is a small sign on your right for Wukoki, the first stop. A 2½-mile (4 km) road leads to the site, which is only about 100 yards (90 m) from the parking lot. The trail is **easy**, but to enter the ruin you must go up a flight of steps.

Wukoki rests on the top of a rock outcrop in the middle of an arroyo and evokes visions of a medieval castle with a turret. Part of the ruin is still two stories high but seems much taller, being perched on its rock. Notice how the walls follow the shape of the natural rock. The Ancestral Puebloans did not have metal tools, and even though sandstone tends to be soft, it was very difficult and time consuming to level the bedrock, so they became adept at following the contours of the rock. You will see good examples of this at Wupatki ruins, too.

If you climb the steps to the ruin, the first thing you'll notice is that the rock outcrop is fairly flat on top, making it a good surface on which to build. You will also have

Wukoki

a great view of the surrounding area. Across the arroyo on the opposite side as well as in the bottom of the arroyo, there had been fields, so from this vantage point it would have been easy to watch the crops for invaders, mostly the four-legged kind. And, in the event of flash floods coming through the arroyo, the pueblo was situated high enough to be safe.

Notice how thick the walls are, which is an indication that there was more than one story. The way the flat, thin stones are placed overlapping one another provides extraordinary strength and support. Some of the rooms can be entered but the doorways are narrow and low, not because the people were small, but to make it easier and more efficient to keep cool in the summer and warm in the winter.

After exploring the ruins, follow the trail around the base of the outcrop and notice all the flat stones lying around that were once part of the structure above. Imagine being an archaeologist and having to figure out where each one came from and then putting them back in their original place.

This site was abandoned by the mid A.D. 1200s as the people moved south of Flagstaff, where there are more reliable water sources. The closest permanent water to this area is the Little Colorado River over 10 miles (16 km) to the east, so it is thought that a decrease in rainfall in the thirteenth century was the cause of abandonment.

There are many rounded-out hollows in the sandstone base and the outcrops next to the trail from the parking lot. This is called honey-combing. Water dissolves the "cement" in the sandstone at different rates and when a hollow develops, it allows more water to sit in the cavity, thus causing more erosion and creating these potholes. Depending on how the sunlight hits the stone, it can create some stunning images.

From the parking lot, return to the main road and turn right. The visitors center and Wupatki Ruin, located directly behind the center, are a short distance along the road on your left.

Wupatki

This is the largest site in the park, and it was occupied from A.D. 1110 to 1220. It consisted of 100 rooms and was four stories high in places. It was an incredible architectural achievement, as the builders wove the walls and structure around and over the large sandstone outcrop in the middle of a narrow canyon. This is the same type of masonry as at Wukoki.

To reach the site you must go through the visitors center, which has a small museum and bookstore, emerging onto a terrace above the shallow canyon, where you have a good overview of the site and surrounding area. The trail is **easy** to the main ruins but there are some steps down. If you continue to the end where the ball court is, the trail is **moderate** with many more steps. You can borrow or purchase a guide to the site, which corresponds to the marker numbers along the trail to which I also refer.

From the terrace, marker 1, you have a good view of the canyon and site. Straight ahead is the main structure; be-

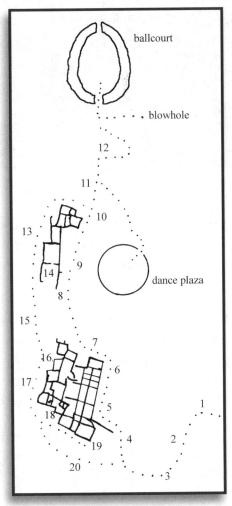

PLAN 5: Wupatki

Wupatki

low and to the right, the "dance plaza"; farther down the canyon to the right is the "'ball court." Across the canyon, looking over the plaza, is another pueblo that is not open to the public. Slightly to your left toward the end of the canyon is where the spring is located, but it no longer has any water. Fields would have surrounded the pueblo and spread out across the desert on the other side of the canyon. Continue down the trail until you come to the Y and turn right. Along the way, notice the black rocks, which are cinders blown out of Sunset Crater 14 miles (22.5 km) to the southwest.

At marker 4 you can see how the Ancestral Puebloans incorporated the natural rock into their building, going around and over in some places but also using it as walls in other places. They built up the slope of the rock to create a multistoried complex that for the most part is no more than one or two stories high but reaches four stories in total. Entrance would have been through openings in the roofs, using ladders.

Much of what you see from marker 5 has been rebuilt and stabilized since the 1930s. Even though stone was the main building component, it was held together with mud mortar, also known as adobe, so sites like this that are exposed to the elements deteriorate and must be stabilized to prevent them from completely collapsing. The large section in front of you where the walls meet has remained standing.

The use of the various rooms is often determined by what was found in them when excavated, though for many rooms their use remains unknown. For example, the room at marker 6 was probably for storing and preparing corn, for you see here two examples of metates used to grind corn into cornmeal, a staple of the residents' diet. Storage areas were generally in the lower stories of the pueblos, with the living quarters above.

In the room at marker 7, a ventilation system was built into the floor, similar to that used in kivas, with a shaft across the floor leading up into a natural crack in the rock. It has been partially buried but runs diagonally to the nearest right-hand corner of the room. If you have a copy of the guide, it has a diagram of this. There was a deflector stone and firepit in the center of the room. As mentioned previously, the inhabitants usually lived in the upper stories but sometimes in the winter they would move into the lower rooms, which would be easier to heat. Most of the Colorado Plateau gets fairly cold through the winter.

Continuing along the path to marker 8 you come to a section that has not been excavated and that gives you an idea of what much of the site once looked like. Archaeologists generally leave part of a site like this unexcavated so that in the future, if and when better techniques or technologies exist, more information can be acquired from a site, because excavation destroys a site.

The Dance Plaza

Below you, at marker 9, is the open plaza that has been compared to a great kiva. Although similar to a great kiva, it was never covered with a roof nor had the characteristics of a kiva. Some speculate that it was used as a type of community center or distribution area for the pueblo, but given the importance of dancing and ceremony in Native American culture, it was probably a dance plaza. The low wall has a bench built around the inside for sitting. If you follow the trail past the ruins and turn right, it goes to the plaza, which may be entered.

At marker 10 you see evidence of later occupations, as some sheepherders enlarged the door and lived in a room behind the wall. Notice that the bottom of the doorway is now filled back in with stone. The room, and other changes, were removed in the 1950s. At this point you can turn left and return to the visitors center on a level trail or continue down to the plaza and the ball court, where the trail is fairly steep.

The "ball court" below you (from marker 12) is influenced by the Hohokam, if not built by them. It is the only one on the Colorado Plateau and the farthest north in Arizona. The Hohokam occupied southern Arizona and built similar structures at many of their sites. They are believed to have been influenced by the Aztecs. The Aztecs played a violent ball game in their courts in which the object of the "game" was to keep a ball moving without using your feet, legs, arms, or hands. The losers would be executed. It is not known what this structure at Wupatki was used for. It is oval with entrances at each end and walls that are about 5 feet (1.5 m) high and 12 feet (3.6 m) thick. An enormous amount of labor went into its construction, so it must have been extremely important to the residents, but its purpose mystifies us.

Next to the ball court on the right is a "blowhole" covered with a metal grate. These were created by earthquakes during the formation of the San Francisco volcanic fields and are called earth cracks. This is a small one but it is connected to miles of underground cracks and no one knows just how vast it is. It either draws in air if there is a high-pressure weather system overhead or expels air under a low-pressure system, which is when it is cloudy and/or raining. It is difficult to tell which way the wind is blowing, but if you have long hair, simply kneel over the hole and your hair will give you the answer. Don't worry, though; it will not suck your head down to the grate. A piece of paper works just as well, but hang onto it so that nothing is pulled into the hole!

Returning to the ruins, turn to your right to continue the tour. At marker 14 is an open plaza that would have been a center of pueblo life, a place to meet, for community work and most likely ceremonies. Behind you and down the embankment is the midden, or trash dump. This is found at all pueblos and was the area where the community threw its rubbish, whether it was a broken pot or bones. At Pecos Pueblo

The room at marker 16

Hearth, deflector stone in Kiva (marker 19)

in New Mexico, the midden is over 100 feet (30 m) deep and created a huge extension to the mesa on which the site was constructed. It is not unusual to find burials in the middens. This midden has not been excavated.

At marker 16 you may enter the room that was almost ready made from the natural rock. Originally the room was used for trash but eventually it was roofed over and a living space created above. Notice the holes in the wall above your head. This is where the ends of the ceiling beams connected to the walls, and it is another example of how the people integrated the natural rock into their construction. Over 5 feet (1.5 m) of debris was excavated from this room.

During the 1930s and 1940s, park rangers lived in the ruins at marker 17, but the rooms they rebuilt were taken down in the 1950s (there are some pictures in the guidebook). Dendrochronology, or tree ring dating, was used on this site, as it has been for many sites in the Southwest, and gives dates that span from A.D. 1100 to 1200. In the back of the room, at marker 18, are examples of a couple of beams that were tested. (See page 423 for more about dendrochronology.)

There is a short spur on the trail at this point that leads to a large, rectangular room believed to be a kiva (marker 19). No household goods were found in the room and there is a ventilation system with a deflector stone and firepit. This room is much larger than the one at marker 7 that has a similar ventilation system. Kivas usually did not have any rooms built over them, which the room at marker 7 did, but there is no definitive proof that this room is a kiva. If the pueblo was inhabited only by the Sinagua (see page 55), they did not use kivas.

This concludes the tour of Wupatki, but there are still four more sites to visit in the park, so return to the visitors center parking lot and turn left onto the highway toward the next stop, Citadel.

Soon after leaving the visitors center you will notice some black cinder cones up ahead. The road winds around these to a turnoff on the left that leads to picnic tables and a trail that goes to the top of the cones. This trail is **moderate** to **difficult**, especially if you climb both cones and the weather is hot. The trail goes up to a ridge where it splits to the left and right, each trail going to one of the peaks. Both are steep, uphill climbs on a fairly smooth surface and end with great views of the surrounding desert, woodlands, and mountains, in particular the San Francisco peaks to the west. Allow at least an hour if you plan to climb both cones. From this stop it is a few miles to the next site, which has two ruins, or just one, depending on the interpretation.

Citadel and Nalakihu

These pueblos are next to each other and contemporary in date but are not physically connected and their relationship to each other is not known.

From the parking lot, which is on the left side of the road coming from the visitors

The trail to Citadel and Nalakihu (foreground)

On top of Citadel

center, a short **easy** trail leads to Nalakihu (a Hopi name which means "house outside the village"), which was built in three different stages over several years. There were around 10 rooms with a second story on part of the pueblo and dates to the late A.D. 1100s. The lower-story rooms have been stabilized and may be entered, but do not climb or sit on the walls. It is most likely that one or two extended families occupied the site, and it might have been an extension, so to speak, of Citadel Pueblo, which had limited space, if it was built after Citadel. If constructed before Citadel, Nalakihu might have been easier to build on the flat ground rather than up on the butte, especially if there were only a few people to begin with, but both scenarios are speculative.

Past Nalakihu, the trail winds around the butte to the only entrance to Citadel. This part of the trail is **easy** but a bit steep at the end. As you go around the site, notice the mixture of red sandstone and black cinderblocks used in the walls. The cinder is hard to work and of uneven shape but readily available, just as petrified wood was convenient for Agate House in the Petrified Forest (see page 29). The entrance is an offset in the wall and would have been easily defended, but if defense was an issue, why was Nalakihu built? Another question about this site is the terracing around the lower part of the butte, which can be best seen in the front (toward the road) along the trail. Were these terraces for gardens?

Citadel dates from the late 1100s to the mid-1250s and was multistoried with 50 rooms, 30 on the ground floor. Some of the exterior wall has been reconstructed, along with a few interior ones, but for the most part it lies in ruins. You see in places where walls have tipped over as the stones are laying edgewise rather than flat. As you walk around the site, look at the patterns of fallen stones and try to imagine how it once appeared. From the south side, where the entrance is, you can see a huge sink-hole that was a natural catchment for water and could be the reason the site was built in this location. The San Francisco mountains can be seen on the horizon.

Box Canyon

From Citadel, continue north on the road, left out of the parking lot, a short distance to the turnoff for Box Canyon and Lomaki, which is on the right. A ¼-mile (0.4 km) road leads to the parking lot and trailhead. Follow the **easy** trail from the parking lot until you see another trail on your left that leads to one section of Box Canyon ruins. From this point you can see the structures perched on the edge of the shallow canyon that is an earth crack. These ruins, the ones directly across from you, and Lomaki,

Box Canyon Dwelling

which is a bit further along the main trail, were probably part of the same community. Notice how they built the structure on the rock ledge, leaving just enough room to walk between the walls and rim. **CAUTION:** Do not attempt to walk around the outside of the building, the rock can be slippery and the ledge is narrower than it looks, with a sharp drop-off to the canyon floor.

Return to the main trail, turn left, and continue to the next junction, where another side trail leads up to the other section of this site. From the second site you can look back to the previous ruins and see how the man-made structure blends in with the natural rock. The main trail goes on to Lomaki, another site built on the edge of an earth crack.

Lomaki

Also known as Lomaki Ruins, this pueblo dates from the late A.D. 1100s and was two stories with nine rooms, some of which have been stabilized and can be entered. It is set on the edge of an "earthcrack" that geologists think was split open by the erup-

Lomaki. Notice the walls at the bottom of the cliff.

tion of Sunset Crater. There are several of these earthcracks in the park. The remains of several rooms below the rim can be seen from this side of the site; that is, from the direction via which you approach Lomaki, a little ways back from the site. Do not get too close to the edge or attempt to go down into the canyon.

This concludes the tour of Wupatki National Monument.

ADJACENT TO WUPATKI

Sunset Crater Volcano National Monument

Established 1930, Sunset Crater Volcano National Monument is 4.8 square miles (12 square km), with an elevation of 6,960 feet (2,120 m) at the visitors center.

Sunset Crater is the youngest example of volcanic activity in the Southwest, having erupted in the winter of A.D. 1064 to 1065, followed by minor eruptions in 1180 and 1250. The cinder cone is 1,000 feet (300 m) high and can be viewed from the trail and highway through the park. Hiking on the cinder cone is prohibited. When it erupted in 1064, the cinders from the explosion covered over 800 square miles (2,000 square km) to the east, north, and south, devastating the region for a short time but benefiting the area in the long run. Volcanic activity can be seen in many places throughout the adjacent countryside.

Touring Sunset Crater

If you enter from the south, you may want to visit here before continuing to Wupatki and then you can exit the park in the north back onto US 89. There is a nice view of the volcano soon after turning off US 89 onto the park road. There is a pullout on the right in which to stop. The visitors center is on the right after the entrance gate and offers information on the geology of the region, along with a bookstore and restrooms. Past the visitors center on the left is the Bonito lava flow, one of two from the eruption. There is a pullout on the left of the road, if you wish to stop for a better view of the lava field.

Beyond the Bonito lava flow a road on the right leads to the **LAVA FLOW TRAIL**, where there are also picnic tables and restrooms. There are two trails: a short, **easy** one that is paved and wheelchair accessible and consists of a ¼-mile (0.4 km) loop; and the longer one, which is **moderate**, with several stairways and low inclines, and which is a 1-mile (1.6 km) loop. From the end of the parking lot, the trail goes across a bridge. Pick up a trail guide at this point and then, in a clockwise direction, follow stops 3 to 6 in the guide. At this point, the second trail turns off on your left, going in a counterclockwise direction. This trail is not too difficult and gives the viewer

Sunset Crater Volcano

a wonderful experience of walking through the lava field and seeing the different formations up close. Stay on the trails as the area is fragile and easily eroded.

The short trail will take about 15 minutes, and for both, allow 45 minutes.

If the last site visited is Lomaki, return to the main road and turn right, which quickly brings you to US 89. Turn left toward Flagstaff. There are many motels and restaurants in Flagstaff. An alternative is Williams, which is about 30 miles (48 km) west on I-40. This is a small town and a good departure point for the Grand Canyon, the next destination. It is also where the Grand Canyon Railroad begins, a daily train that takes passengers to the South Rim. To get to Williams, proceed south on US 89 to Flagstaff and take the first entrance onto I-40 west. Take exit 165 and turn left at the Stop sign. Continue under the interstate and over the hill into town. When you enter Williams, the road divides into two one-way streets. Most of the motels are on the eastbound side (you will be heading west) as well as the other end of town. Soon after you exit the interstate is a new attraction, on the left, called Bearizona. It is a drive-through wildlife park that features bears, buffalo, and other animals. If you like bears, or have kids with you, check it out.

This concludes the third day of the Grand Circle Tour. The approximate timeline is: 2 hours from Holbrook to Wupatki/Sunset Crater; 30 to 60 minutes at Sunset Crater; 2 to 3 hours for Wupatki; 1 hour to Williams (or 30 minutes to Flagstaff).

HISTORY OF THE REGION

Wupatki was excavated in 1933 and 1934 by Harold Colton, who gave the name Sinagua (pronounced *sin'awa*), to the people who lived in this region and around the general Flagstaff area. The word comes from the Spanish *sin agua*, which means "without water," which Colton thought appropriate as he traveled around the territory. The Sinagua date back to at least A.D. 500 and lived in the area until the 1200s. Prior to the first eruption in A.D. 1064 to 1065, the people were thinly scattered across the area in small pithouse villages, a few of which have been discovered under the cinders, though many more were probably destroyed by the lava flows. What becomes more difficult to interpret is what happened after the eruption.

A common theory is that the ash from the volcano blanketed the ground and acted as a mulch, holding the moisture in the soil and improving agricultural conditions. This drew other Native peoples to the area, in particular the Hohokam, Mogollon, and Kayenta, who joined the Sinagua. But recent studies have contradicted this view, suggesting that the ash fall would not have caused a significant gain in agricultural production. In addition, the volcano continued to erupt periodically, though on a smaller scale, until 1250.

There does seem to have been a "building boom" in the 1100s, the period most of the ruins date from, which would seem to indicate an increase in population. The structures show Ancestral Puebloan influence in the building techniques and kivas. And there is the question of the ball court, which is definitely Hohokam in nature. But even if this was not a "coming together" of the various nations into one big happy family, it is still a most unusual site in that it is the only one on the Colorado Plateau that shows these mixed influences. And these influences cannot simply be dismissed as trade among the groups.

The Ball Court, Wupatki

The abandonment of this region poses just as many questions as does its habitation, for by 1290 it seems that everyone had left the Wupatki area, and where they all went is still a mystery. Some people probably moved south to the Verde region, near Sedona, while others went west. It is believed that others migrated to the Hopi mesas to the northeast. The Hopi maintain a strong connection to Wupatki and the San Francisco mountains and have many stories connecting their people to the region. Perhaps future research and excavations will help clarify the story.

Sunset Crater Volcano is part of the greater San Francisco Volcano Fields which formed the mountain range to the west over 400,000 years ago and created more than 600 hills and mountains since then with Sunset being the most recent. This entire region is the result of these eruptions and, though most of the range is extinct, there is still the possibility in the future that the range could expand, particularly in the northeastern extremities. Some volcanologists state there is no such thing as an extinct volcano.

◎ OTHER SITES NEAR HOLBROOK AND WUPATKI

One site that is not on the main tour but should not be missed if possible, is Canyon de Chelly (pronounced *de Shay*) on the Navajo reservation. Although it is a national monument, the land belongs to the Navajo nation and is private property, the only such arrangement in the National Park Service's system and a fact that makes the rules a bit different when you visit the site.

From Holbrook it is about 120 miles (192 km) to Chinle: Take I-40 east to exit 333 and then north (a left turn) on US 191 to Chinle. An alternative route is I-40 to exit 292 to AZ 77 north, which becomes CR 6 on the Navajo Reservation to CR 15, a right turn to US 191 to Chinle. Or, continue north on CR 6 to AZ 264; turn right to US 191 to Chinle. They are all about the same distance but the last one is more scenic.

◎ Canyon de Chelly

is a national monument established in 1931. It is 130 square miles (337 square kilometers), with an elevation of 5,540 feet (1,690 m) at the visitors center.

THINGS YOU NEED TO KNOW: In Chinle, there are signs to the park at the red light. Turn right if traveling north and drive through town until you see the entrance to the visitors center on your right, across the road from the Holiday Inn. The park is open year-round and there is no entrance fee. The visitors center is open from 8 AM to 5 PM, closed Christmas Day. The Navajo reservation observes Mountain Daylight savings time so is one hour ahead of Arizona during early spring, summer, and late

First Ruin, south rim

fall. There are two roads along the rims, with several viewing points of the canyon, and one trail that leads into the canyon to the White House Ruins. These are the only places visitors are allowed without a Navajo guide. If you have a four-wheel-drive vehicle that can go through sand, water, and mud, you can travel in the canyon but you must hire a guide. Otherwise, take one of the organized tours. Remember, all of the land is private, so hiking is not allowed, except on the **WHITE HOUSE TRAIL**.

To reserve a guide, or to join an organized tour, phone the visitors center (928-674-5500), or visit www.nps.gov/cach. During the summer it is best to reserve ahead as space is limited. Sometimes the canyon roads are closed due to high water.

When viewing the ruins from the rims, it is helpful but not necessary to have binoculars.

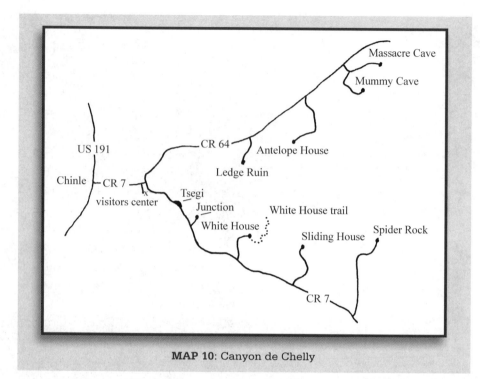

MAP 10: Canyon de Chelly

Touring Canyon de Chelly

How you tour the park depends on the amount of time available, so I will list some options:

If you have 1 hour, stop at the visitors center. There is a traditional Navajo hogan that is open to the public. Next, go to the White House Overlook on the South Rim drive that follows, and to the Spider Rock Overlook, which is at the end of the south road.

In 2 hours, you can see the visitors center, and White House and Spider Rock on the south rim, along with Antelope House Overlook on the north rim drive.

If you have 3 hours, add Mummy Cave and Massacre Cave Overlooks.

Four hours should be enough to stop at all the overlooks. Add 2 hours if you plan to hike down to the White House Ruins.

If you want to tour in the canyons, it takes a half-day for Canyon de Chelly or Canyon del Muerto and a full day to see both. These tours require a Navajo guide.

◎ South Rim

From the visitors center, turn right and then right again to drive along the South Rim road. Just after the campground, the road begins to rise as the canyon walls go from less than 30 feet (9 m) at this point to over 800 feet (245 m) at Spider Rock, and more than 1,000 feet (300 m) farther along the canyon. This drive is 37 miles (60 km) round-trip and all turns are on the left.

The first stop is Tsegi Overlook, which is next to the road. From the pullout you have a wonderful view of the beginnings of the canyons, as well as some of the many Navajo farms that are along the canyon floor.

The next overlook is Junction, where the two canyons separate: de Chelly to your right and del Muerto straight ahead. Two ruins are also visible but they are a bit difficult to find. Look at the north wall of del Muerto, slightly to the left and up from the floor of the canyon. There is a shallow cave in the rock face containing ruins from First Ruin on the left and Junction Ruin to the right. Originally they were probably one pueblo. First Ruin has 10 rooms and 2 kivas, and Junction has 15 rooms and 1 kiva.

The White House Overlook is one of the most popular as there is a good view of the ruins from the rim. This site dates from A.D. 1060 to 1275 and has Chacoan influences in the architecture. Today you see one site on the canyon floor and another in a cave above, but originally the two were connected by a four-story lower structure

White House Ruins

Spider Rock

that had in total 80 rooms and housed at least 100 people. The trail down to the site is 2½ miles (4 km) round-trip and begins to the right of the overlook. This is a **moderate** trail that drops over 500 feet (150 m) in elevation and is well-maintained gravel. In the summer, when temperatures can exceed 100°F (38°C), the trail would be rated **difficult**. And remember, the easy part is going down, then the 500-foot elevation is all uphill! There is no food or water available at the site but there are pit toilets. Be respectful and do not photograph the buildings or people along the trail. **NOTE:** Do not stray off the trail as this is private property and there is quicksand in places at the bottom. If the water is high, it will not be possible to go all the way to the ruins. But if you are able to hike this trail, it will be well worth the effort.

The Sliding House Overlook is at the end of a short road about 1½ miles (2.4 km) from the main road and is the next stop on the South Rim drive. The ruins can be seen across the canyon in a cave near the floor and get their name from the fact that they are literally sliding down into the canyon. In fact, when the original inhabitants were living there, they had to make modifications to the structures to stop them from sliding, so the phenomenon is nothing new. The ruins are hard to see in the morning, as deep shadows fall over the cave.

The Spider Rock Overlook is the last one on the South Rim drive and is about 3½ miles (5.6 km) from the main road. Turn left just before the main road becomes gravel. There is a short, **easy** trail at the parking lot to the viewing area for both Spider and Speaking Rocks. Spider Rock is a rock spire that rises 800 feet (245 m) from the canyon floor and will be the first one visible when you reach the rim. Speaking Rock is to your left across the canyon and is still connected to the canyon wall. Both are sacred to the Navajo.

This ends the South Rim tour. Return the same way you came and at the junction, turn left if you are leaving the park, or right if continuing along the North Rim drive.

◎ North Rim

The North Rim drive is 34 miles (55 km) round-trip from the visitors center and has four overlooks with three visible sites. All turnoffs are on the right and marked. This is CR 64 that continues through to Tsaile. The first turnoff is for the Ledge Ruin Overlook and is about 5½ miles (8.8 km), plus almost another mile (1.6 km) to the rim. The ruins are across the canyon in a small cave a short distance up from the bottom and date from A.D. 1050 to 1275.

The second overlook is about 8 miles (13 km) from the visitors center. A short, **easy** trail winds down to the viewpoint of the ruins (to the right) and also the canyon. Antelope House Ruin is constructed in the Kayenta style and the multistoried pueblo contained 91 rooms, 2 large kivas, and several small ones. Evidence of BM pithouses

Antelope House Ruin

dating to A.D. 690 was discovered at the site. For unknown reasons, this pueblo was the first abandoned in the region. Perhaps its location in the flood plain could have been a contributing factor, as most of the other sites were in caves above the canyon floor. Even the White House had structures in a cave above.

If you follow the trail to the left you can see another canyon that branches off from del Muerto. A large rock formation on the left corner called the Fortress is where the Navajos would flee when being attacked (see page 64). Although it seems to be part of the canyon wall, it is an island completely separate from the surrounding land.

The next turnoff is another 11 miles (17.6 km) farther on CR 64 and leads to two viewpoints. When you come to the Y turn right to Mummy Cave Overlook. The ruins are across the canyon, partway up the wall and easy to spot. The tower and upper buildings to the left were built by Mesa Verdeans in A.D. 1284, after the people had begun to leave the Mesa Verde region. There are 70 to 80 rooms and 3 kivas. The structures on the right that are built down over the edge of the cave are the remains of seven early BM houses dating from A.D. 300 to 400. This is the time period of the mummies that were discovered. Strangely, the cave was not occupied for over 750 years between BM II and the arrival of the Mesa Verdeans.

The other road leads to the overlook of Massacre Cave (see page 64). This cave is on the left just below the viewpoint. This concludes the tour of Canyon de Chelly.

When you return to CR 64, turn left to go back to the visitors center and Chinle, but if you have the time, turn right for a scenic detour to Chinle: Follow CR 64 to Tsaile and turn left onto CR 12 to US 191 south, make another left, and then proceed to Chinle. It is around 80 miles (128 km) back to Chinle this way, but the scenery is spectacular and definitely worth the extra distance as you travel through the rolling red rocks.

From Chinle, retrace the route back to I-40 and Holbrook to continue the tour.

ARCHAEOLOGY OF THE CANYONS

Canyon de Chelly is 27 miles (43 km) long with the Chinle wash running through it, and Canyon del Muerto is 18 miles (29 km) long and watered by the Tsaile Creek. Both canyons' water is runoff from snow melt that originates in the Chuska Mountains to the east and also from occasional thunderstorms during the summer months. The canyons are carved out of the Defiance Plateau that tilts upward toward the east, which is why the canyon walls are low near the entrance just below the visitors center and gradually rise to over 1,000 feet (300 m).

More than 700 archaeological sites have been discovered in the canyons, which span over 2,000 years. In 1870 a photographer by the name of T. H. O'Sullivan took the first pictures of the White House Ruins, which stimulated interest in the region. The Bureau of Ethnology explored the canyons in 1882 and recorded 46 sites, including Mummy Ruins, which the bureau named for the two mummified corpses discovered there. The bureau also named this canyon del Muerto ("Canyon of the Dead"), again for its finds. Another expedition in 1883 increased the known sites to 134 and also mapped the area, but the first publications of the dwellings did not appear until 1897.

The earliest sites date back to the Basketmaker period in the first century A.D., and possibly earlier. Earl Morris, famous for his work at Aztec Ruins (see page 310), excavated Mummies Cave in 1923. He found stone storage cists from Basketmaker times, pre–A.D. 550, and estimated the population at 200. From A.D. 550 to 750, pottery was introduced as well as pithouses, but there is little archaeological evidence from this time period, so there might have been a decline in the population. The development of pueblos and kivas begins after A.D. 750 and the cliff dwellings that are visible today date from 1100 to 1300, when the population peaked at between 700 and 1,000. In the late 1200s, people began to leave, and the canyons were abandoned by 1300.

The Kayenta occupied the canyons, but there is influence of other peoples—the Chacoans in White House and Mesa Verdeans at Mummy Ruins—so it appears that as other areas were being abandoned, some of the people moved here, probably due to the reliable water source. There is no evidence of hostilities among the peoples so it appears that they coexisted peacefully. It is thought that some of the people moved west when they abandoned the canyons to occupy the Hopi mesas. Their descendants still live there today. These people were not the ancestors of the Navajo.

It is thought that the Navajo arrived in this region in the A.D. 1600s or early 1700s. There is, however, some evidence of hogans south of the canyons dating back to A.D. 800, which means it is possible that Navajo were living here at the same time as the Ancestral Puebloans. But there are still questions about Navajo origins, as there is no definitive evidence at the present time. The Navajo were hunter-gatherers and learned the techniques of farming from the Pueblo, and then later, the raising of livestock from the Spanish. They had their own language distinct from that of the Pueblo tongue and they occupied the Dinétah (now the Republic of Dinétah, a sovereign Navajo state).

The Spanish raided the Navajo for slaves, mostly women and children, and in retaliation the Navajo warriors stole cattle and horses from the Spanish. These actions of raid and counterraid continued and in January 1805, a Spanish expedition led by Antonio Narbona was sent into Canyon de Chelly to attempt an end to the hostilities. As they had done many times before, the people fled into hiding, but the Spanish discovered several Navajo in what is now known as Massacre Cave and opened fire, ricocheting more than 10,000 rounds into the Navajo refuge. Narbona reported that his troops had killed 90 warriors and 25 women and children and captured another 35. In fact, there were no warriors, as they were out hunting—only women, children, and elders. When the warriors returned they went after Narbona and his men, but were no match for the Spanish guns and had to retreat.

In 1846, the Americans took over the southwest after defeating the Mexicans in the Mexican-American War and quickly negotiated a treaty with one Navajo headman, assuming he represented all the Navajo, when in fact he only spoke for a few, as there were several headmen. But even with this treaty, limited though it was, the slavery raids continued, as did the retaliations by the Navajo. The situation was so bad that by the mid-19th century, half the Navajo population were slaves. The Americans sent their military into the canyons in 1847 and 1849, but their results were no better than that of the Spanish, as the Indians would simply disappear into the labyrinth.

In 1851, Fort Defiance was built to the southeast of Canyon de Chelly in the hopes that a permanent military presence would bring peace, and in 1855, another treaty was signed. The Navajo traded land for peace but this solution did not work. Between 1856 and 1864, the Navajo were constantly raided by both New Mexicans and other

Native American tribes, and in return they continued to steal livestock. The Americans decided on what was termed a "final solution" to the Navajo "problem": to kill or capture all Navajo and relocate them to a reservation southeast of Santa Fe, New Mexico, called Bosque Redondo ("round forest"), over 300 miles (480 km) from their traditional lands.

Under the direction of General James H. Carleton, the Americans began a program of starving the Navajo into submission. Between December 1863 and January 1864, Colonel Kit Carson led troops on a brutal campaign into the canyons, destroying livestock, food supplies, and homes, and even cutting down 1,000 peach trees. The Navajo began surrendering in large numbers, and in March 1864, the first 1,500 were sent on what became known as the Long Walk to Bosque Redondo. Nine thousand would be sent in total to what can best be described as hell. The farmland was too acrid to grow anything, there were few trees and no shelter from the wind or cold, rations were scarce, and they had to share with Apache, who were their enemies.

Conditions were so bad that when word leaked to the east, there was a congressional investigation in 1865; it would be three more years before the Navajo were allowed to return home. Less than half survived the ordeal. On June 1, 1868, a treaty assigned the Navajo 3.5 million acres, including Canyon de Chelly, only one-tenth of their original lands. Today there are around 160,000 Navajo, who live on 8 million acres.

◎ Homolovi Ruins State Park

Homolovi is between Holbrook and Winslow, just north of the interstate. It was opened to the public in 1993 after several years of excavations and research. Unfortunately the site has been looted extensively by illegal pot hunters.

GETTING THERE: From I-40, take exit 257 to AZ 87 north, a right turn if heading west. The park entrance is a little over a mile (1.6 km) from the interstate and is on the left. Follow the paved road straight to the visitors center where you pay an admission fee.

THINGS YOU NEED TO KNOW: The park is open every day except Christmas. Amenities include a large campground and restrooms, but no services. For more information, phone 928-289-4106; visit www.azstateparks.com/parks/horu; or write to Homolovi Ruins State Park, HCR 63, Box 5, Winslow, AZ 86047.

Homol'ovi is Hopi for "the place of little hills." Over 340 sites have been found in the region. The first archaeological work was done in 1896 by Jesse Walter Fewkes, who also excavated at Mesa Verde. In 1984, the University of Arizona began extensive excavations and surveys and what you see today is a result of its work.

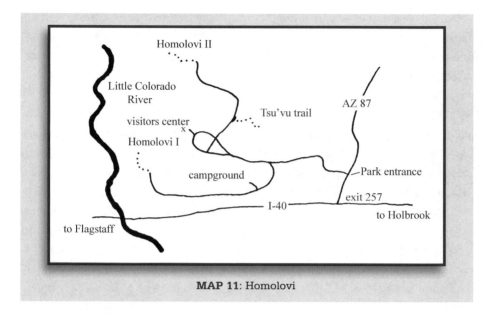

MAP 11: Homolovi

The earliest evidence consists of some pithouses that were inhabited between A.D. 750 and 850 on a seasonal basis. The region was then abandoned for two centuries before being reoccupied around 1050, when the Ancestral Puebloans began to build pueblos. After 1250 there was rapid growth in population resulting in seven pueblos on the east side of the Little Colorado River and two, Homolovi III and IV (neither is open to the public at this time), on the west side. This growth was most likely due to the reliable water source.

After A.D. 1300, the people from the west side moved across the river to the east, where they built larger pueblos. Homolovi I had 200 rooms; Homolovi II, over 1,000, plus 3 plazas and 40 kivas, making it one of the largest pueblos in this region. Extensive trade in ceramics, shells, obsidian, and cotton was conducted at Homolovi II, covering an area from Flagstaff in the west to Zuni in the east, the Hopi mesas to the north, and Phoenix to the south. It was also here that the katsina religious beliefs developed in the 1300s, beliefs that remain with the Hopi today (see page 412). The kivas are rectangular rather than round and probably indicate an influence from the Mogollon to the south. The Hopi still construct rectangular kivas today.

In the late 1300s there were problems that are not understood at present. For some reason the people began to leave, and by the early 1400s the entire region was deserted. Most of the people migrated north to the Hopi mesas, where their descendants still live. These sites are sacred to the Hopi.

In 1993, the state park was opened in cooperation with the Hopi to share the sites with the general public and also to try to stop the terrible looting that was occurring. The many craters you see at both sites are the remainder of holes dug by pot hunters who not only take the artifacts they find but destroy virtually everything in the process.

Touring Homolovi

Follow the park road straight to the visitors center, where you pay an admission fee. If it is not open, continue to the sites and pay before you leave. When you leave the visitors center, the road is one-way, so you must turn right and then left at the first crossroad to go toward Homolovi II. Once on this road you go down a small hill; there is a pullout on the right where the petroglyph trail begins. It is called the **TSU'VO LOOP TRAIL** and is **easy**, but *tsu'vo* is Hopi for "rattlesnake," so you need to be extra wary. Rattlers like to stay under the large boulders along the trail. Never step too close to the shadows by the rocks or reach under any of the stones. Stay at least 5 feet (1.5 m) from any snakes you see and report sightings to the park staff.

There are several petroglyphs along the trail but they are difficult to see and very worn. Never touch any rock art. Near the beginning of the trail is a large rock that is

Homolovi II, west section

flat on top and has two large depressions that were made by the process of grinding seeds into flour. The flour was probably for ceremonial use. Just ahead of this on the left is a petroglyph of bear paws. Next is a petroglyph of three human figures. On the right farther along the trail and below are several images that might depict a migration, but remember, interpretations vary for almost all rock art. The next image is of a large figure with raised arms that has been dated to around A.D. 1200.

The next images appear to be upside down. They were carved on the rock face when it was attached to the side of the butte above, but collapsed and fell into the gully, coming to rest the wrong way up. The last image is of a snake, or possibly a bolt of lightning. You can return to the parking area the same way or follow the marked loop to the right, just after the raised-armed figure, and turn right again where it joins the **DINE POINT TRAIL**. Inquire at the visitors center if interested in following this trail.

Turn right out of the parking area and drive to the end of the road to the Homolovi II ruins. The trail to the site is **moderate** as it is all uphill for about ¼ mile (0.4 km) to the ruins, and then it becomes **easy**. If you are not able to walk up this first part, you are permitted to drive to the roofed shelter that is nearly at the ruins; just be careful of people walking along the path.

At the Y in the trail, turn left to a large restored area of the pueblo. The rooms you see were probably used for domestic activities and were part of the west section. Return to the main trail and continue into the central plaza. This large plaza was the focal point of the pueblo where ceremonies and dances would take place, as well as the location for kivas. The multistoried structure that surrounded this open space, as well as the room blocks around the two other plazas, consisted of over 1,000 rooms and housed between 800 and 1,000 residents. This was the largest pueblo in the region. Notice the many depressions around the site, which are the remains of holes

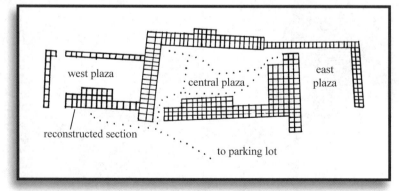

PLAN 6: Homolovi II

Homolovi I

looters dug in search of pottery, arrowheads, and other sellable goods. The trail winds past a rectangular kiva and to the edge of the east plaza, giving you a good idea of the overall size of the pueblo. Return to the parking area by the same path.

To go to Homolovi I, follow the road back past the visitors center and take the first right toward the campground. Stay on this paved road to the end, where there is a parking lot for the site. The trail is **easy**. Walk along the trail toward the mound ahead. This is the site. A small section has been reconstructed but for the most part you see rubble and depressions. Unless you are really interested in archaeology, give this one a pass. There are some nice views of the Little Colorado River, but do not go anywhere near the water as there is quicksand along the banks. Stay on the trails.

It will take about 1 to 1½ hours to see Homolovi II and the **PETROGLYPH TRAIL**. Add another ½ hour for Homolovi I.

day 4

Grand Canyon
National Park
Arizona

■ Established in 1908 as a national
monument, in 1919 as a national park

■ Encompasses 1,900 square miles
(4,920 square km)

■ Elevation ranges from 1800 to 9,161
feet (613–2,792 m)

The Grand Canyon

5. Grand Canyon National Park

GETTING THERE: From Williams, drive east out of town until you cross under the interstate to AZ 64, which leads straight to the south entrance of Grand Canyon National Park. The road is good all the way but if you are driving early in the morning, beware of deer and elk near, or on, the road. If you are going from Flagstaff, follow US 180 to AZ 64, or you can drive north on US 89 to Cameron and turn left onto AZ 64, which goes to the east entrance. **NOTE:** These directions are to the South Rim only, as I will describe the approach to the North Rim later.

THINGS YOU NEED TO KNOW: Words cannot begin to describe the Grand Canyon. Photographs and paintings do not do justice to the grandeur of the spectacle. It is a sight that must be seen, and even then the mind does not seem to be able to comprehend what the eyes see. To paraphrase President Theodore Roosevelt, everyone should see the Grand Canyon.

And there is much to see: The Grand Canyon is 280 miles long (450 km), 18 miles (29 km) across at its widest point, and 1 mile (1.6 km) deep. It is the largest natural cleft in the earth. The elevation on the South Rim is 4,460 feet (1,360 m) and rises to 5,940 feet (1,810 m) on the North Rim. Both rims slope from north to south so everything in the north drains into the canyon, while on the south it drains away from the edge. This results in more erosion on the north canyon walls, which has pushed it farther from the Colorado River, leaving the North Rim much more distant in relation to the river than is the South Rim.

The South Rim is open all year, whereas the North Rim is only open from mid- or late May until sometime in October. High season is May to October. Over 4 million people visit the park each year and many end up asking the same question: Where do I find a parking space? The park is terribly crowded in the high season, with long lines at the entrances, traffic jams and the ever elusive parking spots. It is best to arrive early in the morning, before 8 AM if possible, and visit some of the less popular places, which I describe in this section. There is a shuttle bus to some viewpoints and trails (see page 74), but you still have to park your car first. A pleasant alternative is the day train that runs from Williams to the Grand Canyon and back.

The South Rim has all the amenities, including lodging, grocery stores, gas stations, restaurants, camping equipment, showers, and laundries. There are also a post office, bank, and ATM access. For lodging, call 888-297-2757 or visit www.xanterra .com for reservations, which in most cases must be made several months in advance. There are two campgrounds and an RV park, and reservations for those are recommended from April through October. Call Reserve America at 877-444-6777 or visit www.recreation.gov. Sites may be reserved up to six months in advance.

A permit is required for camping below the rim or in the backcountry, for which there is a fee. Backcountry permits may only be secured by filling out the online form found at www.nps.gov/grca/planyourvisit/backcountry-permit.htm.

One- and two-day mule trips into the canyon are available and require advance reservations through Xanterra (888-297-2757 or www.xanterra.com). The one-day trip goes part way to the river and back while the two-day stays overnight at Phantom Ranch in the canyon. To ride the mules, you must be at least 4 feet 7 inches tall (140 cm) and weigh less than 200 pounds (90 kg) and not be visibly pregnant.

There are several trails that allow visitors to hike into the canyon, but you must be well prepared and know your limitations, as many people must be rescued each year for overestimating their abilities. Be aware of the weather conditions before starting, as the temperature can exceed 100°F (40°C) in the summer and trails can be icy in the winter. Stop at the visitors center for trail conditions before attempting any of them. Bring plenty of water and food with you and be sure to have good sturdy shoes. A list of the major trails follows. Consider all trails **very difficult**! The only exception is the Rim trail.

THE RIM TRAIL is **easy**, with most of it paved and level. **CAUTION:** In many places, there are no guardrails along the edge, which drops off suddenly, and a fall can be fatal. Be especially vigilant with children. This trail runs between Pipe Creek Vista, which is a little over 1 mile (1.6 km) east of Mather point, and Hermits Rest, a total distance of more than 12 miles (19 km) one-way.

THE BRIGHT ANGEL TRAIL goes down to the river and is **very difficult**. Indian Gardens is about 9 miles (14.5 km) round-trip from the rim and has restrooms and water and is the halfway point to the bottom. Allow a full day just to go to Indian Gardens and return. You will have to share this trail with mule trains. The trail begins west of the Bright Angel Lodge.

THE SOUTH KAIBAB TRAIL also goes to the river and is **very difficult**. Skeleton Point is about 6 miles (9.5 km) round-trip from the rim, takes about 6 hours, and is less than halfway to the bottom. The trailhead is on the Yaki Point Road and only accessible by shuttle bus.

THE GRANDVIEW TRAIL does not go to the river and is **very difficult**. This trail is not maintained and is the most difficult in the park. **CAUTION:** This trail is not for the inexperienced. The trail is steep, with high steps in places, very narrow with loose rocks in the path, and many sheer drop-offs. Go down the first few hundred feet before deciding whether to attempt the remainder as it does not get any better! On the plus side, there are no mules and very few people, so it offers some solitude even in the high season.

There is a free shuttle bus system that follows three different routes in the park. You may get on and off the buses at any of the stops that are marked with signs showing a bus symbol. No tickets are required. The routes are color coded and a square beside the door of each bus indicates which color it is and thus the route it follows. Shuttles run at 15- to 30-minute intervals, depending on the season. The Blue, or Village, route makes several stops around Canyon Village, including the parking lots, but does not go to any scenic overlooks. This line connects to the other two, one east and the other west of the village. The Red, or Hermits Rest, route begins at the western extremity of the village and is the only way to travel to Hermits Rest during the high season. It stops at the many scenic viewpoints along the road, all of which are connected to the Rim Trail. The route is 7 miles (11 km) one-way. The Green, or

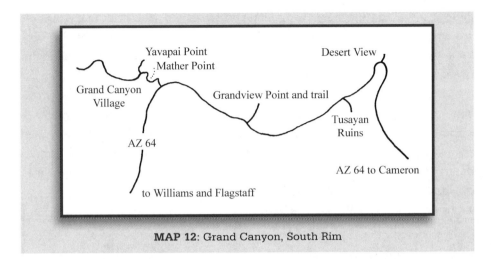

MAP 12: Grand Canyon, South Rim

Kaibab Trail, route goes from the Canyon View Information Center and travels east to the Kaibab trailhead, Yaki Point, and Pipe Creek Vista. It is the only way to get to the Kaibab Trail and Yaki Point, as this road is closed to cars. There is a hikers' express shuttle that goes from the Backcountry Info Center and Bright Angel Lodge directly to the Kaibab trailhead early each morning.

South Rim

If you plan on touring the South Rim, try to arrive early in the morning to avoid the worst of the crowds, especially during the high season. It takes about 1 hour from Williams to the south entrance. After paying your entrance fee, continue north on AZ 64. When you come to the junction for the Desert View Drive, which is a right turn, stay to the left and you will see a sign for the visitors center parking area. The first lot is for RV parking. The next entrance is for lots 2 and 3; if they are full, continue around the bend to lot 4. These serve the visitors center and Mather Point, the first stop on the Tour. If the lots are full, continue to the next stop, Yavapai Point, from which you can walk back to Mather Point and the visitors center. Either of these stops gives a spectacular first view of the canyon.

The next stop is Yavapai Point. Turn right out of the parking lot and then right again less than a mile (1.6 km) farther along onto a short road to the parking lot. There are restrooms at this stop. From this point you can follow the Rim Trail in either direction, east to Mather Point or west. There are unbelievable views from the trail, some of the best in the park.

When you exit from Yavapai, turn left to avoid Canyon Village and continue back to the turnoff for the Desert View Drive, which is on your left. If you choose to go through the village, the many roads wind past stores, lodges, a bank, and a post office, among other buildings. Check *The Guide*, which is given out at the entrances, for a map and list of all the services. **NOTE:** During the summer the roads through the village are congested with traffic and pedestrians.

Once back to the intersection of AZ 64 and Desert View Drive, turn left (if coming from Yavapai Point) toward Desert View, the eastern extremity of the view points. It is about 25 miles (40 km) from Canyon Village to Desert View. There are many view points along this road but be cautious, as they are all on the left (heading toward Desert View) and the traffic tends to be a bit fast for the winding, and sometimes crowded, road. Each pullout offers a different perspective of the canyon with every one as spectacular as the next.

Tusayan Ruins

The next stop on the tour is at Tusayan Ruins, about 20 miles (32 km) from the junction and on the right. The road to the site is clearly marked. From the parking lot, follow the trail past the museum and turn left where the path divides. Continue in a clockwise direction to the back of the small pueblo. Tusayan is U-shaped with living rooms on the west and storage in the north and south arms (see Plan 7). This is a typical shape for an Ancestral Puebloan pueblo but usu-

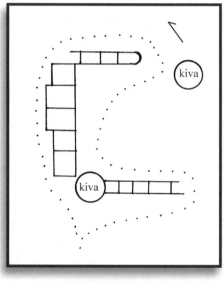

PLAN 7: Tusayan

ally the opening of the U would face south, whereas here it faces east (see the Unit Pueblo, page 398). The five rooms you see along the west side were the living areas, which were two stories high. The many stones lying around are the remains of the collapsed walls. Only the foundations have been restored. Continuing around the corner, you see the storage rooms, which were only one story and smaller than the living rooms. At this point there is another trail that leads to the area that is believed to have been where the fields were located. This is a short gravel loop trail—a pleasant walk, though it is difficult to see where the fields might have been. In fact, fields would have been near almost any of the ancient pueblos in the Southwest.

As you continue on the main trail you see a kiva at the end of the row of storage rooms. At some point during the occupation of Tusayan, this kiva was built to replace the original one that had burned down and had been built into the storage rooms

Tusayan Ruins, one of the living rooms

across the plaza to your right. The path follows the front of the living rooms to the southwest corner of the plaza right in front of the first kiva. The pueblo dates from A.D. 1185 and was occupied by the Kayenta for only 20 years and never inhabited again. Around 30 people lived here.

The Kayenta occupied the South Rim and thousands of sites have been found in the region. This was the western extent of the Kayenta. Tusayan Ruins were excavated in 1930 by Emil Haury, exposing several living and storage rooms along with two kivas. Part of the site was left unexcavated so that future archaeologists, perhaps using new and better technology, might be able to learn and understand the site and culture better, something that is common today but was rare in 1930.

John Wesley Powell's (see page 80) discovery of eight archaeological sites in the canyon bottom in 1869 was the first record of Ancestral Puebloan presence in the region. In 1915, Neil Judd became the first archaeologist to work in the park and surveyed the area, discovering many sites that he believed, as had Powell, were from an ancient Pueblo culture. In the 1930s, while Tusayan was being excavated and studied by Haury, Edward T. Hall surveyed the North Rim. Combined with Judd's surveys, over 500 sites had been recorded. The North Rim had been occupied by the Virgin; and the South, by the Kayenta. Over 1,500 sites are now known from the peak period of occupation between A.D. 1050 and 1150.

Kiva, Tusayan

The ancient people probably lived in the canyon on a seasonal basis, farming during the summer on the alluvial banks near the river and returning to the rim for the winter to supplement their food stocks with hunting. Many granaries have been found in the canyon, as well as terraces on which they would plant their crops. The Kayenta were present by A.D. 900, reaching the peak population around 1050 and abandoning the region by 1200. The Hopi, who are descendants of the Kayenta, claim the canyon is the *sipapu* from which their people emerged. Even though the Ancestral Puebloans lived here only 300 years, people had traveled into the canyon as early as 1000 B.C., the Archaic period. Evidence of this early date comes from split-twig figurines. These are willow branches split in half lengthwise and shaped into animals, such as deer and mountain sheep, using a single branch. They have been discovered in several caves in the canyon.

From Tusayan Ruins, turn right toward Desert View, the last view point before the east entrance. You can get a higher view over the canyon from a stone tower after climbing the narrow, winding staircase that begins inside the gift shop. This climb can be tricky as the stairs are hardly wide enough to meet those going in the opposite direction, but the effort is worth it. A few viewing scopes on top point out specific landmarks. There are many services at Desert View, including a gas station and snack bar.

Visiting the viewpoints and Tusayan Ruins will take the entire morning, so if you have brought lunch along, travel back toward Canyon Village and watch for some picnic tables next to the road just past the turnoff for Moran Point. This is a nice quiet area to stop for lunch and rest a bit before heading over the edge.

The Grandview Trail

The following part of the tour involves hiking partway down into the canyon, and back out. I chose the Grandview Trail to take my students down as this is less crowded than other trails; at times you are the only one on the path. WARNING: Hiking down this trail, or any other, is **very difficult** and can be dangerous if you are not in good physical condition and used to desert hiking. The Grandview Trail is rated as the most difficult in the park, is not regularly maintained, and is very steep and narrow. There are high steps and loose rocks on the trail, as well as sheer drop-offs. If you wish to attempt it, just walk down for five minutes; it does not get any better and, in some places, it is worse. I cannot overemphasize the difficulty of this trail.

Having said this, it is a wonderful experience to hike below the rim on any of the trails. The Grandview Trail does not go directly to the river but has two points to which most people go: the Coconino Saddle, which is 2 miles (3.3 km) round-trip, and Horseshoe Mesa, 6 miles (9.5 km) round-trip. There is no water anywhere on this trail, so pack plenty, along with snacks. To Coconino, allow 2 to 3 hours' return; and for Horseshoe Mesa, anywhere from 4 to 10 hours. Remember a good rule of thumb: Any trail into the canyon is one-third down and two-thirds up! Hiking shoes are recommended; though I know personally of one person who wore sandals, I would not advise this.

In 1883, John Hance made a crude trail to his asbestos claim in the canyon near Grandview. Three years later he advertised his services as the first guide to take travelers down to the river. In 1890, the Grandview Trail was built to go to copper mines on Horseshoe Mesa, followed two years later by the first hotel that was built at Grandview for tourists coming from Flagstaff by stagecoach. At a cost of $20, just for the stagecoach ride, only the relatively wealthy could afford the adventure. A new lodge was constructed at Grand Canyon Village, several miles west of Grandview, in 1901, after the railroad built a spur track into the area, thereby condemning Grandview to obscurity. There are no longer any lodgings there.

Today, several trails descend into the canyon from both the South and North Rims. They average about 8 miles (13 km) to the river and usually take a full day down and another back out. Some athletes training for the Ironman competition run from the North Rim through the canyon to the South Rim! You should consult a doctor before attempting this.

If you do not spend the afternoon hiking into the canyon, there are many other view points to visit, as well as shops and galleries in Canyon Village. This concludes the tour of the South Rim of the Grand Canyon and the end of Day 4 of the Grand Circle Tour.

Grand Canyon from the Grandview Trail

The timeline for Day 4 is: 1 hour from Williams (or Flagstaff) to the South Rim, 1 to 1½ hours for Mather and/or Yavapai point and the drive to Tusayan, 20 to 30 minutes at Tusayan, 30 minutes at Desert View, and, if you hike into the canyon, 2 to 4 hours, and 1 hour back to Williams.

EARLY EXPLORATION OF THE CANYON

In 1540, part of Coronado's expedition arrived at the South Rim (see page 415), guided by Hopi, but after a week of trying in vain to find a route down to the river, the explorers declared the region useless and returned to New Mexico. The first nonnative to penetrate the canyon was Fray Francisco Garcés in 1776. Guided by Havasupai to the river below, he was astonished by the great natural barrier of the canyon. It would be nearly 200 years before another white man would enter the canyon and successfully navigate through the entire length of the Grand Canyon.

Naturalist and geologist John Wesley Powell had a great interest in all things natural from an early age and taught himself geology, botany, and zoology. At age 22, in

1856, he rowed down to the mouth of the Mississippi River alone; the entire length of the Ohio River, the following year; and the Illinois river, the next year, collecting samples of shells, minerals and anything else he discovered of interest.

Powell enlisted in the 20th Illinois Volunteers when the Civil War began in 1860 and lost his right arm in the Battle of Shiloh in April 1862. When his wound had healed, he returned to service in 1863. He was discharged from service with the rank of major at the end of the war in 1865 and was hired by Wesleyan University in Bloomington, Illinois, as curator of its museum. Throughout the state he gave lectures on various scientific topics, but it was on field trips to the West that he developed the idea of exploring the Colorado River through the Grand Canyon.

On May 24, 1869, Powell set out with nine men, four boats, and provisions for 10 months from Green River, Wyoming, on the Green River, to fill in the blank space on maps of the region. After about one month, one of the crew decided to leave the expedition. They had lost one boat and most of their supplies and had no idea what lay ahead or how long the expedition would take. On August 13, after 81 days, they entered the Grand Canyon, one of the last areas of the United States to be mapped. It was a harrowing trip through giant rapids and narrow, granite-lined, sheer canyon walls. In many places they had to portage past rapids as Powell was overly cautious, due to having lost most of the team's supplies early on in the journey. He would stop often to explore the riverbanks and climb up the canyon walls. At one point, while climbing a nearly vertical section of rock, he became stranded, no longer able to continue up or to go back down, as he feared he would fall should he let go of his one handhold. After hearing his shouts for help, one of the other members of the crew managed to climb above Powell and lower down a pair of long johns that Powell, not hesitating for a moment, grabbed hold of with his one hand and scrambled to safety. He was criticized by other members of the party for such reckless behavior.

Exhausted, pounded by the rapids, and nearly out of food, three men would not go on any longer and decided to abandon the expedition and climb out of the canyon to safety. A few days later, on August 29, Powell and his remaining crew emerged from the canyon at the junction of the Colorado and Virgin Rivers. There they found three Mormon settlers and a Native American . . . dragging the river for their bodies! Ironically, the three men who had left a few days before were killed by Indians.

Powell returned to Illinois a hero and began a lecture tour in hopes of raising funds for a second expedition to produce a map and publication, something that did not come out of the first trip. After two years he returned to the Colorado River with a crew of ten to once again successfully traverse the Grand Canyon, this time producing the first maps of the region.

He died on September 23, 1902, and is buried in Arlington National Cemetery.

GEOLOGY OF GRAND CANYON

The Navajo, whose reservation borders the park to the east, speak of a great flood caused by incessant rains: As the waters were rising, an outlet formed—the Grand Canyon—and released the waters. The Navajo survived by being changed temporarily into fish, returning to human form when the waters receded. The geology confirms that the flood had indeed occurred.

The canyon runs in an east–west direction and forms a massive natural barrier to both animals and humans. Most of the carving of the canyon is from the Colorado River, which originates in the western Rocky Mountains and travels 1,450 miles (2,330 km) to the sea. It drops over 10,000 feet (3,050 km) in elevation, drains a watershed of 240,000 square miles (622,000 square km) and carries on average 400,000 tons (365,000 mt) of sand, silt, and debris *every day!* The erosion of the canyon by the river is not caused for the most part by the water but by all this debris that acts like sandpaper, scouring down through the layers of stone to carve what you see, which took only about 5.5 million years, a blink of the eye in geologic terms.

Hoover Dam was constructed in the 1930s at the western end of the canyon, forming Lake Mead. But as soon as the dam blocked the river's path to the sea, it began to fill the reservoir with all the silt, which had previously been forming a huge delta in the Gulf of California. Glen Canyon Dam, upstream from the canyon, was completed in 1963 and created Lake Powell, in part to slow the flow of silt into Lake Mead so as to try to preserve this reservoir for as long as possible. But as a consequence of this dam erosion of the Grand Canyon has virtually stopped. The canyon is still getting wider, due to the erosion by tributaries as well as rainfall and the freeze/thaw cycle, but the Colorado is also becoming clogged with rock falls, as it no longer has the power to push large boulders through the canyon. Also, deltas of sand and silt are forming at the mouths of these tributaries, changing the nature of the inner canyon. Periodic controlled floods have been created by opening the gates of Glen Canyon Dam to attempt and mimic nature and have had limited success, but the inner canyon has been altered considerably by this structure.

The oldest rock at the bottom of the canyon is called Vishnu Schist and is approximately 2 billion years old. This was formed from volcanic eruptions and is extremely hard, trapping the river in a narrow gorge and slowing the rate of erosion, both in depth and width. Just above this is granite, as hard as the schist, which dates to 1.75 million years ago. Both of these types of rock were originally part of a mountain range created by uplift that was eroded over time into a flat plain. This plain was covered in turn by the sea, which filled over time into sedimentary layers that contain fossil algae, one of the earliest-known life forms on earth.

By 500 million years ago, the sea covered the region once more and would advance and retreat five times over the next several 100 million years. This action left coarse sandstone near the shoreline, finer sandstone farther out, and limestone in the deeper areas. Several small animal fossils are found in this layer, including trilobites, brachiopods, sponges, and seaweed. From around 350 million years ago we find the fossils of fish, shellfish, corals, and mollusks. Then, 300 million years ago, the sea began retreating to the west, creating a flood plain that eventually dried and became covered with windblown sand in which are found the footprints of primitive reptiles and trails left by insects and scorpions. This layer is the white Coconino sandstone and dates to 250 million years ago. Rivers flowed through again followed by windblown sand that built up deposits of 4,000 to 8,000 feet (1,200–2,400 m) that have completely eroded away except for Cedar Mountain, which is east of Desert View. This layer is what makes up the sandstone in Zion National Park (see page 107).

Sixty-five million years ago, the Rocky Mountains and Colorado Plateau began to rise, causing cracks and faults in the crust. The Colorado River was flowing into a lake that was draining into the Gulf of Mexico, east of the Grand Canyon region. Five and a half million years ago, the area in the Gulf of California dropped and the Colorado turned southwest, finding an outlet through what would become the Grand Canyon, draining the lake and bringing a tremendous amount of debris through the canyon, carving it in less than 5 million years.

The latest geologic formations occurred 1.2 million years ago, when volcanic eruptions in the western section of the canyon formed dams that created lakes as much as 2,300 feet (700 m) deep before the river cut through the debris, opening up the canyon once more. The remnants of the lava flows remain on the canyon walls.

North Rim

The environment on the North Rim is very different from that of the South Rim due to the higher elevation and the fact that it is more isolated. The road is closed from the first snowfall, usually late October or November, until late May the road can be closed on very short notice, so be prepared if traveling late in the fall. The North and South Rims are only 10 miles (16 km) apart at the narrowest point, but the drive between them is around 230 miles (370 km) and you should not try to visit both in the same day.

There are not many facilities at the North Rim or its vicinity. There is some lodging at the rim that requires advance reservations; Jacob Lake, on US 89A at the junction of the North Rim Road, has gas, groceries, and lodging. The closest towns with all services are Fredonia, Arizona, and Kanab, Utah. Fredonia is about 70 miles (112 km) from the North Rim and Kanab is another 7 miles (11 km).

GETTING THERE: From the South Rim, exit through the East Gate on AZ 64 to Cameron and turn left onto US 89 northbound (toward Page). After about 60 miles (96 km), the road divides to US 89A (left) to Jacob Lake, another 55 miles (88 km), which climbs up onto the Kaibab Plateau and can be a very slow drive, so allow plenty of time. From the turnoff for the park at Jacob Lake onto AZ 67 it is 45 miles (72 km) to the rim. If you are leaving from Williams or Flagstaff, see the directions to Jacob Lake (see pages 88–89).

THINGS YOU NEED TO KNOW: While fewer people visit the North Rim it is still crowded in the summer. This rim, which is less developed than the South Rim, offers the opportunity for a more peaceful visit, and the views of the canyon are just as spectacular. If you have been to the South Rim, your entrance receipt gets you into the North Rim within seven days. There is one lodge inside the park (call 877-386-4383) and two along AZ 67: Kaibab Lodge (928-638-2389) and the Jacob Lake Inn (928-643-7232). There is also one campground in the park and several outside. The lodges have restaurants and fuel; groceries are also available, and there is a post office at the rim. Mule trips go from the North Rim but not to the river (call 435-679-8665 for reservations). There is a shuttle service between the rims that departs from the North Rim at 7 AM, arriving at 11:30 at the South Rim, and leaves the South Rim at 1:30, arriving at the north rim at 6:30 PM (call 928-638-2820 for reservations, which are required; there is a fee).

Touring the North Rim

From Jacob Lake, follow AZ 67 to the visitors center, where two trails begin: The Bright Angel Point Trail is **moderate** and follows a paved, ½-mile (0.8 km) round-trip path to the rim on a peninsula that juts out into the canyon, offering spectacular views to the east, west, and south. The **TRANSEPT TRAIL** follows the rim from Grand Canyon Lodge to the campground and is 3 (4.8 km) miles round-trip. It is **moderate** if you go all the way or **easy** if only partially completed.

The North Kaibab Trail is the only trail that descends into the canyon from the North Rim and is **very difficult**, even if you go only a short distance; it is 12 miles (19 km) to the river. WARNING: Do not attempt to hike to the river and back in one day. This is extremely dangerous, particularly during the heat of summer. You share this trail with mules and if you meet them, move over as far as possible against the cliff face; stand still and do not talk to the mules, move toward them, or attempt to touch them. They can be startled and there have been cases of mules' falling to their death over the edge after an encounter with a hiker. The trailhead is about 2 miles (3.2 km) from the visitors center. Always ask about trail conditions before descending into the canyon, even if only for a short hike down and back.

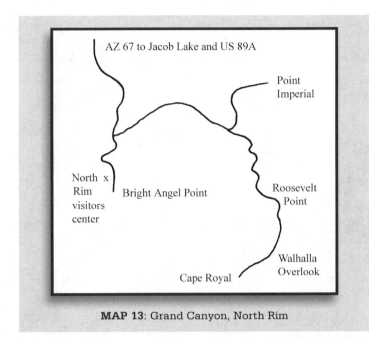

MAP 13: Grand Canyon, North Rim

Driving north from the visitors center, turn right after about 3 miles (4.8 km) to go to the eastern section, which includes Point Imperial, a left turn 5 miles (8 km) from the junction, and Cape Royal. At the end of the road is the **CAPE ROYAL TRAIL**, an **easy** ½-mile (0.8 km) return walk to a view point of the river and Angel's Window. On the return trip there is a view point at Walhalla Overlook, 2 miles (3.2 km) from Cape Royal on the right, and the Walhalla Glades ruins across the road.

This is a small house that was probably occupied during the summer by a single family that moved to the lower canyon for the winter. The two long, narrow rooms are the oldest, whereas the two larger rooms behind them, toward the north, were later additions. Notice the large limestone slab placed edgewise in the foundation of the northernmost room, an unusual feature. The small rooms on the west side were for storage. To the right of the trail when you enter the site are several small rooms that were built after the main structure and are of poorer construction. The site was inhabited around A.D. 1050 to 1100.

A couple of other viewpoints are along this road on your right heading back to the main road. It is 20 miles (32 km) from Cape Royal to AZ 67. There are many other trails along the rim and through the surrounding forests. Inquire at the visitors center for more information.

Pipe Springs National Monument
Arizona

■ Established as a national monument
May 31, 1923

■ Consists of 40 acres (16 ha)

■ Elevation 4900–5100 feet
(1500–1550 m)

Red Cliffs
Archaeological Site
Utah

■ A Virgin site excavated between
1977 and 1979 by the Bureau of Land
Management

■ Elevation 3260 feet (1000 m)

The Colorado from Navajo Bridge

Day 5 is mostly a travel day from Williams to Cedar City, Utah, but there is some dramatic scenery along the route, as well as two small sites plus another interesting stop along the way.

GETTING THERE: From Williams, drive east to the entrance of I-40 eastbound toward Flagstaff. Take exit 201 onto US 89 north toward Page. A good place to stop for a break is the trading post at Cameron, which is about 80 miles (128 km) from Williams. There are restrooms in the large gift shop, gas stations, restaurants, and a post office. An alternate route to Cameron from Williams is to travel along the South Rim of the Grand Canyon, which makes the journey about 120 miles (193 km), but the views from the East Gate to Cameron are impressive.

As you leave Cameron you cross the Little Colorado River via a modern highway bridge but to the west, on your left, is the original single-lane bridge that was built in 1912 and now carries an oil pipeline. Prior to this, the only way to cross the unpredictable Little Colorado was 6 miles (9.6 km) upstream (right) at a place called Tanner's Crossing. North of the river is the Painted Desert Badlands, which you first saw in the northern section of the Petrified Forest, that follows a west-northwest direction across the midsection of Arizona. It is 60 miles (96 km) from Cameron to the junction of US 89 and US 89A.

Turn left onto US 89A, which is the shortest route, and after another 12 miles (19 km) you will come to the Navajo Bridge, which spans the Colorado River. There are two bridges, the modern one that you will drive across and the original bridge (1929) that is today a pedestrian walkway. This was the first bridge to span the Colorado and is 467 feet (142 m) above the river and 835 feet (254 m) long. On the east side are Navajo vendors; and on the other side, a Native American gift shop and bookstore that is open from mid-May to mid-October. The restrooms are open year-round. You can park and walk across the span for a truly inspiring view of the river and canyon below, unless you are afraid of heights. It is approximately 150 miles (240 km) from Williams to the Navajo Bridge.

After crossing the river you see the Vermilion Cliffs on the right that continue until you enter the Kaibab Forest and begin to climb up the winding road to the Kaibab Plateau. The cliffs change color as the sun strikes them throughout the day. Jacob Lake is about 57 miles (90 km) from the Navajo Bridge and is where the access road to the North Rim of the Grand Canyon begins (see Day 4, page 84). Amenities include a service station, grocery store, restaurant, motel, campground, and picnic area, but some services are seasonal. Sometimes this road is temporarily closed in the winter. (If you stay on US 89 to Page and beyond, it will take you to Kanab, Utah, where you can return to US 89A by going south to Fredonia.) It is 32 miles (51 km) to Fredonia and a further 13 (21 km) to Pipe Springs. In Fredonia you will turn left onto AZ 389 toward Hurricane, Utah.

6. Pipe Springs National Monument

This is not a Native American site but was built by Mormon homesteaders and consists of a visitors center, museum, the original home and farm buildings, a couple of horses, and three longhorn cattle (subject to change). There is also a trail behind the buildings that goes over a small hill and has interpretive signs along the way that were put in place by the Kaibab Paiute, who built the trail and whose reservation surrounds the monument. Summer hours are 7 AM to 5 PM; winter, 8 to 5.

Pipe Springs is located in the Arizona Strip, an area bordered by the Grand Canyon on the south and the Vermilion Cliffs to the north. This vast desert has few water sources so the constant flow from the spring at Pipe Springs has made this site an oasis ever since there were people in the region. Traces of Paleo-Indians have been found in the strip and the Virgin used this territory from at least 300 B.C. to A.D. 1250 or later, when they were absorbed, or became, the Southern Paiute. The Paiute were seminomadic, surviving on the natural plants and local game but also growing corn and other crops at Pipe Springs.

In the 1850s the Mormons drove the Paiute from the water source as they continued to expand their control over southern Utah and northern Arizona. In 1863 they brought in cattle and sheep but were having trouble with the Navajo who continually raided their herds. In 1870 they built Winsor Castle, a fortified house, for protection against marauding Native Americans. By 1879 they had over 2,000 cattle, too many for the land to support, which caused overgrazing and the destruction of the natural grasses. The Mormons sold the land and buildings in 1895 to private interests but the Paiute continued to suffer, as they remained cut off from the water.

The late 19th century saw a dramatic decline in the population of Paiute as they were forced from their native territory and water sources and struggled to survive in this harsh region. In 1907, a reservation was founded for them that surrounded, but did not include, Pipe Springs and, even though they were guaranteed a percentage of the water, they never received their proper due and trouble over water rights continued. Pipe Springs became a national monument in 1923 and the government claimed the water rights, "allowing" the Paiute one-third, one-third of what was rightfully theirs in total to begin with.

Today the Paiute work with the National Parks Service. There is a museum at the visitors center that chronicles the Paiute heritage of this region. They also have a campground nearby and a nature trail that goes past some petroglyphs. Contact the Tribal Office (928-643-7245) for reservations, which are required for both the campground and the trail. For more information, phone 928-643-7105; visit www.nps.gov/pisp; or write to Pipe Springs National Monument, HC 65, Box 5, Fredonia, AZ 86022. The park is open all year except for Thanksgiving Day, Christmas Day, and New Year's Day.

TOURING THE PARK

There are guided tours of Winsor Castle every half-hour, which is the only way to see the interior of the structure. The rest of the buildings are self-guided and there are interpretive signs at each location. The trail is **easy** and goes through the orchards, across the pond, and to the two sets of buildings and corral. Much of this remains similar to the way it was originally set out by the Mormon pioneers. There is also the **RIDGE TRAIL**, which is **moderate** and begins past Winsor Castle. It is a narrow dirt path that winds up and around the hill behind the site and offers great views of the desert and surrounding cliffs. **CAUTION:** Watch out for rattlesnakes on this trail.

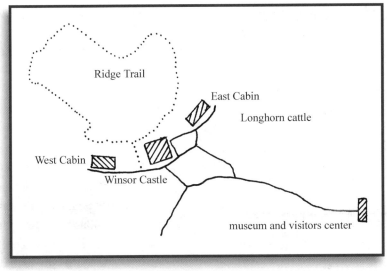

PLAN 8: Pipe Springs

The museum has displays of both pioneer and Paiute material, one of the few locations to see Paiute artifacts. There is also a good bookstore that carries Paiute material that is hard to find elsewhere. Allow an hour for the museum and tour; add ½ hour for the Ridge Trail. There are clean restrooms.

7. Red Cliffs Archaeological Site

Back to AZ 389 turn right and continue to Hurricane, Utah. About 20 miles (32 km) from Pipe Springs is the town of Colorado City, past which you enter Utah and the highway number changes from AZ 389 to UT 59. Also remember that if you are traveling during the summer, late spring or early fall, the time changes when you cross the border and you lose an hour switching to daylight saving time. It is another 20 miles (32 km) to Hurricane.

As you near the town of Hurricane, the road drops down suddenly with a stretch that has many curves, a very steep incline, and a Stop sign at the end. Turn right at this Stop sign and then left at the stoplight and you will be on the main street of Hurricane. Continue out of town heading west for about 9 miles (14 km) until you come to a traffic light past the Quail Creek Recreation Area. There is a large gas station on the right at the light. Turn right onto Old US 91 and drive for approximately 4 miles (6.4 km) along the winding road. At this point, watch for a narrow underpass on the left, where the road dips down into a small valley. There is a sign for the Red Cliffs

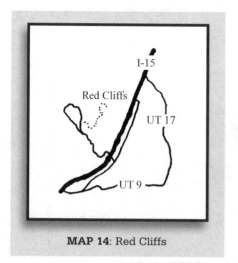

MAP 14: Red Cliffs

Campground but it can only be seen coming from the other direction. There is nothing marking the turn heading north. For more information, visit www .blm.gov/ut/st/en/prog/more/cultural/ archaeology/places_to_visit/red_ cliffs_archaeological.html. After going through the very narrow underpass, turn left and you will cross a stream that has a paved bottom, but do not attempt to cross if the water is high. Continue up a little hill, then along a dirt road that consists of two tracks. Do not continue if the road is wet. Shortly the road divides into a one-way loop; stay left. Drive all the way around through the campground and ignore the signs about paying if you plan to see only the Red Cliffs archaeological site, as the fees are for campers. Just after passing the camp office, watch for a small path on the left, which is not well marked. This is the trailhead to the site. There is no place to park but if you drive a bit farther it is possible to pull off enough onto the left shoulder to allow vehicles to pass. Remember, this is one-way.

The trail first climbs a small hill and then drops down into a dry wash that is sandy and hard walking. The cottonwood trees along this section are indicative of moisture below the surface. Once you are through this section it is mostly uphill to the site but it is not especially steep. Be sure to stay on the trail. Near the top there is a zigzag gate to go through and a short climb to the site. Take time to stop and look around as you ascend because the views of the red cliffs that surround the site are marvelous. The trail is **moderate** but can be **difficult** in the summer as temperatures can surpass 100°F (40°C). Be sure to bring water even though it is not a long hike. It takes 15 to 20 minutes to reach the site. Part of the site has a roof covering it that can be seen from the road.

This is the only Virgin archaeological site that has been excavated by archaeologists, stabilized, and opened to the public. It was excavated in the 1970s by Gardiner F. Dalley and Douglas A. McFadden, Bureau of Land Management archaeologists who also stabilized the site. They published their report "The Archaeology of the Red Cliffs Site" in 1985. The site consists of 27 storage units, including several round structures, that date to BM III. There are two habitation structures, as well as exterior hearths, open work areas, and middens that date to the Pueblo period. About 17 of these

From the trail to Red Cliffs

rooms are open, including some of the round storage rooms. An unusual aspect of the site is that no kivas were found, the kiva being one of the defining characteristic of Ancestral Puebloan sites, though this site is definitely Virgin. The Red Cliffs site is a bit difficult to get to but worth the effort. Watch out for rattlesnakes.

Once you return to the main road, turn left to Leeds, which will take you to I-15 north to Cedar City, a 20-minute drive. There are many motels and other services in Cedar and it tends to be less expensive than services close to Zion. Alternatively, you can return to Hurricane, which also has travel services, or go closer to Zion in Springdale, which is very touristy but closer to the park. Reservations are normally required during the summer in Springdale.

This ends Day 5 of the Grand Circle Tour. The timeline is approximately as follows: 1 hour to Cameron (from Williams); 1 hour to the Navajo Bridge; 30 minutes if you walk across the bridge and visit the gift shop; 1½ to 2 hours to Pipe Springs; 1 hour at Pipe Springs; 1 hour to Red Cliffs; (1 hour lost due to the time change); 1 hour at Red Cliffs; 20 minutes to Cedar City.

day 6

Zion National Park
Utah

- Established in 1909 as a national monument and in 1919 as a national park
- 230 square miles (593 square km)
- Elevation from 3,666 to 8,740 feet (1,120–2,665 m)

Nearby Sites

◎ Parawon Gap Petroglyphs
◎ Cedar Breaks National Monument

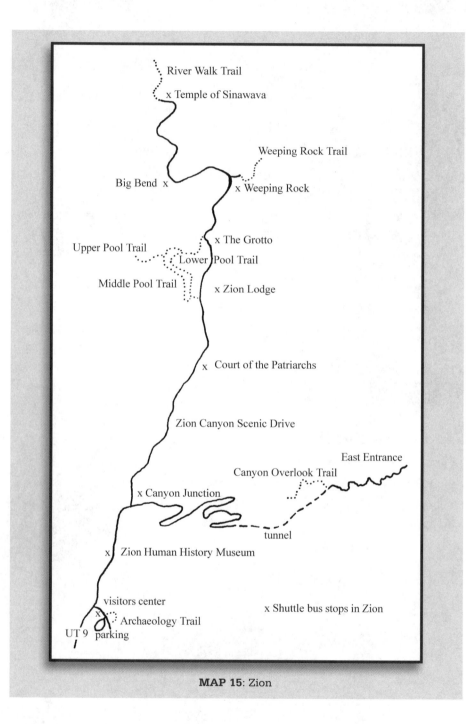

MAP 15: Zion

8. Zion National Park

GETTING THERE: From Cedar City, follow I-15 south to exit 27 onto AZ 17 toward Hurricane to the junction with AZ 9. Turn left, east, on AZ 9 and continue straight through to the south entrance of Zion. If staying in Hurricane, simply follow AZ 9 east.

THINGS YOU NEED TO KNOW: Zion is open year-round. AZ 9 goes through the park and joins US 89 at Mt. Carmel Junction. The road into the canyon is only accessible by free shuttle bus from the end of March to mid-November, unless you are staying at Zion Lodge. The shuttles run from early in the morning until 9 or 10 in the evening, depending on the time of year. Pets are not allowed on the shuttles. If you arrive at the park early in the morning, before 10 AM in the spring and fall, or 9 in the summer, you will probably find a parking space behind the visitors center. There is also parking outside Zion in the town of Springdale. Watch for the signs and if you cannot find them, stop and ask at any of the stores, motels, or garages. If you are staying in Springdale, there are nine Springdale Shuttle stops through town and you can leave your car in the motel lot. This shuttle from town drops passengers at the entrance gate, where you pay your admission to the park and then walk a short distance to the visitors center from which departs the free Zion Canyon Shuttle (a separate system that operates only within the park). For more information, phone 435-772-3256; visit www.nps.gov/zion; or write to Zion National Park, Springdale, Utah 84767-1099.

Zion has the highest sheer cliffs in the United States, rising over 2,000 feet (600 m). The upper level of rock is Navajo sandstone, which was created from sand dunes and is fairly porous. Under this is the Kayenta Formation that is much harder and does not allow water to penetrate, so when it reaches this level, the water travels horizontally, emerging in springs or seeps, such as Weeping Rock.

The canyon has been formed by the erosion of the Virgin River, a small, deceptively placid stream that meanders through the park. The rate of erosion is about 1 inch (2.5 cm) per century. The canyon is widened by slides and rockfalls caused by flash floods and the freeze/thaw cycle.

TOURING ZION

The one-day tour of the park consists of riding the shuttle into the canyon, where you will follow the **RIVERSIDE WALK TRAIL** and then hike up to Weeping Rock and/or the **LOWER FALLS TRAIL** and the **ARCHAEOLOGICAL TRAIL** in the morning. After lunch drive toward the East Entrance stopping to hike the **CANYON OVERLOOK TRAIL** and finally driving to the east gate to see the Checkerboard Mesa.

If you park behind the visitors center, walk across the plaza to the shuttle bus stop and get on the first bus in line. They run about every 10 minutes. Try to sit on the left side of the bus, the driver's side; the views are better. The first stop will be the Zion Human History Museum—skip this for now and stop later if you have time— and then the shuttle will turn into the canyon proper. Watch for wildlife along the side of the road near the river. The stops are Canyon Junction, Court of the Patriarchs, Zion Lodge, the Grotto, Weeping Rock, Big Bend, and, last, the Temple of Sinawava. "Sinawava" is adapted from the Paiute word for the coyote spirit. This is the end of the dead-end canyon road and where the Zion tour begins.

Riverside Walk Trail

The first trail to hike is the Riverside Walk, also called the Trail to the Narrows, that be- gins at the Temple of Sinawava stop. This is an **easy** trail that is level with only a slight change in elevation and is paved. The trail is 1 mile (1.6 km) long one-way. If you begin early in the morning it will be cool as the sun does not shine in the canyon until nearly midday, so bring a light jacket or sweater. There are restrooms at the shuttle bus stop but none along the trail, nor is there any potable water, so be sure to bring along your own. This is a wonderful trail and should not be missed.

The path meanders along the Virgin River and is an oasis in the desert, as water seeps line the canyon walls and create a lush habitation for flowers, moss, and ferns. Watch for deer, especially early in the morning, but do not try to touch them or get too close; remember, they are wild even if they seem quite tame. The same goes for the many squirrels. In fact, it is against the law to feed or touch any wild animal in any national park. This is a wondrous place as the sounds of the water from the river serenade you and the canyon narrows, rising to over 2,000 feet (610 m) and closing in to less than 50 feet (15 m) wide. It is truly an intimate experience as you descend deeper into the canyon.

As you walk along this trail, notice the various colored streaks on the walls of the canyon: the brown shiny desert varnish, the black lichens, the white calcium carbon- ate, and, near the top, the red formations from iron. There are also signs of erosion on the trail as you see the large rectangular blocks of Navajo sandstone that have fallen next to the path and the talus slopes that extend to the river. Notice that in some places, the rock has broken away in the shape of an arch and, in other places through- out the park, the stone behind also falls away, creating a true arch. You will see one example on the road to the East Entrance (see page 103).

At the end of this trail, the pavement ends and the **NARROWS TRAIL** begins, which continues for 16 miles (26 km) before exiting the canyon. This section requires a permit and is sometimes closed due to the danger of flash floods; several people have lost their lives after being caught in the narrow sections that are only 18 feet

The Narrows

Lower Falls on the Emerald Pools Trail

(5.5 m) wide and whose walls rise 2,000 to 3,000 feet (610–915 m) and are eroded smooth, offering no way to escape. Inquire at the visitors center concerning conditions in the narrows before attempting this trail, even if you plan to go only a short distance. The trail also requires that you walk in the river, which can be extremely frigid. The Narrows Trail is not part of the Grand Circle Tour. Instead, return to the bus stop by the same trail that brought you to the start of the Narrows Trail and catch the next shuttle back to Weeping Rock. Alternatively, ride back to the Big Bend stop and then walk along the road to Weeping Rock. This section of road offers spectacular views of Angel's Landing and the White Throne, but be cautious as you walk: watch out for the shuttles and stay on the shoulder of the road.

Weeping Rock

The Weeping Rock Trail is **moderate** as it is not very long, a ½-mile (0.8 km) return walk, but rises steeply and is gravel. The trail begins at the back of the parking lot on the right and splits off to the left. (The right-hand trail, a 2-mile (3.2 km) round-trip, goes to Hidden Canyon and is **very difficult** with high drop-offs; it is not for those afraid of heights.) The Weeping Rock Trail leads to a shallow cave with a rock overhang where the water percolates from the cliff face. It soaks through the softer sandstone until it comes to the impermeable layer of shale, the Kayenta Formation, and exits, two years after it fell as rain on the plateau above. The rock is covered with moss and ferns that hang down from the rock in a surreal Garden of Eden as the water bounces and dances off the rock floor. Expect to get wet.

Emerald Pools Trail

If you have time, or as a substitute for Weeping Rock, get off the bus at Zion Lodge and go across the road and to the left to the trail for the lower falls. This is the Emerald Pools Trail and is **moderate**, being a bit over a 1-mile (1.6 km) return walk with slight elevation changes. The trail passes behind the falls, allowing you to look out across the canyon through the water. This is another beautiful site where the water is usually always running. There are also the Middle and Upper Pools, but the hike to those is more strenuous: If you continue past the lower falls, the trail branches off on the left and goes to the middle section, and then there is another trail that goes to the upper falls. These trails are **difficult** and have high drop-offs. The trail can be slippery in places and people have died from falling off, so use extreme caution.

The Riverside Walk and Weeping Rock and/or the Lower Emerald Pools Trail will take all morning, so if you have brought lunch with you, there are picnic tables at the Grotto stop or return to the visitors center, where tables are scattered around the parking lot. Zion Lodge, across from the Emerald Pools Trail, has a dining room and café.

Archaeological Trail

Near the visitors center is the Archaeological Trail that is disappointing from an archaeological point but offers terrific views of the canyon (see photograph, below). The trail is **moderate** as it is short but quite steep and consists of loose gravel and small stones. It is also difficult to find as it is not well marked. From the visitors center walk to where the shuttles stop, turn right, follow the road for a short distance to the first turn into the parking lot (left side), and look for a small trail directly across the main road (right side); this is the Archaeological Trail. The path goes around to the back of a small hill and then winds up to the top, where there are some interpretive signs and the remains of a few storage units that date to around A.D. 1100. It was excavated in 2000 and all the artifacts have been removed. The views are wonderful and change constantly, depending on the time of day. It is certainly worth the little time and effort it takes to get there, but do not expect much in the way of ruins.

For the next part of the tour, return to your vehicle and follow the main road to-

View from the Archaeology Trail

ward the East Entrance. If you are parked in Springdale, just stay on AZ 9 east. You will not pay to reenter the park if you have kept your receipt. If your vehicle is in the parking lot by the visitors center, turn right when exiting. The road continues past the turn into the canyon and then begins a steep climb up switchbacks toward the tunnel. Soon after you begin to ascend there is a pullout on the right from which you get a good view of the Great Arch. This is the only place to safely stop to see it. **CAUTION:** Watch for pedestrians along this section and for cars parked on the side of the narrow road. If driving in the winter, check road conditions at the visitors center before attempting this section of road.

At the end of the switchbacks is a small building on the left from which the park rangers monitor traffic through the tunnel just ahead. A line of cars may be stopped, so approach with care. Large vehicles, such as campers and RVs, can only go through the tunnel single file, so the traffic is held up in one direction to allow their passage and you might have to wait for 10 to 20 minutes, on average. These vehicles must have a permit and pay a fee for this service. There is no cost for regular vehicles.

Canyon Overlook Trail

As soon as you emerge from the tunnel heading east there is a small parking lot on the right in which to park for the Canyon Overlook Trail. Most of the time, this lot is full, and it is difficult to see the entrance because it appears immediately upon exiting the tunnel, below the road and partially hidden by rocks. If it is full, or you miss the entrance, there is place to park a bit farther up the road on the shoulder, where it is wide enough to get your car off the road, but there are several sharp curves and usually people walking on the road, so be careful. If you cannot find any parking, simply continue on to the East Entrance, enjoying the scenery, and try again on the way back.

The trail begins next to the small ranger kiosk and is **moderate**. There are several steps at the beginning but the rest is fairly level, though it is narrow and winding and there are many high drop-offs along the way. Do not attempt if you are afraid of heights. It is 1-mile (1.6 km) round-trip. A good trail guide, available at the kiosk, points out the vegetation and geology along the way. Near the halfway point is a bridge with chain-link fence on one side and the canyon wall on the other. This brings you to a large overhang where it is always cool, a good place to rest if it is a hot day. This overhang was formed by a water seep similar to that of Weeping Rock that has eroded the soft sandstone. Notice the lush vegetation on the right side of the trail where the water flows.

Walking through this trail enclosed by rock walls you are not prepared for the vast expanse of open space that awaits at the end of the path. Suddenly you emerge onto the edge of the abyss as the slick rock abruptly disappears and the canyon spreads out before you. There are some guardrails but much remains open to the edge, so use extreme caution near the brink as the drop is straight down and very high. Notice the switchbacks in the road below and to the left, which is where you just drove if coming from the west. If you look closely, some of the arched openings into the tunnel are visible. To the right are some sheer cliffs covered in desert varnish; and in the distance, the west wall of the canyon.

Checkerboard Mesa

Return to the parking lot and turn right toward the east entrance. The road is narrow and winding through this section and there are only a few pullouts in which to stop. Watch for cars stopped on the road and people walking along the edge of the highway. The stone shapes along here were formed by windblown sand and there are many marvelous forms culminating in the Checkerboard Mesa just before the gate. Past the mesa is ample parking on the left that allows you to see the formation. The "checkers" or "biscuits" are caused by the bedding planes, thin layers set one on top of the other, and the vertical cracks, that are in fact only skin deep. These checkers are where the face of the rock is eroding away.

From this point, return via AZ 9 through Zion and back to Cedar City. This ends Day 6 of the tour. The timeline is approximately: 1 hour from Cedar to Zion; 45 minutes to the Temple of Sinawava; 1 to 1½ hour for the Riverside Walk Trail; 30 minutes for Weeping Rock; 30 minutes to return to the visitors center parking lot; 30 minutes to the Canyon Overlook Trailhead; 1 hour for the Canyon Overlook Trail; and 1 hour to the East Entrance and back to the tunnel, 1½ hours back to Cedar.

ADDITIONAL ZION TRAILS

If you are visiting Zion for more than one day, there are many other trails to hike but most are very difficult and require planning and proper preparation. Consult with the rangers at the visitors center before attempting any of these.

THE PA'RUS TRAIL is **moderate** and follows the Virgin River from the south campground (just north of the visitors center) to Canyon Junction. This is paved and mostly flat but is about a 3½-mile (5.5 km) return walk, though you can take the shuttle back from Canyon Junction.

THE WATCHMAN TRAIL is **difficult** and begins at the visitors center. It is about a 2½-mile (4.4 km) return walk, has moderate drop-offs along the trail, and ends with some great views of the canyon and the town of Springdale.

Breakfast along the Riverside Walk Trail

ANGEL'S LANDING TRAIL is **very difficult** with high drop-offs, narrow, steep sections (in some places, there are chains to hold on to), and a continuous climb. Not for those afraid of heights or out of shape. This trail begins at the Grotto on the **WEST RIM TRAIL** and branches off about ½ mile (0.8 km) from the top. Not for the faint of heart.

Between Zion and Cedar, exit 40 off I-15, 16 miles (26 km) south of Cedar, is the **KOLOB CANYONS** section of Zion, which has a scenic drive that is 5½ miles (8.8 km) one-way and offers spectacular views of the northern canyons. This section is not usually as crowded as the main canyon during the summer. There are a few trails; stop at the visitors center for info. It takes about 1 hour for the drive, depending on how many stops you make. Your entrance receipt from the main park is good for this section.

THE ARCHAEOLOGY OF ZION

There are no remains within the park from the Paleo-Indian or Archaic periods, but evidence has been found in southwestern Utah and it is likely that these people used this region as well. The earliest known human occupation was by the Basketmakers from around A.D. 500. By A.D. 750, the inhabitants were more dependent on farming and had established many small dwellings throughout the area. The largest site found to date consists of 3 rooms, 12 storage units, and 1 kiva. The region was abandoned by A.D. 1200. The people in this area are known as the Virgin, but the northern sections of the park may have been inhabited by the Fremont, who occupied central Utah, where they lived in pithouse villages. The Virgin were followed by the Paiute who used the region for hunting and gathering and grew corn along the river but did not construct any permanent dwellings. The Paiute may be the descendants of the Virgin.[1]

The first nonnative to explore Zion was Nephi Johnson, a Mormon missionary who in 1858 followed the upper Virgin River into the canyon. Mormons then settled the area, creating settlements at Grafton, Rockville, and Springdale. By 1861 they were farming the canyon along the Virgin River near the present-day Zion Lodge and continued doing so until 1909.

Major John Wesley Powell, the first man to sail through the Grand Canyon, explored Zion in 1871 through 1872. Federal surveys mapped the future park during the 1870s but it was very difficult to reach the area and, once there, still more grueling to enter the canyon. In 1908, a government survey of the area so impressed President Howard Taft in its description of the natural wonders that he in 1909 declared it a national monument called Mukuntuweap. The name was later changed to Zion and in 1919 it became a national park.

It was not until 1923, after a 30-mile (48 km) rail spur line was built by the Union Pacific Railroad from the Cedar City line, that travel to Zion became relatively easy. A gravel wagon road was then constructed into the canyon as far as Weeping Rock, which opened the park to more tourism. Finally, the tunnel was built between 1927 and 1930, connecting the canyon with the eastern section of the park. The tunnel is 5,607 feet long (1700 m).

The first archaeological survey was done in 1933 through 1934 by Ben Wetherill, of the famous Wetherills of Colorado, who found Cliff Palace in Mesa Verde and explored Chaco Canyon, discovering 19 sites and excavating 8 of them. Unfortunately his notes from this fieldwork were all lost in a fire. In 1955, National Park Service archaeologist Albert Schroeder expanded on Wetherill's survey and published an analysis of the finds.

Today, Southern Utah University and the University of Utah continue work in the park, with over 150 sites now recorded in Zion. Only around 30 have structures that include pithouses, storage cists, granaries, overhangs used as shelters, and rock art.

---

2. Personal communication with Barbara Walling and Barry Frank, May 2004.

Other sites comprise scatters of lithics and/or pottery. At this time, very little is open to the public.

THE GEOLOGY OF ZION

During the early Triassic period, around 240 million years ago, the seas that covered the region retreated westward as the land rose and moved northwest, becoming much drier and eventually forming a vast desert that stretched from Arizona to Wyoming. Because the deposits were from windblown sand rather than waterborne, there are no marine fossils in Zion. This is also why Navajo sandstone is the predominant formation on the Colorado Plateau. The Navajo sandstone is mostly white or pink and at Zion over 2,000 feet (600 m) thick, a depth that can be appreciated along the Riverside Walk Trail.

Checkerboard Mesa near the east gate

The way the sand was shaped by the wind is evident in the eastern drive from the tunnel to the East Entrance and also along the Canyon Overlook Trail. In between the sand dunes, clay and silt accumulated and formed into the hard stone layers that are seen in the crossbedding, evident in Checkerboard Mesa in the horizontal ridges.

Below the Navajo sandstone, which is porous, is the Kayenta Formation made of finer grains that erode faster than the sandstone above but are also impermeable to water. This division is where the seeps and springs occur, such as Weeping Rock and the damp areas in the canyon walls along the River Walk. The Kayenta Formation erodes, undercutting the Navajo sandstone, creating the large blocks that break off and are seen in various places in the main canyon. The creation of the canyon is mostly from the Virgin River whose waters originate north of the park from snowmelt in the spring and heavy thunderstorms during July and August. The present erosion rate is around 1 inch (2.5 cm) per century. It was much wetter during the Pleistocene period, 2 million to 10,000 years ago, which greatly increased the volume of the Virgin River and consequently deepened the canyon much faster than today. There are no dams above Zion to curb the flow as has happened with the Colorado through the Grand Canyon. A Paiute story states that the Virgin River once had a much greater flow, substantiating the geological view.

◎ OTHER SITES NEAR CEDAR CITY AND ZION

◎ Parawon Gap Petroglyphs

A few miles north of Cedar City is an incredible and easily accessible rock art site known as the Parawon Gap Petroglyphs. From Cedar, follow Main Street north across the interstate, where it becomes UT 130, or take exit 62 off I-15, and drive a bit over 13 miles (21 km) until you see a road on the right. There is a sign for Parawon. Turn here and go another 3 miles (4.8 km) until you come to the pass. The petroglyphs are on the left, or north, side and there is a small parking area on the west side of the gap and a much larger place on the other side, also on the left.

This pass through the hills was formed around 15 million years ago, when the Red Hills began to be pushed up. At the same time, a river was forming that ran over the hills, eventually eroding down through the rock as fast as the hills were lifting. When this region began to grow drier the river stopped flowing, but a pass had already formed, leaving an access through the mountains that has been used by travelers for thousands of years.

The petroglyphs include examples from the Archaic period to Ancestral Puebloan as well as Paiute, Shoshone, and Fremont. There is a great variety, with geometric designs, dotted lines, animal and human forms, spirals and circles, and several un-

The Zipper, Parawon Gap petroglyphs

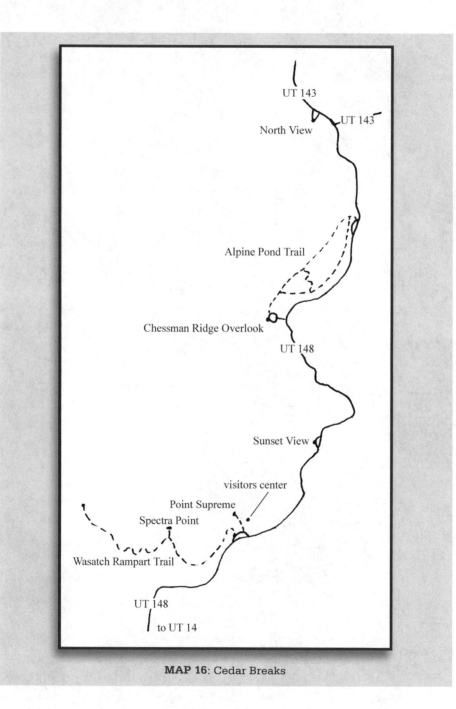

MAP 16: Cedar Breaks

identified symbols. One image that looks like a giant zipper being opened, or closed, is believed to have astronomical significance, as do other markings.

The petroglyphs are mostly on large boulders that have tumbled down the cliff and lie next to the road and parking lot. They are fenced off but easily viewed, even from a car; do not climb on the rocks or touch the artwork, as this damages the images. Please respect the site and do not damage the images in any way. The art is easy to photograph but if it is a cloudy day it can be more challenging, as the rock is very dark in color.

The Parawon Gap Petroglyphs are open year-round and there is no entry fee. It takes about 25 minutes to drive from Cedar City and another 30 minutes to view the site. This is one of the larger and better-preserved rock art sites in this region and worth the short drive.

◎ Cedar Breaks National Monument

Cedar Breaks is located about 22 miles (35 km) from Cedar City. Take UT 14 east over the mountain and turn left onto UT 148 after about 18 miles (29 km). This road is sometimes closed due to ice and snow and the monument opens in late May/early June and closes anywhere from October to December, depending on the amount of snowfall. It is not unusual for several feet of snow to fall over a typical winter. The visitors center is open from late May until mid-October. Call 435-586-9451 for road conditions and closures. Both UT 14 and UT 148 can be dangerous to drive along in the winter, even with four wheel drive. The area is prone to severe thunderstorms, sometimes with hail during the summer. Due to the high elevation, the summer temperatures range from the 50s to upper 60s Fahrenheit (10–20°C) and generally dip below freezing at night. Even when UT 148 is closed in the winter, the park is open for cross-country skiing and snowmobiles.

Cedar Breaks National Monument was established in 1933. It encompasses 10 square miles (25 square km) and the visitors center sits at an elevation of 10,350 feet (3155m). For more information, phone 435-586-9451 (October 14 to May 23) or 435-586-0787 (May 24 to October 13); visit www.nps.gov/cebr; or write to Cedar Breaks National Monument, 2390 West Hwy. 56, Suite 11, Cedar City, UT 84720.

Cedar Breaks is an amphitheater 2,000 feet (600 m) deep and 3 miles (5 km) in diameter that is on the west side of the Markagunt Plateau, which rises to over 10,000 feet (3,000 m) in elevation. The rock contains iron and manganese and these create the reds, yellows, and purples that paint the rock formations. The Native Americans called this place the "circle of the painted cliffs" but it was given its present name by the pioneers for the cedars (which are in fact junipers) and the geological term

Cedar Breaks

Full frame ears

breaks, another word for *badlands*. There are many wildflowers in the surrounding meadows from June through August, as well as bristlecone pines that grow near the rim, which are the oldest living things on earth. The ones here are over 1,600 years old but some in California have been dated to more than 4,000 years in age.

Archaic Indian campsites have been discovered around Cedar Breaks. A nearby source of chert was an important resource for making tools and points and may have been used as trade material. The Archaic Indians hunted the abundant game but occupied the area only during the summer months, as the winter would have been too harsh to survive. Europeans settled the area in the mid-19th century but, as with the Native Americans, their occupation was seasonal. In 1924, Cedar Breaks Lodge was built by a subsidiary of the Union Pacific Railroad that was attempting to form a tourist loop to connect Cedar Breaks, Bryce, Zion and the North Rim of the Grand Canyon, a venture that never became successful, although day trips from Cedar City were popular. In 1937, the Civilian Conservation Corps, or CCC, built the visitors center and ranger cabin. This is just one of many such projects completed during the Depression under a government make-work project that greatly benefited the National Park System and helped to increase tourism by making these remote areas accessible. The lodge was given to the National Park Service in 1970 by the railroad as it was no longer profitable due to the increase in car traffic. Unfortunately, this lodge was torn down by the National Park Service two years later.

Touring Cedar Breaks

The scenery in this often overlooked park is simply stunning; the varying shapes and colors are magical as they seem to dance in the ever-changing light. Although similar to Bryce in both the forms and formation, it is a very different experience. There are four overlooks on the rim along UT 148, all of which will be on your left if you are traveling north, and you should stop at each one as the views are unique from each vantage point. There are also three trails that follow the rim but none descends into the amphitheater, as they do at Bryce Canyon.

The first trail goes by the visitors center to Point Supreme and is **easy**. The **WASATCH RAMPARTS TRAIL** is **difficult** due to the high elevation that makes walking more challenging, and the trail has several elevation changes and narrow, exposed sections. It is 2 miles (3.2 km) round-trip. A short spur leads to Spectra Point and some bristlecone pines. The trail continues past Spectra Point and is **very difficult**. The trail begins at the parking lot to the left of the entrance gate and it is just a short walk to the rim and spectacular views, even if you go no farther.

The **ALPINE POND TRAIL** begins at the Chessman Ridge Overlook, about 2 miles (3.2 km) past the visitors center and also at the parking lot a bit farther on. This is a **moderate** to **difficult** trail that loops around a pond and bog and goes through the woods, making a very pleasant hike in this high country. The trail is a 2-mile (3.2 km) loop. Ranger-guided tours are given for both trails; inquire at the visitors center.

GEOLOGY OF CEDAR BREAKS (AND BRYCE CANYON)

Beginning around 60 million years ago, a large lake formed in southern Utah into which flowed many streams and rivers, depositing sand, silt, and limestone to a depth exceeding 1,000 feet (300 m). This would become known as the Claron Formation. Both Cedar Breaks and Bryce Canyon consist of this formation but at Cedar it is thicker, with more sand and silt and less limestone as well as some volcanic ash, which makes the rocks more colorful and darker. About 10 million years ago, the Markagunt Plateau was forced up to its present altitude, exposing the Claron Formation and causing cracks in the rock. Water, which is slightly acidic, flows into these cracks, dissolving the limestone and weakening the rock. The water also freezes and expands in the cracks, causing the rock to split, a cycle that is enhanced at Cedar Breaks by the high altitude and freezing temperatures even during the summer months. Roots of trees work their way into the cracks and, as they grow, the rock is forced apart, weakening it and adding to the erosion.

As the cracks widen, the rock left behind is formed into fins—long, narrow strips of stone that run parallel to one another. Sometimes arches or small windows, as well as caves, form in the fins and eventually the fins erode down to hoodoos, which are tall rock spires in various shapes. All these stages of erosion can be seen at Cedar Breaks from the rim viewpoints. The amphitheater continues to erode today and is eating back into the plateau at a rate of 9 to 47 inches (24 to 120 cm) per century. What you see at present will eventually be gone . . . in a few hundred thousand years!

day 7

Bryce Canyon National Park
Utah

- Established in 1923 as a national monument
- 1928 designated a national park
- 56 square miles (145 square km)
- Elevation: 6,620 to 9,105 feet (2,018–2,775 m)

Nearby Site

◎ Kodachrome Basin State Park

Wall Street on the Navajo Loop Trail

9. Bryce Canyon National Park

GETTING THERE: From Cedar City, follow UT 14 east over the mountains to US 89, about 40 miles (64 km), and turn left onto US 89 for another 20 miles (32 km), where you arrive at the junction of UT 12 toward Bryce. Turn right, there are signs for Bryce Canyon, and continue for 12 miles (19 km) to UT 63, a right turn, which goes to and through the park. **CAUTION:** UT 14 can be hazardous to travel in the winter, late spring, and early fall, due to ice and snow. Sometimes the road is closed just out of Cedar. An alternate route, though much farther, is to go through Zion (see Day 6, page 97) to US 89 and head north to UT 12.

After a few miles on UT 12 you pass through Red Canyon, a spectacular site in itself and a small taste of what awaits you at Bryce. There are pullouts along the road and trails among the rock formations to explore. Watch out for pedestrians crossing the road—the speed limit is reduced—and also turning traffic and tour buses.

THINGS YOU NEED TO KNOW: The park is open all year, 24 hours a day. The visitors center is open daily from 8 AM to 8 PM, to 4:30 in the winter, and is closed on Thanksgiving Day, Christmas Day, and New Year's Day. For more information, phone 435-834-5322; visit www.nps.gov/brca; or write to Bryce Canyon National Park, P.O. Box 640201, Bryce, UT 84764-0201.

There is a free shuttle bus service in Bryce that operates from late May to late September or early October beginning at 8 AM and ending at varying hours through the season. The route goes from Ruby's Inn, which is outside the park, to the visitors center, Sunset Point, Sunset Campground, Bryce Point, Inspiration Point, Sunset Campground, Sunset Point, Bryce Lodge, Sunrise Point, the North Campground, visitors center, and then back to Ruby's Inn. The shuttle is not mandatory as at Zion but it does save the hassle of finding a parking spot, especially at Sunset Point, as parking is a problem at Bryce, as at other parks.

Bryce is a fairyland of multicolor cliffs, spires, and pinnacles that resemble ancient ruined cities, castles, and fantastic creatures. It is not a canyon but an amphitheater spreading away from the plateau toward the east, and consists of silty and sandy limestone lake deposits that are soft and easily eroded by rain, frost, snow melt, and wind. The capstone layer is of a harder sandstone that wears away much slower than the layers under it, protecting the softer material and creating the fantastic shapes throughout the park. The cliff face is being eroded at a rate of 9 to 48 inches (24–120 cm) per century, a huge amount in geologic time. The pink color is caused by small amounts of iron oxides in the limestone.

There is a road that follows the rim of the amphitheater, with several pullouts to

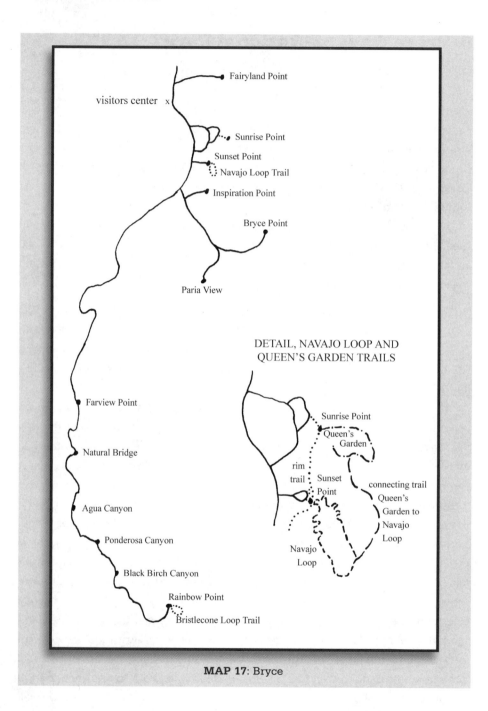

visitors center   x

Fairyland Point

Sunrise Point

Sunset Point

Navajo Loop Trail

Inspiration Point

Bryce Point

Paria View

DETAIL, NAVAJO LOOP AND
QUEEN'S GARDEN TRAILS

Sunrise Point

Queen's
Garden

rim
trail   Sunset
Point

connecting trail

Queen's
Garden to
Navajo
Loop

Navajo
Loop

Farview Point

Natural Bridge

Agua Canyon

Ponderosa Canyon

Black Birch Canyon

Rainbow Point

Bristlecone Loop Trail

MAP 17: Bryce

view the spectacular formations below, as well as many trails that wind through the maze of narrow eroded canyons that make up Bryce.

The full-day tour of Bryce consists of stopping at most of the pullouts and hiking two trails: the Navajo Loop and Bristlecone Loop.

There are many motels in Bryce, which is along UT 12—there is no "town" of Bryce—and in nearby towns such as Tropic. On the Grand Circle Tour we stay in Bryce for one night after touring the park all day, then continue on from there. It can be difficult to find a room during the high season, so reservations are recommended.

TOURING THE PARK

It is about 5 miles (8 km) from UT 12 to the park. After you go through the entrance gate, the visitors center is on your right. The turn for Sunset Point is about a mile (1.6 km) farther, on the left. A short road leads to the circular lot. There are restrooms and picnic tables. Walk out to the rim trail for your first view of the amphitheater, a sight to amaze. It is best to stand for a while and absorb the view, as it takes some time for the brain to comprehend what the eyes are seeing. **CAUTION:** Lightning is a hazard along the rim view points and can be deadly, so always listen and watch for approaching storms and remain in your car if thunderstorms are in the area. You should check the weather info at the visitors center.

The **RIM TRAIL** is paved and **easy** from Sunset to Sunrise Point (both Sunrise and Sunset Points face east). The Rim Trail continues in both directions, and if you are heading south to Bryce Point, be aware that the trail involves a steep climb. Several trails that descend into the amphitheater are the best way to see and appreciate the marvels of the geology.

Navajo Loop Trail

When you get to the rim at Sunset Point and are ready to take the plunge into the abyss, turn right and follow the path to the corner, where there are some steps down and a sign for the Navajo Loop Trail. This trail is **difficult** and has many high drop-offs, is very steep in places, 1.3 miles (2.2km) round-trip, and, lastly, the elevation is over 8,000 feet (2,400 m), which makes the climb back out much harder, especially if you are not yet accustomed to the high elevation. And remember, you are starting at the top and the climb back up is always more difficult. One last point: Be extra careful going down, as there are places where the path is covered with small stones and loose gravel, making it slippery.

This is a loop trail and I have found that it is best to go counterclockwise, so turn right at the bottom of the steps, which will take you down the steepest, and shortest,

In the canyon on the Navajo Loop Trail

section and leave a longer but more moderate climb back up. You begin the descent in a large, open area below which are many switchbacks. Be careful, as the path is not very wide and the tendency is to constantly look up rather than where you are walking. As you descend, the walls begin to close in until they are less than 20 feet (6 m) wide and over 100 feet (30m) high in a section known as Wall Street. This can create a sense of claustrophobia, but it is always nice and cool even on the hottest days. Walking along the path you probably have noticed the lack of vegetation in the canyon: The rock is so unstable nothing can gain a foothold to grow, a fact that does not prepare one for the sight of a massive ponderosa pine, well over 100 feet (30 m) tall, stretching for the sun from beside the trail. At this point in its life the tree is tall enough to reach the sunlight, but how did it survive those first years, growing where the sun only strikes for a very short period each day, if at all?

Near the end of the narrow section of the trail there was a rock fall in 2006 that forced the closure of the Navajo Loop, but a path has been made over the collapsed rocks so that you can continue around the loop. Be prepared to scramble over this slide. From this point, the canyon opens up as it follows a wash around a long bend to the left that allows for great views up to the rim. Also visible are the effects of erosion from the many trees that have collapsed after their footing was washed away, as well as the rock slides in the gullies.

Soon you will arrive at an intersection where the trails divide; bear to the left to continue on the Navajo Loop; go right to gain access to the **PEEKABOO LOOP TRAIL**, which is 5½ miles (8.8km) and **very difficult**; or continue straight toward the Queen's Garden Trail (see below). If you remain on the Navajo Loop Trail it will be a long and steady climb, but a gradual incline, until you near the top, where there is another series of switchbacks but not as many as on the route down. Another point of interest is a small side canyon that has two natural bridges and is on your right as you are going up. This is not far from where the trails divide. You can go into this narrow canyon to see the bridges up close but do not walk on them, as they are fragile.

As you get close to the rim, the walls open up for a spectacular view of the amphitheater and some of the many hoodoos. A couple more switchbacks and you will be back on the rim. Allow 1½ to 2 hours for the Navajo Loop, and probably some time to rest once you're back.

From Sunset Point, walk north ½ mile (0.8 km) to Sunrise Point which is **easy** along the paved rim trail that offers tremendous views out over the amphitheatre. An alternative to the Navajo Loop is the **QUEEN'S GARDEN TRAIL**, which, according to other literature, is the easiest trail that descends into the canyon. But having witnessed the winded hikers on their way back up, I believe that *easy* is relative and there is not much difference in the degree of difficulty between the two trails. The Queen's Garden Trail is not a loop but if you continue past the end it does join the Navajo Loop Trail near the bottom (see above), so you could follow one section back up to Sunset Point, making it a loop that would be **difficult** and take about 2 to 2½ hours. The Queen's Garden Trail, if you turn around at the short spur, is a 2-mile (3.2 km) return walk and **difficult**. If you have time for both, the scenery is very different along each trail and worth the effort, but allow plenty of time and be aware that it is **very difficult** if you hike the two trails in one day.

It will be noon by the time you finish the Navajo Loop and go out to Sunrise Point and back. There are picnic tables by the parking lot at Sunset Point. After lunch, drive to the south end of the park, a left turn onto the main road, without stopping at any pullouts as they will all be on the left as you head this way, so it is easier to stop on the drive back. It is about 17 miles (27 km) one-way. At the very end is Rainbow Point, where another rim trail, the Bristlecone Loop, begins. The trail starts at the right-hand corner of the parking lot, is **moderate**, and is a 1-mile (1.6 km) return walk.

Bristlecone Loop Trail

This trail winds through the forest but occasionally breaks into the open on the edge of the rim for spectacular views out across vast distances to the east and south. Near the beginning of the trail you will come to a crosstrail, but follow the signs of the Bristlecone Loop, which is well marked. At the southern end of the trail are several bristlecone pines, both live and dead examples. The gnarled forms of the dead wood survive for years as the conditions are dry and the wood is extremely dense, due to its slow growth. Looking south you can see a wide dome that is the Kaibab Plateau, north of the Grand Canyon, where Pipe Springs (page 89) is located. **CAUTION:** Rainbow Point and this trail are over 9,000 feet (2,740 m) in elevation, the highest point in the park, and it can be extremely windy.

From Rainbow Point head back north, stopping at the many pullouts, all of which give a different perspective on the amphitheater below. A couple of note include Agua Canyon, one of the best views from the rim, with large hoodoos near the edge and the profile of Navajo Mountain in the distance; and Natural Bridge, where you can see an arch 85 feet (26 m) long and 125 feet (38 m) high. True natural bridges are formed by running water but an arch is created by rain and the freeze/thaw cycle of erosion.

Continuing north you will come to the turnoff for Bryce and Inspiration Points as well as the Paria View. As soon as you turn onto this road, stay to the left for Inspiration Point, which is well marked. The lower view point is next to the parking lot but to get to the upper section you must walk up a steep **difficult** trail that is paved and part of the rim trail. From both the lower and upper viewpoints you look out over the Silent City section of the Bryce Amphitheater from the side opposite Sunrise Point. You can see where the Navajo Loop Trail begins.

Return to the intersection and turn left to Bryce Point, the highest view point in the park and the best place to watch the sun rise. A short walk takes you from the parking area to the rim. Looking toward the northeast you see the Sinking Ship Formation which is a tilted fault block and appears to be rising, or sinking, from the bottom of the amphitheater. Across from here on another short spur road is the Paria View, which overlooks a small amphitheater that was formed by Yellow Creek. This road is closed in the winter to vehicles.

One last view point in Bryce is often bypassed because it is the farthest north. In fact, it is outside the entrance gate, though not the park boundary, and is called Fairyland Point. The road is 1 mile (1.6 km) north of the gate on the right, driving north, and another mile (1.6 km) to the view point. This is one of the finest views in the park with multicolor spires and expansive vistas into the distance. There is also a

View from Inspiration Point

Surreal Spires

trail that is 13 miles (21 km) long, **very difficult**, and ends at Sunset Point. However, you can go down and back on the trail a short distance for a great experience among the hoodoos and other rock formations. The road to Fairyland Point is not plowed in the winter but is open to cross-country skiers and snowshoers.

GEOLOGY OF BRYCE

For the geology of Bryce Canyon, see the section on Cedar Breaks' geology (page 115), as this is part of the Claron Formation that also makes up the scenery at Cedar Breaks.

ARCHAEOLOGY OF BRYCE

Hunter-gatherers during the Paleo-Indian and Archaic periods roamed throughout the region. Basketmaker and Pueblo lived east of the park in the warmer valley, as it was too cold on the plateau, but they did utilize the park for hunting, timber, and wild plants. By A.D. 1150, the region was abandoned for unknown reasons. Following the Ancestral Puebloans, the Paiute used this area until the arrival of the Mormons in the 19th century drove them out. The Mormons grazed cattle and sheep and also founded several nearby towns. Ebenezer Bryce, a Mormon carpenter for whom the park is named, along with his wife, Mary, ran cattle below Sunset Point.

Bryce was first surveyed by John Wesley Powell in 1872. By the late 1870s, overgrazing and woodcutting led to terrible erosion and flooding of the crops in the valley. In the 1890s, a long drought devastated the herds and land, which led to a 1905 restriction on grazing and logging. Tourists began coming to the park but it was a very difficult journey using pack animals. The first automobile arrived in 1915 over a rudimentary road, and by 1919 there were cabins and tourist facilities at Sunset Point.

This concludes the seventh day of the Grand Circle Tour. The approximate timeline is: 1½ hours from Cedar City to Bryce; 1½ to 2 hours for the Navajo Loop trail; 30 minutes to drive to Rainbow Point; 45 to 60 minutes for the Bristlecone Loop trail; 1 to 2 hours for the stops at the various viewpoints; 20 to 30 minutes to the motel.

◎ OTHER SITES NEAR BRYCE CANYON

◎ Kodachrome Basin State Park

One of the often overlooked attractions near Bryce is Kodachrome Basin State Park. It is thought of as only a campground but offers some easily accessible, spectacular, and bizarre rock formations, as well as several hiking trails. From the junction of UT 12 and UT 63, drive east on UT 12 through Tropic, 8 miles (13 km), to Cannonville, 5 miles (8 km), and turn right toward Kodachrome Basin onto a paved road that goes for 7 miles (11 km) to the park. You will have to turn left just before the road becomes gravel and go a short distance to the entrance station. There are clean restrooms and a place to pay your entry fee. Place the money in an envelope and put the receipt in your window if there is no one at the station. Try to have some small bills with you.

Continue on from the visitors center, take the first right, and then go straight on a narrow dirt road that leads to Chimney Rock. In 1949, the National Geographic Society sponsored an exploration of the then little-known Escalante region that begins near Cannonville and runs east and south to the Colorado River. The team that explored the territory came through here and named the place "Kodachrome Flats" (after Kodak's film that was renowned for its brilliant colors) due to the wondrous colors of the formations and stated that this was a photographer's paradise. (You can read the complete article, "First Motor Sortie into Escalante Land," by Jack Breed, in the September 1949 issue.)

The rock spires were formed during the Jurassic period and are believed to have been created when liquid sandstone was forced up into dry sand to become what

are called sand pipes. Chimney Rock is a good example, as it towers 90 feet (27.5 m) straight up from the flat desert surface. There are good views of the massive pink and white cliffs on the north side of the basin. When you return along the same route, there is a road that braches off to the left and goes to the **SHAKESPEARE ARCH TRAIL**, which is one of several trails in the park. The arch is about one-third of a mile (0.5 km) one-way and is best viewed in the afternoon. This trail is **moderate**.

Returning to the main road, turn right toward the campground. There are several trails along this road and you can find information on them at the trailhead station.

Kodachrome Basin

Even if you do not want to do any hiking, at least drive to the end of this road, which winds through many rock spires and hoodoos and has some pullouts to stop and marvel at the beautiful and strange formations. Drive slow, as this is like a small town, with people walking or riding bikes along the side of the road.

An hour is enough time to drive through and see the main sights, or you could spend several days hiking the various trails; either way, Kodachrome Basin is definitely worth the detour.

day 8

**Anasazi
State Park
Utah**

■ Opened in 1970 to preserve,

protect, and interpret the Coombs

Archaeological Site

■ 5.9 acres (2.5 h)

■ Elevation: 6,700 feet (2,050 m)

Goblin Valley
State Park
Utah

- Established as a state park in 1974
to protect and preserve the unique
geological formations

- Elevation 5,000 feet (1,525 m)

Nearby Site

◎ Capitol Reef National Park

10. Anasazi State Park

GETTING THERE: From Bryce Canyon, turn right, east, onto UT 12 to Boulder, which is about 75 miles (120 km) from the junction of UT 12 and UT 63. The site is in the middle of town, which is very small, and will be on the right. The entrance is not well marked, so look for a high chain-link fence next to the road and several large trees. The entrance to the museum is to the right at the back of the parking lot and you must go through it to get to the archaeological site.

There are many spectacular scenic roads on the Grand Circle Tour but the drive along UT 12 from the junction of US 89 to Torrey and UT 24 is without a doubt the most thrilling and overwhelming experience of all. So, given the nature of this drive, I will briefly describe what you can expect on this road, beginning with the first section from Bryce to Boulder. This is not a road on which to be in a hurry as the driving conditions do not allow for speed. It consists of many hills, valleys, and curves, and definitely should not be attempted if there is snow or ice on the roadway.

As you leave Bryce, the road suddenly drops down on a series of switchbacks that take you from the Paunsaugunt Plateau to the valley where the Mormons founded several towns in the late 19th century. The road meanders along the valley floor and through small farming towns before beginning the first of several ascents just after Henrieville. You are surrounded by massive rock walls before finally reaching the summit at 7,400 feet (2,255 m) and descending again to the town of Escalante. As you continue it seems impossible that a road could have ever been built through here, or possibly ever should have been built, but it does eventually come out on the other side, somewhere! The road winds, climbs, and dips for about 12 miles (19 km) to a pull-off on the left with some interpretive signs. Stop for an unforgettable view. At this overlook you can see the Escalante River, below and to the right, which, along with its many tributaries, is responsible for the scenery before you. Now the drive gets interesting.

After leaving the overlook you will head down very quickly to a bridge over the Escalante River in the bowels of the canyon, but do not worry for you will soon begin yet another ascent that leads to the "hogsback." This infamous stretch of the road crosses on a knife edge of rock just a bit wider than the pavement and has drop-offs of 1,000 feet (300 m) on each side. There is one pullout on the left where you can stop, and the only place you should stop, as the shoulders are narrow and there is no guardrail, just those drop-offs. This section is not for those with a fear of heights, nor for the fainthearted! But trust me, once having driven over the hogsback successfully (I do not have figures on how many did not make it), you will never forget the experience.

From the hogsback, the road descends to the town of Boulder and our first stop, Anasazi State Park. I will continue the description of UT 12 later.

THINGS YOU NEED TO KNOW: The park is open every day except for Thanksgiving Day, Christmas Day, New Year's Day. The hours are 8 AM to 6 PM from March to November, and 9 to 5 the rest of the year. For more information, phone 435-335-7308; visit www .utah.com/stateparks/anasazi.htm; or write to Anasazi State Park Museum, 460 North Hwy. 12, Boulder, UT 84716

TOURING THE SITE

You will pay an admission fee inside the museum/visitors center at the cash register on the right as you enter. There are restrooms to the left. Proceed through the building and out the back door to the archaeological site—you will visit the museum afterward—and follow the path to the left, where there is a replica of a pueblo. The Ancestral Puebloans used a combination of stone and jacal, mud and sticks, for their construction. You can see these techniques in the replica and also get a good sense of what the buildings were like by going into and around this pueblo. You will notice that the doors are low and narrow, especially the ones that go from one room to another. They were built this way to conserve heat in the winter, as it gets very cold on most of the Colorado Plateau. The ceilings are low, which was also to keep in the heat. They did not use furniture but sat on skins on the floor, so there was no need for large spaces, and in the summer they spent most of their time outside. When the weather

The replica pueblo

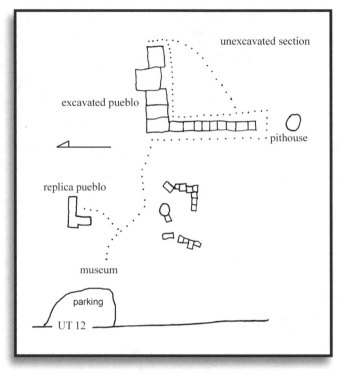

PLAN 9: Anasazi State Park, the Coombs site

was really hot they slept on the flat roofs to keep cool. The doors and windows would have been covered with animal hides.

Most of the rooms would have been used for storage; and the rest, for food preparation, which consisted of grinding the corn and cooking and, in the winter, sleeping. Notice the construction of the ceilings. The builders began by putting large beams across the width of the room, placed smaller sticks crosswise to these, and then finally covered the entire surface with jacal. Jacal is small branches and brush mixed with mud, also called adobe, which creates a well-insulated and strong roof. But there are a couple of problems with this method, the first being that such a roof does eventually leak, even though there is not a great amount of rainfall in the Southwest, so it requires constant maintenance. The second problem, the outcome of which you will see in the ruins, is that this wood becomes extremely dry, and with open fires in the small rooms and only a small opening in the ceiling for the smoke to exit, fire was a danger. If a strong gust of wind blew open the door flap and hit the fire, sparks would be flying all over the room and the chance of the building's burning was high. There are many examples of burned-down pueblos in the Southwest. But one thing to remember is that when one of these structures did burn, it is nearly impossible for archaeologists to determine the cause. It could have been accidental—either from the fire in the interior hearth or a lightning strike. Or, if it was razed intentionally, it might have been by the inhabitants when they abandoned the site or by an enemy attack.

After examining the replica, follow the path to the left toward the covered section of the site. On the right as you are walking along the trail, look carefully and you can see the remains of some structures, though the brush obscures the view somewhat. The pueblo ran straight ahead of you and to the right, covering this knoll, and consisted of over 100 rooms, most of which were used for storage.

The trail now comes to the covered section of the excavated portion of the site. From this first point, looking straight ahead, toward the east, you see the main living areas of the pueblo, the larger rooms, and to your right, the storage area, a configuration similar to that of the Tusayan Ruins (see page 76) in Grand Canyon and typical of Ancestral Puebloan design. You will notice the remains of interior walls that were built of adobe with posts spaced throughout, and the clearly blackened tops of these posts, indicating that fire destroyed the pueblo. There is no question as to how the structure was destroyed but what remains unanswered is why.

The trail goes around the pueblo. At the first corner is a reconstructed pithouse, not a kiva. In fact, no kivas were found on the site, though it has not been fully excavated. This lack of kivas is unusual for an Ancestral Puebloan pueblo (see Red Cliffs, page 91). At the far end of the trail are two manos and metates used to grind the

The excavated pueblo, looking east

The reconstructed pithouse

corn (a third set placed here was stolen a few years ago). From this end of the trail to the east and south the village continues but has not been excavated. Look carefully among the sage and cactus; there are depressions in the ground that indicate more structures: rectangular shapes are room blocks and round ones are pithouses or possibly kivas.

Return to the museum. Notice the exterior wall of the museum, which is modern adobe and looks similar to the original ancient pueblos, without the cow. The museum houses the collection of artifacts from the excavations and has several examples on display. There are also hands-on exhibits, which include an opportunity to grind corn with a mano and metate, identify seeds under a microscope, make rubbings of various pottery designs, and listen to tapes of Native Americans and archaeologists discussing archaeological remains of the Southwest. There are examples of pottery, jewelry, and stone tools, as well as some clay figurines that are characteristic of the culture of the Fremont, who lived to the north. There is also a full-scale model of a typical room and how it might have looked when occupied. The pueblo replica is one-of-a-kind in the Southwest. Although the site is small, it is one of the high points on the Grand Circle Tour.

A large gallery past the gift shop displays artworks with a Southwestern theme by contemporary artists, so check this out before leaving. The displays are periodically changed so even if you have been here before, it is worth visiting again.

ARCHAEOLOGY OF THE COOMBS SITE

A Clovis point was discovered less than 1¼ miles (2 km) from the Coombs Site, and is on display in the museum, proving that the region was inhabited around 10,000 years ago. There is then a large gap in the evidence; in fact, there is nothing until the occupation of the Coombs Site, though there is probably more that has not been discovered yet. The Coombs Site is the northernmost pueblo of the Ancestral Puebloans that has been discovered, and was occupied during the A.D. 1100s. There is no evidence of earlier habitation on the site, nor was it ever reoccupied, so it remains a mystery as to why the Ancestral Puebloans were not here earlier and also why they left after such a short time, which was probably less than 60 years.

The area was ideal for the Ancestral Puebloans, as there were six streams within 5 miles (8 km) that flowed south to the Escalante River 10 miles (16 km) to the south. The region had good land for farming and there were abundant game and wild plants

Room subdivided with upright slabs, the Coombs site

in the nearby hills and mountains. Over 100 structures have been identified, including pueblos, pithouses, and one ramada. There are 96 rooms constructed of either jacal or stone; most of the stone rooms had been used for storage, as one of the biggest problems was to protect the stored seed from rodents. Ten pithouses were found, which proves that both aboveground pueblos and pithouses were sometimes occupied at the same time rather than a complete change from belowground to aboveground habitation. The ramada is a structure consisting of a wooden frame with the roof covered by branches and brush to provide shade and is thought to have been the forerunner of the pueblo (see page 427).

Over 150,000 artifacts have been found including pottery, stone tools, and bones from mule deer, bighorn sheep, rabbit, and the domestic dog. These artifacts give us an idea about building technology, village layout, subsistence, and trade. It has been thought that the Ancestral Puebloans that lived at Coombs were from the Kayenta branch, but some archaeologists now believe that they could have been of the Virgin branch. The pottery is mixed, with many examples of both Virgin and Kayenta. No kivas have been discovered, a characteristic that is more often associated with the Virgin. Geographically, the Coombs Site is separated from the main region of the Kayenta by the Colorado River. The Virgin were physically closer to this area, as they inhabited the valley east of Bryce Canyon. This question might be answered if more excavation is done, or it may remain a topic of debate for some time.

The pueblo was occupied by about 200 people and is the largest excavated site west of the Colorado River. It was destroyed by a fire of unknown origin, after which the people abandoned the region. Where they went and why they left are unknown.

The Peabody Museum at Harvard University did archaeological research and small excavations in the area between 1928 and 1931, but the large-scale excavations were carried out by the University of Utah in 1958 through 1959. Only about half of the entire site has been excavated to date. In 1960, the land was purchased by the State of Utah and the first archaeological state park in Utah was established. The visitors center was built in 1970. Between 1970 and 1988, and again from 1990 through 1991, the staff and volunteers conducted small-scale excavations. The museum houses all of the excavation records.

To the west of the site, another area, which at present is on private land and not accessible to the general public, has the remains of some structures similar to those at Coombs and is believed to be connected to the main site, but its function is unclear. It might have had astronomical uses, similar to the Parawon Petroglyphs north of Cedar City (see page 108).

This concludes the tour of Anasazi State Park.

Goblins

11. Goblin Valley State Park

GETTING THERE: Back on UT 12 to Torrey, turn right out of the parking lot of Anasazi State Park, you will continue the drive through more spectacular scenery, though quite different from the first leg of the journey. Soon after you leave Boulder, the road begins to climb toward the summit of Boulder Mountain at 9,400 feet (2865 m). As you get higher, the terrain changes from the lower desert and scrub brush to alpine meadows dotted with aspens. Two scenic pullouts before the summit are worth stopping at for some wonderful views south over the Escalante region and east to the Henry Mountains. The road then begins to descend in a series of switchbacks until you emerge back into canyon country on the north side. **CAUTION:** This section can be icy or snow covered for a good part of the year, and also watch out for cattle on the road as this is open-range country.

At Torrey, UT 12 ends and you continue on UT 24 east, a right turn at the intersection. Outside Torrey, the wondrous rock formations begin again as you near Capitol Reef National Park, not part of the main tour but described below on page 144 under

"Other Sites." After a short ascent, UT 24 goes down into a breathtaking canyon surrounded by towering cliffs of multi-hued sandstone. There are several pullouts along this section. At the turnoff for the Capitol Reef visitors center, about 11 miles (18 km) from UT 12, turn right and stop at the center if you need a break. There are clean restrooms, but no services. You can drive down the road a little ways and see the orchards and historical buildings before the entrance gate, where you must pay to continue.

UT 24 now winds along next to the Fremont River through a narrow canyon before opening up onto flatlands as you near Caineville, 27 miles (43 km) from Torrey. At Hanksville, a further 19 miles (30 km), stay on UT 24 at the junction, bearing left. Keep an eye out for bandits along this stretch of highway as just south of this area is where Butch Cassidy and his infamous Hole-in-the-Wall Gang, among many other robbers and outlaws, hid in the maze of canyons. From this point the scenery reverts back to just ordinary spectacular as you now cross the San Rafael, or Green River, Desert. After a few miles, watch for some bizarre rock formations on the right, east, next to the highway. They always remind me of something out of the Star Wars films.

About 20 miles (32 km) from Hanksville there is a turnoff on the left, west, for Goblin Valley State Park and Temple Mountain. Turn onto this road. After 5 miles (8 km), turn left again (there is a sign) and you will soon arrive at the entrance gate. The road is paved all the way but some sections have many curves and dips, so drive cautiously; the speed limit is reduced here. Once you have paid the entrance fee, it is only a short distance to the valley, where there is a large parking lot, as well as pit toilets and a covered picnic and viewing area.

THINGS YOU NEED TO KNOW: The park is open year-round from 6 AM to 10 PM and there is an entrance fee for day use (self-pay option if no one is at the entrance station). There is also a campground. For more information, phone 435-275-4584; visit www.stateparks.utah.gov/park/goblin-valley-state-park; or write to Goblin Valley State Park, P.O. Box 637, Green River, UT 84525-0637. For camping reservations, phone 800-322-3770.

TOURING THE PARK

From the entrance gate, follow the road straight to the parking lot. Walk out to the observation deck to orient yourself with the valley. You can see the formations quite well, but to really experience the park you must descend in among the creatures of stone. There are two trails leading down into the valley, one on each side of the observation platform, and they are both **easy** and very short, though steep and sometimes slippery, Once you are in the valley, the terrain is mostly level but there are no trails; instead, you wander around, between, over, under, or through the strange stone beasts

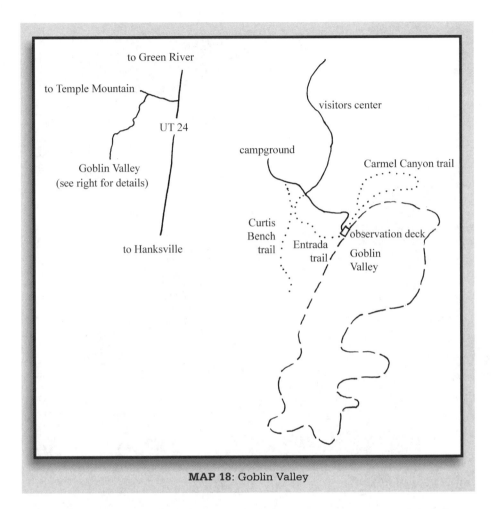

MAP 18: Goblin Valley

that inhabit this place. The valley runs north–south and is 1 mile (1.6 km) wide by 2 miles (3.2 km) long. As it is mostly surrounded by high cliffs, getting lost is not a big problem. However, it is like a maze; if you become disoriented, climb to the top of one of the formations, where you usually can see the observation deck. Be watchful if you have small children. You are allowed to climb on and through the rock formations, but be aware that even though they look soft, this is rock, and a fall can be painful. Also be careful not to get caught in the narrow openings.

Goblin Valley is a constantly changing scene as you walk through formations that evoke thoughts of bizarre and whimsical animals, as well as the turtle, sea lion, and elephant that pop into view. It is a wondrous experience to stroll among the rocks, with each turn bringing a different and unexpected sight. And the views differ, depending on the time of the day and direction when you walk; stop, turn around, and

The Sea Lion

The Turtle

the site looks completely different from what you just saw. This is a place of quiet and solitude, where the mind can roam free and your imagination is the only limit to the experience. There is no other place like this.

Goblin Valley consists of Entrada sandstone, which is made up of weaker mudstone and siltstones and erodes much faster than other sandstones. It was formed between 145 and 170 million years ago in a tidal flat on the edge of a sea. This is the same type of stone as at Arches National Park (see page 173) but here there is no hard capstone to slow the erosion of the softer stone to form arches or hoodoos; instead they form these unusual squat formations.

There are three trails for those with more time to explore the area, but they do not go into the valley, though they offer some nice views. The **CARMEL CANYON LOOP** is 1½ miles (2.4 km), begins at the parking lot, and is **moderate**. The **ENTRADA CANYON TRAIL** also begins near the parking lot and goes for 1⅓ miles (2 km), one-way, ending at the campground. This trail is **moderate**. And the last one is the **CURTIS BENCH TRAIL**, a **moderate** 2-mile (3.2 km) round-trip that begins at the campground and ends with an overview of the valley. But the main reason for coming to this site is to explore the valley itself, so these trails are only if you have extra time or are staying in the campground for a few days.

From Goblin Valley, return to UT 24 and turn left toward Green River. It is about 20 miles (32 km) to I-70, where you head east for 11 miles (17.6 km) to the first exit (158) for Green River. Drive through town as the motels are mostly at the other end. While in Green River don't miss the John Wesley Powell River History Museum on the east

side of the river, a left turn after the bridge. Open from 8 AM–7 PM in the summer and 8 AM–4 PM in the winter. This is a wonderful museum that even has some dinosaurs. Phone 435-564-3427 for information; jwprhm.com.

This concludes Day 8 of the Grand Circle Tour. The approximate timeline is: Bryce Canyon to Anasazi State Park, 1½ to 2 hours; Anasazi State Park, 1 to 1½ hours; Anasazi State Park to Goblin Valley State Park, 2 to 2½ hours; Goblin Valley State Park, 1 hour to "you never want to leave"; Goblin Valley to Green River, 30 to 45 minutes.

◎ OTHER SITES BETWEEN BRYCE AND GREEN RIVER

◎ Capitol Reef National Park

Declared a national monument in 1937 and a national park in 1971, it is 380 square miles (990 square km) and the elevation is 5,500 feet (1,670 m) at the visitors center.

Capitol Reef is located on UT 24 between Torrey and Hanksville (see page 139). The park is open year-round and the visitors center is open daily from 8 AM to 4:30 PM (later in the summer), except Christmas Day. There are picnic areas south of the visitors center and along UT 24. Camping is available near the picnic grounds and there is a fee. Inquire at the visitors center concerning wilderness campgrounds. There are

View from Sunset Point, Capitol Reef

no services in the park but they are available in nearby Torrey, 10 miles (16 km) to the west. For more information, phone 435-425-3791; visit www.nps.gov.care; or write to Capitol Reef National Park, HC 70, Box 15, Torrey, UT 84775.

Touring Capitol Reef

How much, and what you see in Capitol Reef depends on the amount of time you have, the type of vehicle, and your capacity for hiking. Following are some options for a one-day visit. If you will be there longer, consult with the rangers at the visitors center about other trails and, if you are driving a four-wheel-drive vehicle, some of the backcountry roads.

For one-day, easy hiking, no four-wheel-drive vehicle required, consider Panorama Point, the Goosenecks Overlook and Sunset Point; the Petroglyphs on UT 24; the Scenic Drive; and either Capitol Gorge to the "tanks" and/or Grand Wash to the narrows.

NOTE: Check at the visitors center for weather conditions before attempting to hike either Capitol Gorge or Grand Wash, as both of these trails are prone to flash flooding and are sometimes closed by the National Park Service. Cathedral Valley, the

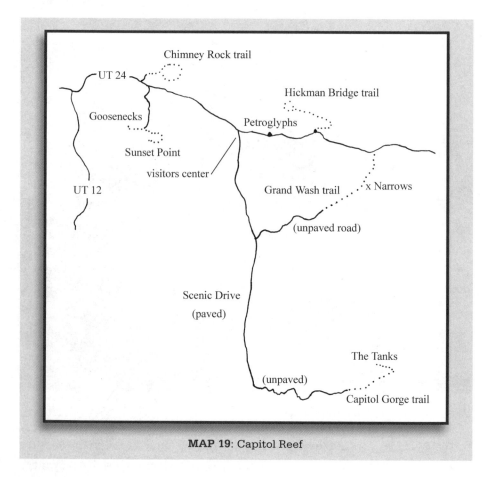

Chimney Rock trail

UT 24

Hickman Bridge trail

Goosenecks

Petroglyphs

Sunset Point

visitors center

UT 12

Grand Wash trail   x Narrows

(unpaved road)

Scenic Drive

(paved)

The Tanks

(unpaved)

Capitol Gorge trail

MAP 19: Capitol Reef

Notom-Bullfrog Road, and Burr Trail Road are impassible when wet; again, check with the rangers first.

A good deal of the park can be seen simply by driving along UT 24—there is no fee for this section—and the Scenic Drive, which runs south from the visitors center and is a fee area. There are many pullouts along both the highway and park drive, allowing ample opportunity to see the superb scenery and rock formations. Several easy or moderate trails lead into the canyons or onto the cliffs, along with several longer and more difficult trails and some backcountry roads for those with four-wheel-drive vehicles.

It is around 9 miles (14.4 km) from the intersection of UT 12 and UT 24 to the Chimney Rock turnoff, on the left or north side of the road, leading to the trailhead. **CHIMNEY ROCK TRAIL** is **difficult** with a steep climb to the top of the cliff and a 3½-mile (5.6 km) loop, but you have a good view of the formation from the parking lot, or if you walk just a short distance along the first section of trail, which is level.

Chimney Rock

Chimney Rock is 400 feet (122 m) high and consists of softer mudstone and siltstone, which is the darker rock, capped with much harder Shinarump conglomerate, the lighter-colored stone. This protects the softer material that would have long since eroded away without it.

Back on UT 24, turn left from the Chimney Rock parking lot, watch for a paved road on the right and a sign for Panorama Point. Turn onto this short road to a parking area and some wonderful views. The dirt road on the left leads to two short, **easy** trails, The Goosenecks Overlook and Sunset Point. For the **GOOSENECKS TRAIL** you must scramble up some slick rock and then walk a short distance to the rim for spectacular views of the 'goosenecks,' where a river turns back on itself to form a loop, on the Sulphur Creek. The rocks near the river are the oldest in the park and date back about 260 million years ago and are known as Cutler sandstone.

The **SUNSET POINT TRAIL** begins on the left side of the parking lot and is a bit over a ½-mile (0.8 km) return if you go to the end. It winds around in a semicircle and has views to the north, east, and south. It is particularly striking in the late afternoon until sunset, thus the name. The trail is fairly level but be extra cautious near the edge, as there are no guardrails and the slick rock can be slippery. Do not go on either trail if there is a thunderstorm in the area.

Continuing east on UT 24, just before the turn to the visitors center, look for the Castle on the left. This formation appears to be several separate pieces of oblong rock carefully placed side by side and precariously perched on the sloping cliff. It is in fact solid rock, and what you see is the result of the forces of erosion working piecemeal on the stone. Drive past the turnoff for the visitors center for now, as there are three more stops within a short distance, all on the left side of the road.

The first stop is the schoolhouse that was used by the Mormon pioneers up until the 1940s. The second pullout goes back much further in time to the original inhabitants, the Fremont (see page 153), who lived to the north of the Ancestral Puebloans, and has examples of their rock art. The last stop is the trailhead to the Hickman Bridge, a **difficult** trail that is 2 miles (3.2 km) round-trip and leads to the largest arch in the park. Natural bridges are formed by running water and arches by erosion. The Hickman Bridge is believed by some geologists to be a true arch and the water flowing under it at present is a result of its formation, rather than its creator.

Return to the turnoff for the visitors center and check the weather info before continuing south on the Scenic Drive. The rangers can tell you whether the two trails, Grand Wash and Capitol Gorge, are safe to hike or closed due to the threat of flash floods. It is always best to check first, even if the sun is shining, as a rainstorm can occur several miles away, or even the night before, and flood the narrow canyons. In some sections there is no place to escape the raging water.

The Castle

From the visitors center, follow the road south past the orchards, where fruit is available during harvest season, and the Mormon buildings that include a blacksmith shop and barn, among others, and stop at the self-pay booth. Try to have some small bills with you. Sometimes fresh baked goods are for sale south of the orchards; ask a ranger at the visitors center. The cliffs become higher, soaring past 1,000 feet (300 m), and closer as you continue along the road, which is 10 miles (16 km) and ends past the Egyptian Temple, a massive formation on the left.

Two trails follow the canyon bottoms and both are **moderate**. The **GRAND WASH** trailhead is at the end of a short dirt road that turns off the Scenic Drive about 4 miles (6.4 km) south of the visitors center. This trail is mostly level on hard-packed sand or slickrock with the occasional soft sand section. It goes through to UT 24, 2¼ miles (3.6 km) in total, if you can arrange for someone to pick you up at the other end

Sandstone Domes

and bring you back to your vehicle. If not, it will be a 4½-mile (7.2 km) return walk. However, the Narrows section, where the canyon is only 20 feet wide (6 m) and 500 feet high (150 m), is 1 mile (1.6 km) from the trailhead and goes on for about ½ mile (0.8 km), so if you turn around, the hike is cut almost in half. Allow 1½ to 2½ hours, depending on what point you turn around at on the trail.

The other trail, Capitol Gorge, is at the end of a dirt road that is narrow, winding, and rough. When you reach the end of the paved road, keep left and you will soon arrive at the trailhead. There are restrooms. Although it is hard to believe the road continues on from where the pavement ends, it does, and, not only that, this used to be the only road from Hanksville to Torrey until 1961, when the present road, UT 24, was built and paved. (After every heavy rain, the old road had to be repaired.)

The **CAPITOL GORGE TRAIL** is a 2½-mile (4 km) return walk if you go to the "tanks" section and back. Watch for petroglyphs on the left as you go in, as well as pioneer inscriptions, and many bullet holes and vandalism. There are several places where you must walk through soft sand, which can be difficult. In some places, slick-rock is exposed next to the canyon walls, where you can get out of the sand, but sometimes you cannot avoid it. And remember while going in that you have to come back the same way.

There are signs for the "tanks" at the end of the trail, a 1-mile (1.6 km) walk, and a short trail on the left climbs up and over the rock to get to them. The tanks are hollows in the sandstone that form pools of water, or tanks, and can hold a tremendous amount of precipitation for long periods of time. There are steps cut into the rock and the trail climbs moderately through a narrow side canyon until the tanks suddenly appear. You can continue up the wash, but in some places the pools go completely across the trail, necessitating a scramble around the edge of what can be very deep "puddles." Do not drink this water or enter it. Allow about 1½ to 2 hours for this portion of the tour.

This ends the brief tour of Capitol Reef.

The Geology of Capitol Reef

Capitol Reef contains the Waterpocket Fold, a geological formation created when the Colorado Plateau experienced a huge uplift around 65 million years ago. The fold is 100 miles (160 km) north–south and 3 miles wide (5 km), sloping down toward the east. Only four canyons go through the fold and all are subject to flash flooding. The white domes are of Navajo sandstone.

This area was a vast desert 260 million years ago, larger than anything on earth today. By 240 million years ago, the sea covered the region and was open to the west-forming tidal flats. Sediments of sandstone, siltstone, and mudstone, with some layers of limestone that contain fossil shellfish, built up to over 1,000 feet (300 m) in the area around the visitors center, becoming thinner toward the east. Volcanism produced some bentonite, the dark gray stone northeast of the visitors center. Again the region became a vast desert, forming the Wingate sandstone, and above this, deposits of fine siltstone came from rivers flowing into the area to produce the Kayenta Formation. 190 million years ago, sand dunes formed the Navajo sandstone, which was followed by several incursions of the sea and also some lake deposits.

Sixty-five million years ago, the Colorado Plateau was rising, forming the Wasatch Mountains to the west and the Rocky Mountains on the east. The uplift was generally horizontal but in a few places, such as at Capitol Reef, the land was pushed together and tilted at a very steep angle, exposing the horizontal layers nearly vertically. This is why as you go from west to east through the fold, the different types of rock slope down into the ground and disappear from sight, where they are replaced by the next-younger formation. This can be seen driving along UT 24 and in the two canyon trails. The differing rates of erosion for each formation has resulted in the unique scenery in Capitol Reef.

Waterpocket or 'tank'

Human Settlement

The Fremont were first identified as distinct from the Ancestral Puebloan in the Fruita area of Capitol Reef. The Fremont occupied central Utah and were the northern neighbors of the Ancestral Puebloan. Characteristics of their culture include unpainted grayware pottery, the wearing of moccasins instead of sandals, living in pithouses, and building separate masonry storage rooms in nearly inaccessible places among the cliffs. They did not use kivas and maintained a greater dependence on wild game and plants than on agriculture. They did grow corn but a different variety from the Ancestral Puebloan that was better suited for a shorter season. They also tended to move more frequently. Their rock art is also stylistically different. There are a few examples in the park and appear in abundance throughout their territory, though most are difficult to get to. (See Sego Canyon, page 179.) The Fremont produced unfired clay figurines that are unique; a few are on display in the museum at Anasazi State Park (see page 136).

The origins of the Fremont are not well understood and there is much controversy over the issue, as well as what happened to them. By A.D. 1500 they had left the region and seemingly vanished. Some archaeologists believe they migrated to the east or southeast and are associated with the Ute from southwestern Colorado, but there is no substantial evidence at this time. The Fremont are probably the least understood and most mysterious of all the ancient Southwestern peoples.

After the Fremont had left the area, both Paiute and Ute utilized the resources until driven out by the Mormons in the 1870s. The Mormons established towns to the west of Capitol Reef, including Torrey, and by the 1880s they had founded Fruita, located in the park, and both Caineville and Hanksville to the east. The orchards in the park were planted by the Mormons, who occupied the region until the 1940s.

In 1937, Capitol Reef National Monument came into existence with the preservation of 37,000 acres (15,000 h), and the Mormons who were still living there slowly drifted away, abandoning the protected land. By 1970, the monument contained over 250,000 acres (100,000 h), and the following year, Capitol Reef became a national park encompassing 241,904 acres (98,000 h). The name is a combination of two sources: "Capitol" after the similarity between the whitish domes of sandstone and the Capitol in Washington; and "Reef," a nautical term referring to a barrier, normally in the sea. But even though it is landlocked, the long fold of rock certainly was a barrier to travel through the region.

Capitol Reef, though not on the main tour due to time restraints, is certainty worth exploring either via a simple drive along the highway and Scenic Drive or by hiking some of the many trails or traveling off-road.

day 9

Arches
National Park
Utah

- Established in 1929 as a national monument and in 1971 as a national park
- 125 square miles (323 square km)
- Elevation: 3,900–5,700 feet (1,195–1,723 m)

Newspaper Rock State Historic Monument
Utah

- Established as a state monument in 1961 to preserve the petroglyphs
- Elevation: 6,111 feet (1,860 m)

Nearby Sites

◎ Sego Canyon Petroglyphs

◎ Canyonlands National Park

12. Arches National Park

GETTING THERE: From Green River, take I-70 east for 20 miles (32 km) to exit 180 and go south on US 191 25 miles (40 km) to the park entrance. The entrance road will be on the left and there is a turning lane, so when you begin to descend between high cliffs, work your way into the left lane. The highway is four lanes in this section and divided, but at times there can be traffic congestion near the turnoff. A short road leads to the entrance gate and just past it on the right is the visitors center. The park is 5 miles (8 km) north of Moab.

THINGS YOU NEED TO KNOW: The park is open 24 hours a day, every day. The visitors center is closed on Christmas Day. Visitors center hours vary with the season but are open by 9 AM at the latest, which is during the winter. There are no services in the park but you can find everything in Moab. For more information, phone 435-719-2299; visit www.nps.gov/arch; or write to Arches National Park, P.O. Box 907, Moab, UT 84532-0907.

Arches has the largest collection of natural arches in the world, with over 200 within park boundaries. Many of the arches in the park are easily accessible from the

The Windows Section

paved roads, but to visit Delicate Arch, the most spectacular of all, a hike of about 1½ miles (2.4 km) is required on a trail beginning at Wolfe Ranch.

TOURING ARCHES

The full-day tour consists of making a stop at Balanced Rock, hiking to Delicate Arch, and exploring the Windows section.

From the entrance gate, proceed to the visitors center, where there are clean restrooms, a bookstore and gift shop, and an exhibition about the geology of the park. Past the visitors center, the road climbs a series of switchbacks to the plateau. As you ascend, the "Penguins" are above on the left and there are a couple of pullouts, one left and one right, where you can stop for a better view of this formation. Once you are at the top, the road straightens out, somewhat, and you soon come to the Park Avenue viewpoint and trailhead on the left. Continue past but watch for turning traffic. The road goes around a sweeping corner and you get a view of the La Sal Mountains to the east, as well as your first sight of the massive fins in the Courthouse Towers section. Opposite these fins, look on the left for the Three Gossips and Sheep Rock. Past

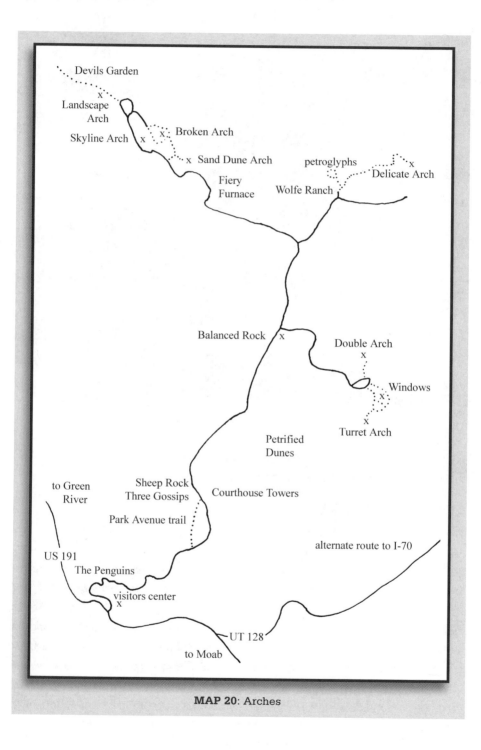

MAP 20: Arches

Three Gossips (center) and Sheep Rock (right)

this point, on the right, are light-colored petrified dunes and on the left towering cliffs. After a few more miles, look to the right for a wonderful view of the Windows section in the distance. As the road begins to ascend, watch for the Balanced Rock parking lot on the right. Drive in the first entrance, as the lot is one-way and you exit out the other end. This is the first stop on the Arches tour.

Balanced Rock

A short, **easy** trail around Balanced Rock is about ⅓ mile (0.5 km). The classic photo of Balanced Rock shows a teardrop-shaped stone perched on a very small pedestal, but as you walk around it you quickly see an ever-changing form and that the true contour of the rock is more circular. This is a good example of differential erosion, whereby the lower Dewey Bridge mudstone is eroding much faster than the upper Slick Rock sandstone, until finally gravity will win out and Balanced Rock will collapse. If you follow the trail counterclockwise past Balanced Rock, look for a short, heavily eroded stump with a small rock nearby. This was Chip-Off-the-Old-Block, a Balanced Rock in miniature, that collapsed in the winter of 1975/76. And past this are two larger stones that retain a substantial base for now but will eventually become "balanced rocks."

When you walk around Balanced Rock you can appreciate the true scale and size of it, and how small the pedestal is on which it rests. In fact, you might not want to

Balanced Rock

linger for too long under it, as it appears ready to fall at any moment. It is truly a wondrous sight to see firsthand and is only the beginning of your voyage through this surreal rock garden. The trail is mostly level with only a slight upgrade and a few steps.

Delicate Arch

From the Balanced Rock parking lot, turn right and drive past the Windows turnoff. The road now meanders down a hill and bears left in a long curve. As you come out of this curve there is a road on the right for the Delicate Arch trailhead, which is located at Wolfe Ranch. About a mile (1.6 km) down this side road you come to a Y. If you plan to hike to Delicate Arch, turn left to the parking lot; if not go right to the viewpoint, which has two trails. One is **easy**, paved and with wheelchair accessibility; the other is **moderate**, a 1-mile (1.6 km) return walk, with hilly terrain. You can see Delicate Arch across the canyon about a mile (1.6 km) away. This is a good alternative if you cannot make the hike to the arch. Binoculars are useful.

The trail to Delicate Arch is **difficult**, a 3-mile (4.8km) return walk, with no shade and about half or more overexposed slick rock uphill. In the summer heat, this trail is **very difficult** and should not be attempted during the midday, only early morning or late afternoon. Carry plenty of water and a flashlight, as you do not want to be walking after dark without a light.

The trail begins at Wolfe Ranch beside the parking lot. There are pit toilets but none along the trail. The ascent is 480 feet (146m) but this is deceiving, as the first part of the trail goes up and then down again a few times before you arrive at the long, steady climb up the main section of the trail. Watch for the rock cairns marking the trail. There is no relief until you reach the top—it just keeps going up—and in the hot

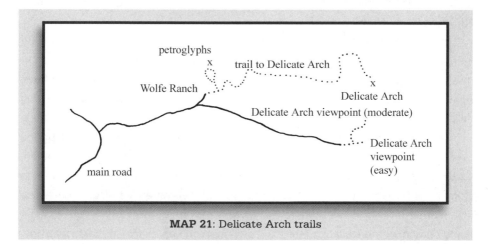

MAP 21: Delicate Arch trails

sun, this section can be brutal. Once you reach the top, the remainder is not too bad, as it snakes its way around and over the rocks and scrub trees until you reach the last part. The trail then skirts along a cliff on a narrow ledge with the cliff face on the right and a significant drop on the left. And after all this effort you still have not been able to catch even a glimpse of the arch. I believe the best part of this trail is the fact that just when you begin to lose hope and are wondering whether you are on the right trail, you round a corner and there it is, only a short distance away, this magnificent creation of nature, a spectacle that is hard to believe even when you are standing under it. This is probably the greatest natural phenomenon, Delicate Arch.

However, before you can get up close to it, there is one last barrier, a 4-foot (1.2 m) -high fin of sandstone that you must crawl over. This can be difficult and sometimes people need assistance, but there are usually others there willing to help. It is easier to cross if you walk over to the left, where some outcrops of stone serve as steps. The top is about 5 feet (1.5 m) wide and flat but you must scramble down the other side, which is a bit higher, and the sandstone slopes away from the ledge at a steep angle; you do not want to fall when you climb down. The arch sits on the other side of a large bowl that slopes down but the surface is rough, so the footing is good, but be careful as you must walk around the rim of this bowl to get to the arch.

Delicate Arch is truly Mother Nature at her best: massive, fragile, overwhelming, unbelievable, incomprehensible. How was this created? What keeps it from collapsing? Emotions sweep over you as you gaze in awe at this formation. It cannot be real,; the mind will not accept it; it must have been built of paper and glue in some studio back lot in Hollywood. But it is real, a product of millions of years of water and chemical reactions, erosion. In a land of mind-boggling scenery and fantastic geologic formations, Delicate Arch stands out. It would be difficult to find a more impressive rock anywhere.

You will want to sit for a while in the presence of this formation before the long journey back, so take your time. Walk around and through the arch; notice what a narrow pedestal it rests on and the shape of the stone. It appears to be made up of three separate rocks: two bases, one larger than the other, and the sweeping arch resting delicately on these bases. It is difficult to believe it exists, even when standing under it.

Return to the parking lot the same way you came, but just before the small bridge over the creek near Wolfe Ranch another trail branches off to the right (as you are walking toward the parking lot). You may have noticed this on the way out. It leads along a short distance to some Ute petroglyphs. This is an **easy** trail and worth the few minutes it takes to see the images. There is a group of mountain sheep that are being herded, or more likely hunted, by some men on horses accompanied by a dog. The Ute did not have access to horses until at least the 1700s, so this fact helps to date

Students at Delicate Arch

the petroglyphs to a certain degree. We still do not know how many years after 1700 the work was done, but as rock art is so difficult to date, any little bit helps.

The remains of Wolfe Ranch are next to the parking lot and consist of a corral, originally built in 1888 (marker 4), a root cellar for storing food (marker 6), and a cabin (marker 5). This is not the cabin built by John Wolfe in 1888 for himself and his son, which is long gone, but a second house constructed for his daughter, son-in-law, and their two children in 1906, when they joined him and lived here for two years. Wolfe stayed for 20 years altogether, running cattle and establishing a garden (marker 8) that was watered by an irrigation system consisting of a dam near the present bridge, a pond, and ditches into the garden. It is difficult to believe that cattle could have survived in this area but it is much changed. A few years after Wolfe left, sheep were brought in and within two years, the land had been stripped of its grass from over-grazing, and has not been farmed since.

Once back at the parking lot return to the turnoff for the Windows section, turn right out of the parking lot, then left at the junction with the main road, and left again at the top of the hill. There are no services in the park but if you have brought a picnic lunch, there are picnic tables across from the Balanced Rock parking lot. A favorite place of mine to stop for lunch is the first turnoff on the Windows road, an area known as the Garden of Eden. After you turn onto the Windows road there is a sharp curve to the right, followed by another to the left, and as you enter this second curve, there is a road on the left; turn here and go up a short distance to a small parking area. This stop is usually not very crowded so it is a good place to stop for lunch, though there are no picnic tables. In fact, there are not many anywhere in the park, and if it is near noon, they will be full.

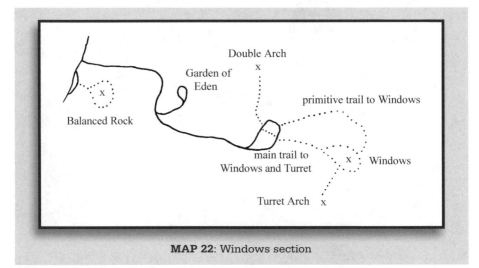

MAP 22: Windows section

You can see many various formations near this parking area, including
the large elephants to the east. They can
be difficult to see, depending on how
the light strikes them and the angle at
which you are viewing them but I believe
they definitely look like elephants, even
though my students have never seen
them as such. Sometimes they agree,
but I believe they are just humoring me.
But I still think there are elephants here.

Windows Section

From this stop, continue on to the
Windows, a left turn at the bottom of the
hill. The Windows section is usually very
crowded and finding a parking space
is difficult unless you arrive early in the
morning, but if you are following the
Grand Circle Tour you should be used to
this scenario from other national parks.
There are two areas to park and the road
is a one-way loop, so if you cannot find a

An elephant?

place in the first, or upper, lot, try the lower section. There is a stairway that goes from
one to the other. Once you have parked, there are three arches to see: the Windows
and Turret Arch along the upper trail, and Double Arch near the lower parking area.

The trail to the Windows is **moderate** as you climb a small hill and some steps,
and is a 1-mile (1.6 km) return walk if you go past Turret Arch. There is another trail
that begins by the South Window and loops down behind the Windows and back to
the parking lot, which is a bit harder than the main trail but affords some nice views.
The Windows consist of two arches, the North and South, that have eroded out of
one fin and are also referred to as the "Spectacles" because they look like a pair of
eyeglasses from a distance. You may climb into the arches but there is a steep drop-
off behind. The trail continues to Turret Arch, which is opposite the Windows. This was
named for what looks like a turret on a castle that is on the left side of the arch. Here,
too, you may climb up into the opening but it is difficult, so use caution and remember, it is much harder to come back down. There are some beautiful views over the
petrified dunes and of the La Sal Mountains from this point.

Turret Arch

Return to the lower parking lot, where the trail to Double Arch begins beside the large sign. This trail is **easy** but parts of it are loose sand and can be a bit hard going. Double Arch produces an amazing play of light and shadow as the sun changes position through the two bands of stone that make up the arch. In one of the Indiana Jones films, near the beginning, a young Indiana rides through the desert and then enters a secret passage under a double arch, this arch. (There is no entrance in reality.) But Hollywood aside, Double Arch is a spectacular sight to see and one of the highlights of visiting Arches.

Return to the main road and turn left toward the visitors center. Down the hill from Balanced Rock is a pullout on the left; stop for great views of the petrified dunes and the Windows area as well as the Great Wall on the right side of the road. The next stop is the Courthouse Towers viewpoint on the left. There is a sign across from the Three Gossips and Sheep Rock, the latter named for its sheeplike appearance, though I have always thought it looks more like the profile of a monkey. At this stop you can appreciate the immensity of these fins called the Organ and the Tower of Babel. This is also the end, or beginning, of the **PARK AVENUE TRAIL.** This is a **moderate** 1-mile (1.6 km) distance, one-way, that goes up over 300 feet (91 m) in elevation. The starting point is the other end, which is fine if you have someone to drive around and pick you up at Courthouse Towers. If not, it is better to begin at this end, making the first half uphill and the return downhill. The trail goes between two massive cliffs with some balanced rocks along the way.

Double Arch

The Egyptian Queen (left) along the Park Avenue Trail

The next stop is the La Sal Mountains viewpoint at the end of a short road on the left past the curve. This concludes the one-day tour of Arches, but if you have more time, at least another day, there are two other areas worth visiting: the Fiery Furnace and Devils Garden. To reach these areas, continue past the turn to Wolfe Ranch on the main road. The Fiery Furnace is about 2½ miles (4 km) from this turnoff and the Devils Garden is at the end of the road, a further 3½ miles (5.6 km).

OTHER AREAS WITHIN ARCHES

Fiery Furnace

The Fiery Furnace viewpoint is the second pullout on the right past the Wolfe Ranch turnoff and at the end of a short road. You can see the maze of fins and walk a short distance on the trail, but to hike into the valley and among the fins you must go on a ranger-guided tour or obtain a hiking permit. For either option, you must sign up at the visitors center prior to arriving at the trailhead. Too many people were getting lost, so they do not allow anyone to walk through without a permit or guide. As there are no trails and you wander around among the fins, it is best to go on one of the tours rather than on your own. Rangers offer 3-hour guided tours for which there is a fee. In November and from late February to early March tickets may be bought at the visitors center. For the high season they can only be obtained online at www.recreation.gov. Type in "Arches" and follow the directions.

Between the Fiery Furnace and Devils Garden are three arches, all of which are easy to reach. Sand Dune and Broken Arch are on the same trail that begins about 2 miles (3.2 km) from the Fiery Furnace turnoff and are on the right. There is only a small pullout with enough room for a few cars. Sand Dune Arch is in a narrow canyon and is impressive, but while the trail is short—it has a (0.5km) ⅓-mile return walk—you must walk through deep sand in places, so the trail is **moderate**, though kids love it. The arch is on the right and difficult to see until you are right on top of it, but it is worth the hike. Allow 20 to 30 minutes. If you continue on to Broken Arch, the two trails branch off a short distance from the parking area; it is almost 1½ miles (2.4 km) round-trip on a **moderate** trail that is mostly flat but sandy in places. It takes about an hour-plus to see both. Broken Arch is also accessible on a trail from the Devils Garden campground.

There is one more arch on the way to the end of this road and it is on the right about ½ mile (0.8 km) from the Sand Dune Arch parking lot. Skyline Arch is at the end of an **easy** ⅓-mile (0.5 km) trail that climbs a small hill at the beginning but is then level. Erosion is usually a slow process but in 1940 a massive boulder fell from the opening of Skyline, more than doubling the size of the arch. If you go to the end of the trail, you can see the remnants of this stone. No one witnessed the phenomenon

Sand Dune Arch

nor did it fall on anybody (though I do not know if anyone ever checked under this massive chunk of rock), but it makes you pause to think as you stand under this cliff . . . though usually not for long.

Devils Garden

At the end of the road is the Devils Garden parking lot and trailhead. There is one main trail, plus several side trails to arches and a wilderness loop. Altogether there are eight arches in this area and to see all of them takes over 7 miles (11.25 km) of hiking and a half-day or more. The difficulty of the trail depends on how far you go and on which trail. I will describe the main trail and each branch as you come to it. The trail begins in a narrow canyon with smooth, dark walls and then quickly opens up with terrific views of the rock formations. About ¼ mile (0.4 km) in there is a branch to the right that goes to two arches, Tunnel and Pine Tree. This is a **moderate** trail and is ½ mile (0.8 km) round-trip.

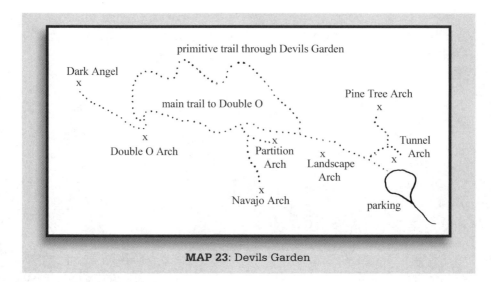

MAP 23: Devils Garden

As you continue on the main trail it is a little over a 1 ½-mile (2.4 km) return walk to Landscape Arch, the most famous in this section, a **moderate** trail with several small changes in elevation and some soft sand along the way. Landscape Arch is 106 feet (32 m) high and 306 feet long (93 m), the longest span in the park and one of the longest in the world. At its thinnest point it is only 11 feet thick (3.3m) since a 5-foot-thick piece that was 60 feet long (18m) fell off in 1991. Debris from the rockfall is visible on the slope below the arch. If you look up to the right another arch is visible, Partition Arch, which is reached by a spur trail a bit farther along the main trail.

If you continue past Landscape Arch, the trail becomes **difficult** with many changes in elevation, though none is very high, plus you must scramble up and over sandstone fins and walk along narrow bands of stone that have sharp drop-offs. However, there is another arch, the Wall Arch, a short distance past Landscape, which is not too difficult to reach. This is similar to Sand Dune Arch in the fact that it is in a narrow canyon and you can almost walk right by it and not notice it. **NOTE:** Wall Arch collapsed in 2011.

About ¼ mile (0.4 km) past Landscape Arch, the trail branches off again, this time on the left, and goes to Partition Arch, the one you saw from near Landscape, and Navajo Arch. This section is **moderate** and almost a 1-mile (1.6 km) return walk. The main trail continues on to Double O Arch, 4.2 miles (6.8 km) return from the parking lot, and then another 0.8 mile (1.3 km) to the Dark Angel, a rock spire and the end of the trail. Past Double O Arch is a turnoff for the primitive loop that winds through the fins; it is **very difficult** and not maintained and about 3 miles (4.8 km) back to the main trail near Landscape Arch.

This concludes the tour of Arches National Park. From the visitors center, turn left back to US 191 south toward Blanding. The next stop is a short detour to Newspaper Rock, a wonderful petroglyph site between Arches and Blanding.

HUMAN ACTIVITY AT ARCHES

The earliest signs of human use of this region are some Folsom points that date to around 8000 B.C. There is a little evidence of activity during the Archaic period, 6000 to 500 B.C. This area was the northern extremity of the Ancestral Puebloans and where they shared territory with the Fremont (see Capitol Reef, page 153). One element that brought both peoples to the region was some veins of chert used for making tools and points. There are also petroglyphs from both the Fremont and Ancestral Puebloans. An extensive drought in the 13th century A.D. forced the Ancestral Puebloans to abandon the area and move south, a time when the Fremont were also leaving the region. Following this, the Ute occupied most of eastern Utah, until driven out by the Mormons in the 19th century.

The earliest inscription in Arches dates to June 9, 1844, by Denis Julien, a mountaineer and explorer who sailed down both the Green and Colorado Rivers 30 years before Powell. In 1855, the Mormons established a town near modern Moab but were soon driven out by the Ute. It was over 20 years before they would return and found the towns of Moab, Monticello, Blanding, and Bluff.

In 1888, John Wesley Wolfe and his son Fred moved to Utah from Ohio, looking for a healthier climate, and purchased 150 acres along Salt Wash, establishing the Bar DX Ranch. They built a small one-room cabin, a corral, and a dam across the Salt Wash Creek. They had an irrigation system for a small garden and grazed cattle on the surrounding land. In 1906 they were joined by Wolfe's daughter Flora, her husband, Ed Stanley, and their two children. A new cabin was constructed, along with the root cellar, which are the structures seen today at the site. The original cabin and dam were washed away. In 1910 everyone moved back to Ohio. There were several owners after this, including one sheep farmer whose animals overgrazed the region, leaving it barren of natural grasses and causing much erosion, which accounts for the way it appears today. In 1948, the land was sold to the federal government.

GEOLOGY OF ARCHES

Arches National Park was created to preserve a unique landscape containing over 200 arches as well as many balanced rocks. The geologic story begins 300 million years ago with a sea that left 2,000 feet (600 m) of salt deposits and are the reason arches form here more than anywhere else on the Colorado Plateau. Around 250 million

Courthouse Towers

years ago, the sea had retreated and deposits from rivers created a huge delta that was later covered with windblown sand dunes. When, 210 million years ago, mountains rose in western Utah, the region became a massive desert with what would become the Navajo sandstone. This in turn was covered by finer silt and mud and then another layer of sand dunes to form the Entrada sandstone.

Between 290 and 200 million years ago, the first phase of anticline began to form the landscape. Anticline is where the rock is pushed into a fold, causing an upward dome. From 60 to 5 million years ago, the second phase of anticline caused a collapse of the surface in places. The reason behind this was the salt. As it was forced up, it began to move toward the southeast like toothpaste being squeezed from the tube. When the Colorado Plateau was uplifted 20 to 5 million years ago, the area became a bulging dome that caused the rock to crack and split into long vertical sections, or fins, such as Courthouse Towers, the Fiery Furnace and Devils Garden. The valley around Wolfe Ranch is where all the salt collapsed, dissolved, and was flushed into the Colorado River. The water in the Salt Wash was too salty for Wolfe to drink but he found a spring higher up and to the north that was still salty but tolerable, a consequence of the thick layer of salt that once covered the land.

The unique combination of this unstable salt deposit, the softer Dewey Bridge mudstone and the harder Slick Rock sandstone is what produced—and continues to produce, as this is an ongoing process—the many arches in the park. As the rock was pushed up by the salt, the narrow fins were created—think of turning an orange inside out; this is stage one. The sandstone of these fins is held together by a natural calcium cement that is dissolved by water, which is slightly acidic; this is stage two. However, the cement is not spread evenly throughout the sandstone, so it erodes faster in some places than in others, forming the arches. You will notice round hollows in the stone, that are caused by the wind. Once a weak spot has eroded a bit, the wind swirls sand around in the tiny hole, creating an ever larger one. Eventually all of the arches you see in the park today will collapse, but this will take several million years for this to occur, and they will be replaced by different ones. Most of the arches in the park were formed in the last 2 million years.

The other element at work is differential erosion; a good example of this is Balanced Rock. The softer Dewey Bridge is composed of mudstone and erodes faster than the overlying Slick Rock made from fine-grained windblown sand. The harder rock protects the softer Dewey Bridge to a certain degree, but when the weight of the upper stone becomes too much for the Dewey Bridge to support, it comes crashing down.

The Slick Rock tends to erode in large slabs that fall from the sides of the cliffs as moisture seeps down into the many vertical fissures in the rock. You will notice large boulders and flat pieces of stone at the base of the cliffs and under certain arches. Skyline Arch lost a large chunk of rock in 1940 and Landscape Arch became much thinner in 1991, but most of the erosion is not as dramatic as this and is imperceptible to the casual observer.

13. Newspaper Rock

GETTING THERE: From Arches National Park turn left on US 191 (south) and drive around 40 miles (64 km) to the turnoff for Newspaper Rock. Watch for a road on the right and signs for the Needles section of Canyonlands National Park. This is UT 211 but the turn is not well marked. After you turn, it is about 12 miles (19 km) to the site, which is at the bottom of a hill past a sharp curve to the right. There is a large parking

Newspaper Rock

lot behind some trees. The site is to the right of the parking area and fenced off, but you can get very close to the rock art.

THINGS YOU NEED TO KNOW: This site is open year-round and there is no fee for visiting. Do not cross the fence or touch these or any other rock art images, as the oil from your skin contains acids that damage the art. There is a short **easy** path to the site.

There are many "newspaper rocks" in the Southwest, as the early settlers thought of these sites as being "read" like a newspaper. The Navajo call this place Tse Hane, "the rock that tells a story," if only we could read the story. This site is unique in that it contains images from the Archaic, Basketmaker, Fremont, Pueblo, Ute, Navajo, Spanish, and American periods, though the pictures are all jumbled together and in some places superimposed over one another, which makes the job of sorting and attempting to decipher them all the more difficult. And, as with most rock art images, it is nearly impossible to understand most of the signs, so any interpretation or "translation" is usually an educated guess.

The canyon was carved by Indian Creek that drains into the Colorado River. The cliff face has a dark patina from desert varnish, allowing a nice contrast with the underlying rock to produce petroglyphs that are easily seen. There is also an overhang of rock to protect the images, which accounts for their beautiful state of preservation. The site has not been vandalized, as many others have, so this improves the condition as well.

As this site was a crossroads of many cultures over time there are numerous examples of varied images, including anthropomorphs with horns, deer, elk, sheep, buffalo, men on horses, animal and human tracks, and hand prints. Among the more interesting images are a herd of deer in a long line on the top left side, interspersed with three "flying squirrels," and ending with a bear track; a lizard/man with either horns or a headdress, on the bottom left; a human figure that has long lines attached to each side of his head and is wearing what appear to be chaps, which would make this figure from after the 16th century; another figure with horns above what could be a prayer wheel, an important element in many Native American rituals; and a beautiful set of deer tracks going up the rock, just to name a few. The images that are near one another might be related but they could also be from differing time periods so there may not be any connection between them. No one has yet discovered a way to date petroglyphs.

There are so many images that you could stay for hours and still not see each individual picture, and this is what makes Newspaper Rock such a special place to visit. This, along with the great variety, makes for an astounding sight well worth the small detour. Newspaper Rock is one of the finest examples of rock art in the Southwest that is easily accessible.

Return to the main highway and turn right toward Blanding, your next stop on the Grand Circle Tour. It is around 30 miles (48 km) to Blanding.

This ends Day 9 of the tour. The approximate timeline is: 45 to 60 minutes from Green River to Arches; 10 minutes to Balanced Rock, 30 minutes at Balanced Rock; 10 minutes to Wolfe Ranch; 1½ to 2 hours to Delicate Arch and back, including the petro-

Left side of Newspaper Rock

glyph site; 10 minutes to the Windows section, 1 to 1½ hours at Windows, including Double Arch; 1 hour return to the visitors center, including stops at all the pullouts between Balanced Rock and the center; 1 hour to Newspaper Rock; 45 minutes to Blanding.

◎ OTHER SITES NEAR ARCHES

When you exit from Arches onto the main highway and head south, there is a road on the right, US 279, just before the bridge over the Colorado River, that leads to some petroglyphs. They are about 5 miles (8 km) down the road on the right, but are rather difficult to see. There is a pullout on each side of the road and most of the images are high up on the cliff face, but if you like rock art, they are worth the time to see; if not, then skip these.

◎ Sego Canyon Petroglyphs

Another petroglyph site that is definitely worth a visit if you are staying longer in the area is Sego Canyon. To get there, take I-70 east from Green River for about 25 miles (40 km) to exit 187 for Thompson and CR 94. Turn toward Thompson and follow the paved road through town for about 4 miles (6.4 km). Watch for a small parking area on the left just after you go through a deep gully. If you hit dirt road, you have gone too far. There are picnic tables and a pit toilet at the site. There are two separate sites with Fremont-, Ute-, and Archaic Barrier Canyon–style images. The site is open year-round and there is no admission fee.

The Ute images include some shields, horses with and without riders, and buffalo, among others. The triangular human figures with elaborate headdresses are Fremont, as are the hunter and mountain sheep. But the most impressive images are the ghostly Archaic figures painted in shades of red and brown. These are known as Barrier Canyon style, are pictographs, and are common throughout this region, but most are in inaccessible places or very difficult to get to. However, these at Sego Canyon are easy to find and observe as they are next to the road; you do not even have to get out of the car.

The figures are large, sometimes over life size, without arms or legs, and have huge

Fremont, Sego Canyon

Archaic, Sego Canyon

holes for eyes, giving them a ghostly appearance as they seem to float through the air. Some have horns or appear to be wearing a cape. There is one that looks like a silhouette of Batman. It is believed that these figures represent shamans' visions during a ceremony, possibly induced by a lack of sleep and food or by a hallucinogen. Another interpretation is that the large figures are the shamans and the small figures near the main images are their spirit helpers. The reason or purpose they served for the creators will probably never be known, but the images stand on their own as haunting works of art and excellent examples of this style.

An alternate and much more scenic, though longer, route from Green River or Sego Canyon to Arches is UT 128 along the Colorado River. Take I-70 east to exit 204 and follow UT 128, which traverses rolling desert, until you cross the Colorado and begin to follow the winding river with the water on one side and towering cliffs on the other. This is an exhilarating drive but not one for the faint of heart.

◎ Canyonlands National Park

was established in 1964 to preserve one of the most rugged wilderness areas in Utah. It encompasses 527 square miles (1360 square km).

GETTING THERE: Canyonlands comprises four separate areas: two, the Island in the Sky and the Needles, are easily accessible by car; the others, the Maze and Horseshoe Canyon Unit, are remote and difficult to get to even with a four-wheel-drive vehicle. The Island in the Sky is the most accessible. To get there, take UT 313, which is 8 miles (12.8 km) north of Moab on US 191 on the left (driving north) or 21 miles (34 km) south of I-70. From the turn it is about 20 miles (32 km) to the visitors center. The Needles visitors center is located on UT 211 (the same road that goes to Newspaper Rock, see page 175) and is about 30 miles (48 km) from US 191. For the other two sections, inquire at the visitors centers or contact the park.

THINGS YOU NEED TO KNOW: The park is open year-round and the visitors centers hours are 9 AM to 4 PM with extended hours in the summer. It is closed Thanksgiving Day, Christmas Day, and from late December through February. For more information, phone 435-259-4712 for the Island in the Sky visitors center, 435-259-4711 for the Needles visitors center, or 435-719-2100 for park administration, visit www.nps.gov/cany; or write to Canyonlands National Park, 2282 S. West Resource Blvd., Moab, UT 84532-3298.

There are many trails and four-wheel-drive roads to explore either on your own or with an organized tour, but you can see some spectacular scenery just from the paved roads. The Island in the Sky is a high mesa located between the Colorado and Green Rivers, both of which can be seen from the viewpoints along the road. The main road goes past the visitors center before dividing after 6 miles (9.6 km), with one road continuing south to Grand View Point Overlook, 6 miles (9.6 km), and the other heading northeast to Upheaval Dome, 5 miles (8 km), which is a crater of unknown origins. There are several pullouts along the way and some short trails leading to Mesa Arch (just before the junction), an **easy** ½-mile (0.8 km) loop, Whale Rock, a **moderate** 1¼-

Canyonlands Island in the Sky section

mile (2 km) return trail that has great views of Upheaval Dome, and the Crater View trail, an **easy** ½ mile (0.8 km) plus return that goes to the rim of Upheaval Dome. At the end of the other road is the **GRAND VIEW OVERLOOK AND TRAIL**, a **moderate** 1¾-mile (2.8 km) return walk that offers views of both the Green and Colorado Rivers and probably the most spectacular sights anywhere in this section of the park.

The Needles district is mostly known for its red rock spires with white bands. There are also many arches and some ruins, though many of them are only accessible by four-wheel-drive or on primitive difficult trails. The visitors center is beside UT 211, 24 miles (38.6 km) beyond Newspaper Rock on the same road. This is an easy drive on a paved road surrounded by sweeping vistas. Past the visitors center, the road becomes winding and hilly but the scenery is even more interesting. A short distance from the entrance is a trail to the Roadside Ruin. This is a ⅓-mile (0.5 km) **easy** loop to a granary that is tucked into a shallow cave and in remarkably good condition. Pick up the trail guide that explains what the various plants and bushes are beside the numbered markers.

Continue along the road to a pullout on the left, which is the viewpoint for the Wooden Shoe Arch, an arch that looks like, well, a wooden shoe. Stay on the main road, as the loop to the south does not allow views of this arch even though it is closer. Continue on the main road to the **POTHOLE POINT TRAIL** parking. This is an **easy** ½-mile (0.8 km) loop trail past several potholes that sustain a variety of aquatic life after it rains, plus there are some interesting rock formations.

The road ends just past the Pothole Point Trail but another short route a bit farther back toward the visitors center leads to nice views and a four-wheel-drive road. The scenery is worth the drive if you have the time, just remember that travel with a regular car is limited in this section.

The Maze and Horseshoe Canyon are only accessible with a four-wheel-drive vehicle, and even then the roads are sometimes impassable. Contact the visitors center before attempting to enter this region.

Geology of Canyonlands

The region of Canyonlands is the result of the two major rivers, the Green and Colorado, especially their many tributaries that fan from the rivers like the branches of a tree, forming numerous canyons and making travel through the area difficult. But long before these rivers created this scenery there was a similar story as at Arches (see page 173): the depositing of huge amounts of salt as the sea retreated, followed by mudflats from a coastal plain, a delta and then sand dunes, river deposits, and a massive desert covered with dunes. Next was the great uplift of the Colorado Plateau, which increased the flow and speed of the rivers, leading to the erosion that resulted in what you see today.

The Island in the Sky is a Y-shaped mesa rising 2,000 feet (600 m) above the rivers. It connects to the "mainland" by a narrow neck of land that is being undercut by erosion and will someday disappear. The Colorado is to the east, on the left side as you enter the park, and the Green is to the west. Both are visible from view points along the road. This is the highest area of the park and offers the best views over the canyons of the effects of erosion, which has created a layered design. When you look out over the canyons, there is a prominent shelf of white along the lower rim just above the river, which is called the White Rim sandstone. Most sandstone is red or pink from hematite, an iron oxide mineral whose color leaches into the porous sandstone that is originally white in most cases. So this white sandstone is not an aberration but is in fact the natural color of the rock.

An unusual feature is Upheaval Dome, in the western part of the park. It was believed that this formation was caused by the collapse of the rock due to instability of the salt underneath, but another theory is that this is the result of a meteor strike around 65 to 60 million years ago, the time of the extinction of the dinosaurs. It is thought that the meteor crater was 5 or 6 miles (8 or 9 km) in diameter and as much as 4 miles (6 km) deep. More than 3,000 feet (1,000 m) of overlying rock, including the rim of the crater, has eroded away and the hole would have partially filled from the shattered sides immediately after impact. What remains is the remnants of this massive impact, if this was in fact created by a meteor.

The Needles section was formed in a similar way as was the geology in Arches, but from a much older level of sandstone. The vertical cracks, rather than going mostly parallel as in the fins of Arches, also have perpendicular joints that produce spires rather than fins. This layer is known as the Cedar Mesa sandstone and has stripes of red and white. All the spires and arches are formed in this type of sandstone.

The two rivers meander slowly through the northern reaches of the park, and even though you cannot get close to them from the main roads, you can see both up close in other easily accessed places: The Colorado runs next to US 279, Potash Road, on the western side of US 191 just before the bridge to Moab (see page 178 for the directions to the petroglyphs on US 279 near Arches), and the Green River passes through the middle of Green River (the town). Where the two rivers meet can be seen from Confluence Overlook in the Needles section at the end of a very long and difficult trail or a short trail and difficult four-wheel-drive road. Not long after the two placid rivers become one, the Colorado, their waters enter Cataract Canyon, a stretch of the most turbulent rapids in any of the parks. Powell described this part of the river as the roughest his team sailed through. The lower section is now under Lake Powell, but in the southern boundary of Canyonlands, the river still roars unchecked.

Edge of the Cedars
State Park
Utah

■ Designated a state historical
monument in 1970 and a state park
in 1974

■ 16 acres (6.5 h)

■ Elevation of 6,200 feet (1,890 m)

Hovenweep National Monument
Utah/Colorado

- Established as a national monument in 1923
- Comprises 784 acres (317 h) in six separate areas on Cajon (pronounced *Cahone*) Mesa
- Elevation 1,585-2,060 feet (485-630 m)

Nearby Sites

- Butler Wash Ruins
- Mule Canyon Ruins
- Natural Bridges National Monument
- Monument Valley

14. Edge of the Cedars State Park

GETTING THERE: The park is on the western edge of Blanding, Utah. When US 191 makes a sharp left turn in the center of town (heading south), go straight on Center Street for about 6 blocks and turn right on 600 West Street for a short distance to 400 North, and turn left again. You will see the museum and large parking lot. The route is well marked to the site.

THINGS YOU NEED TO KNOW: The park is open every day except Thanksgiving Day, Christmas Day, New Year's Day, and Sundays. Hours are 9 AM to 5 PM. There are no services at the park but Blanding has motels, restaurants, service stations, and grocery stores. For more information, phone 435-678-2238; visit www.stateparks.utah .gov/parks/edge-of-the-cedars; or write to Edge of the Cedars State Park, 660 W 400 North, Blanding, Utah 84511-0788.

Part of the pueblo has been excavated and reconstructed, including a kiva that may be entered. There is also a museum that is one of the finest in the Southwest.

Museum guard

TOURING EDGE OF THE CEDARS

Before entering the museum you are greeted by some wonderful whimsical sculptures that play among the shrubbery to the delight of visitors. Look carefully as sometimes they like to hide behind the bushes and must be sought out. These sculptures are based on the animal and human figures that inhabit rock art in the region. Inside the museum is a bookstore in the back to the right, as well as a gallery over to the far left past the stairs, in which contemporary Southwestern artists display their work. The exhibitions change on a regular basis, so be sure to stop in and see the latest show. The cash register, where you pay the entrance fee, is to the right upon entering.

To get to the ruins you must go

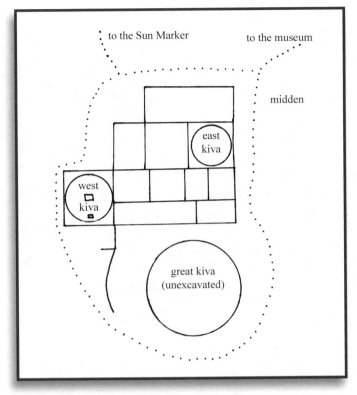

PLAN 10: Edge of the Cedars

through the museum, but I will begin with the archaeological site and then return to the permanent display. The stairs are to the left of the entrance and the walls are decorated with a series of rock art figures based on images from the nearby region. Ascending the stairs is like walking through a canyon of sandstone walls and is a marvelous introduction to the site. Once you are at the top of the staircase—there is only one flight—go to your left and across the museum to the hallway that is in a tower and has beautiful panoramic views out over the ruins and surrounding countryside. Follow the hall around and exit on the other side. Turn left and continue straight to the double doors that lead to the site. A sign over the doors indicates the way, and you must return by the same way. If the rooms are dark, don't worry; the lights come on automatically whenever someone enters a room and shut off when the person leaves, which helps conserve electricity.

There is a paved **easy** trail around the ruins and then down to the Sun Marker. As you walk toward the structure, stop where the trail divides and look to the left. This low mound is the midden, or garbage dump. To your right, the village continued

Northeast corner

along the ridge but to the far right, the section was severely looted and has never been mapped. You are at the northeast corner, where there is a long, narrow room directly in front of you that was probably used for storage, as it is on the back side of the pueblo.

There were three building phases at this pueblo, two between A.D. 1025 and 1125, after which it was abandoned, and then a third around 1215, when it was reoccupied for only a few years. The long room and west kiva, the reconstructed one, and its surrounding building, plus a few of the central rooms and the great kiva, are from the second building phase. The row of rooms next to the long room in the central area are from the first phase, and the east kiva and rooms on the north side of the great kiva are from the last stage of building, though not all archaeologists agree with this timeline.

Walk counterclockwise around the pueblo, stop at the opposite corner, and look out over the valley. All of this was farmed by the village inhabitants and some of it is still used for agriculture, especially toward the west. There probably were other pueblos within sight of this one, but any evidence has for the most part been destroyed over the last few centuries. The high wall on the northwest corner, in front of the long room, is part of the first pueblo and goes across the full width of the structure as well as continues south, forming a tradition L-shaped pueblo. From this point you can see the end of the wooden ladder emerging out of the reconstructed west kiva. There is a short stairway up to the plaza where the entrance is for the kiva.

Once you are at the top of the stairs, notice the small, square hole south of the entrance. This is the ventilation shaft for the kiva, and from inside you will see how it is constructed. This is a keyhole kiva (see Plan 11) that is typical for the Mesa Verdean branch of the Ancestral Puebloan. Enter the kiva, being careful on the ladder as the rungs tend to be slippery from use. Remember whenever you enter a kiva that these are sacred places, so treat the kiva with respect. Once you are inside and your eyes have adjusted to the low light, you can see the various parts of a typical kiva and how they were constructed. The hearth is directly under the entrance and ladder, so the people would have entered through the smoke of the fire. You can see where it was by the ring of stones in the floor directly under the entrance, which also serves as the chimney. The walls are plastered but you can see the stonework under it in places that were left bare. The Grand Circle Tour includes kivas that can be entered at other sites,

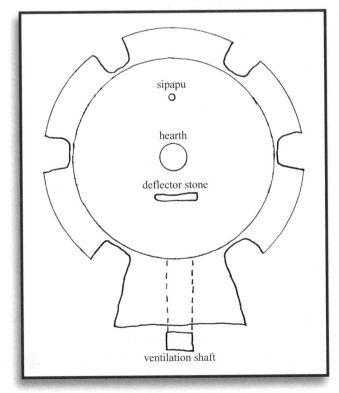

PLAN 11: Mesa Verdean kiva

Ventilation shaft (under planks), west kiva

but most do not have the plastered walls and you will see that in comparison they look dramatically different.

Along the walls near the roof there are niches that were used as shelves for the sacred objects used during the ceremonies, though we know very little about either. On the south side you see the ventilation system, which consisted of an underground, wood-covered shaft that led to the small, square hole on the roof. Fresh air would be drawn down into the shaft to provide oxygen for the fire as well as for the people inside, though even with this method it tended to get rather smoky. There would be a deflector stone at the end of this shaft so the air would not hit the fire directly thus preventing the smoke and hot embers from blowing around the room. There is also the *sipapu*, a small hole filled with clean sand, which was the exit/entrance to the lower world. This is placed on the north–south axis of the kiva and is near the bottom of the ladder.

Look up at the ceiling and notice how it is constructed. The way the beams are fitted together along the edges is called cribbing and it creates a roof that is very strong and rises toward the center allowing more headroom, though by now you realize just how low the ceiling is. They began with large beams set in a circular form, with each circle becoming smaller until they closed the opening (Figures 4 and 5 on page 428).

Next, they covered these beams with small branches and brush, along with flat stones and mud, to create a very strong roof that could be used as a plaza. This is a small example, but the same technique was used for the great kivas, those that are over 40 feet (12 m) in diameter, though the larger ones had four support posts near the center. Although the primary building material for the pueblos was stone, a great amount of timber went into the construction of even these small abodes. If you have taken notice of the terrain, in most areas where they built, there are not many trees. On the one hand, this is due to the desert conditions surrounding many of the pueblos; on the other hand, much of the deforestation was caused by the Ancestral Puebloans, especially around the larger centers, such as Chaco Canyon (see page 322).

When climbing out of the kiva be careful not to bump your head as the opening is small. Imagine going in and out when there was a fire below and smoke coming out the entrance. Walk over to the far left corner of the plaza to see details of the masonry. The wall next to the kiva is original and if you look over the edge to the left, the low foundation that is visible is from the later construction, while the tall wall with the small door and wooden beams sticking out is from the second phase. This section also had a second story just above the kiva plaza where you are standing.

Great Kiva (foreground)

The Ancestral Puebloans always tried to build a kiva below ground level, but in some cases the rooms around it were raised to give the impression of the kiva being sunken, as illustrated here. The large circular depression to the right of the lower wall is the great kiva that has not been excavated. The small kivas, called kin kivas, were for the immediate family to use, while the great kivas were for large ceremonies and celebrations at which people from the surrounding communities would join with the locals.

Directly south of the kiva is a rectangular room. In the corner toward the great kiva is another room that has a straight wall on the west side and a semicircular wall on the east that follows the contour of the great kiva. A second room south of this one has contoured walls on both sides, an unusual feature.

Go back down the steps and continue on the path around the southern end of the pueblo and the great kiva. More structures have been found south of the main pueblo, including a few rooms and possible kivas, indicating the village stretched along the ridge, but this section has not been completely excavated at present. In fact, the site continues outside the park boundaries as more rooms and pottery have been found there. The trail continues around the great kiva and along the eastern side of the pueblo, where you can see good examples of the walls and how they were constructed, and also the second kiva that was a later addition. You will now be back at the Y in the trail where you began. Instead of returning to the museum at this time, go toward the reconstructed kiva again, left, and turn right onto a path that goes down a small grade to a modern structure that has ancient leanings: the Sun Marker.

This rather bizarre-looking structure at the end of the path is a combination of art and practicality, of the modern and ancient world. Created by artist Joe Pachak, it is an homage to the astronomical aspects of Ancestral Puebloan society that were of great importance to these peoples' everyday life. Many places throughout the Colorado Plateau were used by the people to follow the movements of both the sun and moon as a guide to planting and harvesting as well as the timing of different festivals. The Parawon Gap petroglyphs would have served a similar purpose (see page 108). If it is a sunny day, watch the ever-changing light and shadow on the monument for a while to experience the effects of this sculpture. If you happen to be here on the summer solstice, a sliver of light travels across the spiral until it pierces the mountain sheep. It is a remarkable creation and a wonderful addition to this site.

Return to the museum, and upon entering the building, turn left into the archaeology room. In this room is a display of the tools used in archaeological excavation and descriptions of the techniques, along with photos and records of the dig at Edge of the Cedars. In front of this room is a large, glassed-in room that holds row upon row of every type of pottery created by the Ancestral Puebloan, along with other artifacts found at this and other sites in southeastern Utah. There are some beautiful examples

Southeastern section

of bowls, mugs, cooking pots, and storage vessels, mostly done in the black-on-white Mesa Verde style.

Continue into the main hall of the museum. As the exhibitions are periodically rearranged, I will point out some of the highlights of the collection. There are many examples of pottery, including some effigy vessels in the form of birds and ducks that were probably used in ceremonies, plus several miniatures of unknown use. There are some artistic examples of Mesa Verde painted mugs and corrugated ware that seems to simulate basketweave. Most examples are dated and their find location given in the display. There is a comparison of the different types of pottery by region with a corresponding map.

Some of the rarer objects include a few well-preserved baskets from the Basketmaker period, wooden tools and weapons, nets for capturing small game, the rope from a spring pole snare, sandals, bone tools, gourds, jewelry, and corn cobs. There is also a large collection of lithics, including manos and metates; arrowheads and spearheads from Clovis to P III, several of whose points are still tied together with a yucca cord; and flake cores. All are well marked with dates and type.

But of all the fine examples from the ancient world that are on display, the highlights of the collection are three objects of which there are virtually no others like them in the world; two turkey feather blankets and a macaw feather sash. One of the blankets is almost completely intact with the woven yucca cords still wrapped with the turkey feathers. The other lacks the feathers but illustrates how the underlying cords were woven together. Turkeys were domesticated and used mostly for their feathers early on, but in the later Pueblo period they also became a source of food. The Macaw sash dates to A.D. 1150 and is from the Canyonlands region to the north. This is of indescribable beauty with red and blue feathers wrapped around yucca cord and is in remarkable condition. Macaws and their feathers were highly prized by the Ancestral Puebloans and came all the way from central Mexico in trade. These three objects alone are worth the trip to the museum.

This concludes the tour of Edge of the Cedars archaeological site and museum.

ARCHAEOLOGY OF EDGE OF THE CEDARS

Edge of the Cedars is the northern boundary of the Northern San Juan Basin, which stretches from Chimney Rock (see page 312) in the east to the Coombs Ridge in the west (this is southwest of Edge of the Cedars) and the San Juan River to the south. All of the rivers and washes in the region drain south into the San Juan River, which in turn empties into the Colorado River just north of the Utah-Arizona border. This territory is further divided into an area called Montezuma's Valley that encompasses the most fertile region that the Ancestral Puebloans inhabited and stretches from Mesa Verde to the Edge of the Cedars. The farmland was, and is, much better in the eastern part around Cortez, Colorado, than near Blanding, which is at the western extremity of the area. The Mesa Verdean branch occupied this region.

Between Mesa Verde and Edge of the Cedars are 2,500 square miles (6,500 square km) of land that had an estimated population of over 30,000 Ancestral Puebloans living in eight large towns that never exceeded 2,500 to 3,000 residents, and many small villages built in clusters. Edge of the Cedars was one such small town, with a population around 250. It was occupied from A.D. 850 to 950 and again from 1025 to 1125. There were six residential complexes and ten kivas, as well as one great kiva. One of the most interesting discoveries was a copper bell that had to have been imported from Mexico, as the Ancestral Puebloans never worked metal. Only part of the village has been excavated. In the surrounding territory, several irrigation ditches and check dams have been reported by local farmers over the years, but a thorough investigation of the land has as yet to be completed.

The construction is in the Mesa Verdean style, using large stones for the walls, which are one, two, or three stones thick and have the exposed edges ground or pecked smooth. You can see this detail in outside corners and especially the round structures that you will see in Hovenweep, where the stones are carved with a rounded edge that creates the circumference of the building. The thicker walls allowed them to build two- and three-story pueblos by A.D. 1100. The walls were held together with mud mortar and chinking was placed in the small spaces between stones to help prevent cracking of the mortar. The outside was covered in a mud plaster as was the interior though sometimes the inside walls were also painted solid colors and occasionally had geometric, human or animal figures on them. You can see an example of the mud plaster inside the reconstructed kiva at Edge of the Cedars.

15. Hovenweep National Monument

GETTING THERE: From Blanding, head south on US 191 for about 15 miles (24 km) to the turn onto UT 262 (on the left) at the bottom of a long hill. Continue straight on this road until you see the signs for Hovenweep, make a sharp right turn and then a left—again there is a sign—and finally a right to the monument's visitors center.

CAUTION: UT 262 is open-range country and it is not unusual to find animals, especially horses or donkeys, in the road. It is about 45 miles (72 km) from Blanding to the visitors center and the road is paved all the way. When you leave Hovenweep for Cortez, Colorado, turn right and stay on this road to the four-way intersection, turn right and continue to US 461, right again, and this will take you into Cortez and is paved all the way. For a slower, more scenic route, though of equal distance, turn left from the visitors center and left again at the Stop sign and yet another left at the next intersection, and then go straight through to Cortez. You will come out onto US 461 by the airport. Turn left toward the center of town and then right onto US 160, where the majority of motels and other facilities are.

THINGS YOU NEED TO KNOW: Hovenweep is open year-round and the visitors center's hours are 8 AM to 6 PM May to September, 8 to 5 October and April, 9 to 5 in the winter, closed Thanksgiving Day, Christmas Day, and New Year's Day. There is a 30-site campground near the visitors center, with a first come, first served basis, but no other facilities in the park. There is an entrance fee to the park and to use the campground. For more information, phone 970-562-4282; visit www.nps.gov/hove; or write to Hovenweep National Monument, McElmo Route, Cortez CO 81321.

As you drive up the short road to the visitors center and Square Tower Ruins, turn right into the parking lot, continuing straight goes to the campground. There are picnic tables beside the parking lot. The visitors center entrance is on the left under the canopy and restrooms are on the right. On the left by the center is a large map with di-

Along the road to Hovenweep

rections to the other sites and whether the roads are closed. It is also advisable to ask a ranger about the road conditions before attempting to visit any of the other five sites. If you arrive early in the morning and the visitors center is closed, you can pay when you return, as the trailhead begins by the door. There is also a self-paying option.

"Hovenweep" means "deserted valley" in the Ute language, a name that is appropriate for this isolated region. As you stand on the canyon rims it is hard to believe that a once thriving community survived here, a testament to the resourcefulness of the Ancestral Puebloans.

The Ancestral Puebloans occupied these shallow canyons from A.D. 1100 to 1300, but before this period, going back to Basketmaker, they lived scattered on the surrounding low mesas. There are six sites in the monument: Square Tower, near the visitors center, and Holly, Horseshoe, Hackberry, Cutthroat Castle, and Cajon Groups. More than 2,500 people probably lived in the area at one time and many sites are still unexcavated. The shallow canyons had springs that were a reliable source of water, which explains the popularity of this region for habitation. The people built along the rims, down the canyon walls, and in the bottom of these fingerlike depressions.

There are no great kivas in Hovenweep but the residents did construct many towers and D-shaped buildings, the use of which is still not understood: Were they kivas or houses, used for defense, or for astronomical purposes? What is known is that the architecture is Mesa Verdean in style and the towers are some of the finest examples of this type of construction. The largest site, and most accessible, is the Square Tower

Group. Hovenweep Castle stands on the rim near the end of one canyon and was part of a much larger complex of two- or three-storied buildings. Several ruined buildings fill the canyon just below the rim and a three-story tower is located on a prominent boulder near where the ancient spring emerged. There are several other well-preserved structures farther down the canyon on both sides.

During the P III period, the Ancestral Puebloans seemed to have been fascinated with towers and Hovenweep has many examples. One of the best is Holly Tower located at the Holly Group site, not far from Square Tower. It is two stories high and sits on an almost inaccessible rock outcrop near the end of the canyon. Footholds were

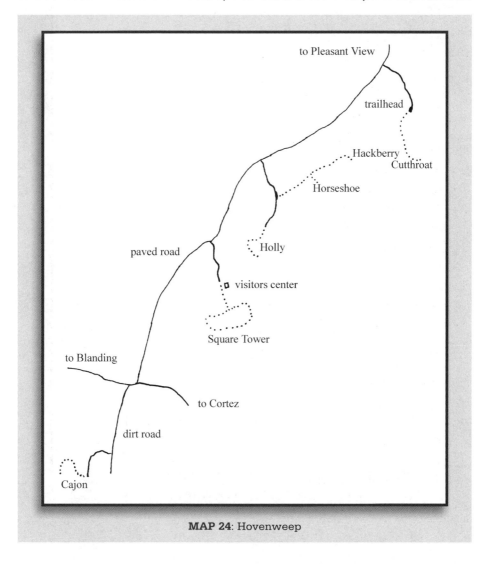

MAP 24: Hovenweep

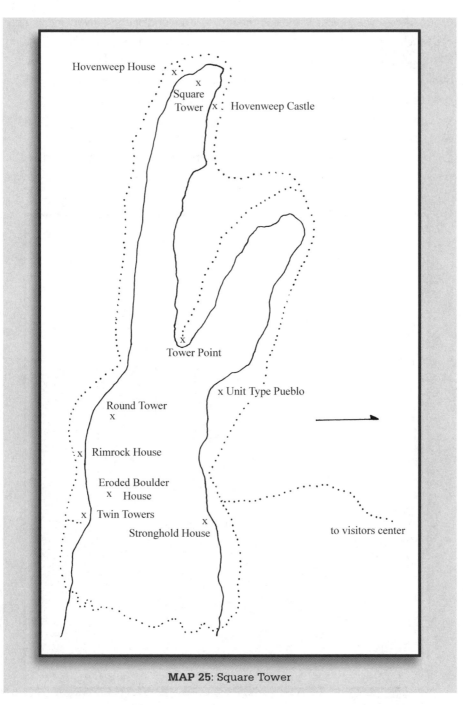

MAP 25: Square Tower

carved into the rock to gain entry to the tower. The towers remain one of the great enigmas of this ancient civilization.

TOURING HOVENWEEP

The tour consists of visiting the Square Tower, Holly, Hackberry, and Horseshoe Groups. I also describe the other two groups, Cutthroat and Cajon, but they are not part of the main tour.

Square Tower

The easiest site to visit is the Square Tower Group, which is located behind the visitors center along a paved trail that goes as far as the canyon rim. The trail continues around the canyon on a gravel surface and finally there is a very rough section that goes into, and back out of, the canyon forming a loop. The first section is **easy**; the part around the canyon is **moderate** if you turn around and retrace your steps, but is **difficult** if you continue on the loop through the canyon (see map 25).

Walk under the canopy and follow the paved path to the canyon rim for your first view of Hovenweep. This is a wonderful place, silent, peaceful, and beautiful with

Stronghold House and Tower (left)

what seem to be the bluest skies in the Southwest. As you look across the shallow canyon you can see, from left to right, Twin Towers, Eroded Boulder House just below the rim, Rimrock House, and below that, Round Tower. All of these structures were part of the same pueblo and you can see the rubble on the rim and down the slope of what was probably the largest community in this section.

On this side of the canyon is Stronghold House and Tower. The house appears to be isolated, perched as it is on its split rock pedestal, but in fact it is the top section of a large pueblo that was built mostly under the rim and all connected together. One

Twin Towers, left, Rimrock House, top right, Eroded Boulder House, right center

side of Stronghold Tower has collapsed into the canyon as it was built on wooden beams that bridged a gap in the rock and when the wood rotted away the tower lost part of its support. The trail continues to the right toward Unit Type House, which was part of a larger section of buildings below the rim and to the left and was possibly connected to the Stronghold pueblo, forming one continuous village. There are good views across the canyon from this point.

The trail divides a short distance past Unit Type House and the path to the left

Hovenweep House (left) Square Tower (center) Hovenweep Castle (right)

goes out to Tower Point, where a tower remains on the rim with much rubble below. This is a good viewpoint down the canyon but can be bypassed if you do not have the time or desire to do the extra walking. Stay straight on the main trail to the largest ruin, Hovenweep Castle.

This section consists of Hovenweep Castle and Hovenweep House on the rim, and Square Tower in the canyon. Hovenweep Castle was not a castle but part of a large pueblo, most of which is on the slope below the rim and can best be seen from the trail on the other side of the canyon. The remains are impressive not only for their size but the quality of the masonry. There are not many places in the Southwest that achieved the high level of quality and beauty of stonework as at Hovenweep, and the Castle is a fine example. The entrances to these towers were on the canyon side and there are some T-shaped doors that remain. One section is a D-shaped tower; you can see the curved surface of the exterior wall and how the stones were carved to the contour of the building. The use of large stone and fine dressing is the Mesa Verde style.

Past the Castle you can see Square Tower down in the canyon. This tower was originally three stories and sits on a block of sandstone, though it is difficult to see the base due to the growth of brush. There is a T-shaped door on the other side. The spring was to the right of the tower. As you continue past Hovenweep Castle, the trail goes around the end of the canyon, where there are the remains of a check dam that held back the runoff from rainstorms, allowing the water to soak slowly through the Dakota sandstone and supplement the spring below.

The next structure is Hovenweep House, which is in fact a D-shaped tower that was part of a larger and separate pueblo. As you walk toward the tower, notice all the stones strewn on the ground; they are the remains of the many rooms that surrounded the tower and once formed the pueblo. Do not pick up or disturb any of these because the pattern of the fallen stones can give clues as to the size of this pueblo, number of rooms and kivas, and other information that is lost if they are moved or disturbed in any way.

Continue past the site and look across the canyon to see the extent of the Castle site. The structures on the rim were only a small part of the whole and there is rubble below the rim and around a large boulder. There were several kivas along the slope and a great number of rooms, some of whose rooftops reached the rim and allowed access to the towers from the canyon side. Now it seems that these doors lead out into thin air and there is speculation that the reason was defense, but when the buildings were still standing it made sense that the entrances should be on this side rather than the back, as the main rooms were in the canyon.

Also from this point the T-shaped door in Square Tower is visible. And if you look

Hovenweep Castle

carefully, and the sun is at the right angle, the remains of some cliff dwellings to the left of the Castle are visible just under the rim. These were separate from both the Castle and House pueblos. You will also notice that the vegetation is greener and more lush at the head of the canyon as there is still a seep there, though the spring no longer runs.

It is a fair distance along the trail to the next ruin, Rimrock House, but there are wonderful views along and across the canyon. You can see the tower on Tower Point and the remains below it as you progress down the path. Watch for the remains of ancient walls in the canyon wall opposite, as the Ancestral Puebloans built small granaries in the many hollows.

Rimrock House is part of the much larger village that hugged the rim and descended nearly to the bottom of the canyon and stretched from the Round Tower to well past the Twin Towers. Below and to the left is the Round Tower, and to the right is Eroded Boulder House, which was about the center of the pueblo. Eroded Boulder House is hard to see from the trail but you can see the rubble on top of the boulder, indicating that the structure was built around and over the rock incorporating it into the pueblo. This was common practice, as it was easier to build around than try and remove these massive stones. You see the same technique used at Wupatki and Mesa Verde.

Eroded Boulder House

Twin Towers

The last structures along the trail are the Twin Towers, which were not towers but two residential building, each two stories. The shape was determined by the boulders on which they sit rather than from any desire to build round structures and they are a marvel of construction, some of the finest examples at Hovenweep. The masonry is remarkable in its quality and craftsmanship and is a testament to the skill of the people who built it.

Much of these sites have not been excavated, as is the case with Hovenweep in general, so it is difficult to estimate population, but most archaeologists place it around 400 to 600 for Square Tower.

From this point you can either return by the same route to the visitors center or continue along the trail, which soon descends into the canyon over a very rough trail, including several high steps, both going down and back up, that you must scramble over. However, if you go into the canyon there are some good views of the nearby ruins and you get a very different perspective on the canyon itself; just be warned that it is not easy. The only good part is that the canyon is not very big, so the hike is short. Watch out for rattlesnakes. This ends the tour of the Square Tower Group.

Holly

Before heading to the Holly Group check with the rangers at the visitors center for road conditions because, if it has rained recently, the road will be impassable. It is better if you have a high-clearance vehicle, but if the road is dry, a regular car will make it; nevertheless, always inquire at the visitors center before attempting the drive. The off-roaders go even when the road is wet and consequently cut it up terribly leaving deep ruts. The road is rough and narrow, with only a few places to meet oncoming vehicles, and some sections of slick rock that either drop or climb steeply and suddenly. The road is also difficult to find and not well marked.

To get there from the visitors center, return to the main road and turn right. Check the mileage on your odometer, as it is about 4 miles (6.4 km) to the turnoff. Around the 4 mile (6.4 km) mark, watch for a road on the right, which has a very small wooden post with a carving of a bird on it; this is the way to Holly. Just before the turn is another road on the right that is in better condition than the one to Holly, but it is a dead end that goes to an oil well and not any archaeological site. Don't ask how I know this.

It is less than a mile (1.6 km) to the pull-off for the trailhead to Horseshoe on the left, though it seems farther, but continue past to Holly, which I describe first. A bit past the Horseshoe trailhead, the road divides in a Y; keep right. Now the road gets worse. You go up a steep hill followed by a steeper descent and you cannot see

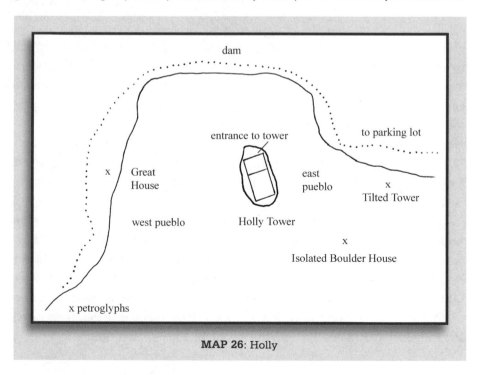

MAP 26: Holly

Tilted Tower, Holly

oncoming traffic, and there is no place to meet. At the bottom is the parking lot, and I use the term loosely, as it is a section of slick rock that is very uneven, rough, and small. Once you arrive, the trail to the site is **easy**. There is a pit toilet beside the parking lot.

The trail is on the opposite side of the parking lot and winds through the trees before you soon emerge on the edge of Keeley Canyon and the site. First you come upon some room blocks on the rim and a large boulder that is tipped at an angle where it split off from the rim and has some ruins on it. This is Tilted Tower, which was attached to the rim during the occupation but broke away after abandonment; exactly when is not known. The room blocks and Tilted Tower were originally connected and part of a large pueblo that continued down in the canyon and had at least three kivas.

Next you see Holly Tower, a two-story tower built on an isolated boulder near the head of the canyon, similar to Square Tower from the previous site. The towers were extremely difficult to construct and this one is a high point of Ancestral Puebloan architecture. It is molded perfectly to the rock and the masonry is beyond reproach. Notice the square corners and their alignment, and this after 800 years of exposure to the elements. There is only one entrance, on the north, and you can still see the handholds that were pecked into the rock. No one knows how the people built this tower but it stands as a stellar example of their great skill and artistry in architecture.

The trail goes around the head of the canyon, where there was a spring that is now covered by the collapse of the rim. There are the remains of a dam and reservoir in the corner of the canyon directly in front of Holly Tower. The next ruin is Curved Wall House, which has a beautiful curved exterior wall enclosing a rectangular room. This was not a house but most likely a ceremonial room, as there is a tunnel under the building through a natural crack that leads into the canyon, where there are seven kivas below the rim. This entire side of the canyon was one large pueblo from this point to beyond the curve in the rim. Past the Curved Wall House is the remains of the Great House, which was two stories and residential. The pueblo extended past the Great House and was connected to this house through a door on the canyon side of the building.

Entrance, Holly Tower

Walk past the Great House to see the entire canyon and the relationship of the two pueblos, one on this side and another opposite with Holly Tower in between. All the rubble in the canyon is the remains of these villages. The population was around 100 to 150. Another ruin visible from this side is the Isolated Boulder House, a small building constructed over the crest of a fallen rock. Its use is unknown but it is clear that the house was built after the rock tipped over as opposed to Tilted Tower. The walls are perpendicular, whereas those of the Tilted Tower are slanted to the degree the rock tilts.

If you continue down the path past the ruins, there are some petroglyphs in

Isolated Boulder House

the edge of the canyon, but they are not too easy to find. Look for a large rock that is perpendicular to the cliff and has a small ledge jutting out at the top and about 4 feet (1.2 m) of clearance between it and the boulder to the left. The petroglyphs are in a row below the ledge and consist of a spiral, three concentric circles one inside the other, and then another spiral. They were used for astronomical sightings. During the spring and fall equinoxes and the summer solstice, a shaft of light pierces the petroglyphs, but nothing occurs at the winter solstice.

This concludes the tour of Holly. Retrace your steps to the parking lot and then drive back to the pullout for the Horseshoe and Hackberry trailhead (both are located on the same trail). This trail is **moderate**, a 1-mile (1.6 km) return walk to Horseshoe, and traverses slick rock, so there are several minor changes in elevation.

Horseshoe Tower

Horseshoe

was a small pueblo of about 50 to 60 people, with most of the living spaces and kivas below the rim and in ruins. A large D-shaped structure and the remains of a tower, both located on the rim, are worth the walk. The D-shaped building, known as Horseshoe House, was probably used for ceremonies, and the central room appears to be a kiva. This circular central room was surrounded on three sides by an outer concentric wall and the space in between divided into three rooms; there are no connecting doors to any of the rooms. On the north side are several small holes in the masonry that do not seem to have had any practical purpose. Some archaeologists think they were for ventilation, but the largest of the three rooms has only one. Another theory is that they were "watch holes" to see an approaching enemy, but given the thickness of the walls and small size of the holes, and the fact that they point at most in only two directions, this is highly unlikely. The other theory is that they have something to do with astronomical observations, but this has not yet been proven, so the use of this structure remains a mystery. Any suggestions?

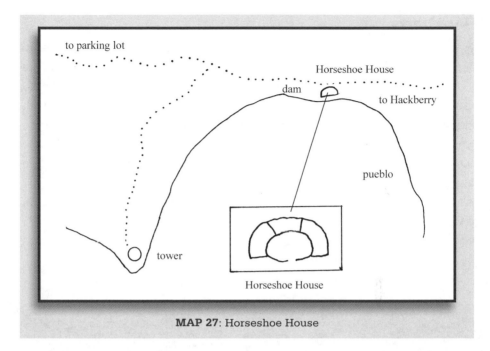

MAP 27: Horseshoe House

On the right side of Horseshoe House (facing the canyon) are a dam and a reservoir that runs for a fair distance along the rim, and farther along in the same direction is a round tower. From this side of the canyon you can see the rubble under the rim where the main pueblo was to the left of Horseshoe House. There is a spring under the rim directly below Horseshoe House.

Horseshoe House from the north

Hackberry

If you follow the path past Horseshoe, you will arrive at Hackberry Ruins, a large pueblo but one that has not been excavated. It is mostly in ruins, though there are some standing remains on the far side of the canyon. It is about another 1-mile (1.6 km) round-trip beyond Horseshoe. Hackberry had a population of 250 to 350, with structures on the rim and in the canyon. The canyon is overgrown with trees and brush because the spring that the Ancestral Puebloans used still has water. At the end of the canyon you will see the large cottonwoods, which only grow where there is an abundance of water. There are at least 14 kivas and numerous rooms, and if you follow the path around the canyon, you walk past some of the rubble to the standing structures at the end of the trail. There were also rooms under the overhang beside the spring, but this section is closed as it is too dangerous getting down into it. From Hackberry, follow the same trail back to the parking area.

This concludes the Day 10 of the Grand Circle Tour. The approximate timeline is: 1

Hackberry, east pueblo

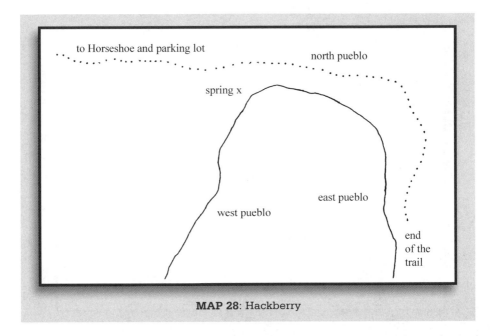

MAP 28: Hackberry

to 1½ hours at Edge of the Cedars; 1 hour from Blanding to Hovenweep visitors center; 1 hour at Square Tower; 1½ to 2 hours for Holly, Horseshoe and Hackberry; 1 hour from Hovenweep to Cortez, Colorado.

OTHER SITES IN HOVENWEEP

Cutthroat

If you plan to visit Cutthroat Castle, be sure to inquire at the visitors center about the road conditions, as this is the most difficult site to get to and requires a high-clearance vehicle. From the visitors center, turn right on the main road and drive about 8½ miles (13.6 km) before watching for a road on the right marked by the infamous wooden post and carved bird, as at the Holly Road. The first section of road is similar to the Holly Road, except the slick rock is rougher and sage and juniper trees line most of it and drag along the side of your vehicle, adding cool racing stripes to your paint. About 2 miles (3.2 km) in (seems *much* farther) is a parking area on the right where the trailhead begins, but the road continues down closer to the site. For this second part you need an off-road four-wheel-drive vehicle. If you do not believe this, just stop at the parking lot and walk down the next 100 feet (30 m) of the road; you will be convinced. From the parking lot, it is a 1½-mile (2.4 km) return walk on a **difficult** trail that winds down a hill and across the road to the site.

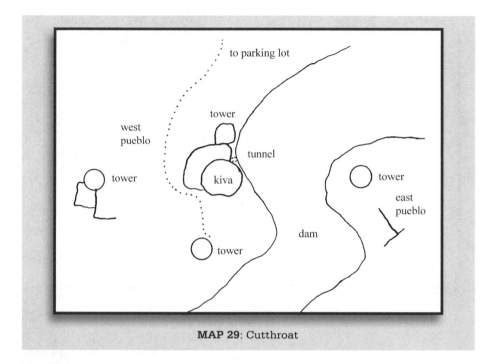

MAP 29: Cutthroat

Unlike the other sites at Hovenweep, Cutthroat does not sit at the head of a can-yon but in the middle of Cutthroat Gulch and straddles a stream that was dammed. This is a large site that housed a population around 150 and was situated on both sides of the canyon. The larger section includes Cutthroat Castle, which sits promi-nently on a huge outcrop of sandstone and consists of a two-story kiva, the round room, surrounded on one side by a D-shaped room with a tunnel in the floor through a natural crack to a two-room structure below the rock. There are other rooms, includ-ing a two-story square tower connected to the back of the D-wall and another kiva just beyond the structure to the north. West of this structure (opposite side to the tun-nel) is a round tower connected to several rooms and at least three kivas that are the round depressions. South of the castle is another round tower, five more kivas, and an extensive section of rubble. Across the stream is another round tower, some room blocks, and five more kivas. The streambed is dry but cottonwoods are growing there, indicating moisture below the surface. The remains of a dam are located between the south tower and the section of wall across the canyon.

This is an isolated area and there are many rattlesnakes around, so caution is re-quired when walking around the site. Remember, they like shady places during the heat of the day. Do not move or disturb any of the rocks or sit, stand, or walk on the walls. Return to the parking area by the same trail.

Kiva (top left) and tunnel (lower center)

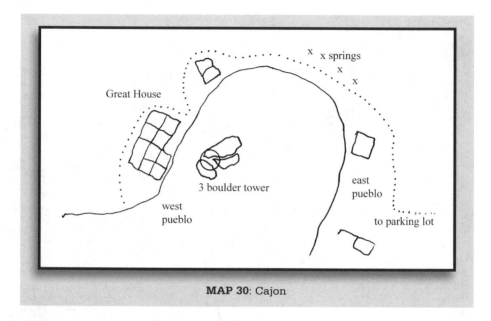

MAP 30: Cajon

Cajon

To get to Cajon, turn left out of the visitors center road and drive to the intersection, a distance of about 6 miles (9.6 km). Turn right and then left in less than ¼ mile (0.4 km), onto a dirt road. Ask about road conditions, as this section is impassable after rain, even with a four-wheel-drive vehicle. Continue on this dirt road for about 3 miles (4.8 km) and watch for a turnoff on the right past the large oil tanks. Be careful, as the road sometimes washes out where you first turn in and you don't see it until it is too late. Once on the road, keep left at the Y and you will be at the parking area. It is less than ½ mile (0.8 km) from the main road. The trailhead is beside the sign and through the gate on an **easy** trail that goes in a semicircle around the canyon.

When you approach the site there is a lot of rubble and some standing walls. This is the east side, and there was a large pueblo that stretched out along the rim and into the canyon. There was at least one kiva on the rim and three more in the canyon, as well as some cliff dwellings under the edge toward the head of the canyon. As you walk past this section you can see the standing structures along the west side of the canyon, which is much better preserved and includes a two-story room block and, beyond this, a large multistory block on the rim near a tower in the canyon. There are several springs at the head of the canyon beyond the east-side ruins that were supplemented by a large earthen dam about 100 yards (95m) back from the rim, as well as dams near the rim.

The first building on the west side was at least two stories and marked the beginning of the west pueblo that stretched along the rim and in the canyon past the large structure. There were at least seven rooms on the ground floor. The large building was two, and probably three, stories in the section away from the rim and had 10 or more ground-floor rooms. There are three kivas immediately in front of the structure in the canyon, as well as the round tower. This tower was built around and over three separate sandstone boulders and is a remarkable example of Ancestral Puebloan masonry (see photo on right, page 219). It was two stories, and has a door on the canyon side and another toward the rim that was most likely connected to another room, as evidenced by the visible rubble. These round towers are very difficult to build on flat ground and a work of architectural genius to construct it between these boulders, following the contours and creating a building that is an extension of the natural landscape. Why the Ancestral Puebloans built towers remains a mystery, and this one is the biggest mystery of all. It seems the most difficult location to construct a tower. Perhaps the builders wanted to showcase their ability.

Across the canyon you can see some cliff dwellings under the rim below the standing walls on the east side. There were several rooms in the low caves, including

Great House, Cajon

storage and living areas, but this section is closed, in part because the remains are very unstable and it is a perfect place for rattlesnakes.

This is the last site open to visitation at Hovenweep.

THE ARCHAEOLOGY OF HOVENWEEP

Hovenweep is on the Cajon Mesa, which is part of the Montezuma Valley in the Northern San Juan Basin. The mesa runs in a southwest direction from Pleasant Valley, Colorado, past Cajon Ruins and slopes southward from an elevation of 6,800 to 4,800 feet (2,080 to 1,460 m) with Hovenweep occupying the southern half. Numerous shallow canyons dissect the mesa.

In the Montezuma Valley there were over 180 large villages between A.D. 600 and 1300 and tens of thousands of small sites. During the 1200s, there were 70 large villages from Mesa Verde to Blanding on the best farmland in the Southwest. The elevation ranges from 5,500 to 7,200 feet (1,675 to 2,200 m) and there was more rain due to the higher elevation. Hovenweep was in the center of the valley and has some of the best-preserved exposed sites in the Southwest. Earlier settlements were widely dispersed near the best farming areas but the population later moved into larger villages near springs at the head of canyons.

A few points from the Paleo-Indian period around 11,000 years ago have been found, but there is more evidence of Archaic hunter-gatherers, such as several seasonal camps, hearths, stone tools, and projectile points. There were no ceramics during this time. By 2,000 years ago there was agriculture in the San Juan Basin, with corn being the first crop, followed by squash. In BM II, people lived in pithouses; one site, plus possibly three others, have been found near Cutthroat. BM II ended around A.D. 500.

BM III, from A.D. 500 to 700, saw the introduction of beans, domesticated turkeys, the bow and arrow, and the beginnings of ceramics. The people lived in larger pithouses and pithouse villages and the population grew considerably. There are three BM III sites in Hovenweep. In the P I period, A.D. 700 to 900, they began to build above ground structures and kivas. Cotton was grown and an abundance of pottery was made. Twelve P I sites were discovered at Hovenweep.

From 900 to 1100, P II, the population spread throughout the mesa and began constructing larger masonry buildings in small, widely dispersed pueblos. Pottery has decoration painted on it and kivas were lined with stone. There are 67 P II sites in Hovenweep.

There are 318 P III sites in Hovenweep that date from 1150 to 1300. The Ancestral Puebloans began in smaller villages spread throughout the territory, but in the early 1200s began to move to the canyons from the mesa top. The total population of the six pueblos was around 2,500, and although the people built many kin kivas, there

Holly Tower

Three Boulder Tower (east side), Cajon

are no great kivas; however, each village had towers. All the ruins visible in the monument date from this period.

The towers are one of the mysteries of the Ancestral Puebloans. They are found in other places, such as Mesa Verde, but nowhere else are found towers the quantity and quality of those that are at Hovenweep. The towers in the late P II period were associated with residential buildings, but in early P III they were sometimes connected by a tunnel to kivas or were built next to them. In the late P III, large towers were built on the rims and single boulders as at Holly. There are round, square, D-shaped, and rectangular ones, and some that follow the contours of boulders. They can be one, two, or three stories, with single or multiple rooms. The excavated contents have not helped in understanding their use, as both ceremonial and everyday objects have been discovered, such as pottery. There is also evidence of storage and food preparation in the structures. They were multipurpose structures used for everything from religious ceremonies to storage to living quarters and astronomical observations. Whatever their purpose, or the reason they were built, they stand as evidence of the skill and technical abilities of these people. The towers are a true marvel of architecture.

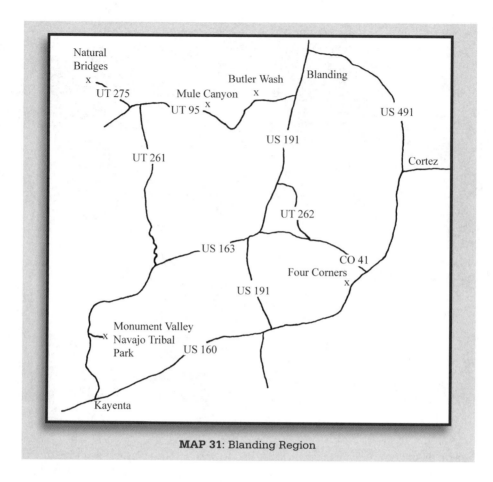

MAP 31: Blanding Region

◎ OTHER SITES NEAR BLANDING

From Blanding there are four sites that can be visited in a day, depending on the extent of your explorations, and they are more or less in a circle. The sites are Butler Wash Ruins, Mule Canyon Ruins, Natural Bridges National Monument, and Monument Valley. Also, if you are interested in dinosaurs, there is a wonderful museum in Blanding. Located on a side street across from the Comfort Inn and open Monday thru Saturday from 9 to 5, April 15 to October 15, it has an extensive collection of fossils.

◎ Butler Wash Ruins

From Blanding, drive south on US 191 about 4 miles (6.4 km) to UT 95 and turn right. The first site, Butler Wash, is just over 10 miles (16 km) from this intersection to the parking area. The site is open year-round and there is no fee. The trail to the view point is over a 1-mile (1.6 km) return walk and **moderate**, with several slight changes in elevation and mostly on slick rock. One problem is that the trail is not well marked and you must constantly watch for the rock cairns on the slick rock through an area that appears much the same with no distinguishing features. The trail ends at the rim of a small canyon where there is some chain-link fence along the edge. From this point you can see the ruins to your right and across the canyon. There is no access to any of the ruins. Binoculars are useful.

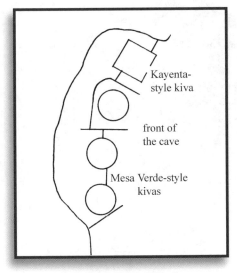

PLAN 12: Butler Wash

The canyon is U-shaped, with the main ruins at the end, to your right, and continuing along the opposite wall. Beginning at the far right is the largest site in a cave just below the rim. It consisted of several living and storage rooms and four kivas. Three are round and Mesa Verdean in origin, but the fourth is square and shows influence from the Kayenta group to the south. To the left and slightly above is a small cave with the remains of a wall along the front and another structure that is visible inside. Next to that is a long, shallow opening with more ruins along the front and a wall farther in that is hard to see. Below these, there is a lot of rubble on the slope, which could have originated from these structures or possibly there were more buildings on the ledge.

If you continue looking to the left, there are more ruins in a small depression that is lower down the canyon wall and was probably for storage. Above and to the left are more remains in another small cave, and just above this a large opening with many rooms in the cave and on the slopes, though it is mostly rubble.

These cliff dwellings date from the A.D. 1200s and are only a few of the hundreds of sites located in this region, which is on the western fringes of the Montezuma Valley and would have had contact with Edge of the Cedars and the many other surrounding sites. This site has been determined to be Mesa Verdean because of the three round kivas, plus the pottery that was found. However, the square kiva and the remains of Kayenta pottery indicates influence from the Kayenta branch, though the Mesa Verdean pottery far outnumbers that of the Kayenta, which could have been obtained from trade. This mix is found throughout the area. The site was abandoned prior to 1300.

This site is not accessible and can only be viewed from the rim of the canyon after walking over ½ mile (0.8 km). You will need binoculars; otherwise the ruins are difficult to see, but the country is beautiful.

Butler Wash Ruins, Square Kiva

Kiva, Mule Canyon. Notice the small door at the bottom left that leads to the room in the background, left.

◎ Mule Canyon Ruins

Ten miles (16 km) farther along UT 95 brings you to an interesting site, Mule Canyon Ruins, which is open all year and has no entrance fee. There are signs on the road marking the turn on the right driving west. The site is next to the parking area, so no hiking is required. Mule Canyon is Mesa Verdean but with strong Kayenta influence, as at Butler Wash. The site was occupied as early as A.D. 750 but the main habitation period was from 1000 to 1150. There are 12 rooms in an L shape facing south, with 2 kivas and a tower. One kiva, the tower, and the room block have been excavated and stabilized and are visible.

What makes this particular tower different is that the kiva was connected to it by an underground tunnel and also to the room block by another tunnel that leads to the southeast room in the pueblo. Although there are other towers in the region, and tunnels connect towers and kivas in Mesa Verde, the two tunnels are unusual and it is not known why they were built in this manner. The kiva is typical Mesa Verde style, but if you look at the ventilation shaft, there is another opening to the left and above that is the entrance to the tunnel that goes to the tower. Now walk around to the other side and you will see another entrance near the floor on the left, which goes to the pueblo (see photograph, above). In the remains of the two-story tower you can see the exit of the tunnel, which was probably the only way to get into it, as there were no doors or windows in the lower floor. Although the use of these towers is not known for certain (see Hovenweep, page 219), this one might have been used as a signal

Tower, Mule Canyon. Entrance to tunnel on left.

tower, as there is another tower about 1 mile (1.6 km) away to which there is a clear line of sight. It has been shown in other parts of the Northern San Juan (see Chimney Rock, page 312) that fires can be easily seen from one tower to another over long distances, though there were probably other uses for them as well.

Mule Canyon is a wonderful small site that has easy access.

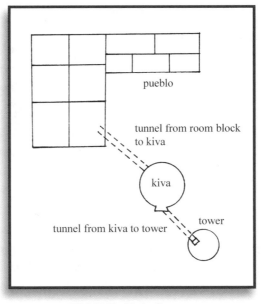

PLAN 13: Mule Canyon

◎ Natural Bridges National Monument

was established in 1908 and covers 12 square miles (31 square km). The elevation is 6,500 feet (1,980m) at the visitors center. The park is open every day and the visitors center hours are 8 AM to 6 PM May to September, 9 to 5 November to March, 8 AM to 5 PM in April and October, closed Thanksgiving Day, Christmas Day, and New Year's Day. For more information, phone 435-692-1234; visit www.nps.gov/nabr; or write to Natural Bridges, HC-60 Box 1, Lake Powell, Utah 84533-0001.

This is a site where you can see the main points of interest in about an hour with little effort, or spend a day or more hiking into the canyon to the bridges and archaeological sites. The turnoff for the monument is about 16 miles (25.7 km) past Mule Canyon Ruins on UT 95 onto UT 275, which goes to the visitors center. The road becomes a one-way loop that is 9 miles (14.4 km) around. The monument is about 44 miles (70.8 km) from Blanding.

There are three natural bridges in the monument—Sipapu, Kachina, and Owachomo—and a large ruin, Horse Collar. The three bridges can be seen from roadside stops and the ruins can be viewed from the rim at the end of a trail, plus there are trails down to each bridge and a loop trail to all three bridges and the ruins. The three bridges are named from the Hopi language: Sipapu is "the emergence from, and entrance to, the lower world"; Kachina are the dancers that represent spirits in religious ceremonies; Owachomo means a "rock mound."

Dimensions of the bridges:

- Kachina spans 203 feet (62 m), is 108 feet (33 m) from the base to the stream, 44 feet (13 m) wide and 93 feet (28 m) thick.
- Sipapu spans 268 feet (82 m), is 167 feet (50 m) from the base to the stream, 31 feet (9 m) wide and 53 feet (16 m) thick.
- Owachomo spans 180 feet (55 m), is 100 feet (30 m) from the base to the stream, 27 feet (8 m) wide and 9 feet (3 m) thick.

The first stop will be the viewpoint for Sipapu Bridge with all pullouts on the right. From this point you can see the bridge, but if you want to hike down to it, the trailhead is farther along at the next stop. The trail down into the canyon to Sipapu Bridge is **very difficult** and requires descending stairs and ladders plus switchbacks, and is over a 1-mile (1.6 km) return walk.

The next pullout leads to the viewpoint of Horse Collar Ruins, which is at the end of a **moderate** trail just over a ½-mile (0.8 km) return walk. The viewpoint is on the rim and does not go down to the ruins but still gives an excellent view of the site. It is best if you have binoculars. The site stretches along near the bottom of the canyon, and if you scan the cliffs, you can spot other small structures in the shallow recesses.

Kachina Bridge is the next stop. A short, **easy** paved trail leads to the viewpoint. If you want to hike down to this bridge, the trail is **very difficult** and about a 1½-miles (2.4 km) return walk. Another option is to descend to Kachina and continue along past the bridge in White Canyon to Horse Collar Ruins and Sipapu Bridge. This is about 3 miles (4.8 km) from the trailhead. Next, hike out of the canyon at Sipapu, cross the road, and follow the trail on the mesa back to the parking lot for Kachina, for a total distance of around 5½ miles (8.8 km) on a **very difficult** but highly rewarding hike.

The last stop is for Owachomo Bridge, the easiest to visit. A short, **easy** trail leads to the viewpoint of the bridge, and a **moderate** trail of less than a ½-mile (0.8 km) return walk goes to the bridge, which is the oldest of the three. There is a change in elevation of less than 200 feet (60 m) on a path that is mostly slick rock. If you descend past the bridge to the bottom of the canyon, there is a trail that goes to Kachina Bridge that is about 3 miles (4.8 km). You can then continue through the canyon on the loop described for Kachina. The total distance to all three bridges plus returning on the mesa is over 8 miles (12.8 km).

CAUTION: Be aware of the danger of flash flooding in the canyon. Talk to the rangers at the visitors center before descending into any of the canyons. You also need a copy of the map of the trails issued by the National Park Service.

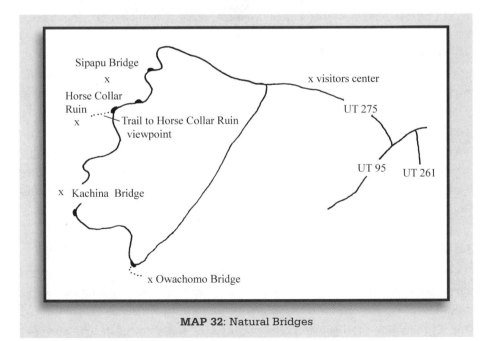

MAP 32: Natural Bridges

Human Occupation

There is evidence, including rock art and stone tools, from the Archaic period that hunter-gatherers lived in the region. Over 200 sites have been discovered from the Ancestral Puebloan period, showing three different occupations, the first from A.D. 200 to 400, and the second from 650 to 725, both of which were on the mesa. During the final occupation, between the mid-1000s and the late 1200s, they were living in the canyons. This last period is when Horse Collar was built. The people were from the Mesa Verdean branch, but as at Butler Wash and Mule Canyon, there is a strong influence from the Kayenta.

Geology

This formation is called Cedar Mesa sandstone and was formed 250 million years ago on the edge of an inland sea. This sandstone is not strongly cemented and thus erodes fairly easily, and you can see many tributaries into the main canyons due to this fact. This also explains the creation of the bridges, as the water flowed in a meander pattern, turning back onto itself in goosenecks that isolated narrow fins of stone and, as

Horse Collar Ruins

water always takes the easiest path, holes developed in the lower side of the stream that eventually cut through. These small holes enlarged over time and, together with erosion from rain and the freeze/thaw cycle, the results are the three bridges. There is no longer a stream flowing under Owachomo, so all erosion now is the same as effects arches, such as those in Arches National Park (see page 173). They are still a bridge as opposed to an arch, as they were originally created by a stream. Eventually all these bridges will collapse under their own weight, but new ones will take their place somewhere in the area.

◎ Monument Valley

From Natural Bridges, return to UT 95 toward Blanding and then turn right on UT 261 after 2 miles (3.2 km). This road has some great scenery, but one stretch is gravel and a series of switchbacks as it winds down the mountain, and some sections are only one lane wide. It may not be passable if there has been a recent rainstorm or it is foggy. Check the road conditions at the visitors center in Natural Bridges.

Mexican Hat rock formation

UT 261 comes out onto US 163. Turn right toward Mexican Hat. Near this small town is a side road that leads a short distance to the "Mexican Hat" rock formation. You can see the "Hat" from the highway on the left and there is a sign for the road that goes to the site. It is worth the short detour to see this strange formation up close. The town of Mexican Hat is where you cross the San Juan River through a dramatic canyon of red rock and then emerge onto a plateau that is the northern edge of Monument Valley.

If you are a fan of western movies, you have seen the scenery of Monument Valley used as the backdrop of numerous films. The mesas, buttes, and spires emerge from a flat, rolling landscape to create one of the most beautiful scenes in the Southwest. Only a small section is in Utah, with the majority in Arizona, and all of the valley is on Navajo land. You can see a great deal of the valley by simply driving along US 163, but there is one place where you can drive among the rock formations: the Monument

Valley Navajo Tribal Park. Because the valley is on Native American land, you are not allowed to travel off the main road without a guide, but in the Tribal Park is a loop road on which you can go on your own to explore deep into the monument. The Monument Valley Navajo Tribal Park visitors center is open from 6 AM to 8 PM from May through September and from 8 to 5 in the winter. Daylight savings time is observed on the reservation. It is closed Thanksgiving afternoon, Christmas Day, and New Year's Day. For more information, phone 435-727-5874, -5870, or -5879; visit www.navajo nationparks.org/htm/monumentvalley.htm; or write to Monument Valley Navajo Tribal Park, P.O. Box 360289, Monument Valley, Utah 84536.

When you first see the monuments in the distance, the road begins to descend a long hill and then flattens out. At first they appear to float on the horizon, dark shapes against a clear blue sky. But as you draw near, the stone figures rise up out of the flat, shapeless landscape, creating the strange forms that inhabit the valley. They loom ever larger as you approach until you become an insignificant speck walking among giants. There is no other place like this. Most of the formations will be on your left as you drive south, and there is a sign at the intersection for the Tribal Park, which is a left turn. A short, paved road leads to the visitors center. There is an entrance fee. The

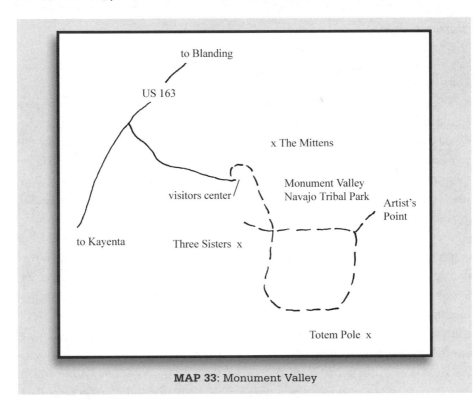

MAP 33: Monument Valley

The Mitten (left)

visitors center includes a restaurant, a gift shop selling Native American works, a museum, and restrooms. There is also a campground.

The road in the park is unpaved but passable with a regular car unless there has been a recent rainstorm. There are some rough spots and short, steep grades, but overall it is not a problem. Inquire at the entrance gate or visitors center. If you do not want to venture in with your vehicle, there are regularly scheduled tours leaving from the visitors center whereby you ride in the back of open four-wheel-drive trucks. The road is only a partial loop, as you drive a few miles before you arrive at a one-way section that circles around one of the many mesas.

If you decide to drive through the park on your own, the entrance to the valley road is to the left of the parking lot. Ask at the entrance gate or visitors center. The road descends down a moderate hill with a few curves and then levels off. Stop in the designated pullouts and be cautious of the soft sand shoulders. You will first see, to the left, the Mittens, and next to them Merrick Butte. As you continue, Mitchell Mesa looms high on your right and Elephant Butte on the left. As you approach a four-way intersection, the three rock spires on the right are called the Three Sisters and a short spur road goes closer to them. Straight ahead, the road becomes one-way in a loop around Raingod Mesa. The road continues between this and Thunderbird Mesa past where you see the Totems, probably the most spectacular spires in the park. Another short spur leads to Artist's Point for some wonderful views. From there, the road returns to the intersection. Turn right to return to the parking lot. The total distance from the visitors center is 17 miles (27.3 km). The map you will get at the entrance gate lists the names of the various formations not only along the road but throughout the park. Monument Valley is an experience not to be missed.

The mesas, buttes, and spires in Monument Valley are formed from De Chelly sandstone, which flakes off in large pieces. The De Chelly sits on a base of the Organ Rock Formation, which is of harder shale that has no permanent waterways cut into it, producing the effect of the valley, being flat except for the monuments. There are none of the canyons that you find just to the north in such places as Natural Bridges or Canyonlands, only some dunes from the windblown sand. And the "valley" is in fact part of the Monument Upwarp, an upward fold of rock much higher than the surrounding landscape where the softer stone has eroded away, leaving the "monuments" on the harder underlying stone.

From the Tribal Park, return to the main highway. Depending on how much time you have, there are several alternative routes back to Blanding or on to Cortez, Colorado, the next stop on the Grand Circle Tour. The shortest way to Blanding is to turn right and follow US 163 to US 191 north (left turn) or turn left for a more scenic, though longer, route. If you go left stay on US 163 to Kayenta and then turn left onto US 160. At Mexican Water you can turn left again onto US 191 north or continue on US 160 to the Four Corners Monument. This is the only place in the United States where four states have a common border. There is a platform with the borders indicated on it where people are photographed (on hands and knees) "standing" in all four states at once. Mostly it is a market whose Native American vendors sell pottery, jewelry, rugs, and many other handcrafted objects.

After the Four Corners, you can take CO 41, on the left, which becomes UT 262 in Utah and goes back to US 191 and Blanding, or stay on US 160 through to Cortez, Colorado. This ends the tour of other sites around Blanding.

day 11

Mesa Verde
National Park
Colorado

- Established 1906
- 81 square miles (211 square km)
- Elevation 6,025 to 8,305 feet
(1,836–2,531 m)

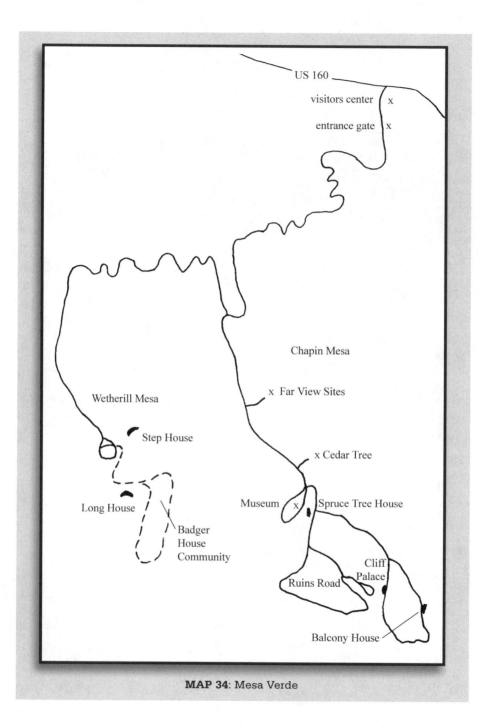

MAP 34: Mesa Verde

16. Mesa Verde National Park

GETTING THERE: From Cortez, follow US 160 east for 10 miles (16 km) to the turn-off for the park on the right. It is well marked. The visitors center is on the left soon after turning off US 160 and the entrance gate a short distance farther.

THINGS YOU NEED TO KNOW: The park is open daily, year round. Many of the sites are closed in the winter and sometimes the roads are not passable because of snow or ice. The visitors center and Chapin Mesa Museum are open all year, closed Thanksgiving Day, Christmas Day, and New Year's Day. Visitors center hours: Late May to September, 7:30–7; September to November, 8–5; November to April, 8:30–4:30; April to late May, 8–5.

In the winter, the only cliff dwelling open is Spruce Tree House, but this site must be visited on a free ranger-guided tour. The rest of the year the site is self-guided. The Mesa Top Loop Road, or Ruins Road, is plowed and open, weather permitting. The road to Cliff Palace is not plowed but can be skied or hiked to the overlook. The site itself is closed. The Far View sites are open, but the entrance road is not plowed so you must park by the gate and walk in, though this is only a short distance. Cliff Palace tours begin in early April and run to November. Balcony House is open from early April to November. Wetherill Mesa, which includes Long House (ranger-guided only), Step House, and Badger House, is generally open from late May to early September. Due to the possibility of heavy snowfall and severe winter conditions, it is best to contact the park about accessibility if you plan on traveling there in the winter.

There is camping at the Morefield Campground, a few miles past the entrance gate. Spaces are on a first-come basis. There is also Far View Lodge, open from mid-April to late October, for which reservations can be made by phoning 800-449-2288 or online at www.visitmesaverde.com. A restaurant–gift shop is located by the lodge; another can be found at Morefield campground; and one that is open all year is near the museum. The others are seasonal.

Three cliff dwellings—Cliff Palace, Balcony House, and Long House—require tickets for the ranger-guided tours. These must be purchased at the visitors center before going to the sites. Tours generally depart on the hour or half-hour, depending on the time of year.

Trailers and towed vehicles are not allowed past the Morefield campground, and large vehicles over 8,000 pounds (3636 kg) and/or 25 feet (7.6 m) in length are prohibited from the Wetherill Mesa Road.

For more information, phone 970-529-4465; visit www.nps.gov/meve; or write to Mesa Verde National Park, P.O. Box 8, Mesa Verde National Park, CO 81330-0008.

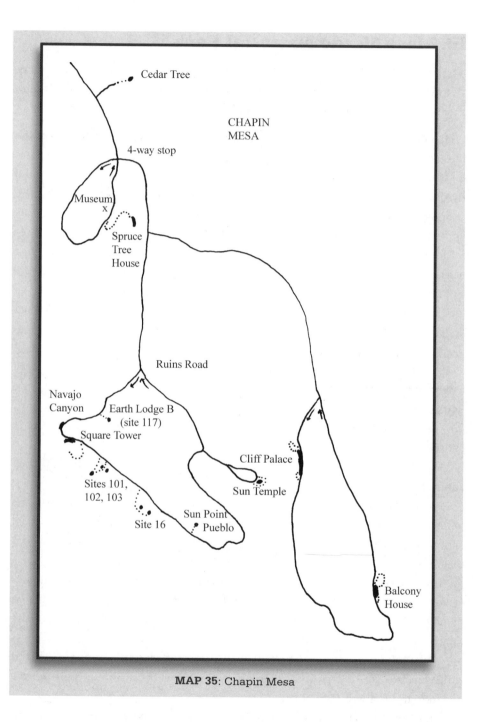

Cedar Tree

CHAPIN
MESA

4-way stop

Museum
x

Spruce
Tree
House

Ruins Road

Navajo
Canyon

Earth Lodge B
(site 117)

Square Tower

Cliff Palace

Sites 101,
102, 103

Sun Temple

Site 16

Sun Point
Pueblo

Balcony
House

MAP 35: Chapin Mesa

Mesa Verde, whose name is Spanish for "green table," is one of the most important archaeological areas in the Southwest. Over 4,000 sites from pithouse to pueblo to cliff dwellings are visible within park boundaries, though only a few are open to visitors. The earliest evidence dates to BM III, around A.D. 550, and is found in pithouses within caves. Soon after, pithouse villages were built on the mesas, followed by pueblos, and finally the cliff dwellings, which date to the 1200s.

TOURING THE PARK

The Grand Circle Tour includes a full day at Mesa Verde and visits two cliff dwellings—Cliff Palace and Spruce Tree House; the Ruins Road, where you will follow the evolution of architecture from pithouses to pueblos and kivas; the Far View Community, a series of five sites plus a large reservoir; and the Chapin Mesa Museum. The sequence is: Cliff Palace, Ruins Road and the museum in the morning, followed by Spruce Tree House and the Far View complex after lunch. It is a long but rewarding day.

Cliff Palace

Your first stop should be the visitors center to purchase tickets to Cliff Palace (and also Balcony and Long House, if you plan to visit these). Allow 45 to 60 minutes from the visitors center to Cliff Palace. After you pass through the entrance gate, the road begins to climb onto the northern end of the mesa by a steep and winding road that can be congested with traffic so you do not want to be in a hurry. There are several

Speaker Chief Complex, Cliff Palace

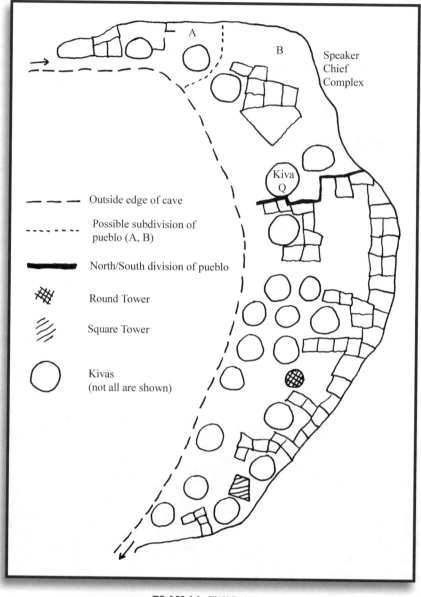

Outside edge of cave

Possible subdivision of
pueblo (A, B)

North/South division of pueblo

Round Tower

Square Tower

Kivas
(not all are shown)

A

B

Speaker
Chief
Complex

Kiva
Q

PLAN 14: Cliff Palace

pullouts along the way to admire the views out over the valley. For the tour I try to arrive early enough to go on the 9 AM tour of Cliff Palace for which tickets must be purchased before 8 AM. The center opens at 7:30 AM in the summer and you can expect a line, especially in the summer. **NOTE:** Cliff Palace will be in the shade during the morning hours; the sun hits it by midafternoon.

With tickets in hand, return to the parking lot and head for Cliff Palace. Once you reach the Far View Lodge on the top of the mesa, continue straight for about 6 miles (9.6 km) until you come to the four-way stop, where you will turn left. Turn left again in less than ½ mile (0.8 km) onto the Cliff Palace Loop Road that soon becomes one-way in a counterclockwise direction (simply bear right) and watch for the parking areas that line both sides of the road. There are restroom facilities (but none at the site) and picnic tables. The path to the overlook, where the tours begin, is on the right and down a few steps. This section is **easy** and you can get a good view of the ruins from the overlook even if you are not able to proceed to the site itself.

The trail to Cliff Palace is **very difficult** and consists of several steep stairways for the descent, a paved path along the front of the ruins with some slight elevation changes, and a very steep climb back up to the mesa on the original path that includes using toeholds notched into the cliff face, squeezing through a narrow crevice, and climbing up some ladders. It is not recommended if anyone has heart or breathing problems, among other conditions, and there are signs at the overlook that warn visitors of the dangers. **NOTE:** Even with the warnings there are still some people who go down that should not, you may encounter a long wait on the ascent.

Cliff Palace is one of the largest cliff dwellings in the Southwest and consists of 150 rooms; 75 open spaces such as courtyards, plazas, and work areas; and 21 kivas. Twenty-five of the rooms had hearths and are considered living rooms. The population is estimated at 100 to 125 full-time residents. It was occupied only during the A.D. 1200s, with most of the construction completed between 1260 and 1280. There are some stone slab structures that date to BM III and P I but they most likely were storage bins.

The stairs are on the right of the overlook. There is a locked gate that the ranger opens and then relocks after the last person has gone through, so if you are late, you will miss the tour. Once you reach the bottom of the stairs the trail winds around the cliff, entering the site from the north end. Where the cave begins to open up to your left were several rooms, including two kivas, one on each side of the standing wall, and an open area with four grinding stones to the far left of the left-hand kiva. This section over to the rock outcrop, including a third kiva to the far right in the front, was probably one unit occupied by an extended family (it is labeled section A on Plan 14).

Past this you see the remains of a three-story structure abutting the cave ceiling (section B on Plan 14; photo on page 239), which is referred to as the "Speaker Chief Complex" and was one of the predominant areas of the pueblo. Two of the room blocks were three stories high and appear even higher due to the fact that they are built on an outcrop of rock well above the trail. There were several room blocks and courtyards and also a round room in the back that was the only access to the rooms on the upper ledge (see next paragraph). There is a kiva to the right of the main structures beside the rock (known officially as Kiva Q) that was painted inside with two different colors exactly half and half, divided north–south. This is believed to represent the division of the pueblo between the northern and southern parts, a common feature of pueblos ancient and modern. The "northern" people were in charge of the winter festivals and religious ceremonies, whereas the southern people looked after the summer events. This fact was reflected in the architecture (see Chaco Canyon, page 333) by a dividing line in the pueblo, and there is one here but it is difficult to find (see Plan 14). It begins on the southern edge of Kiva Q and goes toward the back of the cave, then south around a room, east again past a second kiva and room, and then zigzags north and east to the back wall of the cave. So when you stand in front of this kiva, everything to the left is in the northern section; and to the right, in the southern.

Also from this point you can look up and see the walls on the ledge above the main ruins. The ranger may point out this feature, which does not look like much but in fact consisted of several large rooms used for storage, most likely corn. The door on the left is the only way to enter these rooms and you could only get to this door from room 68, the round structure in the Speaker Chief Complex, so whoever lived in this section controlled access to a large food store. The big gap in the center once had a wall but it collapsed when part of the ledge fell into the village below during the time Cliff Palace was occupied. This must have been a terrifying event, possibly injuring and/or killing some people. The drywall section enclosed an open area that led to two large storage rooms on the southern end.

Next you come to the first of three kivas in a row, all at the same level, near the front of the cave. Behind them, to the left of the rock outcrop, are two large retaining walls that support two more kivas in back. Three more kivas rise in steps along the front; all would have been roofed to provide open spaces along the lip of the cave. From this area you can see the round tower toward the back of the cave. This is an example of the great skill of the masons; the tower tapers in toward the top and all of the stones are rounded to the circumference of the structure. The tower was two stories.

To the right of the tower are two more individual sections, containing room blocks and kivas, which extend to the four-story building that looks like a square tower but was a room block. This might have been built to mirror the four-story Speaker Chief Complex at the opposite end of the cave. The interior of this structure was painted, as were many of the rooms and kivas, and the third-floor paintings are well preserved. The bottom half is red with a mountain range at the top; the upper section is white with a red rectangle filled with vertical zigzag lines and rows of dots in the center; these may represent lightning and raindrops, respectively. There is an opening on the

Square "tower," south end, Cliff Palace

front that you are allowed to look through to see the painting. From this point you have a good view of the village looking back toward the north.

Past this point is the exit that travels up through a narrow crevice in the cliff face, using ladders. A short trail leads back to the parking area.

From the parking area, continue around the one-way loop toward Balcony House (see page 267 if you are stopping there). Three pullouts between Cliff Palace and Balcony House offer spectacular views over the canyons as well as several cliff dwellings dotting the opposite canyon walls. The first is less than ¼ mile (0.4 km) from the parking area on your right and is the Cliff Canyon Overlook. You can see a series of dwellings on the other side of the canyon that include (from left to right) the House of Many Windows in a long, narrow opening, Site 634 in an alcove below a sweeping curved overhang of sandstone, Sun Point Dwelling, consisting of only three rooms along a very narrow ledge, the opening into Fewkes Canyon and, on the mesa top to the right of Fewkes Canyon, the Sun Temple. A short distance from here is the second stop that gives a better view of the House of Many Windows directly across the canyon. About a mile (1.6 km) farther on is another stop on the right with a view over Soda Canyon and the cliff dwelling called Hemenway House. This is just before the parking area for the Balcony House tour, which is usually congested with cars and pedestrians. Continue past unless you are visiting Balcony at this time.

When you come to the Stop sign at the end of the road, turn left to the Mesa Top Loop, which also becomes one-way. On this loop you can see the changes in architecture from the earliest pithouse to the latest cliff dwelling, all within about 6 miles (9.6 km).

Ruins Road

The first stop is on the left (remember, this is one-way) a little over ½ mile (0.8 km) from where the road divides. A short, **easy** trail leads around the covered structure known as Earth Lodge B, or Site 117, and dates to A.D. 595. This BM III pithouse is one of eight in total from this village but the only one excavated and open. It consists of two rooms: the main living area, which is 20 feet (6 m) in diameter, and the smaller antechamber. Entrance was through the antechamber that was also for ventilation and storage. The main room had a stone slab deflector in the doorway, separating the two rooms, and another before the hearth, the large, slab-lined hole in the floor. The "wing" walls on each side of the entrance divide the food preparation area from the rest of the room. The four smaller holes near the edge were where the support posts stood, hold-

Earth Lodge B (stop 1). The antechamber is top left.

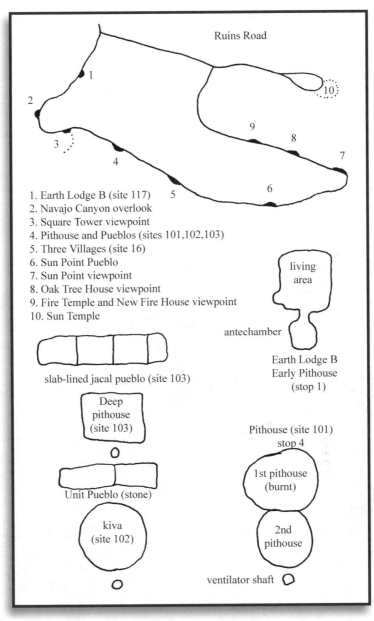

Ruins Road

1. Earth Lodge B (site 117)
2. Navajo Canyon overlook
3. Square Tower viewpoint
4. Pithouse and Pueblos (sites 101,102,103)
5. Three Villages (site 16)
6. Sun Point Pueblo
7. Sun Point viewpoint
8. Oak Tree House viewpoint
9. Fire Temple and New Fire House viewpoint
10. Sun Temple

living area

antechamber

Earth Lodge B
Early Pithouse
(stop 1)

slab-lined jacal pueblo (site 103)

Deep
pithouse
(site 103)

Pithouse (site 101)
stop 4

1st pithouse
(burnt)

Unit Pueblo (stone)

kiva
(site 102)

2nd
pithouse

ventilator shaft

PLAN 15: Ruins Road

ing a square roof frame on which the side walls were built at a steep angle. Both the roof and walls were constructed with large framing beams crossed with smaller sticks interwoven into branches and finally plastered with adobe. There were also storage cists in the walls and floor, as well as a *sipapu*. The pithouse was only 12 inches (30 cm) below the surface and is typical of the type of house being built at this time all over the Colorado Plateau. There are also several hearths around the exterior of the houses, as the people lived mostly outside, especially during the warmer months.

The next pullout, on the right, offers a beautiful view of Navajo Canyon and the typical landscape of Mesa Verde, a large south-sloping mesa dissected by many canyons, such as this one.

A short distance from this stop is the trail to the Square Tower House Overlook on the right. The trail is **easy** with some change in elevation but nothing steep. This overlook affords a wonderful view of Square Tower, a cliff dwelling tucked into a shallow alcove in a corner of the cliff face. It is not a tower but part of a larger room block that

Square Tower (stop 3)

Pithouse, site 101 (stop 4)

has collapsed. There were originally around 80 rooms; about 60 remain. This structure dates from the early A.D. 1200s, to between 1280 and 1300, the last phase of construction before abandonment.

The next stop illustrates the transition from living in pithouses to aboveground structures. The sites are on the right and there is a short, **easy** trail. Two protective shelters cover three different ruins in total. First follow the loop trail to the farthest structure from the road, as this is the oldest structure. Site 101 looks like a single pithouse with an antechamber but there are two structures: the larger was built just before A.D. 700 and destroyed by a fire, and then, just after 700, the second, smaller structure was constructed in the antechamber of the original. Both were dug into the ground about 4 feet (1.2 m), much deeper than earlier pithouses, and the second added a ventilator shaft, which was a new design feature. There was no antechamber in the second pithouse and the entrance would have been through the roof over the hearth in the same way as a kiva, although kivas did not exist at this time. Other features of these pithouses remain the same as Earth Lodge B. Continue on the trail to the right toward the large pavilion.

Under the roofed structure next to the road are some examples of the earliest aboveground structures, Sites 103 and 102. Site 103, on the left (north) when you enter from the back (opposite the road), consists of a series of rooms slightly below

Slab lined jacaj pueblo, site 103 (stop 4)

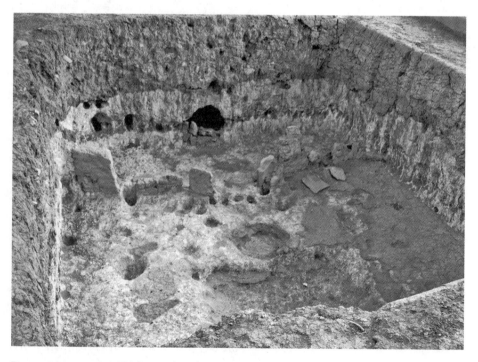

Deep pithouse, site 103 (stop 4)

Kiva (bottom) and stone room block (top) site 102 (stop 4)

ground level, with an upright lining of slabs on which were built jacal walls. A few rooms are exposed, with many more adjacent but unexcavated. This structure dates to the A.D. 830s. To your immediate right is a deep pithouse that was contemporary with these aboveground rooms, illustrating the fact that the Ancestral Puebloans lived in both pithouses and surface structures within the same village. Two of these deep pithouses were excavated, but one has been backfilled to protect it while this one has been left open for viewing. This pithouse is square and 6 to 7 feet (1.8–2 m) deep, so it probably had a flat roof. Although it looks like a kiva, there are some differences. We still have the low wall room divider to create separate food preparation and living areas, and there is no banquette or pillars. Some elements of the kiva are present, including the ventilator shaft, stone deflector, and central hearth. It would be an easy transition from deep pithouse to kiva.

Site 102 is just south of the deep pithouse and appears to be part of it but is a completely separate pueblo and dates to A.D. 950. There are two rooms of what was the first attempt at stone construction and, to the south, a kiva. Notice the banquette around the inside of the kiva and the stone pillars for the roof supports, as well as the lack of any dividing walls, which are elements that differentiate this from the deep pithouse on the other side of the stone room block. By looking at both you can easily see the differences between a pithouse and kiva. This site is an example of the unit pueblo, with the room block on the northern side and a plaza, kiva, and trash

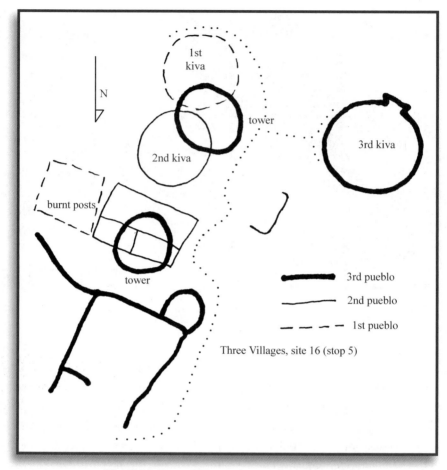

PLAN 16: Three Villages (Site 16), Ruins Road

mound to the south, which would be the basic architectural layout for all later pueblos, whether large or small.

So at this one site you can see 250 years in the evolution of Ancestral Puebloan architecture from the shallow pithouse of A.D. 700 to the unit pueblo of 950. Nowhere else in the Southwest can you find this architectural timeline in one place.

The next stop, again on the right, is Site 16 and consists of three different pueblos built one on top of the other in a sequence from A.D. 900 to 1075. There is a short, **easy** trail to the sites. The first thing you will see is a wide foundation wall with trees growing in it, and then a round structure. Ignore these for now, and look for the second tower next to the shelter. Just past this to the left are some burned pole stubs from the first pueblo that was constructed of jacal (refer to Plan 16). This structure ran parallel along the front of the modern shelter. You are standing at the west end. Inside the shelter on the left at the back is a kiva that was part of this earliest pueblo and is a standard kiva, except for the fact the when it was excavated everything was backward: the dirt on the surface was from a deeper level in the ground, whereas what was removed from the bottom of the kiva came from the surface. What had happened was that when the people built a second village on the same spot sometime after the first had burned down, they dug a new kiva, the one now between this kiva and the shelter wall, and took the dirt from this second one and simply filled in the first with it, thus the reverse order when excavated. So even though they built another village in the same place as the original, they did not reuse the kiva but constructed a new one next to it.

This second kiva and the single-course walls that are outside and next to (and under) the tower were the pueblo from the second set of buildings that sat on the same location. This structure was smaller and dates from around A.D. 1000.

The last structures built on this site are the wide multicoursed stone walls that include the tower next to the shelter (outside), a second tower inside the shelter on the left that was built on the two original kivas, a large kiva on the right inside the shelter, and the unusual large, rectangular building outside, which has another tower on the

Three Villages, Site 16. 1st village, burnt posts top right; 2nd village, single course stone wall, center; 3rd village, double course stone walls

Kiva, 3rd village

southwest corner. It is thought that this last structure was not a building but an open platform used for ceremonies and that what had been a village for over a century was converted in the late A.D. 1000s to a religious site. Altogether, this consisted of the plaza/platform, two towers, and a new larger kiva. The kiva is stone lined with eight pilasters (the "standard" in this region is six), and two rectangular cists on either side of the hearth, which were either for storage or foot drums. We do not know why they built on the site of the previous pueblos, but it may have been a way to show reverence for their ancestors.

At this site you see the change from the use of posts and adobe for the first village to the single-course masonry on the second to the wide multicoursed walls of the third structures, a change that took place over almost two centuries.

The next stop on Ruins Road is the Sun Point Pueblo, on the left near the road. This is the final example of pueblo construction on the mesa before the people began moving into the cliffs. There were 20 rooms, a tower, and kiva, and it was built in the late 1100s or early 1200s but only occupied for about 10 years. The kiva has a banquette, ventilator shaft, hearth, and *sipapu*. There is another hole to the right and above the opening of the ventilator shaft, which is a tunnel leading into the tower, a feature you will also see at Cedar Tree and Far View (see pages 261 and 270). Although the construction and use of the towers is not well understood (see Hovenweep, page 219), some of them do seem to be extensions of the kiva and were most likely used for religious purposes, which of course does not rule out other uses, as kivas at times served as weaving rooms and living quarters.

Beyond Sunpoint Pueblo, the road turns back sharply to the left and there are three pullouts to see more cliff dwellings. The first stop is Sun Point on Cliff Canyon, across from the Cliff Canyon Overlook. Scan the cliff face opposite for the remains of structures in the many caves and openings, and to the far left you can see Cliff Palace. The remains below the Sun Temple, where the two canyons meet, is Mummy House, perched mainly on a ledge with one structure in the small cave directly above. The next stop, just a short way farther, has a good view of Oak Tree House, the second largest pueblo in this area after Cliff Palace. This site contains around 54 rooms and 6 kivas built on a steeply sloping ledge that required the construction of retaining walls to level the floor and increase the usable space. There are also several storage rooms on the upper ledge, in the same manner as at Cliff Palace.

The last pullout has views of Fire Temple, on the left, and New Fire House. New

Oak Tree House (stop 8)

New Fire House (detail)

Fire House has around 20 rooms and 3 kivas on two separate ledges. To the left of the large structure on the upper ledge you can see some toeholds carved into the cliff face where the inhabitants traveled between the two levels (photograph, left). A ladder connected these to the buildings below.

Fire Temple was a great kiva. The large, open, rectangular room has a central firepit and two stone-walled cists in the floor for storage or use as foot drums. The walls were plastered and painted red and white, decorated with figures of rain clouds, cactus, humans, and animals. There are attached rooms on each end but no evidence of anyone's living there. The ceremonies held in this kiva would have served the entire community from the surrounding canyons and mesa.

From the Fire Temple pullout, continue to the intersection and turn right toward Sun Temple. The road has two-way traffic for a short distance after turning and then divides into one-way again as it loops around the edge of the mesa to the parking area for the Sun Temple. This structure is D-shaped with a double wall and the space between these walls divided into several rooms that are connected by doors (see Plan 17). The walls are 4 feet (1.2 m) thick in some sections and surround two kivas on the east end. The long, straight wall is the south side. On the west end are two more kivas and a few other rooms. The walls are of the highest quality with pecked masonry and extreme precision in the joints. Unfortunately, you cannot enter the building nor is there anyplace to get a bird's eye view, so all you see is the outside of the structure. At one time you could walk along the thick walls that were capped with concrete but this is no longer possible, so visiting the site is disappointing. In fact, the best part about stopping here is the view across the canyon of Cliff Palace from the exact spot Richard Wetherill stood when he first saw the ruins (see page 285). At the southwest corner of the temple is what is thought to be a solar marker that would have been

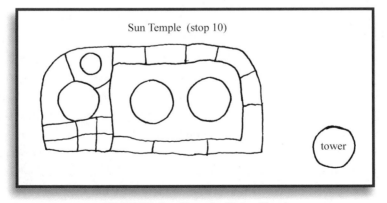

PLAN 17: Sun Temple, Ruins Road

used in the same way as we have seen with some petroglyphs where shafts of light shine across them at specific times of the year. There are also the remains of a tower to the east of the temple.

This structure bears some similarities to other structures visited on the Grand Circle Tour, such as Horseshoe House in Hovenweep (see page 210), also D-shaped with a double wall and enclosed kivas, though part of one side is open. There is no evidence of any roof, so it must have been open to the sky but no artifacts were found in the structure and some archaeologists think the building was never finished, which could also explain the lack of a roof. But there seems to be no doubt that it was constructed for religious purposes, even if it was never used.

This is the last site to visit on Ruins Road, so follow the road back past the turnoff for Cliff Palace to the four corners and go straight toward the museum. If you have brought along lunch, look for the large picnic area set among the trees along some narrow dirt roads on the right just past the four corners. There is also a small restaurant past the museum on the left. In this section are the museum and trailhead for Spruce Tree House.

The museum is on the right across from the parking lot. As with other national parks, there is an acute shortage of parking space and it can be nearly impossible to find anything near the museum, so you might have to circle a few times. There is some space near the picnic area and it is not too far to walk.

Chapin Mesa Museum

The museum has a wonderful collection of artifacts from both Mesa Verde and surrounding regions. A series of dioramas at the entrance examine the history of habitation in Mesa Verde and give a good sense of the changes that have occurred and what the communities looked like when they were in use. The Folsom (though there is no evidence they ever occupied Mesa Verde), Basketmaker, and Pueblo time periods are each represented and the dioramas are nicely done and informative.

The main sections of the museum hold examples of nearly every type of object ever discovered, including wooden crutches for a child, an atlatl, sandals, cradle boards, dog hair sashes, pottery from the earliest period to Mesa Verde Black on White, the last type produced, pieces of cotton blankets, arrows and points, stone and bone tools, digging sticks, corn, beans, and gourds, and numerous other objects. The collection is well laid out with interpretive signs and good lighting throughout. There are also examples of artifacts and artworks from modern Native American artisans, some of which illustrate the continuation of traditions as well as the influence the ancestors have on the present inhabitants. A bookstore and gift shop are attached to the museum.

Spruce Tree House

This is one of the best-preserved cliff dwellings in the park and the only one open all year. You may visit the site on your own in the summer, but during the winter months it is only accessible on the free ranger tours. The trail to the ruin is **difficult** due to the steepness of the paved path; going down is not too bad but remember you must come back up the same way. The trail descends about 100 feet (30 m) and is a ½-mile (0.8 km) return walk. There are around 114 rooms and 8 kivas. It is one of 14 sites in this canyon that were occupied between A.D. 1200 and 1276.

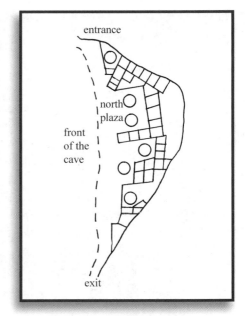

PLAN 18: Spruce Tree House

As you descend below the rim, notice how thick the vegetation is and the variety of trees and plants. Do not wander off the trail as you might damage the natural flora, and there is poison ivy. One of the best springs in Mesa Verde is at the head of this canyon and is the reason for the lush growth.

The site is on the other side of the canyon and the trail winds around and past the spring and one of the original ways into this pueblo, a series of hand- and toeholds carved into the canyon wall on the left between sign posts 1 and 2. The other entrance is at the south end of the site. You approach the ruin from the north and the first structures are three-story room blocks that reach up to the cave ceiling. Notice the outside corners, a good example of the excellent quality masonry work, as well as the way they followed the contours of the natural outcrops of stone too large to remove.

Next to this is the northern courtyard that comprises two kivas behind a low wall over which refuse was discarded, now under where you are standing. Both kivas have their roofs reconstructed because they had originally collapsed, as is the case with most kiva roofs. Their reconstruction is based on one of the very few that remained intact and was discovered in Square Tower ruins. Now that they have been restored to their original state, you can see what a large plaza is formed over the kivas with only their small entrances, where the ladders protrude, and ventilation shafts disrupting the floor space. The surrounding room blocks were two and three stories and had balconies extending from the roof/ceiling beams, some of them can be seen in the

Spruce Tree, north court

back to the right. The third-floor rooms could only be entered from the balcony. This area is the second of what were probably three separate sections in the northern part of the pueblo.

Continuing along the path there is a large room block adjacent to the plaza. Look for sign post 4, where you can see some of the original plaster on the back interior wall. There is sort of an X pattern design on this wall but it is hard to see. Look for the two holes just below the horizontal beam; the design is to the left and a bit below the right hole. Many of the rooms were covered with different-colored plasters inside and out, and more has been preserved at Spruce Tree than at any other site in Mesa Verde. There is an open kiva to the right of the room and you can see, in the back left corner, part of a balcony that originally ran all the way across the back wall. There are three room blocks behind this kiva, as well as a large refuse area in the back of the cave.

Next is a reconstructed kiva that may be entered. Be cautious when entering or exiting the kiva, as this ladder is the only way in and you do not want to step on anyone's fingers or have yours crunched. These ladders can be slippery, as they have been worn smooth, so hang on tight. Remember as you enter that this is a sacred place.

Beyond this is another kiva that is the division between north and south. The line is to the left of the kiva and follows the "main street" to the back wall of the cave. The rooms near the front open toward the north; the first row in the back face south. There are two kivas and two round structures in the southern part, and several room blocks that make up about one-third of the entire pueblo. At the south end is a wall that was topped with dry-laid stones, which was intentional but we do not know why. There is a similar section in Cliff Palace (see page 242). This concludes the tour of Spruce Tree House. Return to the rim on the same trail.

From the parking area, turn left—the road is one-way—and go straight at the four-way stop heading back toward the visitors center. About 5 miles (8 km) from the stop is a road on the right that goes to the Far View Community. There is a sign if you are driving the other way but for some reason there is not one on this side, so watch carefully for the road. The short road leads to some parking, but mostly you just pull off the edge of the road wherever you can. There are six sites at Far View, all within easy walking distance.

Far View Community

Although most people think of the cliff dwellings when they visit Mesa Verde, and they are wonderful to see, an often overlooked aspect of the park are the mesa pueblos in the Far View section. There are six sites within a short walking distance of one another along level gravel trails that are all **easy**.

Pipe Shrine, north (older) section. Notice the single course walls.

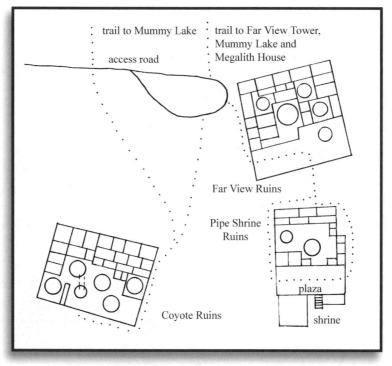

PLAN 19: Far View 1, south section

Far View occupied the northern section of Chapin Mesa, which included around 50 villages inhabited from ca. A.D. 900 to the abandonment of the region about 1275. By A.D. 1100 there were 400 to 500 occupants. So far, 18 sites have been found totaling around 375 rooms, 35 kivas, and some towers. The first pueblo is Far View House, which you will see at the end of the access road. This pueblo dates from A.D. 1100 to 1275 and had 40 rooms on the ground floor plus some second-, and maybe third-, story sections. There are four kivas built within the room block: three that are small kin kivas, a large one with eight pilasters and stone cists in the floor, and another on the southern side outside the pueblo in the courtyard. The large southern plaza has terracing along the front to level the ground. There are a few places in the front where you can enter the pueblo, but access is limited and the walls are still very high, so you cannot see the interior well. You are able to walk around the pueblo and admire the high quality of the masonry work, but then move on to the next site.

Pipe Shrine House is a short distance south of Far View House and probably had a connection to it as they are so close. There were 22 ground-floor rooms plus a second story and one kiva and a tower. The northern section of the pueblo is built with single -course walls and dates to the A.D. 1000s, while the southern rooms are of double-course stone construction, indicating the 1100s for this remodeling, which included a large kiva and tower enclosed by additional rooms. There is also a terrace to the south with steps leading down to a shrine where several pipes were discovered by Jesse Fewkes, thus the name. Pipes were, and continue to be, important in Native American ceremonies for the smoking of sacred tobacco.

From Pipe Spring, return to the parking area and you will see a trail to your left that leads into the woods. Follow this to Coyote Village, also known as Site 820. This is

the most interesting of the three pueblos in this area, not only for what is there but also for the fact that the pueblo is accessible, giving people an opportunity to walk around the plaza and through some of the rooms and, as the walls are low, you can see the layout of the village. There were 30 ground-floor rooms, a second and a third story with an unknown number of rooms, 5 kivas, and a tower. The site was excavated in 1968 to 1969 and dates from A.D. 800 to 1100. The walls are of both single- and double-coursed masonry and the tower was built over an earlier pithouse.

Four of the kivas are in an enclosed plaza surrounded by rooms, with another incorporated into a room block. Next to the southwest kiva is an attached room with six stone slab–lined grain-grinding bins. The tower, adjacent

Coyote Ruins, grinding bins

to the milling room, is connected to the central kiva by a tunnel. In the southeastern kiva, between the pilasters, are wooden poles that were probably used as shelves or for hanging things. They are over the banquette, or bench, that goes around the interior of kivas, illustrating the fact that these benches were not made for sitting; people would sit on the floor. All in all, a very interesting ruin to explore.

Instead of returning to the parking lot, turn left by the northeast corner of Coyote Pueblo and follow the path through the woods and across the access road, watching for traffic. Continue along near the main road until you come to an open area. This is Mummy Lake, which is not a lake but a reservoir. It is 90 feet (27.4 m) in diameter by 12 feet (3.6 m) deep and holds approximately half a million gallons (almost 2 million

Coyote Ruins, east kiva with intact wooden poles

liters) of water. It was first constructed around A.D. 900 and enlarged twice, and used up to 1275. The water would enter in the southwest corner through a long, sweeping, stone-lined curve where the silt would settle to be periodically dredged out. The entire reservoir has a stone wall around the outside. A set of steps, to the right of where the entrance is, lead down to the bottom, allowing easy access to collect the water. It is believed that this water was only for personal use and not irrigation, as there is no outlet. However, at times, especially during droughts, it was not uncommon for the people to water plants individually, carrying the water to the fields. It seems that the amount of water held in this reservoir, though it is not possible to know whether it was ever full, would have been sufficient for both the inhabitants and crops.

A long canal that ran along where the main road is now had a series of smaller channels feeding it to supply the reservoir. Unfortunately, most of the main ditch was destroyed when the road was built, as the canal was only discovered afterward. Later surveys have found another canal, built in the late 1100s or early 1200s, which went past Mummy Lake to the east and south to supply water to Cliff and Fewkes Canyon, where many of the inhabitants were building and moving into the cliff dwellings. The water would have come from melting snows and summer rains and drained most of the mesa to the north.

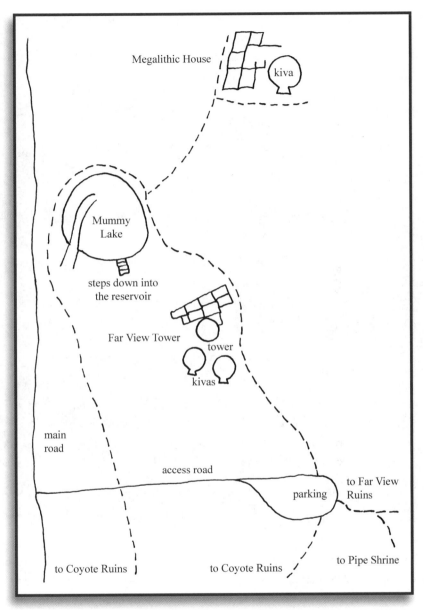

PLAN 20: Far View 2, north section

You can walk around the reservoir and join another trail on the east side. Turn left to go to Megalithic House, a 5-minute walk. This site is a typical unit pueblo with nine rooms and a kiva that was built in the A.D. 1200s. The unusual aspect of this site is the large stones used for the base of some of the walls. Using upright stone slabs had been common going back to pithouse construction, but using boulders of this size was rare. When Fewkes excavated the site in 1922, he referred to the wall as "Cyclopean," a term used to describe the massive stones used in the construction of Mycenaean Greek fortresses around 1400 B.C. and believed to have been built by the one-eyed giant Cyclops. These large stones seem strange and out of place in Ancestral Puebloan

Megalithic House

architecture and raise questions as to why they were used, which always makes a site more interesting. Notice the high quality of the masonry in the kiva.

Follow the trail back but go past Mummy Lake, staying to the left and not the original way you came, as there is one more site to see on the path to the parking area. A short distance past the reservoir is the Far View Tower site, a ceremonial complex. There are two kivas and a tower, plus some rooms. The room block, where there were 16 rooms and 1 kiva, is constructed of single-coursed masonry and dates to the A.D. 1000s. The tower is of double masonry and was built on top of the older village in the

Far View Tower, the tower sits on the original rooms built of single course stones, foreground

1100s, as was one of the kivas while the other was remodeled. This earlier pueblo was converted into a ceremonial site just as we saw at the third stop on Ruins Road Loop (the Mesa Top Sites, Site 16, page 250). This tower is one of around 60 found throughout Mesa Verde.

Follow the trail back to the parking area. From the access road, turn right to exit the park. This concludes the one-day tour of Mesa Verde. The approximate timeline is: from Cortez to the visitors center, 20 minutes; to Cliff Palace, 40 to 60 minutes; 1 hour to tour Cliff Palace; 1 to 1½ hours for the Ruins Road section; 45 to 60 minutes for the museum; 1 hour to see Spruce Tree House; 1 to 1½ hours for the Far View Community; 60 minutes to return to Cortez.

ADDITIONAL SITES WITHIN MESA VERDE

If you have more than one day at Mesa Verde or wish to see other sites than those in the Grand Circle Tour, there are several options, including, (on Chapin Mesa), Balcony House cliff dwelling and Cedar Tree Tower; and on Wetherill Mesa there are two cliff dwellings—Step House and Long House—and the mesa community of Badger House, in total another full day.

Balcony House

This is the most adventurous and difficult cliff dwelling to visit but also the most spectacular and interesting, even though it is small. The site is open from late May to mid-October, depending on the weather, and can only be visited on a ranger-guided tour. The tours are scheduled for every half-hour in the summer and on the hour in spring and fall, and you must purchase tickets ahead of time at the visitors center. After walking down a short trail you must climb a 32-foot (9.7 m) wooden ladder to gain access to the ruin; and to depart, you are required to crawl through a 12-foot-long (3.6-meter-long) tunnel that is 1½ feet (0.4 m) wide by 3 feet (0,9 m) high, before you climb up steep stone steps and two more ladders to return to the parking area. There is no other exit. (Sometimes a wooden box the size and shape of the tunnel is placed near the entrance door to the visitors center, so you can crawl through before buying your ticket to Balcony. If you cannot get through this box, do not go to Balcony.) The trail is **very difficult**, and if you have a fear of heights, ladders, and/or enclosed spaces, or health problems, do not go on this tour.

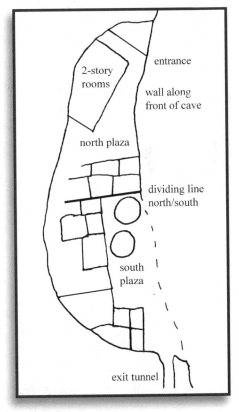

PLAN 21: Balcony House

Balcony is the most defensible of all the cliff dwellings and seems to have been one of the last occupied. Among 12 sites located on the west side of Soda Canyon, there are 80 rooms and 6 kivas in total. Balcony consists of 45 rooms and 2 kivas. At the bottom of the trail you arrive at the long ladder below the ruin, which is up and to your left. To the left of the ladder were some turkey pens and a spring in the cliff face. This was the original path into the site that followed the talus slope past the south end of Balcony and then up the cliff, using toe-holds carved into the stone. The modern trail to this point largely follows the original way to the top of the mesa.

Balcony House, entrance

North plaza, protecting wall (right)

Once up the ladder, you enter the north plaza of the pueblo. There is a room block with four rooms and a balcony between the two stories, which is a continuation of the floor. The rectangular openings are doors, not windows; the only access to the second story was from the balcony in front that was reached by a ladder. An unusual feature of this plaza is the wall along the front of the cave, built to offer protection against falling over the edge. What is unusual about it is that this is the only such wall found on any of the many cliff dwellings in Mesa Verde. Given the precarious positions of all these pueblos, it is perhaps surprising that more were not built. Imagine small children running around these plazas with no protection at all from slipping over the edge; it makes one wonder why the people did not construct more of these retaining walls, as they certainly had the ability to do so. There is some reconstruction but this section was remarkably well preserved.

On the south end of the plaza is a dividing wall separating the pueblo into north–south. There is a small window through which the two sides could communicate, but the only way from one side to the other was by a doorway at the very back of the cave near the location of another spring. The tour goes through this area and you can see the black soot on the ceiling from the fires, with the only exit for the smoke through the small square holes in the front walls. You will see examples of this farther on.

Southern plaza, kiva 1, foreground; kiva 2, lower right

From the back of the cave you emerge into the south end, where the two kivas are located. Notice that there is no wall along the front in this section. The kivas, now open, would have been roofed, creating another plaza in this end. The long beam projecting from the room block behind the kivas was originally part of the roof of a room that separated the two kivas. Also in this wall is a T-shaped doorway with two small square holes just above and on each side, which are not windows but smoke holes. The kivas are typical Mesa Verdean keyhole with six pilasters but the orientation is off somewhat. The Ancestral Puebloans usually placed the ventilation shaft on the south side but in these caves the best source of fresh air is the front—in this case that would be east—so the shafts had to be changed from the norm.

Balcony House exit

On the south end of this section is the original entrance. A massive piece of stone separated from the cliff face at some point long before any people were here and formed a tall, narrow V. The Ancestral Puebloans closed each end with masonry, leaving a small passageway, the only access to the pueblo, which was easily defended if need be. The tunnel is the only modern exit; knee pads would be helpful! Once through the tunnel, you exit up stone steps, holding a chain railing, and then the two ladders. A good workout, but worth the effort.

Cedar Tree

This is one of the easier sites to visit, as it is small and next to the parking area. If you are driving north, toward the visitors center from Chapin Mesa, the turn is on the right but the sign is difficult to find, so watch for the first turn past the four-way stop. It is a short distance. The access road leads to the site, which was similar to the Far View Community, but the only part excavated is a kiva and tower that are connected by a tunnel. It is nicely preserved and the tunnel is easy to see; it

Cedar Tree, tower entrance on left

does not take long to visit. This is another of the many towers at Mesa Verde whose function and purpose continue to puzzle archaeologists.

Wetherill Mesa

This section of the park is open from late May to Labor Day between the hours of 9 AM and 4 PM. There are three separate sites: Long House Cliff Dwelling, which may only be visited on a ranger-guided tour; Step House Cliff Dwelling, self-guided from the parking lot; and the Badger House section on the Mesa, also self-guided, to which you can walk or ride the tram.

The road to Wetherill is on the right before the parking lot for the Far View Lodge. It takes between 30 and 45 minutes to drive from this point to Wetherill on a winding, hilly road with several switchbacks. Long campers and towed trailers are prohibited.

Next to the parking lot at Wetherill is a visitors kiosk and canteen with trail guides, rangers, shade, restrooms, food, and a place to sit down. The area has suffered several

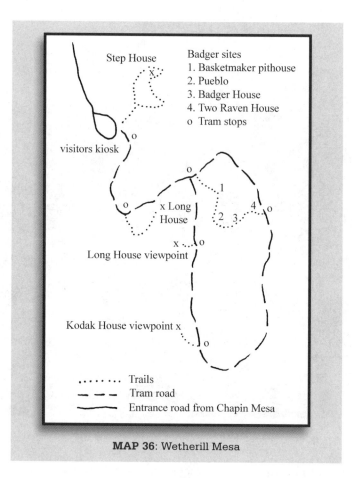

Badger sites
1. Basketmaker pithouse
2. Pueblo
3. Badger House
4. Two Raven House
o   Tram stops

Step House

visitors kiosk

x Long House

Long House viewpoint

Kodak House viewpoint x

· · · · · · · ·   Trails
– – –   Tram road
———   Entrance road from Chapin Mesa

MAP 36: Wetherill Mesa

fires over the past years and today is an eerie landscape of dead trees and burned stubs, very different from Chapin Mesa.

There is no charge for the tram that takes visitors to the Long House trailhead, Badger House community, and the overlooks for Kodak House and Long House. **NOTE:** For the Long House tour itself, you must purchase tickets at the visitors center before driving out there. The first tour is at 10 AM.

Approximately 900 sites have been recorded on Wetherill Mesa, with a population between 1,000 and 2,000. Nearly 1,000 check dams were built, as well as extensive terracing to increase available farmland.

Step House

The trailhead for the Step House Cliff Dwelling is on the right of the parking lot between where the tram departs and the visitors kiosk. This is a **difficult** trail that descends on several switchbacks to the site and then returns to the mesa in a loop. It is all exposed to the sun and there is no shade except at the site itself, so it gets very hot; carry plenty of water. The trail goes along the mesa for a short distance to a Y—keep right—and then begins to descend. Soon you will catch sight of the ruins in the cave ahead, only to lose them as you drop lower. The trail enters the cave from the left, or south end, allowing a good view of both sites. The cave opening faces east.

There are two villages at this site. A pithouse village from the early A.D. 600s comprised six pithouses, four of which have been excavated and stabilized, while the other two are under the later pueblo. The cliff dwelling is a P III pueblo from the 1200s, built on the boulders in the north end of the small cave.

When you first reach the site, before you come to the pithouses, look to the left for a set of steps built up the talus slope to the mesa top. It appears rather rough but you can still make out the stairs of the original entrance to the later pueblo. These steps give the pueblo its name.

You are now in front of the four pithouses. The earlier inhabitants lived in the caves, but generally by the mid A.D. 450s, most people began establishing villages on the mesas (see the first stop on Ruins Road, page 244) but a few continued living under the overhangs and this is the best-preserved example. One of the houses has been partially reconstructed to illustrate how they were built, and in the two on the left you can see the remains of burned beams. It seems that most pithouses were

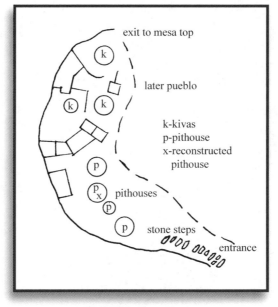

PLAN 22: Step House

Step House, with pithouse village in the background

burned, but whether from accidental causes or otherwise is impossible to know. Of course, a house covered mostly with very dry logs and branches with an open fire in the center is probably predisposed to burn at some point.

Continue along the path to the large boulder with marker 2 in front of it. On the left side are some toeholds notched into the rock to make it easier to climb to the rooms above and on the right are grooves caused by the people's sharpening of stone axes, knives, and points. Grooved markings like this can be found at many sites, though they are not often visible to the public. Imagine how many times these were used to leave the deep marks you see. Now climb up a short ladder to the later village.

At the top of the ladder are some petroglyphs, one of the larger panels in the park. You can see the difficulties of construction as the walls snake around and over the many boulders that litter this end of the cave. You have to wonder why they did not build over the other pithouses on the south side, where the floor is fairly level and rock free.

The next stop, marker 4, is one of the kivas. In some places you can see traces of the plaster used to cover the walls, and in this one a line of mountain sheep was painted around the lower section below the pilasters. Some of the room blocks rose two stories and possibly a few were three. The quality and skill of the builders is evident from the many obstacles they had to overcome, probably more so here than in any other cliff dwelling.

At marker 6 is another set of toeholds that go up to some small rooms used for storage. This is also a good vantage point to look back across the cave to see the steps on the south end and the layout of the pithouses. Step House, though small, is a remarkable feat of engineering and building skill and should not be missed if you come to Wetherill Mesa.

Continue along the path out of the north end of the site and back up onto the mesa to return to the visitors center and parking lot.

Long House

This cliff dwelling may only be visited on a ranger guided tour and you *must* purchase tickets at the visitors center *before* coming to Wetherill Mesa. The first tour is at 10 AM and each one takes about 90 minutes. The trail to the ruin is **difficult** and requires climbing up and down two ladders. Wait at the ranger kiosk until the departure of the next tour is announced, and then you ride the tram to the trailhead, which takes about 5 minutes.

Long House is the second-largest cliff dwelling in the park, with 150 rooms and 21 kivas. It probably housed between 125 and 200 people and was occupied during

Long House, trail to the upper section

the A.D. 1200s. The site faces south so takes advantage of the winter sun, which would have made it much more comfortable, as the winters can be very cold at this altitude.

The trail winds through the trees, offering beautiful views out over the canyon as well as a few glimpses of the ruins. You enter the site from the west end and can see along the entire village as the cave curves in a semicircle. This pueblo is more open and the rooms less crowded together than at Cliff Palace. The site is divided north–south by the great kiva that forms the central plaza. The rooms on this end were from two to four stories, with some rising five stories in the east end. Notice the storage rooms high in the cave built into the small crevice similar to those at other cliff dwellings.

The trail goes along the front of the village and then up two ladders just before the great kiva and into the back of the pueblo. The earliest rooms were built in the back and then they gradually expanded toward the front. As you continue along, there are some depressions in the rock that were used for sharpening tools, and a spring in the

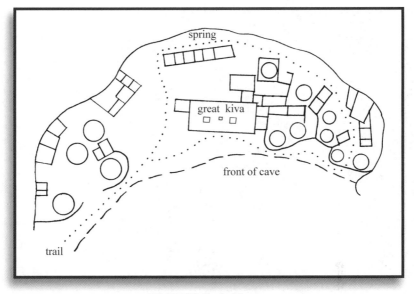

PLAN 23: Long House

back of the cave, where the people pecked small channels in the floor to direct the water into deeper holes that made collecting it easier. The water still runs but not as well as it did when occupied by the Ancestral Puebloans. One reason is that a check dam was built directly above on the mesa to collect the runoff so it would filter down through the sandstone and increase the flow of the spring, rather than simply running over the edge into the canyon. This same technique was used in many places throughout the southwest. There are also some petroglyphs along the back wall that are hard to see, but the ranger will point them out, including the hand with six fingers.

You come down through the east end, which occupies a smaller section of the cave even though there are as many rooms and kivas as in the west section. As at other pueblos built in the caves, the people had to level the floors by building retaining walls and constructed around and over large boulders they could not remove. Above this section is another wall that encloses the space on the upper ledge, but it was never divided into rooms, and there are many small holes along the front. Some speculate it could have been used to watch the village below but more likely it had something to do with astronomical observations, though this has never been proven.

The trail comes back down along the front of the large plaza. This is referred to as a great kiva but there were no walls or roof, so it is also called a dance plaza but probably served the same functions as a great kiva. The central hearth is lined with stone slabs, as are the two shallow cists and even the *sipapu*. On the left end of the east wall is a door leading to a room block that went up five stories to the roof of the cave.

Depressions from sharpening tools

There is another similar plaza in Fire Temple, which can be seen from the last overlook on the Ruins Road (see page 253).

To exit the site, you follow the same trail back up to the mesa to the tram stop. From this point you can either go back to the visitors kiosk or continue to the Badger House community, described next. The trams pass by every 30 minutes.

Badger House Community

There are four sites on the mesa that make up the Badger House Community and these share some similarities to the Ruins Road sites. However, there are also many differences, so a visit to one does not preclude seeing the other, though Badger is more difficult to get to than the Ruins Road.

Take the tram from the Long House trailhead, or from the visitors kiosk if you are not going to Long House, to the first stop (second stop from the visitors kiosk), where the driver may orient you to the layout of Badger. You follow the path, an **easy**, paved, level trail, from one site to the next and end up on the opposite side where the tram will pick you up, near Two Raven House, for the return trip to the visitors kiosk, after two short stops. Do not follow the branch trails that point to tram stops, as they are no longer used (see Map 36, page 272).

Antechamber (top) and addition (bottom) (site 1, Map 36, Baskermaker pithouse)

Early pueblo. (site 2, Map 36).

The first site (site 1, Map 36, page 272) is visible from the tram stop and is a pit-house from the mid–A.D. 600s. It was originally a typical pithouse with the main room and an antechamber for storage and entry into the dwelling, but at some point this antechamber was converted into living quarters. Another hearth, *sipapu,* and dividing walls were added, plus an antechamber, turning the building into a duplex occupied by two families. It is also possible that an entrance through the roof was added so that the inhabitants could enter without having to go through the other smaller house.

Continue along the path to the second site (site 2, Map 36), the Developmental Pueblo Village. These structures date from around A.D. 750 to 1000, and the long arc of rooms exposed are from after 800. These are some of the earliest masonry walls, with rough stones and upright slabs topped with jacal. The structure was destroyed by fire and at marker 4, archaeologists found the remains of an adult who had been overcome by either the smoke or flames and had perished before a wall collapsed onto him. At the end of the row of rooms is a kiva, referred to as a great kiva although it appears small for the designation, though I do not know the diameter. The kiva was destroyed by fire and eventually filled in, with houses being constructed over it. You can see the stratigraphy of the kiva; that is, the different layers of soil, along the side. The light-colored soil at the bottom is where the original hole was dug for the kiva, and the blackened area above is from fires that were built over the filled-in structure and has nothing to do with the fire that burned the building. The last is fill placed in the depression on which the people built the houses.

Kiva (site 2, Map 36)

Badger House (site 3 Map 36) Older single course walls under younger double walls

The third site is Badger House (site 3, Map 36, page 272). As you walk toward the covered site, the first thing you see is the remains of a tower to the left of the path. This tower was connected by a 40-foot (12 m) tunnel to a kiva, both of which were built in the mid-1200s as part of the second village at this location. A previous village had been occupied between A.D. 900 and 1100 at the same site, and once inside you will see the distinction in the architecture. At marker 7 is a mazelike configuration of walls that make it very difficult to sort out the layout of the two separate villages, but you can tell the difference between the earlier and later construction by the build of the walls. The single stone–thick sections are from the earlier pueblo, whereas the double stone walls are the remains of the second occupation. You can clearly see how they built over the first village, a common practice.

The last site on the mesa is Two Raven House (site 4, Map 36, page 272). This pueblo was occupied from the early A.D. 900s until sometime in the 1100s. The remains do not fit the pattern of a standard pueblo and there are some unusual aspects to the site. At marker 10 is a small, round structure believed to be an oven in which hot rocks would be placed on the floor. The food to be cooked was set on these and then covered, probably with earth. To the right of this structure is a small, round pit that seems to be a very small kiva but its size and location suggest that it might have

Two Raven House, oven

Two Raven House, small kiva?

served another purpose, though exactly what is unknown. Both of these structures are unusual.

Farther along the path is a kiva and plaza for the L-shaped pueblo, and just beyond this are the remains of a wooden palisade thought to have surrounded the pueblo. The purpose of this fence is unknown. These seem to be rare but they are also difficult to find, as the exposed wood does not survive well over time and require a great deal of effort archaeologically to discover, so they may have been built more often than is believed. It might have been a windbreak. One theory is that it was used as a fence to keep turkeys in although they could have easily flown over it. Another idea is for defense, but it does not seem to have been substantial enough for this purpose either. Any thoughts? The last unusual element at this site is a small, triangular structure on the left as you exit the roofed section. It was possibly for storage.

The path continues a short distance to the road, where there is a bench and shade at which to wait for the next tram. From this point, the tram winds along the mesa to a stop at the overlook for Kodak House. This cliff dwelling had around 70 rooms built on two ledges and is not open to the public. Kodak House is one of the most looted at Mesa Verde; many of the walls were destroyed in an effort to find whole pots and other objects to be sold. Nordenskiöld used to store his cameras in the pueblo during his pioneering archaeological work in the park in 1891 (see page 286), thus the name. There is a short, **easy** trail to the overlook.

Kodak House

The next, and last, stop on the tram line on Wetherill Mesa is at the overlook for Long House, which has an impressive view of the site. This is another short, **easy** trail, but for both of these the tram only stops about 5 minutes, just enough time to walk to the edge, snap a couple of quick pictures, and return. If you miss the tram, it will be 30 minutes before another and they do not like people walking on the road.

This concludes a look at the extra sites in Mesa Verde.

ARCHAEOLOGICAL HISTORY OF MESA VERDE

The origins of Southwestern archaeology are intertwined with the discovery and exploration of the ruins of Mesa Verde. The impact on the rest of the country, especially with the eastern policy makers in Washington, would have long-term positive effects on the exploration and preservation of other ruins in the Southwest.

In 1874, photographer William Henry Jackson, working for the US Geological and Geographical Survey of the Territories, traveled into the area and managed to find and photograph two cliff dwellings. These were the first images to be produced of the ruins in the future Mesa Verde Park. Three years earlier, his photographs of western Wyoming had been instrumental in influencing Congress to pass a bill that created Yellowstone National Park in 1872.

The next person to venture into the forbidding canyons of the green mesa was Virginia Donaghe McClurg, who would be a driving force in the creation of the park. A reporter from the east, she traveled to Colorado in 1877 because of her health. She was not able to visit the ruins until 1886, locating three at that time and becoming enthralled with the sight. This would begin a 25-year campaign to preserve the ruins and create Mesa Verde Park.

On December 18, 1888, Richard Wetherill and his brother-in-law, Charles Mason, while searching for some stray cattle, walked to the edge of a cliff and peered across the canyon. Although a snowstorm reduced visibility, they could just make out the outlines of several structures, some three stories high, in a large alcove opposite. Amazed at the sight, they quickly forgot about the cattle and rode north, working their way around the head of the canyon and over to where the ruins lay below them. Using tree limbs tied together, they managed to scramble down the cliff face and into the cave, most likely becoming the first non–Native Americans to see the pueblo they named Cliff Palace. They would soon introduce the world to the cliff dwellers.

Richard Wetherill was one of five brothers and a sister who were the children of Benjamin Wetherill, a homesteader who settled near Mancos, Colorado, in 1881 on the Alamo Ranch. The Wetherills were not the first to explore the canyons of Mesa Verde but were the first to dig and explore individual sites. Richard and his brothers Al and John were the most interested in the ruins and did the majority of the work.

They would dig in the ruins and search the canyons during the winter, and by 1890 had found over 200 cliff dwellings.

The ranch suffered hard times, so the brothers advertised themselves as tour guides, which attracted tourists to their ranch for the grueling three-day pack trip into the canyon to see Cliff Palace. They also did a brisk business selling the visitors artifacts. They put together collections of artifacts that were sold to educational institutions, including the Denver Historical Society, the University of Pennsylvania Museum, and the Colorado State Museum. Between 1889 and 1901 they guided over 1,000 tourists to the ruins, including several writers and scientists.

Through their extensive explorations and digging, the Wetherills began to see patterns emerging and recognized the differences between earlier inhabitants and the later cliff dwellers. They distinguished the earlier "basket people," named for some well-preserved baskets they found, and the "cliff dwellers," who had built the pueblos in the caves along the canyons. They were ridiculed for their views at the time, but in 1927 at the first Pecos Conference organized by Alfred Kidder at his dig at Pecos Pueblo, the archaeologists agreed on a chronology of the earlier Basketmaker and later Pueblo cultures, which more or less was the same as the Wetherills'.

In 1891, the Wetherills took Gustaf Nordenskiöld, a Swedish citizen living in Finland who had come to the Southwest for health reasons, to see Cliff Palace, with which he became enchanted. Although not formally trained in archaeology, he did come from a scientific background and became the first person to use a scientific approach to do research at Mesa Verde. He spent the summer among the ruins and taught the Wetherills a more systemic method of removing objects and recording what they found. He took many photos. Kodak Ruin acquired its name because he stored his equipment there while working around Wetherill Mesa. He made drawings as well as surveyed many of the ruins. The large numbers carved in the caves by many cliff dwellings are his. Nordenskiöld, with the help of the Wetherills, dug at Longhouse, Kodak House, Mug House, and Step House on Wetherill Mesa, and Spruce Tree House on Chapin Mesa. Nordenskiöld would also have a huge impact on the future of not only Mesa Verde but of almost all the ruins of the Southwest, though not intentionally.

Before he left the west he shipped back to the National Museum in Helsinki, Finland, a large collection of the objects he had recovered from Mesa Verde. This was legal, but it caused a backlash against the plundering of Southwestern sites that led to the introduction of the Antiquities Act of 1906, protecting all ancient ruins on public lands and preventing the exportation of artifacts.

The Wetherills had tried to impress the East Coast academics with their work at Mesa Verde but were harshly criticized for their methods and the fact that they were uneducated. At the same time, the major museums and universities from the east were doing the same thing by sponsoring "scientific" expeditions to the Southwest that were nothing more than the looting of sites to fill their collections. The Wetherills were forced out of Mesa Verde when it was made a national park in 1906, but Richard went to Chaco Canyon, where he set up a trading post and continued exploring ruins in the area. He was killed in 1910 during a dispute with a Navajo and is buried in Chaco near Pueblo Bonito.

When Nordenskiöld shipped his collection of artifacts home, it became a catalyst in the drive to preserve the heritage of the Southwest. Virginia McClurg was one of the first to appreciate the beauty and historical significance of the Mesa Verde region at a time when prospectors and others could only see the dollar value of the Southwest. She would fight for 25 years to have Mesa Verde permanently protected. She formed the Colorado Cliff Dwellers Association, which gained the support of numerous women's clubs to lobby Washington politicians to have Mesa Verde declared a national park.

Long House, great kiva, Wetherill Mesa

During the 1870s there was a growing movement to preserve certain areas of natural wonder and unique beauty, and when Yellowstone became the first national park in 1872, a precedent had been set for conservation efforts. The drive to save Mesa Verde and its ruins continued to gain support among members of Congress as well as the general population after the Nordenskiöld incident, culminating in the introduction of a bill in 1904 to create the national park. However, it died amid a fight over who would have the rights to excavate in the protected areas.

Another bill introduced in 1905 again perished, along with an antiquities protection act, but both were gaining in support. In early 1906, the two associations—one led by McClurg for Mesa Verde and the other by those pushing for the creation of the Antiquities Act—joined forces to support each other's bill. On the verge of success to create a national park in Mesa Verde McClurg, who had almost singlehandedly brought the debate to this point after 25 years, withdrew her support for a national, or government-controlled, park in favor of a state park that would be run by the Cliff Dwellers Association, making McClurg the one who would be in charge. This caused a split between her and Lucy Peabody, second in authority in the association, who supported a national park. Fortunately there was enough momentum in favor to push the bill through Congress, creating the first national park for the preservation of archaeological ruins. This would soon be followed by the Antiquities Act, which made it illegal to remove artifacts from any public land. Unfortunately, the last-minute change in McClurg's position left her out of the victory that followed and pushed her aside as far as the new park was concerned. She continued to support Mesa Verde through fund-raising efforts until her death in 1931 and was the driving force that created Mesa Verde National Park and preserved for the future what you see in the park today.

With the creation of Mesa Verde National Park and all the publicity surrounding its founding, tourism increased and there was a new push to stabilize and reconstruct the ruins for visitors. In 1908, Jesse Walter Fewkes was hired to excavate and restore some of the ruins. He had been trained as an ethnologist, and after becoming interested in Southwestern Native peoples, became one of the first to study the Native Americans in the region, gaining their trust and much knowledge about their culture. In 1909 he restored and stabilized Cliff Palace and was very critical of the Wetherills and what they had done to the ruins. However, Fewkes would be criticized by later archaeologists for his failure to keep records for most of the changes he made, with the restorations sometimes being made according to what he thought it should look like rather than based on what remained. He also supposedly had conversations with the spirits of the people who had once inhabited the sites and who gave their approval for his work.

Jesse Nusbaum, an archaeologist from Santa Fe, stabilized and restored Balcony House in 1910. It is not known whether he gained the approval of the spirit world. The first road into the park was completed in 1913, bringing many more tourists into the sites. By 1934 the ruins had began to deteriorate again and more work was needed at Cliff Palace.

Earl Morris, who had excavated Aztec Ruins (see page 310), was in the process of reconstructing the great kiva at Aztec, when he was placed in charge of the new stabilization project at Mesa Verde. Morris hired Al Lancaster, a farmer from Pleasant Valley, near Lowry Ruins, who was experienced in excavation and stabilization and had worked on several sites. Although a self-taught archaeologist, Lancaster had a knack for the work, especially stabilization and reconstruction.

Morris and Lancaster reconstructed the structures to what they thought the buildings had originally been like but there was still much speculation. They redid some of Fewkes's work at Cliff Palace, but unlike Fewkes, they documented their work, including photographing each section of repair before and after the work. They concentrated on the Speaker Chief's House in the northern end and the painted tower on the south. Morris left after this to continue his work at Aztec but Lancaster stayed on at the park and is responsible for most of the stabilizations along Ruins Road. He received a Distinguished Service Award from the Department of the Interior in 1962 for his work at Mesa Verde.

Today, stabilization work is an ongoing process, as the ruins must be continually monitored for damage from the elements and, especially for the cliff dwellings, water seepage that destroys the adobe. Another problem has been caused by the methods used in the 1930s to secure the walls; mortar. The trouble is that the mortar, used to "point," or fill the gaps between stones in the walls, and also as a cap over the top of the walls, does not allow the water to seep out of the walls as did the original adobe, but traps it inside and causes the sandstone blocks to deteriorate. The hard caps also crack over time, which allows more water to infiltrate the walls compounding the problems. Mortar was used on many stabilizing projects over the years so it has become a widespread problem, not just at Mesa Verde. At the time, it seemed like the best solution, and no one could have foreseen the result. Today, a special mix of mortar and adobe allows water to seep out of the walls, offering better protection.

The increase in tourism, especially over the past two decades, has been hard on the sites. Most people follow the rules and do not touch, stand, or sit on the structures, but there are still some who disregard the fragility of the sites and cause damage. These ruins have stood for over 800 years and it is everyone's responsibility to help in their preservation by not causing any undue harm.

Lowry Pueblo
Colorado

- Established in 2000
- Within the Canyons of the Ancients National Monument, in southwestern Colorado and extending to the Utah border
- Elevation 6,700 feet (2,050 m)

Anasazi Heritage
Center
Colorado

- Established in 1988 by the Bureau of Land Management for the storage, display, and preservation of ancient artifacts from the Four Corners region

Aztec Ruins
National Monument
New Mexico

- Established as a national monument
in 1923
- 320 acres (130 h)
- Elevation 5,700 feet (1,740 m)

Nearby Site

◎ Chimney Rock

17. Lowry Pueblo

GETTING THERE: From Cortez, follow US 491 (formerly US 666) north, a right turn if you are on US 160 west, about 18 miles (29 km) to Pleasant View, where a small sign indicates the turn onto County Road CC on the left. This road is paved for the first section and then dirt the rest of the way to the site, which is almost 9 miles (14.5 km). Just before reaching the site you must turn left, where the road divides in a Y. Recently there was not a sign for Lowry, but the parking lot is shortly after the turn. When driving north toward Pleasant View, you can turn at the sign for Hovenweep, CR BB, and then turn right at the four corners and go left to Lowry.

As you drive north out of Cortez and along the road to the site, notice the rich farmland and you will understand why the Ancestral Puebloans settled in this part of the Southwest. It is the most fertile and thus had the largest population density. There is quite a difference from Hovenweep or even Mesa Verde, which today is covered with sage and trees and does not look too prosperous from an agricultural perspective.

THINGS YOU NEED TO KNOW: The parking lot is close to the ruins and connected by a short, **easy** trail. The site is open daylight hours year-round but the road may be impassable after heavy rains. There is no fee nor any services, except for pit toilets and picnic tables.

Lowry was one of eight major towns in the Montezuma Valley region that date to the A.D. 1100s and 1200s. It is believed to be a Chacoan outlier (see Aztec Ruins,

North section, Lowry

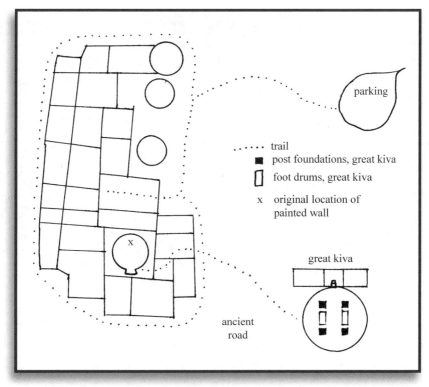

PLAN 24: Lowry Pueblo

page 311). The excavated structure is a great house in the tradition of Chaco and Aztec, among others, and was occupied between A.D. 1030 and 1140. It is the northernmost outlier and contains several Chacoan features, such as interior kivas, the type of masonry, a great kiva, and roads. Over 100 sites are nearby, including smaller pueblos, shrines, storage structures, reservoirs, and irrigation systems, although this is the only one to have been excavated. It was discovered in 1919 and excavated during the 1930s by Paul S. Martin from the Chicago Field Museum of Natural History.

TOURING THE SITE

Lowry was part of a greater area that consisted of 40 separate structures, covering nearly 1 square mile (2.6 sq. km) and was the second largest in the Montezuma Valley. The 24 living sites comprised 2,400 rooms with an estimated population of 1,500 to 1,800. There were two sections, one on each side of the water supply, connected by roads. The remains visible are in the northwestern section of the town and the great kiva was part of a large, open plaza with more buildings to the north and east.

The trail leads to the pueblo and you have a view of the ruins that are on an el-

North rooms, entrance to great kiva

evated site, though in past years the brush has grown to partially obscure the scene. The pueblo had 37 ground-floor rooms and a second, and maybe a third, story, for a total of 65 to 80 rooms and 8 kivas. Not all rooms were occupied at the same time. On the right as you approach are the remains of 3 kivas, with another directly in front of you. Continue through the low door into the interior of the pueblo, but do not walk or crawl over any of the walls. As you walk around inside, notice the size of the rooms and masonry. The larger rooms are Chacoan influenced and date to A.D. 1090, and the smaller ones Mesa Verdean, dating from the early 1100s. The Chacoan sections feature masonry finished with small even-coursed stones, whereas the Mesa Verdeans used larger stones in uneven courses. By the early 1100s, most building techniques were Mesa Verdean in style. Some of the doors are T-shaped and many of the rooms do not have connecting openings and would have been entered using ladders from above.

The higher walled section to the left (south) encloses a kiva that may be entered by a side door. There is a skylight to illuminate the interior of this kiva. The reason it was covered and preserved in this way was to protect a painted mural around the lower part of the banquette that could be seen at one time. Unfortunately, efforts to preserve it in place have not worked, so it was removed and is on display in the museum at the Anasazi Heritage Center. The original entrance into this kiva would have been by a ladder through a central smoke hole in the roof.

Continuing along the trail around the pueblo, notice that the west side, opposite the path from the parking lot, is one continuous wall with no openings. This is the back of the pueblo and is a common feature on Chacoan structures. In fact, there was most likely only one ground-floor entrance, which was on the east, with ladders going up to the top of the first story. This could have been for protection, convenience, or just the preference of the inhabitants.

As you walk from the pueblo toward the great kiva you are crossing a road that was 30 feet (9 m) across and possibly connected into a system of roads that led to Chaco Canyon. There is an outline of this road but it is nearly impossible now to tell where it was. It was built by the Ancestral Puebloans and is one of many in the area.

The great kiva has an interior diameter of 45 feet (13.7 m) with a low banquette around the wall and was built in A.D. 1106. There are four large stone bases on which the support posts sat that held the roof, with cists between each that were probably covered with animal skins and used as foot drums. The entrance would have been down a stairway connected to the rooms on the north side. This kiva was part of a large plaza used for ceremonies and rituals that involved the surrounding communities. Earlier P I and P II kivas are under this P III structure, as well as pithouses where the pueblo was built indicating a continued occupation of over 400 years. Although the site has become somewhat overgrown in the last few years it is still a wonderful and worthwhile ruin to visit.

The great kiva looking north, Lowry

Dominguez Pueblo

18. Anasazi Heritage Center

GETTING THERE: If you are at Lowry, return to the highway and turn right. Stay on CO 491 for about 10 miles (16 km) to the turnoff for CO 184 to Dolores, on the left, and continue about 8 miles (12.8 km) to the museum which will be on your left. If you are coming from Cortez take CO 145 north, which is on the eastern end of town, or from the east branch off US 160 onto CO 184 at Mancos.

THINGS YOU NEED TO KNOW: The museum is open daily from 9 AM to 5 PM in the summer and 10 AM to 4 PM from November to February. Closed Thanksgiving Day, Christmas Day, and New Year's Day. There is an entrance fee for the museum. For more information, phone 970-882-5600; visit www.co.blm.gov/ahc/hmepge.htm; or write to Anasazi Heritage Center, 27501 Hwy. 184, Dolores, Colorado, 81323.

This museum was the result of the largest archaeological project ever undertaken in the United States. From 1978 to 1983, the area along the Dolores River was surveyed for archaeological sites ahead of the construction of a large dam that would create the McPhee Reservoir. More than 200 archaeologists discovered over 1,600 sites and tested 120. The majority of the artifacts are in the museum, which also has a "hands-on" section where people may grind corn with a mano and metate, weave on a loom, and use computer simulations to see what the region was like when the Ancestral Puebloans lived here.

The center also has two archaeological sites: a small one near the museum entrance, and a larger one that is a short walk up the hill. These two P III sites were named after the Spanish Franciscan priests Francisco Atanasio Dominguez and Silvestre Vélez de Escalante who reported seeing the ruins as they traveled west in 1776, searching for a route from New Mexico to California, which they never found.

TOURING THE SITE

Dominguez Ruins

The first thing you will see is the Dominguez site, located next to the parking lot and beside the entrance walkway into the museum. There are only three rooms and one kiva in this pueblo, which was probably occupied by a single family, but the small size is not indicative of the importance of the site. In one of the rooms, a significant burial was discovered of a woman who was about 35 when she died and was buried with a large amount of jewelry, pottery, and other artifacts, including a necklace with 6,900 beads (some archaeological assistant had to count and record each one). The

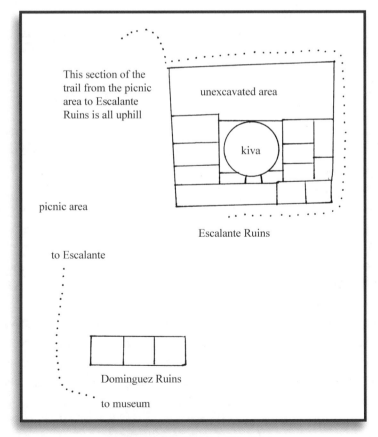

PLAN 25: Dominguez–Escalante

relative importance of this burial does not fit into the typical version of the Ancestral Puebloans as an egalitarian society. Finds of this nature have been exceedingly rare, so this woman's role or position remains a mystery. The construction is in the Mesa Verdean style and is one pueblo of many that surrounded the ridge.

Escalante Ruins

To visit the Escalante site you must follow a paved trail that is a 1-mile (1.6 km) return walk, almost all uphill, on a series of switchbacks. It is **moderate**, but more difficult in the heat of summer. Beware of approaching thunderstorms, as they move in fast and the site is on a high, exposed ridge.

Escalante was occupied from around A.D. 1129 to the early 1200s and had between 20 and 25 rooms with 1 kiva. A double row of rooms surround the kiva on three sides, with a single row on the south. The kiva is Chacoan but the masonry style is Mesa Verdean, as was the pottery discovered there. The mixture from both Chaco Canyon and the San Juan is not understood at this time, though there are many theories, including one where a Chacoan man (the mason) married a San Juan woman (the potter), but I have problems with this (see page 442).

Several rooms in the east-southeast corner, plus the kiva, have been excavated and the foundation walls on many more can be seen in the unexcavated sections. You approach the site from the northwest and the trail goes around the pueblo. There is also a spectacular view out over the McPhee Reservoir. Notice the T-shaped doors and large stones placed in uneven courses. The kiva has a low banquette and bases for eight pillars, which is typical of the Chacoan style, but the masonry is Mesa Verdean. Return by the same trail to the museum.

The Anasazi Heritage Museum was built to house the artifacts discovered during the excavations prior to the filling of the McPhee Reservoir and for the interpretation and study of the history and culture of the Pueblo people occupying the Montezuma Valley. Over 3 million artifacts are stored there and available for research, with some examples on display, but for the general public, the best aspect of the museum is the hands-on section.

When you enter the museum, the bookstore/gift shop is on the right; an auditorium is to the left; the kiosk for information and to pay the fee is straight in; and the main collection is behind the lobby. Down the hall to the right, beyond the restrooms, is a large gallery where varying exhibitions are displayed; some are good, others not so much, but they are always worth a look.

The main features to see include the full scale reconstructed pithouse, which can be viewed from above and at eye level; a large display of archaeological tools and

East side, T door, Escalante ruins

instruments accompanied by explanations as to their use; and the hands-on section. You can grind corn as the Ancestral Puebloans did, using a mano and metate, which is not easy, weave on a loom, view artifacts through a microscope, and explore drawers filled with objects from the excavations, many of which you may pick up and handle, except for the ones that have been stolen. There are interactive computer programs for kids of all ages to use and information on the ancient Pueblo people and their culture. One can easily spend hours here. **NOTE:** This museum is very popular with school groups and at times can be crowded and noisy.

South side, Escalante ruins

19. Aztec Ruins National Monument

GETTING THERE: From the Anasazi Heritage Center follow CO 184 to Mancos and US 160 east toward Durango, a left turn. After about 15 miles (24 km), watch for CO 140 on your right and turn here. The road number changes to NM 170 when you cross into New Mexico. Turn left onto NM 574 in La Plata to Aztec, left in Aztec onto NM 516, then left again just before the bridge at the first red light—there are signs for the monument—and follow the winding street past a school to the parking area on the right. You can also stay on US 160 through Durango to US 550 south and follow this highway into Aztec to NM 516. Watch for the signs to the monument as soon as you cross the bridge and turn right.

When you leave Aztec, if you are staying in Bloomfield, the closest town with lodging to Chaco Canyon, turn left at the light on NM 516, cross the bridge, and then turn right onto US 550 south to Bloomfield. Turn right onto US 64 to get to the center of town.

Bloomfield does not have many places to stay, but Farmington does, though it is about 15 miles (24 km) farther to Chaco and back. From Aztec, turn right at NM 516 and continue on this road to Farmington.

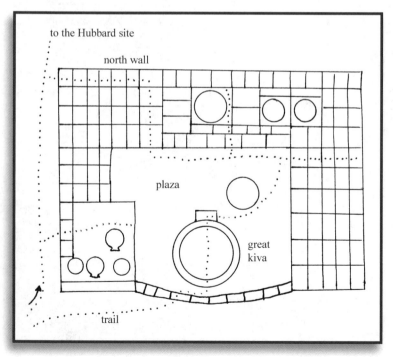

PLAN 26: Aztec

THINGS YOU NEED TO KNOW: The monument is open all year, except Thanksgiving Day, Christmas Day, and New Year's Day, from 8 AM to 5 PM September to late May and 8 AM to 6 PM during the summer. There are picnic tables and restrooms. The visitors center has a small museum collection, bookstore, gift shop, and a video presentation about the site and the people who occupied Aztec. The monument contains several ruins but only two have been excavated and are open to the public: the West Ruin and the Hubbard Tri-Wall Site. For more information, phone 505-334-6174; visit www.nps.gov/azru; or write to Superintendent, Aztec Ruins National Monument, 84 County Road 2900, Aztec, New Mexico, 87410-0640.

In the late 1800s, when this site was discovered, and partially looted, it was not believed that the Native Americans were capable of having built something as monumental as this structure; thus, it was called Aztec in the mistaken assumption that Mesoamericans had constructed it.

There are 12 structures in the immediate area of Aztec. They are mostly P III with a few late P II. Aztec was built around A.D. 1100 by Chacoan or Chacoan-influenced peoples, and abandoned by 1150. It was reoccupied for a short period of time in the 1200s by people from Mesa Verde, before being left for good. It consists of over 400 rooms, 28 kivas, and the only great kiva in the Southwest that has been fully restored. It was rebuilt in 1934 by archaeologist Earl Morris, who spent many years excavating the site. The inner part of the great kiva is 41 feet (12.5 m) in diameter and set partially below ground. A short distance behind the pueblo is the Hubbard Site.

TOURING THE SITE

A short, paved, **easy** trail winds through the ruins, giving you access to both the interior and exterior of the structure. From the parking lot, enter the visitors center and pay the entrance fee at the ranger desk straight ahead. The museum, to the right through the door on the right side of the theater, contains a small collection of artifacts. Exit through the back doors on the left to reach the trail.

Outside, it is cool and shaded as you get your first sight of the ruins. Follow the trail to the left, which places you beside the west wall of the West Ruins, an impressive structure still rising two stories. Follow the path up a few steps to marker 2 for an overall view of the pueblo and plaza. On your immediate right is a Mesa Verdean kiva and to the left you see many rooms stretching away along the west wing toward the north, as well as the remains of some other interior kivas. Straight ahead is the great kiva, the reconstructed round building, and the large, open plaza where most activities would have taken place. You see the shape and size of the pueblo with rooms along the east on the far side of the plaza past the great kiva and across the north,

Northeast corner

to your left, connecting east and west. The narrow row of rooms encloses the plaza on the south. Where you are would have been two stories, and possibly three on the outside, with the same configuration on the north and east sections.

Go back down the steps and continue to the right. The sandstone used in the construction came from quarries several miles away as there is no suitable rock nearby. Notice the two rows of dark green stone, one at ground level and the other just below eye level, a feature used along this wall and in a few rooms. No one knows why these colored stones were placed like this, especially considering the fact that the walls were plastered with adobe so any features of the masonry would be obscured. The waviness of the courses is due to the movement of the subsoil over time; originally they would have been laid in straight rows. The west wall is 278 feet (85 m) long with few doors or windows.

Marker 4 (this refers to the sign posts along the trail and correspond to the Aztec

Ruins guidebook the ranger will loan you at the front desk) is at the northwest corner, where you have a view of the north, or back, wall, which is 360 feet (110 m) long and, like the west and east sides, contains few if any ground-level openings. Aztec shares many architectural features with the buildings in Chaco Canyon (see page 322), including its large size, a long north wall, kivas in the room blocks, at least three stories and thick walls. Most of the structure was built between A.D. 1110 and 1130, around the time Chaco was in decline, and was a major center in and of itself.

Continue past the pueblo to the Hubbard Site, named after a one-time owner of this property. This is a tri-wall structure that still baffles archaeologists as to its purpose, though most agree it was ceremonial in nature. It consists of a central kiva surrounded by two concentric circles of rooms: 8 in the inner ring and 14 in the outer. A few of the rooms have connecting doors, but most would only have been accessible through the roof. There is another such structure to the east of the pueblo but it has not been excavated; and in Chaco Canyon, one is found next to Pueblo del Arroyo

Hubbard tri-wall structure

(see page 349). As well there are similarities to the Sun Temple at Mesa Verde and Horseshoe House in Hovenweep (see pages 210 and 255). It was built over at least three older kivas, including a Chacoan one where the center room is now. The building is 64 feet (19 m) in diameter. It was excavated in 1953 but had to be backfilled in 1979 due to the deterioration of the walls, so now you see only part of the top section.

Return to the corner of the pueblo, where you enter the ground floor. Several of the doors you pass through, including the entrance, are modern, framed around holes punched into the pueblo by pot hunters in the late 19th century. Watch your head, as the doorways are low and some rooms are fairly dark.

At marker 7, and throughout the other ground-floor rooms, you can see some of the original beams in the ceiling, which are spruce or pine and came from a distance in excess of 20 miles (32 km) to the north. These large beams support smaller crossbeams with interwoven brush mats and mud on top to produce the upper floor. These lower-floor rooms would mostly be used for storage or sometimes for garbage as the ventilation was poor and the rooms were dark, but if you see blackened ceilings it indicates hearths, which means they were occupied. It was also common to place the dead under rooms, and in the room marked 9, thirteen skeletons were discovered in 1881 by looters. The deceased had been placed in the flexed position and the room sealed off.

Not all of these rooms would have been in use at one time as it was common to fill the lower rooms with trash or burials and then build new structures on top or in front of them, making it difficult to estimate population numbers for these pueblos. They were not like apartment buildings; rather, a series of small pueblos, each occupied by related clans, constructed together in what became a single entity. But even in large villages, such as Aztec, elements of the standard unit pueblo can be seen: south facing, small kin kivas built into rooms to give the appearance of being below ground; and south of the room blocks, an open plaza and a U-shape of room blocks.

When you exit the covered rooms, the trail turns right and you are in what was the highest section of Aztec, going up at least three and probably four stories. On the walls you can see where the floors were by the recessed stones and small round holes for the crossbeams (see photograph, below) and larger openings where the main support beams once were. You will notice in some rooms that the ceilings seem low, but this is because you are standing on unexcavated ground or, in some cases, backfill rather than on the original floor. The backfill is purposely placed in the rooms to stabilize and preserve them.

After leaving these open rooms you will be in the plaza, which was the heart of any pueblo. The great kiva and another smaller one are exposed, but Morris found buried below the surface others that had been abandoned and covered over. This is where everyday activities took place, including most of the cooking and, on sacred days, celebrations and dancing, features that have always been, and still are, an important part of Native American life and culture.

As you continue along the path, the rooms next to the plaza on this side are later Mesa Verdean and were added to the original Chacoan. At marker 14, the T-shaped door, you can see the difference in the two types of masonry: the exterior wall is later; and the interior wall, earlier Chacoan.

Detail of floor insert, top

The path goes up a few steps to the interior of the north section and a Chacoan kiva. This type has a low banquette, generally eight posts and no "keyhole" by the ventilator shaft, whereas the Mesa Verdean kiva, of which there is a good example at the beginning of the tour, has a high banquette, six posts, and the outward "keyhole" shape by the ventilator (see page 426). By using the masonry style and type of kiva, you can gain some insight into which section was built when, the Chacoan being earlier. Looking toward the east you see two more Chacoan kivas and the rooms along the east side.

Return to the main path and continue left to the corner of the plaza where the trail enters the east side of the pueblo through a T door. The trail goes to the back room—watch your head, as the doorways are low—giving you a good look at the masonry and changes that were made over time. One door was sealed and there is an unfinished wall. Today we call it remodeling.

Back in the plaza you arrive at a kiva where a few beams are placed across one another, resting on the stone posts. This is called cribbing, and if you continue laying in beams around and around the kiva, a domed roof is created, a technique that requires many more beams than does a flat roof (this is described in on 427, Figures 4 and 5). The advantage with the cribbed style is that a larger opening can be spanned. If you lay the beams flat, they require support posts if the space is large. The next stop is the great kiva.

This is the only completely rebuilt and restored great kiva in the world. Many people believe ruins should not be rebuilt but it is difficult to argue against reconstruction once you have walked through this building. It is magnificent, and even though

The reconstructed great kiva (looking east)

it may not have been exactly like this when original, it is certainly very close and captures the feeling of what it was like being in such an important place. There is a serenity and calmness inside, a coolness from the heat of the plaza, a sense of well-being. Even though the space is large, it is not intimidating or overwhelming but welcoming. Entering this structure is one of the highlights of any tour of the Southwest.

You enter from the north into a fair-sized room where people would prepare for the ceremony in the kiva proper. On each side is a small door that leads to the outer ring of 15 rooms that surrounds the inner main chamber and has openings with steps down into the central kiva. These rooms were originally connected to the outside by exterior doors that were eventually sealed up. When you walk down some steps, you are in the main chamber of the kiva. Directly in front of you is the hearth made of raised stones in a square. Look up: The smoke hole is over the hearth, and if the sun is shining, a shaft of light dramatically pierces the dark interior. Notice the roof. Morris studied many examples of kiva roofs that were intact before designing what you see here so that it would reflect the original as closely as possible.

On each side of the hearth is a large cist whose use is unknown, but they were probably covered with animal skins or wooden planks and used as drums. Drumming is an important part of Native American ceremonies as it represents the heartbeat of Mother Earth. The four large support posts each rest on four limestone disks set into the bedrock and were quarried about 40 miles (64 km) away. Under each of these were placed sacred objects before construction. A few of the original disks are on the floor next to the northeast post. Each weighs around 350 pounds (150 kg). The posts were built of stone interlaced with small beams, an example of which can be seen on the northwest post (first one on the right coming down the steps) facing the foot drum. The interior is plastered and some kivas were painted with murals but no evidence of painted designs was discovered here, only traces of red and whitewashed solid colors.

Great kivas were the center of a community, the center of the earth, its navel, where life first emerged. They are the first house built by the people and a place of the six sacred directions: north, south, east, west, below, and above. They are a place where the people came together to celebrate and renew their ties to the earth and sky. This is a sacred place; respect it when you enter.

The trail exits through the southern door onto the plaza once more and then crosses a row of rooms that enclosed the south end of the pueblo. This long, narrow row of single rooms is common on Chacoan pueblos and Morris discovered many Chacoan artifacts in these rooms but their construction using river stones is unusual, though there are flat sandstones and mud mortar as well. They were probably used for storage but some archaeologists believe there is a defensive element to them, though there does not seem to be much evidence for such a claim.

Why the people left this region where they had successfully farmed and thrived for more than two centuries is unknown, and even though many areas of the original Ancestral Puebloan territory were abandoned around the same time, being situated near the Animas River would have made for a much more stable water supply. Although the land was better than most other regions, by A.D. 1300, Aztec was deserted.

This concludes the tour of the West Ruins at Aztec.

ARCHAEOLOGY OF AZTEC

One of the earliest reports concerning Aztec was a geological paper by John S. Newberry in 1859 that described some visible walls at least 30 feet (9 m) high. The region was proving popular for settlers as it had a good water supply and fertile ground, the same reasons the ancient people had been drawn to this location several centuries earlier. By the 1870s widespread looting was occurring, which is when the holes were made in the north block where the trail goes today, and the ruins began to suffer damage. In 1889 the owner of the land, John R. Koontz, banned digging in an attempt to keep pot hunters away from the ruins, and when he sold out in 1907 to H. D. Abrams, the new owner continued the no-dig policy. When he agreed to let the American Museum excavate the site in 1916, Abrams insisted that some of the artifacts be housed on-site and not shipped back east, as was commonly happening at other digs.

Earl Morris was 27 when assigned the task of excavating the West Ruin at Aztec in 1916 and would prove to live up to the challenge. In four years, using mostly local farmers as hired help, he managed to open up and stabilize the massive ruins and to survey the nearby area, locating a much larger community of which the West Ruin is only a small part. Born in Chama, New Mexico, he became the first local archaeologist in the field of Southwestern archaeology. He also has the distinction of being the only archaeologist to reconstruct a great kiva, which was rebuilt between 1934 and 1936.

Among his many discoveries at Aztec were tens of thousands of beads, 200 bushels of corn, a large quantity of pottery, and numerous burials, including one of a 6-foot 2-inch man (188 cm)—the average height of an Ancestral Puebloan man was 5 foot 4 (162 cm)—wrapped in a turkey feather blanket with pottery, jewelry, and a shield.

Morris found what he believed to be two distinct occupation layers: the oldest, Chacoan; followed by a narrow layer of abandonment and a subsequent reoccupation by people from Mesa Verde, or the local San Juan region. However, some archaeologists dispute this theory and believe the site was continuously occupied with a period in which both bands occupied Aztec at the same time.

At this time, many questions remain concerning Aztec, as with most other ancient Pueblo sites, which await further excavations and study.

OUTLIERS AND GREAT HOUSES

The West Ruins of Aztec are part of a much larger complex near the Animas River that includes 37 buildings, 7 great houses, 13 great kivas, and a road system all within 2 miles (3.2 km). This is only what is known, as there are most likely still-undiscovered sites plus others that were destroyed over time. This collection of sites is known as an outlier community, a term connected to Chaco Canyon (see page 322).

An outlier community consists of several structures, both large and small, which share similarities to the sites in Chaco Canyon, such as the masonry, style of kivas, overall design, and roads. The masonry is core and veneer, whereby a thick wall is built with larger stones of various size in the center and smaller, flat stones placed in even rows on each side. The kivas are round with a low banquette and 8 pillars, sometimes lacking a *sipapu*, and are usually built into a square room within the room block. The design of Aztec is a south-facing U-shaped pueblo with a narrow row of rooms on the south side completely enclosing the plaza. And finally, there is a road that goes toward Chaco Canyon.

The term *great house* refers to a structure such as the West Ruins, a large complex

West wall, exterior, Aztec

that was preplanned, at least partially, before its construction, as is indicated by the tapered walls. These are wider at the bottom, tapering toward the top to support several stories, at the same time reducing the weight and materials required. These structures were described as *pueblos* since their discovery, but in recent times it has been changing to the use of *great house*, a term I find misleading.

These buildings, such as the West Ruin at Aztec and Pueblo Bonito, as well as several others in Chaco Canyon, were not houses and I feel the use of this term, which will continue, gives the impression of wealth and status by implying they are mansions built and occupied by an elite faction among the ancient Pueblo peoples, for which there is no evidence. These are villages that were built over many years, and in most cases, many centuries, which have the same characteristics as the unit pueblos when broken down into their smaller components.

This concludes the Day 12 of the Grand Circle Tour. The approximate timeline is: 30 minutes from Cortez to Lowry; 30 to 60 minutes at Lowry; 20 minutes from Lowry to the Anasazi Heritage Center; 1 to 1½ hours at the Heritage Center; 1 hour from the Heritage Center to Aztec; 1 to 1½ hours at Aztec; 20 minutes to Bloomfield (or Farmington).

◎ OTHER SITES NEAR CORTEZ/BLOOMFIELD

◎ Chimney Rock National Monument

This is a very unusual and spectacular site not too far from Cortez or Bloomfield. To get there from Cortez, follow US 160 east through Durango, 45 miles (72 km), and onward toward Pagosa Springs, turning onto CO 151, 40 miles (64 km) past Durango, on the right. The entrance road is a couple of miles along on the right. Before you arrive at the turn for CO 151 you will see the Chimney Rock formation on the right. There is also a very good view as you approach the visitors center.

From Bloomfield, New Mexico, follow US 64 east to NM 511, which is 3 miles (4.8 km) past Blanco. This scenic road follows the San Juan River crossing on the Navajo Dam. At Ignacio, turn right onto CO 172 to CO 151. The road to the visitors center is on the left and there are signs.

The site is open from May 15 to the end of September. Tours at 9:30 and 10:30 AM visit all sites, but 1 and 2 PM tours only go to the upper pueblo. A tour of the lower site is self-guided between 10:30 and 2:30. There is an entrance fee. The visitors center, a small log cabin beside the lower parking lot, has books and gifts for sale as well as an archaeological display. There are picnic tables and restrooms. Wear something red and you'll be surrounded by hummingbirds. The tour begins at the upper parking lot,

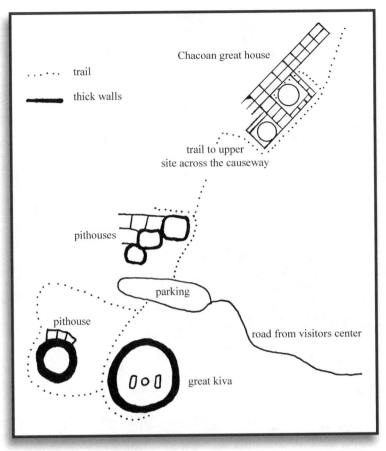

PLAN 27: Chimney Rock sites

a short drive up a steep road from the visitors center. There are three different areas to visit: The first is below the parking lot and has an **easy** trail that is paved and winds through the trees and past several ruins; the second is beside the parking lot on the opposite side (east) and is **easy**, steep but very short; the third is at the end of the causeway near the top of the mesa and is **difficult** (**very difficult** in the heat of summer), and consists of a gravel path that goes continuously uphill and is fairly steep. The guide generally stops at least twice to rest but temperatures do exceed 100°F (40°C) in the summer. The ridge is very narrow and the sides drop off steeply, so this trail is not recommended if you are afraid of heights.

The site is protected by the USDA Forest Service but is operated by the Chimney Rock Interpretive Association, and is run mostly by dedicated volunteers who give the tours and maintain the site. Without these services, the site would not be open to the

Chimney Rock

public. For more information, phone 970-883-5359 during the summer; in the winter, phone 970-731-7133, leave a message; www.chimneyrockco.org.

The area surrounding Chimney Rock was first occupied around A.D. 850, when people moved upriver from the San Juan. After A.D. 1000 there was a large population increase as more people came from the south. Eight areas have been identified, including the high mesa of Chimney Rock. One of the larger sites was on Peterson Mesa, to the west across the river. There are 16 sites on the high mesa, with around 100 rooms. There was no water on Chimney Rock and it had to be carried from an elevation of 600 feet (182 m) up to 1,000 feet (300 m). As evidence of this, a large number of pots for storing water have been discovered. The fields were also a long distance, but much sandstone was available for building, as well as pockets of clay, used to make mortar, and many trees on the mesa, used for beams. The people continued to build

pithouses well into the 11th century but placed thick stone walls on the surface rather than sinking them into the ground: A pithouse without the pit.

The mesa was first excavated in 1921 but was left exposed to the elements, which caused considerable damage. In 1968, excavations began again and the ruins were redug and stabilized by a crew of Navajo.

Chimney Rock is 300 feet (91 m) high and towers 1,000 feet (300 m) above the valley floor at an elevation of 7,600 feet (2,300 m). It is composed of sandstone known as Pictured Cliff.

Touring the Site

You may visit the upper site only with a guide, but the lower site may be visited on a self-guided tour. A free trail guide to this section is available on the website, www .chimneyrockco.org. In the first site to the west and below the upper parking lot is a

Three pithouses on the site above (east) the parking lot

great kiva that is 44 feet (13.4 m) in diameter, with a bench only along the north section, foot drums, a hearth, and 14 subfloor storage cists. There is no *sipapu* but not all
kivas have one, and this is particularly true for Chacoan-influenced designs. It is not
known whether there was a roof over the structure.

Near the great kiva is a pithouse that has some unusual aspects to it but is also
characteristic of this area. Because the soil is very thin here, the pithouses could not
be sunk into the ground but sit on the bedrock and have very thick stone foundation
walls that form the "pit" along with rectangular rooms attached on the north side. In
one of these north rooms are three grinding bins.

To the west of the pithouse is a stone basin, a nearly perfect circle carved into the
bedrock, about 10 to 12 inches (25–30 cm) in diameter and 3 to 4 inches (7–10 cm)
deep. The purpose of these basins is not understood, but there are several at Chaco
Canyon (see page 359) as well as other sites. One theory is that they have something
to do with astronomical observations, as the basin lines up perfectly with the north
wall of the Great House, the site on top of the mesa, at the summer solstice sunrise.
Whatever their purpose, they are another of the many anomalies that surround the
Ancestral Puebloans and raise questions about these wonderfully skilled and intelligent people.

The second site is above the parking lot and consists of three round rooms and
a few rectangular ones. The pithouse structures have extremely thick walls, like the
pithouses below the parking lot; in fact, they are thicker than anything else in the
southwest. The reason for this is unknown. The eastern room, on the right as you head
uphill, is the earliest and dates to around A.D. 950, while the other two are contempo-

rary and date to 1075. All three were two stories. The rooms in the northwest corner seem to have been common working areas for the three pithouses. If you look at the interior of the rooms you can see that they are not round, especially the center, and largest, one, but have rounded corners and almost straight walls in between. These structures, like so much at this site, are in many ways not typical Ancestral Puebloan buildings, though they follow the general patterns, perhaps adapting to the location.

From here to the last site is a long uphill hike across a narrow causeway with spectacular views all around, as there is nothing on either side to impede your vision. This site is the Great House Pueblo. It is very different from the lower structures but remarkably similar in construction to Chacoan outlier great houses (see page 311). It was built in two sections: the western end, around A.D. 1076, and the eastern and larger section, in about 1093. The outside walls were constructed first and then the interior space was divided into rooms. The walls were perfectly straight, the corners square. Small chinking stones fill in the gaps and the inside and outside walls were

East end of the Great House, kiva in the foreground

Detail of masonry, Great House

plastered. The kivas are constructed in a square room, a feature typical of Chacoan design. The north section, behind the kivas, was two stories. There were over 50 rooms and 2 kivas in total. In some places, the walls still stood over 14 feet (4.2 m) high in 1921 when first excavated. The east kiva, the bigger of the two, is a perfect circle and has a low banquette with eight pilasters, again typical of Chacoan kivas, and probably had a cribbed roof. The other kiva has a high banquette and most likely had a flat roof. Neither had a *sipapu*, a characteristic of nearly all the kivas in this region.

The western end is of poorer construction than the eastern side and was filled with refuse. These tend to be large buildings with an extensive number of rooms, but only some of the rooms were in use at any given time, a fact that distorts the image of these large structures as to their number of inhabitants.

Between the Great House and the twin towers is a place where extensive burning took place to signal other pueblos. In fact, it has been shown that a signal could, and still can, be sent from here via intermediate pueblos all the way to Chaco Canyon, connecting all the outliers. This is a distance of more than 90 miles (145 km). These sites were abandoned between A.D. 1130 and 1135.

Chimney Rock is an unusual and interesting site with wonderful views of the hills, valleys, and mountains that surround it and well worth the detour to visit.

The trail across the causeway, looking back down

day 13

Chaco Canyon National Historical Park New Mexico

- Established in 1907 as a national monument, 1980 as a national historic park
- 53 square miles (138 square km)
- Elevation: 6,000 to 7,000 feet (1,830–2,135 m)

Nearby Sites

◎ Pueblo Pintado
◎ Salmon Ruins

20. Chaco Canyon National Historical Park

GETTING THERE: From Bloomfield follow US 550 south (toward Albuquerque), about 43 miles (69 km) to the turnoff for Chaco Canyon on the right. There is a large sign for the park. This is CR 7900 and is paved. Stay on this road to the Y and then turn right, there is a sign for the park. This is CR 7950, though you probably will not see any signs. The first section is paved; then there are 17 miles (27 km) of dirt road, very rough, extremely dusty dirt road, unless it has rained recently and then it will be mud and most likely impassible, especially with a regular car. There are also several dry washes that you must drive through and which are prone to flash flooding. WARNING: They must never be crossed if any water is flowing in them. For road conditions, phone the visitors center 505-786-7014. It is 68 miles (109 km) from Bloomfield to the visitors center. **NOTE:** Do not turn at the Blanco Trading Post onto NM 57, as the park is no longer accessible from this road.

As you near the park, watch for Fajada Butte to rise out of the desert in front of you. When you are once again on paved surface road, you have entered the park, where all the roads are blacktop. You might want to check your fillings as the washboard section you have just passed through can be a truly bone-jarring ride. There are a couple of pullouts on the left if you want to stop and admire the view or take

Una Vida

pictures. The campground is on the right, near the canyon wall and the rangers' dwellings. The canyon runs east–west with Fajada Butte at its eastern entrance. The road bears to the right in a long curve; the visitors center is on the right. This is the most difficult of all the Grand Circle Tour main sites to get to, but also one of the three most important archaeological areas in the Southwest, the others being Mesa Verde and Hovenweep.

THINGS YOU NEED TO KNOW: The official name is the Chaco Culture National Historical Park, which I refer to simply as Chaco. The park is open from 7 AM to sunset year-round. The visitors center is open from 8 AM to 5 PM except on Thanksgiving Day, Christmas Day, and New Year's Day. There is an entrance fee. Stop at the visitors center first to pay your entrance fee and receive a sticker to place on the windshield of your vehicle. There is a campground in the park. **NOTE:** No food, lodging, gas, or any other services are available in the park. The visitors center has water and restrooms. There are also pit toilets at some of the sites. Bring lunch as it takes a full day to see the main sites. For more information, phone 505-786-7014; visit www.nps.gov/chcu; or write to Chaco Culture National Historic Park, P.O. Box 220, Nageezi, New Mexico, 87037-0220.

As you travel the 25 miles (40 km) from the main highway to Chaco Canyon, observe the landscape. What do you see? No towns, no houses, no trees, no vegetation, no water. Few live in this region today, but during Ancestral Puebloan times, the population was between 6,000 and 12,000, and the climate, rainfall, and general environment were not that much different from what you find there today.

The time period of the Bonito Phase is A.D. 920 to 1130 and covers P II and P III. P III began 50 years earlier in Chaco Canyon than it did anywhere else for the Ancestral Puebloans, and waned 100 years earlier. The great houses, such as Pueblo Bonito and Una Vida, were begun as early as A.D. 850 and built along a 7-mile -long (11.2-kilometer-long) canyon. Extensive irrigation systems utilized runoff from the cliffs by means of ditches, dams, and canals. By A.D. 1020, the Chacoans were on their way to creating the greatest pre-European society north of Mexico, excelling in architecture, pottery, jewelry production, astronomy, road construction, and agriculture. The peak of their culture was A.D. 1055 to 1083 and the most intensive building period.

Around A.D. 1140, the Chaco culture collapsed. First, the outliers were abandoned, followed by the canyon sites. The reasons are not known but the amount of rain did diminish about this time and, as the population had continued to expand for 200 years and the residents had cut down nearly all of the trees in the vicinity, it appears that the number of people had exceeded the resources. The canyon was briefly reoccupied from A.D. 1250 until 1300, probably by people from Mesa Verde, before being finally abandoned permanently.

I include a timeline for Chaco as it differs from the standard Pecos chronology that applies to the other branches of the Ancestral Puebloans.

Late BM III	A.D. 600–700	Shallow pithouses
Early P I	700–800	Deep pithouses
P I	800–850	Aboveground slab stone houses
Early Bonito	850–1020	First great houses (Bonito, Una Vida), small houses
Early Classic Bonito	1020–1050	Hungo Pavi, Chetro Ketl
Classic Bonito	1050–1070	Pueblo del Arroyo, Pueblo Pintado
Late Classic Bonito	1070–1125	Great houses remodeled and enlarged
McElmo	1070–1150	Mesa Verdean style construction, Kin Kletso
Late Bonito	1120–1200	No new construction
	1200–1250	Abandoned
Mesa Verde	1250–1300	Reoccupation, some remodeling
	1300–	Abandoned permanently

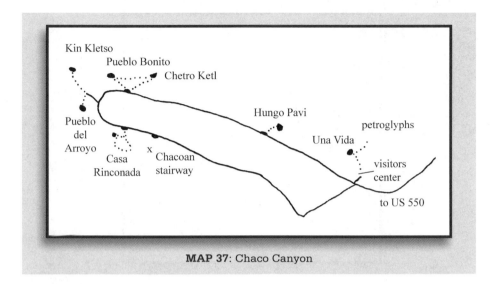

MAP 37: Chaco Canyon

TOURING CHACO

Chaco Canyon is one of the easier sites to visit, even though it is large with much to see, as the ruins lie close to the loop road and most of the trails are level and short. The tour begins with Una Vida and some petroglyphs, then Pueblo Bonito and Chetro Ketl in the morning, followed by Pueblo del Arroyo, Kin Kletso, and the Casa Rinconada sites in the afternoon.

Una Vida

The first site to visit is Una Vida (Spanish for "one life"), which is behind the visitors center on a short, **easy** trail. This site has not been excavated, just stabilized, and gives you a good idea of what all the ruins once looked like in Chaco before any excavations. As you approach the site, the trail divides and becomes a loop. Go to the left at the division. This is near the southeast corner of the great house, which had approximately 100 ground-floor rooms and 6 kivas, plus an unknown number of rooms on the second and probably third floors. The pueblo is L-shaped with one section north–south, directly in front of you, and the other east–west, ahead and to the left. A narrow row of rooms connected the two ends of the room blocks and enclosed the plaza. Some of the walls are dry laid, which means no mud mortar was used, indicating they were built much later in the A.D. 1800s by scavenging stones from the original walls. These sections were constructed by either Navajo or Hispanic shepherds as temporary housing when they brought their flocks into the canyon for winter grazing.

As you enter the plaza, past marker 2, you can see the layout of the pueblo with

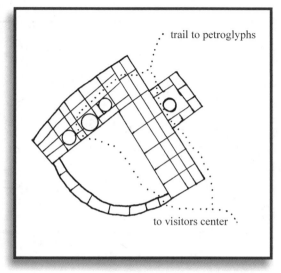

PLAN 28: Una Vida

the room blocks to your right and straight ahead and, sweeping around you and to the left, the single row of rooms enclosing the plaza. The depression to your left is a great kiva. At marker 4 in the north central section is an example of Chacoan masonry. This is the core and veneer style, which has a rubble center with cut stones on the outside. The style of facing changed over time, see pages 330 and 331 for examples. These changing styles are used to date the construction of each phase of a site along with the use of dendrochronology. Una Vida dates from around A.D. 850 to 1100 and was one of the first large structures in the canyon, along with Pueblo Bonito. The walls are wider at the bottom than at the top, to support several stories, and this is indicative of a preplanned structure.

At marker 5 you are outside the pueblo again and at the northeast corner. To your right is a bump-out on the back of the eastern wing that seems to have enclosed a small plaza with a kiva. The trail divides at this point, with the right branch returning to the visitors center, and the left going to the petroglyphs. There are several interesting images at the end of this trail (see photograph, left) but the climb up to

Petroglyphs near Una Vida

them is **difficult**. **CAUTION:** The petroglyphs are viewed by walking along a narrow ledge partway up the canyon wall.

If you go to the petroglyphs, return by the same trail to marker 5 and then continue back to the visitors center.

Exit the parking lot and turn right onto the one-way loop road through the park to the next site, Pueblo Bonito. A short distance from the visitors center is Hungo Pavi, another unexcavated ruin. This is not on the Grand Circle Tour but can be included or visited instead of Una Vida, especially if you do not plan to go to the petroglyphs, so I will briefly describe the site.

◎ A SITE NEAR UNA VIDA

◎ Hungo Pavi

(the meaning of this name is unknown) is seen along a short, **easy** trail from the parking area next to the main road. The great house is U-shaped and has an enclosing wall on the south of the plaza built in a semicircle. There are over 70 rooms, 2 kivas on the ground floor, plus a second and probably a third story. The site dates from around A.D. 950 to 1050. At the division in the trail, turn right. You are walking over the west side, which brings you into the plaza. There is a depression on the right, which is a great kiva, and you see the standing remains to the left, stretching down to the east section. The trail continues across the plaza past some open rooms, crosses the east wing and brings you to the northeast corner where the long north wall is still visible. Also from this point, if the lighting is just right, you can see a stairway carved into the cliff face over a little to the right. The stairway is not accessible.

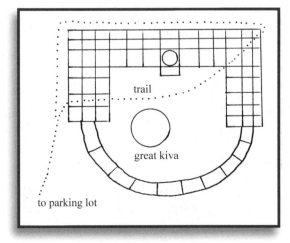

PLAN 29: Hungo Pavi

North wall, Hungo Pavi

Continue along the north wall. This long wall is another characteristic of Chacoan structures (see Aztec Monument, page 305, and Chetro Ketl, page 347). This site will not be excavated in the foreseeable future, as the role of the national parks today is to preserve rather than dig. There are several reasons for this, including the expense to excavate and preserve the structures afterward, as well as the politics of the region to-day. Many of the Pueblo do not want any excavations on these sites as they consider this a desecration of their ancestral homes and believe that everything should be left to decay and return to Mother Earth. For more on this topic, see page 424.

Return to the parking lot and continue along the loop road to the next stop, which is for both Pueblo Bonito and Chetro Ketl.

Pueblo Bonito

(Spanish for "beautiful town") is without a doubt the most impressive archaeological site in the Southwest. The largest completely (or nearly so) excavated Chacoan ruin was comprised of 800 rooms, 37 kivas, and 3 great kivas of which as many as 600 rooms were in use at one time. It is estimated over 1 million stones were used in the veneer faces alone, with countless others for the rubble fill, plus more than 15,000 large wooden beams, all the smaller trees, and the immeasurable amount of mortar. Most of the trees were cut between 40 and 60 miles (64 and 96 km) from here. Bonito is only one of 12 great houses in the immediate area.

Bonito was constructed and renovated over a period from A.D. 850 to the early 1200s in at least four stages, but there would have been continual maintenance during this time. I will briefly discuss these stages but remember that not all archaeologists agree with the time periods for the stages, nor that there were only four.

Bonito I. The earliest part is in the north section (see Plan 30) and was semicircular in shape and built in three separate sections on a north–south axis. Several kivas and one great kiva were built in the typical unit pueblo design. The Chacoans used type I masonry (see top photograph, next page), which consists of widely spaced stones placed in a lot of mortar. It was three stories in parts and the rooms were 6½ feet (2 m) high, which was much larger than the norm at the time. The layout was asymmetrical. This construction dates from the A.D. 820s to the 950s. An interesting point about these earliest rooms is that this is where almost all of the burials were discovered, as well as a large part of the artifacts, including pottery from the early to late periods. In the early 700s, a Ponderosa pine was growing in the west court near where the south rooms would eventually be. It is thought that this tree was sacred, which could have been one of the reasons the pueblo was built in this location.

Bonito II. Type II masonry (see bottom photograph, next page) was employed in this construction, which consisted of a long arc of 30 single-wide rooms four stories high that encircled the original room blocks and can be seen along the back (north)

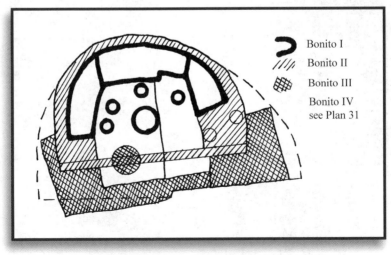

Bonito I
Bonito II
Bonito III
Bonito IV
see Plan 31

PLAN 30: Pueblo Bonito construction stages

Top: Type I masonry; Bottom: Type II masonry

Top: Type III masonry; Bottom: Type IV masonry

side next to the trail. There was a balcony on the exterior. The rooms were only accessible from the outside, with no entrances from the Bonito I rooms. It is thought that these rooms were buttressing for the older section, as the type I masonry is not very strong. The Chacoans also added rooms along the front (south), enclosing the plaza by connecting both ends of this new arc forming the classic D-shape, built great kiva Q (marker 9), and raised the plaza with fill. This addition dates to the A.D. 1040s.

Bonito III. Both the east and west sides were extended southward and many kivas were built, especially in the east block. The rooms across the south were filled in and new ones were constructed, joining the new extensions to create a form very similar to what is visible today. Another great kiva was built in the west plaza next to the south rooms, and a dividing wall was placed through the plaza. This construction dates from 1050 to 1070. Possibly an ominous event occurred during this time, as this is when the Ponderosa pine died.

Bonito IV. This was the most intensive construction and remodeling period and lasted from A.D. 1070 to the early 1100s (see Plan 31). The great kiva in the west plaza near the south rooms was filled in and another was built in the southeastern corner of the east plaza. The latter is known as kiva A (marker 10) and bears many similarities to the reconstructed great kiva at Aztec. New rooms were built across the south end and each side, giving the structure the shape you see today. Much of the older north section and many lower-floor rooms were no longer used. The builders tore down and then rebuilt most of the southeast section, reusing much of the stone and beams for the new construction. This is where activities were now focused.

In the late 1100s and first half of the 1200s, most of the rooms were no longer used, except for the kivas. New kivas built during this time exhibit Mesa Verdean characteristics and there is a shift from a majority of Chacoan pottery to a mixture of Chacoan/Mesa Verdean and finally almost all Mesa Verdean. The row of rooms dividing the plazas was also constructed at this time. It is thought that most Chacoans abandoned the area after 1150, as people from Mesa Verde moved in, at first living together with the Chacoans and then completely occupying the great houses.

There is still much debate about Bonito and the Chacoans in general after more than a century of study; in fact, there are more questions than answers. There are three main theories, all of which have many points con and few pro: First, that Bonito was a center of trade, controlling a vast territory in the San Juan region and connected to the canyon by roads; second, that the canyon was a major religious center and controlled the region with its priests, and there were huge pilgrimages into the sites; third, that the people were farmers, as were all other Ancestral Puebloans. Each will be discussed further on page 360.

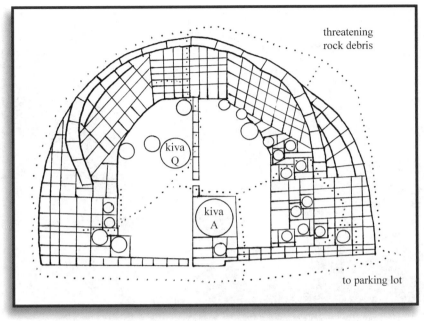

threatening
rock debris

kiva
Q

kiva
A

to parking lot

PLAN 31: Pueblo Bonito

Touring Pueblo Bonito

This is the largest of the great houses and the only one that has been completely excavated and stabilized, which makes visiting the site a rewarding experience. From the parking lot on the right side of the road are two trails, and both **easy**. The one to the left goes to Bonito; the one on the right, to Chetro Ketl. I will begin with Bonito. Plan on spending between an hour or two there.

You approach Bonito at the southeast corner. The trail goes counterclockwise along the east exterior, then climbs some steps and crosses the debris of Threatening Rock, follows the north wall, turns south through the northern section and into the west plaza, and crosses the east plaza into and through the southeast part, exiting near the southeast corner where you began.

At this first stop, the walls overwhelm, as they still rise to the third story with massive thickness and beautiful masonry. To the left is the south wall in two sections at differing angles (more about this later), and the east wall to the right disappears under the rubble of Threatening Rock. Even as a ruin this structure is impressive.

As you walk beside the east wall, notice the veneer finish of the masonry, which would have been hidden under adobe, giving the structure a much different appearance. Which type is this stonework? (If you said type IV, you get an A. So what is the

Pueblo Bonito, southeast corner

date?) The small holes in the exterior wall are for ventilation, but the ones in the interior are doorways. Continue along the trail to the large pile of rubble. To the right are some mounds that stretch to the east and north and are the remains of the Hillside Ruins and date to the later period, the mid-1100s to 1250. A few excavations have been done in this area, but for the most part, the site is known from subsurface imaging (see page 422). There are many rooms and kivas in a long, narrow structure that seems to have been connected to Bonito. Its function remains unknown. (The park's guidebook to Chaco states that one mound is a great house, but this is doubtful). At the bottom of the cliff in front of Threatening Rock, when it was still standing, were raised platforms of clay and rubble surrounded by retaining walls that were believed to have been built to support the rock and prevent its collapsing. New theories suggest the walls were not structural but probably part of a religious structure. Most of these remains are now under the rubble.

At marker 2 are the remains of Threatening Rock, which collapsed in January 1941, destroying around 30 rooms in the northeast section of Bonito. Interestingly, the first building, Bonito I, was within range of this rock, so the people were well aware of the dangers when they chose the site. The massive hunk of rock was approximately 100 feet (30 m) high by 150 feet (45 m) long and 35 feet (10.5 m) thick, weighing over

30,000 tons (27,000 mt). The Chacoans had placed prayer sticks in the space between the rock and cliff so as to prevent the collapse, a tactic which seems to have worked, as archaeologists removed them in December 1940 and it fell the very next month. Coincidence? (The National Park Service states that it was a particularly rainy winter and this was the cause of the collapse, but I'm not so sure.) Of course, one benefit of its collapse is a raised platform from which there is a wonderful view out over the ruins.

The trail winds through and over the broken remains of Threatening Rock and branches off on a short side trail to an overlook of Bonito at marker 4. As you look out at the ruins, the east wing and plaza are straight ahead and the west wing and plaza are to the right. You can see the many rooms and kivas and also get an appreciation for the size of Bonito. Across the canyon and slightly to the right is South Gap, the only opening in the south wall of Chaco Canyon. Continue along the main trail to marker 5 (photograph, page 336). This is a cross-section of the core and veneer walls that illustrates the skill of the masons and the great number of stones used in construction. This wall is from Bonito II, which sweeps around the exterior of the Bonito I room blocks. The wall is wide at the bottom to support several stories and tapers toward the top to reduce both weight and material. This is a second-story room.

The trail follows the north wall past this unusual arcing construction that consists of 30-plus rooms lengthwise, four stories in height but just one room wide. There are

Chacoan masonry

no connecting doorways to the interior rooms or the plaza and the only access was from the exterior, where you are now. A balcony protruded above the ground-floor rooms, another similarity to the great houses. Many of the rooms had narrow platforms the width of the room and midway between floor and ceiling, a feature also found in several other rooms throughout the structure. They could have been for storage or even sleeping platforms, but their purpose is unknown at this time.

You now enter the north section, where a path branches to the right into the oldest part of the site, Bonito I. This segment had around 100 rooms over 3 stories and 5 kivas. The type I masonry can be seen at the end of the side trail. This masonry required more maintenance and was not as strong as succeeding types, which could be why they built those rooms around the outside, for support. Other types of masonry are visible as this section had numerous remodels over time. The trail is directly over where the northern burials were located. **CAUTION:** The trail now goes past several open kivas, and there are no barriers around them, and they are deep.

Exit the north room block and enter the east plaza, where you have a good view of this large, open space. There are several open kivas in and around the plazas but you must imagine these covered with flat roofs that made the space even larger. The rooms around the outside would have been three and four stories high, except on the south, where they were only one story, enclosing the plazas forming a secluded space. At marker 9 is kiva Q, the oldest great kiva at Bonito.

The trail goes over the central row of rooms which separates the plazas and past kiva Q which is in the west plaza. Straight along the central row of rooms, on the west side, is where the original, and only, entrance was and beside this was the location of the Ponderosa pine. There was another great kiva in the south of this plaza but it was filled in during the Bonito IV remodeling and there is no trace of it now. The path crosses the west plaza toward the west wing and branches off to the right in front of the five rooms where most of the western burials were found. It continues into the southwest corner through some of the last construction at the pueblo. Return to the plaza and turn right, following the room block around to the southeast corner. This is where the original entrance was into the pueblo. It was 7 feet (2.1 m) wide originally but was later reduced to 3 feet (0.9 m) and finally sealed up completely, most likely in a closing ceremony when Bonito was abandoned.

Return to the trail and cross into the east plaza to marker 10. This is great kiva A and is similar to the reconstructed kiva at Aztec (see page 308) and also the great kiva at Lowry (see page 295). It has a northern entrance, raised stone hearth, cists on either side of the hearth, bases for four posts, a low banquette around the interior, and niches in the wall. Although the top is even with the plaza now, it probably rose above the ground when built.

Great kiva A, north entrance top right

The opening you can see in the south wall to the left of Kiva A, where the trail exits, is modern, originally there was no entrance from the outside into this plaza. Before continuing on the trail, walk to the north of the plaza, where there are several kivas and a good view of the architecture in the standing walls. Imagine the walls intact, rising from one story in front of you to four stories at the back and covered with reddish adobe gleaming in the sun, wrapping around the plaza like embracing arms. This would have been a wondrous place, and remains so.

Return to the trail that enters the east wing. Between this point and the exit are two sets of stairs, one up and the other down, and several low, narrow doorways to crawl through, so anyone with mobility problems should avoid this section and exit by the opening south of great kiva A (marker 10). Also, at the beginning, the trail goes along side some open kivas, so use caution.

The rooms in this section were rebuilt during the Bonito IV period after the previous ones had been torn down. Notice how high the ceilings are and the large size of the rooms, a characteristic difference between Chacoan structures and other Ancestral Puebloan buildings. Some of the ground-floor rooms have been partially backfilled to preserve original floors, so the ceilings appear lower for the first floor. In some rooms, the remains of the beam construction can be seen protruding from the walls. The large beams, called vigas, are the main support and were primarily of pine, spruce, or fir. On top of these were placed perpendicularly the latillas which were juniper or willow, and finally small branches, brush, and a coating of mud to complete the ceiling/floor.

At marker 13 there is a corner door in the second-story room, another feature of Chacoan construction. This is an architectural element that is difficult to incorporate and requires a great deal of skill as it reduces the strength of the corners in the building. The ends of the vigas are visible in this room and the line of small holes along the side walls are where the latillas were placed. The function of a room is partly determined by what is found in it when excavated; hearths indicate a living room; manos and metates, a food-preparation room. Lower interior rooms such as this were probably for storage as they were dark and had no ventilation. Many of the rooms at Bonito had few or no artifacts so their purpose is unknown. Rooms like this add to the mystery and lead to more questions about Bonito and the people who inhabited it.

As you continue through this part, notice the corners of the rooms. If the masonry is continuous, they were all built at the same time, but, if the stones of one wall abut those of the other, then this is a later addition. Archaeologists use this to assist in determining the construction sequence. Also look for the outline of door-

North section from the east plaza

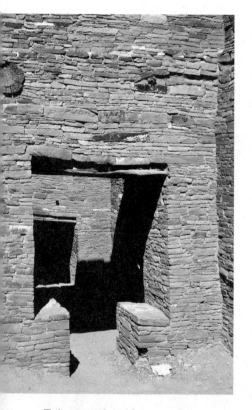

T door, marker 16

Corner door, marker 18

ways that have been filled in with stone, a possible indication that the function of a room changed. At marker 16 is a T-shaped door, a type used at many other sites and believed by some archaeologists to have originated in Chaco Canyon. The reason the Ancestral Puebloans built doors in this shape is not known but there is speculation that they may have been symbolic, though there is no evidence of that. In the room with marker 17 are original vigas and latillas in place. Samples were taken from the vigas for dendrochronological dating (see page 423) and if you see a small round plug with a number on it, this is an original beam. Taking these samples does not damage the beam. At marker 18 there is another corner door in the second story and the ends of the vigas and latillas are visible.

You exit the structure near the southeast corner where the trail begins. Turn right and follow the southern wall to the opposite corner. To the left, in front of Bonito, are the remains of two mounds divided by a road that led across the canyon to the great kiva of Casa Rinconada, directly to the south. At first it was thought these mounds were middens, trash dumps, but upon more investigation it has been discovered that they were purposely built structures surrounded by masonry retaining walls filled with sand and debris and paved on top with clay. There were also steps up the 10-foot-high (3-meter-high) mounds. It is now believed they had a religious or ceremonial function as others have been found, including the aforementioned mound in front of Threatening Rock. Another mystery surrounding Chaco Canyon.

As you walk along the exterior of the south wall you will notice that it is in two sections at differing angles. It is not known why it was built this way but one theory suggests an astronomical connection. The eastern section is in line with sunset at the spring and fall equinoxes, and if you sight along the western section toward the west, the sun sets there several days before the fall equinox, a fact used in some modern Pueblos to announce and prepare for the ceremonies at the equinox. If you sight along the western section toward the east the sunrise at the equinoxes is observed. Of course, there is no evidence the Chacoans built the walls for this reason, but if not, it is an interesting coincidence. Continue along the trail past the south wall and around the west side if you wish to walk around the entire structure.

Exterior, south wall

This ends the tour of Pueblo Bonito, one of the most fascinating ruins in the southwest and one that raises many questions about the people who built and used this structure. Allow between 1 and 2 hours to visit and appreciate Bonito.

Return to the parking lot by the same trail. There are pit toilets beside the parking lot. The next site on the grand Circle Tour is Chetro Ketl.

Chetro Ketl

(whose meaning is unknown) is the second -largest great house in Chaco Canyon but the largest in square footage and is only ½ mile (0.8 km) southeast of Pueblo Bonito. It contained around 400 to 500 rooms, at least 12 kivas, and 2 great kivas. Counts vary as the site has only been partially excavated. The ruins have been dated by us- ing dendrochronology from over 300 samples (see page 423), producing one of the most accurately dated sites in the canyon. It was built in 15 major construction phases between A.D. 1010 and 1117 and abandoned shortly after this last date. The structure is U-shaped, with a single row of rooms arcing across the south side, connecting the east and west wings. Chetro Ketl was built and remodeled many times over a period of a century or about three generations. The site was partially excavated by Edgar Hewett's field school students in 1920 to 1921 and again from 1929 to 1934.

From the parking lot, follow the **easy** trail on the right to the ruins. You enter the site along the southern end of the mostly unexcavated west section. A branch trail on

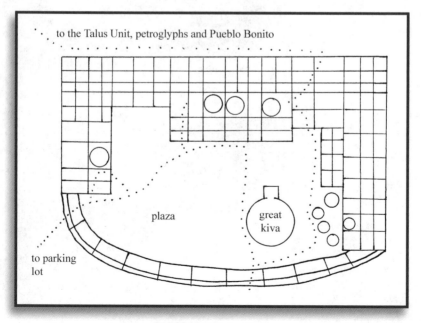

PLAN 32: Chetro Ketl

Great kiva, looking north

the left leads to a kiva and rejoins the main trail at the southeast corner of the west side. In front of you is the large open plaza that was not divided as at Bonito. An interesting fact about this plaza is that the ground level was raised 12 feet (3.6 m) above the surrounding terrain to literally elevate the site and probably make it appear even more impressive.

Continue along the trail toward the north central section to the point where the trail branches off, again on the left. To the right near the center of the plaza lies a great kiva that has been backfilled. The branch trail leads to marker 2 and the oldest section of the pueblo. Behind protective glass are the remains of some plastered and painted walls. This is a second-story room and was the level to which the plaza was raised. Return to the main trail in front of the south wall. This is an unusual and unique wall because of the pillars that are clearly apparent. Originally, the low wall had several square posts built on it, behind which was a long, narrow open-air room, but

Colonnade

the spaces were filled shortly after construction, and the interior divided into smaller rooms and a roof added. You can see that the pillars are part of the wall and the fill stones in the spaces were separate (see photograph, above right). This colonnade was built around A.D. 1087. Some archaeologists suggest a Mesoamerican influence on Chacoan architecture because of this element, but, while it is true that colonnades were employed in Mesoamerican buildings, they were not constructed on low walls as here. And the presence of only one element does not lend itself to a very strong case for outside influence. This seems more of an experiment in architecture, one that did not last long or catch on.

Past the colonnade is a broken section of walls that reveals the masonry. If you have been to Bonito, you can see the same technique employed here and also at the other great houses. The trail now goes past the great kiva. The same features are

Detail, colonnade

Stone disks and stone lined post hole, great kiva

present as you will find at Bonito or Aztec Monument: northern entry through an antechamber, a raised stone hearth, floor cists on each side of the hearth, four bases for
the supporting posts, a low banquette around the interior, and wall niches. The kiva is
60 feet (18.2 m) in diameter and 14 feet (4.2 m) below the plaza. The round sandstone
disks placed under the posts (see photo above) are 3 feet (0.9 m) in diameter; there
are several on the floor of the kiva, next to the post holes. Four disks were placed below each post, under which were two alternating layers of adobe and lignite, and at
the bottom, a circle of sand with a leather pouch that contained turquoise dust. The
great kiva was built over a previously existing kiva and was part of the many remodels
of Chetro Ketl.

Past the kiva, the trail crosses the southern row of rooms. This one-story section
arced around from the east to west wings, enclosing the plaza. There were plastered
walls and ventilation holes, indicating that the rooms were roofed, but their use is unknown. Outside these rooms, and attached to them, were two walls about 2 feet (0.6
m) apart and 7 feet (2.1 m) high, running the entire length of the southern rooms. As
the plaza was built up these single rooms would become retaining walls, as probably
was this exterior double wall. The trail continues along the southeast section and past
several kivas.

You now enter the northern section and come to three kivas aligned east–west and called Kiva Complex G. There was extensive remodeling in this area, with at least six previous kivas in or near the same spot as the one at marker 8. You can see the elevated position of the kiva, which sat inside square walls on the second-story level. Similar kivas are found at Aztec Monument, where the rooms are built up around the kiva to give the sense that they are set belowground. There are also some tower kivas in Chaco; these are multistoried round rooms that may or may not have been separated by floors and are rare.

Past marker 9 you have a good view down the interior of the north wall toward the west and can see the many room divisions and the great length of the complex. The trail exits the structure on the north. Look to the right toward the end of the canyon. This entire area was fields watered by an extensive irrigation system. Smaller structures were built against the canyon wall behind Chetro Ketl, utilizing the side of the canyon as a back wall. The many round holes in the canyon wall are where the ends of the wooden beams were attached. To the left is the 500-foot-long (152-meter-long) north wall, an exquisite example of Chacoan masonry. There are no doors on the ground floor but there was a balcony along the second and third stories with doors that allowed access to the exterior, the same as the northern exterior at Bonito. The

Raised kiva, Kiva Complex G

Talus Unit, altar, east side

balconies are gone now, their wood used for firewood and modern construction, but you can see where they were attached to the wall in the notch just above where the vigas protruded through the wall.

The trail continues along the wall and past the pueblo, then turns toward the cliff to the Talus Unit. The name is from the talus slope, an accumulation of debris that sheds off the cliff face and is common along the bottom of most canyon walls throughout the Southwest. But notice that there is not much debris at present because it was used in the construction of the great houses and is absent from Chetro Ketl west to Pueblo del Arroyo.

The Talus Unit is in two sections connected by a single room. The eastern section, the first you will come to, is later than the other, larger site and had eight ground-floor rooms and two kivas. A very unusual room in this unit is on the left side directly behind marker 12. The front room led into a second through a wide doorway and three steps with a low dividing wall on each side, and seems to have been roofless. Directly behind and higher up the cliff wall is a series of hand- and toeholds carved into the sandstone, which would be reached by a ladder from this room. It is thought that this room was connected to the road system as some sort of altar. There are no other instances of this type of architecture.

The larger unit to the west, left, had around 30 rooms in two stories and 5 kivas built on an elevated terrace, probably to level the ground, which is a common feature in Ancestral Puebloan architecture. This room block exhibits typical unit pueblo construction.

From the Talus Unit you can return to the parking lot—turn left by marker 12—or continue along the bottom of the cliff to Pueblo Bonito and then back to the road from there. Several petroglyphs line the canyon wall between the two great houses and you can see them beside the trail. Some are difficult to spot, so keep searching the rock face as you walk.

This concludes the tour of Chetro Ketl and it should be around lunchtime, so if you have packed lunch and want to sit at a table to eat, and have running water to wash up, follow the loop road back to the visitors center. If you did not bring any food, it is going to be a long day, as there is none available in the park or between the park and the main highway.

Pueblo del Arroyo

(Spanish for "village by the wash") is another great house that shares many of the characteristics of the others, but there are also a few differences: There is no great kiva, the pueblo does not face south, and a tri-wall structure is connected to the exterior of the west wall. The pueblo is U-shaped and has a curving row of rooms enclosing the plaza. This is on the east side instead of the south, orienting the structure

The tri-wall structure, Pueblo del Arroyo

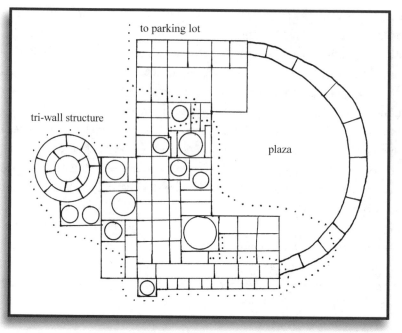

PLAN 33: Pueblo del Arroyo

toward the east, but the reason is unknown. The ruins date from the mid A.D. 1000s to the early 1100s and have evidence of Chacoan and Mesa Verdean construction. This pueblo was one of the last built in the canyon and the only one that is not against the cliffs but in a flood-prone area. There were nearly 300 rooms and 12 kivas, and it is the fourth-largest great house. It was excavated from 1923 to 1926 by Neil Judd.

The site is located at the western end of the loop road, on a two-way spur road to the right. The trail is short and **easy** around the ruins. This parking lot is also the trailhead that goes to Kin Kletso, the next site on the Grand Circle Tour.

From the parking lot you approach the northwest corner and follow the west wall past the unexcavated mounds of the northern section, on the left. You will see both Chacoan and Mesa Verdean–style masonry, which used larger stones without the small chinking stones in the cracks. The trail turns to the right and comes to the tri-wall structure at marker 2. There are three concentric ring walls. The two outside rows are divided into separate rooms with the central circle undivided and most likely a kiva. It was two stories and had between 70 and 80 rooms. This structure dates to A.D. 1109 and was possibly built by people from Mesa Verde, as the tri-wall form is more prevalent in the northern San Juan region (see page 305). Its purpose is unknown.

The trail goes around the tri-wall building toward the southwest corner, but between markers 3 and 4 are two kivas connected to the side of the tri-wall. There had been rooms here that were torn down to build the kivas, and prior to this, two kivas were filled in to build the rooms. Although some suggest that these great houses were preplanned, and the large tapering walls certainly were, the overall structure is the result of many remodels during the occupation of these pueblos, rather than a master plan. At marker 4 you have a good view of the massive walls and multiple floors that were common to all great houses.

Around the corner and along the south wall, a series of small rooms were built in the later style of masonry. Originally these were buttresses for the south wall behind them, which is a 100-foot-long (30.5-meter-long) room that Judd excavated. It seems that the wall began to tilt outward during construction, thus the need for the buttresses. This room is unusual even by Chacoan standards, where much larger rooms are common, but there are no others like this. It also shows that even the highly skilled Ancestral Puebloan masons made mistakes, occasionally. Perhaps this was another

Interior, south wing

experiment akin to the colonnade at Chetro Ketl. You can see the T-shaped doorways on the second floor and a groove where a balcony was, the same as along the north wall at Chetro Ketl.

At marker 6, the southeast corner of the southern wing, a trail branches to the left into the room block. This is some of the late Chacoan construction and you can see many rooms and a kiva. This area gives one a good idea of the construction with exposed cross sections of walls, the notches for the ceilings, and even a partially intact ceiling, illustrating how the vigas and latillas were placed (see photograph, page 351).

Return to the main trail to marker 10. This is on top of the enclosing rooms; in front of you is the plaza. The trail enters the plaza and follows the north side of the south wing. There is a door that can be entered but it is a tight squeeze. Veering to the right along the front of the west section is a long, narrow room between the kiva and plaza where the skeletons of three scarlet macaws were found. This species is not native to the Southwest but was imported from southern Mexico and highly prized for its beautiful feathers.

The kiva to the right of marker 13 is Mesa Verdean in style and is from the later period of remodeling in the A.D. 1100s. Compare this to the one on the left, which is Chacoan (see page 426 for a comparison). A side trail goes straight to marker 14 in the oldest section of the structure that dates to the mid- to late 1000s. The room on the right has several grinding bins with manos and metates and was remodeled in the early 1100s.

Mesa Verdean kiva, marker 13

Mesa Verdean masonry, Pueblo del Arroyo, west side, beside the trail

The trail exits through the unexcavated north section. Turn right to return to the parking lot. The next site is Kin Kletso.

Kin Kletso

(Navajo for "yellow house") is about ¼ mile (0.4 km) past Pueblo del Arroyo down an **easy** trail. Kin Kletso is a McElmo structure that was built between A.D. 1075 and 1130 in two square units. The western part is the earliest followed shortly after by the eastern. There were around 130 rooms and 5 kivas. The two northern rows of rooms were three stories high; the remainder, two stories. Two of the kivas, one in each end, are Chacoan, and the other two in the east end are Mesa Verdean, which is from the last construction at the site. The other kiva in the west end is a tower kiva that is two stories high with a hearth in the floor and ground level T-shaped door on the east. The Chacoan kivas are built in the second story on top of fill in the ground floor.

The McElmo period is late in the occupation of Chaco Canyon and the last before the abandonment of the area. This is when people originating from both Chaco and the Northern San Juan region coexisted in the canyon. The period is characterized by key-hole kivas, large stone masonry, smaller rooms, and the square unit construction without an open plaza or enclosing wall. It is also when the tri-wall structures were built.

You approach the ruins at the southeast corner and the trail circles around the site. Turn right. In the extended room on the east end is one of the last kivas built, a

South side looking east, Kin Kletso

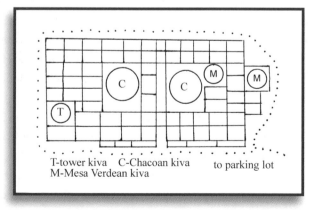

T-tower kiva   C-Chacoan kiva   to parking lot
M-Mesa Verdean kiva

PLAN 34: Kin Kletso

keyhole design. Along the back side, the wall closest to the cliff, is a double row of rooms that was three stories high. Around the corner on the west end and one room back from the south side is the tower kiva that went from the ground to the top of the second story. Only a few of these have been discovered. Why they were built is unknown; there might be a connection with the towers in Mesa Verde and Hovenweep, as they were built by the same band.

Along the front, or south, side there are a row of small rooms that extend partway and a gap where the two sections are joined. To the left is the older and larger west unit. The impressive workmanship is visible in these later buildings, but they are much smaller than the great houses. It was first believed that the canyon had been abandoned by the Chacoans before the Mesa Verdeans arrived, but sites such as this illustrate the two peoples lived and worked together for a short period of time before everyone left the canyon by the mid- to late 1100s.

Return to the parking lot the same way and drive back to the loop road, turn right, and continue to the next stop at the Casa Rinconada community. The parking lot is on the right.

Casa Rinconada

(Spanish for "house within a corner") In this part of the canyon south of Chaco Wash are the ruins of the "small houses" as opposed to the great houses on the north side. Three units have been excavated near the great kiva that is set on a sandstone ridge to the west. Each of the small houses had from 10 to 50 rooms of one or two stories, plus kivas. It is estimated the population was around 300 in 50 pueblos that would be larger than any of the great houses except Pueblo Bonito and Chetro Ketl. The masonry is not of the same high quality as at the great houses and, when first discovered, these units were believed to have been earlier than the great houses. It was thought that the people moved from the small houses to the great houses, but it is now known that the two were in fact contemporary. There is another small house community to the east, near Fajada Butte, but it has not been excavated. These three units were excavated from 1936 to 1947 by the University of New Mexico.

The parking lot is a short distance past the road to Pueblo del Arroyo and on the right. An **easy** trail goes around the three pueblos and great kiva. The trail goes straight to the unit known by its excavation number, Bc50. (**NOTE:** The term "Bc" has nothing to do with a date.) As you walk toward the ruins, notice the mounds scattered around the canyon floor; these are other small house sites that have not been excavated.

The first site had 26 ground-floor rooms and 4 kivas. The ruins you see date from

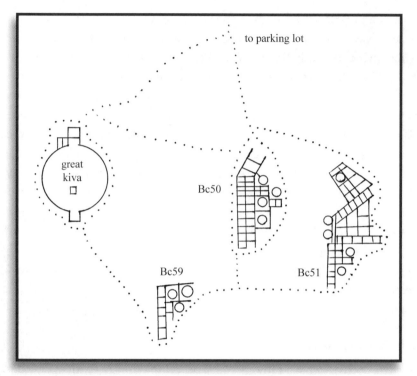

PLAN 35: Casa Rinconada small house sites and great kiva

A.D. 1050 and were some of the last remodeling at the site. These structures were built over older remains, including a pithouse village, and were continually changed over time. There was also a pithouse village under the west plaza of Pueblo Bonito, indicating the people continued to live in the same locations over time. Some of the walls are only single course, which is not found in the great houses and are indicative of a single story. Walk counterclockwise around the site. The west side contains a double row of rooms running north–south and the kivas are on the east side, which is not the way pueblos were usually oriented. In fact, none of the three sites follows the standard pattern of a pueblo.

Follow the trail past the kivas and turn right toward the larger ruins, site Bc51. This pueblo had around 45 rooms and 6 kivas. The site was also remodeled several times during its occupation and has a strange shape and orientation. Again the room blocks are north–south, but some of the kivas are to the south with others in the north and west. Their layout defies what we consider the unit pueblo construction. The trail goes south along the east side. At marker 6 is a backfilled keyhole kiva, indicating that the Mesa Verdeans lived in the small house sites as well as the great houses.

The trail continues to site Bc59, which had around 20 rooms and 5 kivas (see photo page 361). The orientation of this village is similar to the first one, Bc50. At marker 9 are the remains of three kivas built one on top of another over a period of time, showing that they were constantly being changed (see photograph page 410). The oldest kiva is at the bottom; and the latest, from around A.D. 1050, is at the top. At the south end of the pueblo the trail branches off to the left and goes onto the South Mesa on the **KIN KLIZHIN TRAIL.** Walking along any of the longer back country trails requires a free permit from the visitors center. More on these trails follows.

Continue to the right toward the great kiva. The great kiva is 63 feet (19.2 m) in diameter inside and is the largest in Chaco Canyon and one of the largest in the Southwest. It has two entrances: a single room on the south and several on the north, the usual entrance for great kivas. The north door is T-shaped, there is a low banquette around the interior and a second one on the east side, a raised stone hearth with cists on each side, and four stone-lined post holes. The kiva is on a north–south axis. Two unusual features are a tunnel under the floor from the north antechamber, leading

Site Bc51

toward the west side of the interior, which was 3 feet (0.9 m) square and 39 feet (11.9 m) long, and the other is a double spiral stone-lined ditch around the northwest post by the end of the tunnel. The tunnel was probably used in ceremonies where a figure would suddenly emerge from the floor, perhaps as a representation of the emergence through the *sipapu*. The spiral stone design is unique and its purpose unknown. What you see exposed is the second kiva, which was built over an earlier; this remodeling filled in and covered the tunnel. There are 34 niches in the wall and an altar in one of the northern rooms.

As you walk back toward the parking lot there are two mounds, one on each side of the trail. These are unexcavated small house villages. From the parking lot turn right on the loop road and drive a short distance to a pullout on the right. There is a stairway visible at this stop that was carved into the canyon wall, one of several stairs leading into Chaco Canyon. If the sun is overhead you will have a good view of it, which is to the right a bit looking toward the canyon wall.

This ends the tour of Chaco Canyon. The approximate timeline is: 1½ hours from Bloomfield to the visitors center; 30 minutes for Una Vida and the petroglyphs; Pueblo Bonito, 1 to 2 hours; Chetro Ketl 30 minutes; Pueblo del Arroyo 30 to 45 minutes; Kin Kletso 30 minutes; Casa Rinconada ½ to 1 hour; 1½ hours return to Bloomfield.

The great kiva, Casa Rinconada. The tunnel is seen below the T door, the hearth is at the lower left

OTHER SITES IN CHACO CANYON

There are several other great houses in and around the canyon but none of them has been excavated. They are along or at the end of hiking trails, most of which are long, and all require a free permit that you can obtain at the visitors center, where you will be given information about the trail conditions, distance, and time to complete.

The **PUEBLO ALTO TRAIL** skirts the mesa along the north cliff face and provides wonderful views of the canyon and ruins, especially Pueblo Bonito. The trail begins behind Kin Kletso and a permit is required. The first section that climbs the canyon wall is **difficult** but then it levels out and is **easy**. The first part of the trail, and I use this term loosely, ascends through a cleft in the wall and climbs up and over rock fall (see photograph, right), is narrow in places, being less than 2 feet (0.6 m) wide; some steps are high and there are loose rocks.

The Pueblo Alto Trail to the mesa

Oh, and beware of rattlesnakes. Once on top you must watch carefully for the rock cairns, as they are hard to follow in places. Along the trail are some stone circles as well as basins, both marked with signs. These basins are perfect circles carved into the bedrock and are thought to have been connected to astronomy, but their use is unknown. Basins are found at other sites, including Chimney Rock (see page 316).

From on the mesa you can see the canyon east to Fajada Butte with a bird's-eye view of Pueblo Bonito and other ruins toward the south. This is the only place to appreciate the size and location of Bonito, short of flying over the canyon. You can also see the relationship of the sites to one another, which is more difficult while you are in the canyon. It will take about an hour or more to hike from the parking lot to the viewpoint of Pueblo Bonito and back, but it is well worth the effort. The other two trails are the Casa Chiquita and Wijiji. To hike them all would take about 2 days.

THE CHACO PHENOMENON

Over the past century of studying Chaco Canyon, a differing picture has emerged of the people and culture compared to other Ancestral Puebloan communities, but this picture is still very fuzzy and confused, with many unanswered questions and conflicting theories. However, it is generally agreed that what happened over 1,000 years ago is of such a magnitude as to be referred to as the "Chaco Phenomenon."

The great houses. These structures are characterized by their overall size, large rooms with high ceilings, enclosed plazas, a D-shape floor plan, masonry, and great kivas. But even with these differences there are also similarities to the standard Ancestral Puebloan structures, including a north–south axis; south facing; many smaller kin kivas; multiple stories; and the construction techniques. Some have suggested a Mesoamerican influence and/or presence at Chaco, but the underlying architecture is definitely Ancestral Puebloan and evidence of outside influence is extremely weak at best.

The small houses. These are located mostly on the south side of the canyon and include the community around Casa Rinconada and most likely the Talus Unit near Chetro Ketl, as well as the building east of Pueblo Bonito. These pueblos consist of small, individual units of rooms and kivas that were probably part of a larger connected village and were contemporary with the great houses.

The outliers. These are structures built in a manner similar to that of the great houses in Chaco Canyon but they lie outside the canyon, in some cases, a great distance from Chaco. Outliers include Aztec, Salmon Ruins, and Chimney Rock to the north and Casamero to the south, plus many others in all directions. Some of these, such as Aztec, are considered great houses as they have all the architectural elements found at Pueblo Bonito or Chetro Ketl. However, others, such as Chimney Rock, have some similarities, including preplanning, tapered walls, masonry, and in-room kivas, but are much smaller and do not have an enclosed plaza. These should be considered Chacoan-influenced, or -built, but not great houses, which term implies something different. Their connection to Chaco is not understood.

The burials. One problem that emerged early on in the excavations at Chaco was a lack of burials. Even though population estimates for the canyon and surrounding areas go as high as 12,000, only around 135 burials were discovered at Pueblo Bonito, and about the same number in the small house community of Casa Rinconada. It was customary to bury the remains in middens or under rooms, and if there was a cemetery, it has not been discovered, so where were the inhabitants buried? The common theory is that the cemetery has not been found yet, or that it was washed away by flooding from Chaco Wash. It could also be that for some unknown reason, this

Site Bc59, Casa Rinconada

place was different and most bodies simply were not buried here but transported elsewhere. The lack of burials has lead to small population estimates, some as low as 70, for Pueblo Bonito.

The majority of burials at Pueblo Bonito had tremendous amounts of funerary goods, including turquoise, pottery, shells, prayer sticks, jet, arrowheads, worked bone, baskets, and copper bells. The quantity and luxury of these objects are rare outside of Bonito.

The burials occur in two separate areas of Pueblo Bonito, but coincidentally both are in the original part of the pueblo, the northern section which had the richest burials, and the western section. It appears that the people in each section were related to one another but not to the people in the other section. The remains from the north were connected to the small house settlement near Fajada Butte, whereas the people buried in the west were related to people from the Casa Rinconada unit. This shows that the great house communities were not separate but part of, or an extension of, the small house villages, at least in the case of Pueblo Bonito.

The roads. Much has been made of the extensive road system which seems to radiate out of Chaco in all directions and connect the canyon to the outliers. These roads range from 6½ feet (2 m) to 33 feet (10 m) wide, and in places the ground was

leveled by cutting down hills or filling gullies. They are straight and have embank-
ments of rough stone, masonry walls, or berms along some sections. Steps were cut
into or formed with adobe in canyon walls, but this occurs mostly in Chaco Canyon.
Some connect the great houses to outliers; others, to quarries, and still others seemingly lead nowhere.

There is much controversy about the road system. Why would a people without
the wheel or animal transport build roads? But the answer is not as straightforward
as some suggest. The roads are wide, but only where they are close to a great house
or kiva, and then narrow quickly as they spread out into the desert. They are not continuous but were built in short, broken sections no more than 1¼ to 1¾ miles (2 to
3 km) in length, not the 31 miles (50 km) ascribed to the north road from Chaco to
Salmon. Given that the Chacoans did not need roads and that the roads themselves
do not seem to have been constructed for practicality, it comes back to the question
of *why*. Perhaps the purpose is not in the final product but in the construction; that
is, they were a symbol of something and their use was incidental. Given the evidence
of the importance of astronomical knowledge to the Ancestral Puebloans, the roads
might be a representation of the star system. Or they may relate to religious beliefs
about the arrival and/or departure from this level (Mother Earth) to the world below.
Perhaps the answer lies not so much in the destination as in the journey.

The culture. There are only two major differences in the culture of the Chacoans
as compared to other bands of Ancestral Puebloans. They differ in the amount and
type of funerary goods from the burials in Pueblo Bonito and in the size of the architecture.

In almost all cases of burials throughout the Colorado Plateau, few goods were
placed in the graves, the one exception being at the grave of one woman at Dominguez Ruin, beside the Anasazi Heritage Center Museum (see page 297). But the remains from Pueblo Bonito were interred with both a large quantity and a high quality
of goods. This usually signifies a high status in life and goes against the view of the
Ancestral Puebloans as a society without rulers or an elite. Much has been made of
the fact that this implies a hierarchy in Chaco, probably based on a kinship priest-
hood; but for any of the large sites, such as the Far View community in Mesa Verde,
there would have to be someone in charge, as simple human nature soon leads to
chaos if no leader is present. This does not mean that there were "rulers" in the sense
of those of today's world, but for the structures in Chaco Canyon to have been built
and maintained, I believe a hierarchy was necessary, as at the other large Ancestral
Puebloan sites.

Given the amount of religious objects, it seems natural that the leaders were priests or priestesses, or more likely both, and that the Chaco community grew and prospered because of their abilities and knowledge of this and the other world. As the prosperity of the canyon increased over time, more people would be drawn to the region and the leaders, probably kin based, would illustrate their power and/or control and/or understanding of nature and the gods by building and enlarging the great houses, improving the irrigation system, performing numerous ceremonies and building the "roads." The society would still be agriculturally based, as were all other Ancestral Puebloans, but held together by a personality or cult embodied in the families at the top of the hierarchy.

Religious beliefs also explain the reason that so much broken pottery from various sources is found in and around the canyon. People would come here, or be sent by their pueblos, to take part in the ceremonies in hopes of gaining some of whatever it was that helped the Chacoans to prosper. This does not imply large-scale pilgrimages into Chaco, for which there is no tradition among the Pueblo, but only the movement of a small number of people at differing times of the year. It seems that most of the goods were coming into the canyon with few going out, which does not imply trade but an end use at Chaco. There is also no tradition of large-scale trade among the modern Pueblo.

Whatever took place in Chaco Canyon a millennium ago, it was one of those events in history where all the elements come together at the same time and place to create—what shall I call it—a phenomenon. This was, and is, Chaco Canyon.

THE ARCHAEOLOGY OF CHACO CANYON

There is some evidence of Paleo-Indians in the Canyon from 10,000 years ago, as well as Archaic finds from 4,000 years ago. During BM II there was some farming, along with hunting and gathering. By BM III, around A.D. 490, there was a small permanent population in pithouse villages. The first aboveground rooms date to P I, A.D. 700 to 900, and at this time the development was similar to that of other areas in the Southwest.

In the A.D. 900s, the people began to enlarge some pueblos and there were large amounts of pottery and turquoise. There was tremendous growth in the mid-1000s and the population was at its peak between 1100 and 1130. From 1130 to 1180 there was an extended period of drought and the last construction dates to around 1132; the canyon was abandoned by 1150. In the mid-1200s there was a reoccupation by Mesa Verdeans before it was abandoned permanently around 1300.

The Spanish military traveled through the canyon in the mid-17th century and Chaco is on a map from 1774. The first written accounts come from the 1800s. In 1849,

James H. Simpson and illustrator Richard Kerns passed through, wrote about, and drew the ruins. These were the same two who left inscriptions at El Morro (see page 15). In 1877, photographer William Henry Jackson mapped and photographed the sites in Chaco. He found the stairway east of Chetro Ketl that today bears his name. He took 400 pictures but, unfortunately, he was using a new, experimental film and not one of his images turned out—a great tragedy. The honor of producing the first images of the Canyon goes to Victor Mindeleff of the Smithsonian Institute in 1888.

Richard Wetherill (see page 285) arrived at the canyon in 1895 after being forced out of Mesa Verde. The following year he received the financial support of the Hyde brothers, Talbot and Frederick, wealthy businessmen from the east. F. W. Putnam from the American Museum of Natural History at Harvard was appointed director and George Pepper, a 23-year-old graduate student, was made field director of what became known as the Hyde Exploring Expeditions. Richard Wetherill was the foreman in charge of a Navajo and Zuni crew but, as Putnam was rarely at the site and Pepper had no field experience, Wetherill ended up running the dig. He also set up a trading post in the canyon.

The expedition dug out over 200 rooms and kivas in Pueblo Bonito and discovered several burials in the northern section. The men found more than 10,000 pot sherds, 5,000 lithics, 1,000 pieces of bone and wood, 50,000 pieces of turquoise, copper bells, prayer sticks, sandals, and preserved cloth. There was no way to date the site at the time and they soon came under pressure to stop the dig, due to reports that they were only looting the ruins to send artifacts back east. The excavations lasted from 1896 to 1901.

What was done in Chaco led to pressure to pass the Antiquities Act in 1906 to preserve archaeological sites and prevent "excavations" like the Hydes' and especially the removal of finds out of the Southwest. The Hydes did eventually donate their collection to the American Museum. Richard Wetherill was killed not far from the canyon in an altercation with a Navajo in 1910 and is buried, along with his wife, just west of Pueblo Bonito.

In 1907, Chaco Canyon was made a national monument and in 1916 came under the control of the newly formed National Park Service.

The National Geographic Society chose Neil Judd, an experienced archaeologist, to lead its sponsored excavations in the 1920s. He began in 1921 and worked for the next seven years at Pueblo Bonito and Pueblo del Arroyo in the first professional dig at Chaco. Judd mapped the building sequence by the changes in masonry and used the newly introduced field of tree ring dating, known as dendrochronology (see page 423), to establish the first dates for the site. He discovered the western burials at Bonito, as well as the road system. An account of his work is recorded in a series of articles published in *National Geographic* during the 1920s, which still make for fascinating reading.

Judd was followed by Edgar Hewett, who taught anthropology at the University of New Mexico and set up a field school to train students in archaeological excavation at Chaco in 1929 after the National Geographic Society team had left. He focused on Chetro Ketl, which became the most accurately dated site in the canyon due to the abundance of in situ beams. Over 300 samples were dated by using dendrochronology. He also dug on the south side of Chaco Wash, excavating the great kiva and small house sites of Casa Rinconada.

In 1933, Gordon Vivian, one of Hewett's archaeologists, was hired by the National Park Service to stabilize the ruins. He used a Navajo crew who were excellent craftsmen at this profession and continue to be employed for this task. One thing he was not able to do was prevent Threatening Rock from collapsing in 1941, destroying between 30 and 70 rooms in the northeast section of Pueblo Bonito.

The Park Service excavated Kin Kletso in 1951 and built the visitors center and ranger housing in 1957. It teamed up with the University of New Mexico in 1971 to form the Chaco Center for the continuing study of Chaco Canyon. The center's first task was a survey of the entire canyon system, which had never been done before. More than 2,200 sites were recorded, and the center also excavated several areas. In 1980, the park was expanded to its present boundaries to enclose additional sites. Studies of the Chaco Phenomenon continue, as does stabilization, but there are no ongoing excavations.

◎ OTHER SITES NEAR CHACO CANYON

◎ Pueblo Pintado

GETTING THERE: From Bloomfield, follow US 550 south to the exit for Chaco Canyon. At the junction with CR 7950 for Chaco Canyon, stay straight instead of turning right toward Chaco and continue on this dirt road for about 18 miles (29 km). The road is rough and similar to the dirt section to Chaco. When you reach the paved road at the T, this is the town of Pueblo Pintado. Turn right and watch for the water tower on the right. Just past the tower, turn right onto the road by the school. This goes to the ruins but there are no signs. The road curves left and then right before heading out of town. Look for the ruins on a ridge to the left. About a mile (1.6 km) out there is a short road on the left that leads to the site. This road is impassable if wet; and when dry, is very rough with some ruts. Drive slowly.

From Chaco Canyon, turn right at the end of CR 7950 instead of left toward US 550 and follow the above directions.

You can also reach the ruins from the south on a paved route from I-40. From Grants, take I-40 west to exit 79 and turn right. At the lights, turn left onto the divided highway and then right at the junction with NM 605 toward San Mateo. Stay on NM 605 for 13 miles (21 km) and then turn left onto NM 509 north. It is 35 miles (56 km) to the junction with CR 9, turn right, and go another 15 miles (24 km) to Pueblo Pintado (Spanish for "painted town"). Once in town, watch for the water tower—it will be on the left as you come from this direction—and follow the above directions to the site.

The site is open year-round and there is no entrance fee. There are some services in the nearby town of Pueblo Pintado but nothing at the ruins. For more information or to check road conditions, phone 505-786-7014 (the visitors center in Chaco Canyon).

Pueblo Pintado is an unexcavated great house at the eastern extremity of Chaco Canyon that is still an impressive ruin, with some walls rising three stories from its position on a ridge overlooking a great expanse of desert. It lies 3 miles (4.8 km) east of

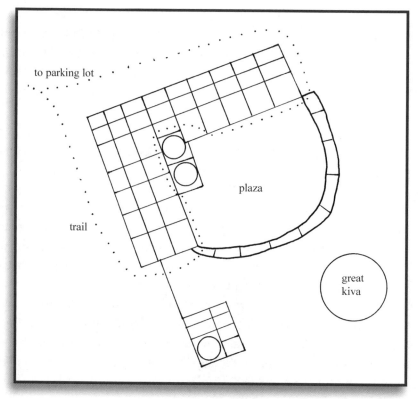

PLAN 36: Pueblo Pintado

North exterior

the entrance to Chaco Canyon and 16 miles (25.7 km) from Pueblo Bonito and was the first large structure one would encounter traveling from the east toward Bonito. This remained true into later times, as both the Spanish and Americans passed by Pintado on their travels west. Simpson and Kerns were the first to record and draw the ruins on their journey to Chaco and beyond.

There were around 60 ground-floor rooms and more than 130 rooms overall in three or four stories, plus 4 kivas in the room blocks and 15 in the plaza and a great kiva south of the plaza, outside the southern enclosing wall of rooms. The pueblo is L-shaped with rooms on the north and west sides and an enclosing row of rooms to the south and east. The northern wall is 200 feet (61 m) long and the western wall is 150 feet (45.7 m) long. There is also an unusual mound in the plaza that appears to be an L-shaped room block but as it has not been excavated, what it is remains a mystery. This might be why the great kiva is outside the plaza, as there would not have been room inside.

The earliest structures are from the late A.D. 800s and early 900s, but the great house was built between A.D. 1060 and 1100. Several small house sites surround the great house, and a road leads to the west. There was more rainfall here than in Chaco Canyon, which could be the reason for establishing the great house, as the people expanded the farmland with population growth. One problem, however, is a shorter growing season, due to the pueblo's higher elevation.

Touring Pueblo Pintado

There is no formal trail but a narrow path winds around and through the site. Do not walk on the walls or the rubble of collapsed walls, as rattlesnakes like this rubble. **CAUTION:** Some open rooms and kivas are deep. Do not pick up or collect any pieces of pottery or stone.

There is a fence surrounding the site, with a gate beside the parking area. As you approach the pueblo at the northwest corner, the ruins are striking even in their present state. The path follows along the west wall toward the south where the interior walls are exposed, illustrating their thickness and the masonry. The small holes in the walls are for the ends of the latillas, and the notch held the floor. As was typical of great houses, there were no doors in the exterior wall on the ground floor and there was only an entrance or two into the plaza.

Past the end of the west wing is another set of rooms that was separate from the great house and consisted of several rooms and a kiva in an almost square building. There was a narrow wall between this structure and the main pueblo, where the path crosses through to the interior of the pueblo. Ahead of you are some remains of the enclosing rooms on the south; to the right is a depression a short distance from these rooms; this is a great kiva. Where the path goes into the plaza by the southeast corner

West exterior

West interior looking north

of the west wing might have been one of the original entrances into the plaza, with another on the east side.

The path goes through the west side, where you can see the large size of the rooms and how the building was constructed. There are two kivas in the corner of the L; one has been partially cleared and stabilized. The plaza stretches out from this corner and you can see the mound where the enclosing rooms are, as well as the depressions of several kivas, possibly as many as 15. It is more difficult to make out the mound of the L-shaped rooms. You also see many piles of rubble from the fallen walls. If you examine them closely, notice what nice building blocks they make with very little work, as the sandstone flakes off in thin slices almost ready to use. Look at some to see whether you can distinguish the worked edges from what is natural (see photograph page 429). Past the enclosure toward the east are some ruins, but their function and relationship to the pueblo are unknown.

The trail goes around the eastern end of the north section and back toward the gate, following along the exterior of the north wall. This ends the tour of Pueblo Pintado. Although this site is not excavated it is still a wonderful experience to see the ruins and their location in the landscape. You should allow a half day for travel and visiting the pueblo.

◎ Salmon Ruins

GETTING THERE: Salmon Ruins is located on the western edge of Bloomfield, heading toward Farmington, on the south side of US 64. If you are coming from Bloomfield, it is a left turn across two lanes of traffic and the site is tricky to find as it appears suddenly on a small rise. Watch for signs.

At the visitors center you'll find a museum and research library, picnic tables, and restrooms. There is an entrance fee to see the ruins. The site is open from 8 AM to 5 PM Monday to Friday and 9 to 5 on weekends. It is closed Sunday mornings during the winter, as well as Thanksgiving Day, Christmas Day, and New Year's Day. For more information, phone 505-632-2013; visit www.salmonruins.com; or write to Salmon Ruins Museum and Research Library, 6131 US 64, P.O. Box 125, Bloomfield, New Mexico, 87413.

Salmon is a Chacoan outlier about 30 miles (48 km) directly north of Chaco Canyon and 12 miles (19 km) south of Aztec Monument. The earliest construction, on the east side, dates to A.D. 1068 to 1072, but the main building period is between 1088 and 1095, a very short time span for such a large structure. It is believed that residents from Chaco came, or were sent, here, possibly to relieve population pressures in the canyon, which accounts for the quick construction. It was not occupied too long after completion, as they abandoned the pueblo around 1150. As at Chaco, the site was reoccupied by Mesa Verdeans about 1200 and abandoned permanently around 1270.

The great house is in a U-shape facing south. There is no enclosing row of rooms as we find with most great house construction. The north wall is 400 feet (122 m) long,

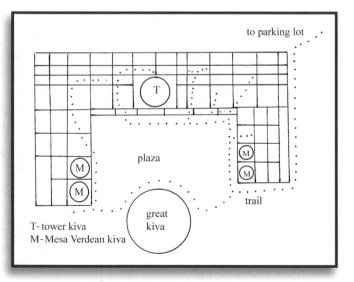

PLAN 37: Salmon

Great kiva, entrance and antechamber top

the east side is 160 (48.7 m) feet, and the west side 180 (55 m) feet. There were over 300 rooms in three stories, several kivas, one great kiva, and a tower kiva. The population is estimated at 200 to 300.

The great kiva is 46 feet (14 m) in diameter, with an antechamber and entrance on the north, and was remodeled. The tower kiva was two stories and located in the north section in a direct north–south alignment with the great kiva. In A.D. 1250 a fire destroyed the tower kiva in which 16 children and 4 adults were killed. Another more devastating fire in 1270 burned a large portion of the pueblo and probably led to its final abandonment. Several small sites have been located in the surrounding area. Salmon Ruins was excavated by Cynthia Irwin-Williams between 1972 and 1978.

Touring Salmon

When you enter the visitors center to pay the entrance fee, on the right you will find a museum that has a collection of artifacts discovered at the site. The display is set around the outside of a large, circular room with temporary exhibitions in the center. Beyond a bookstore and gift shop on the left is the research library. The library contains all the excavation notes and records for Salmon, along with other material, and is open to anyone, but research can only be done on-site as nothing may be borrowed.

From the museum you can walk to the ruins down a short, paved path, out the door to the left of the counter. The path is steep and winding, so be careful not to slip, and remember, you must walk back up the same way. There is also a paved road down to the lower parking lot but it is narrow, winding, and steep, only wide enough for one vehicle. The road is to the right of the visitors center. You can park next to the ruins and the flat, **easy** trail that goes around the site. Picnic tables are located beside each parking lot.

The trail approaches the ruins at the northeast corner, where you can see the length of the north and east exterior walls and the Chacoan core and veneer masonry. You will find examples of later Mesa Verdean stonework in other areas of the ruins. At the south end of the east wing, marker 2, is a long, narrow room that is rare but similar to, though shorter than, the southern room at Pueblo del Arroyo in Chaco Canyon (see page 351). An infant burial in a painted pot was discovered in the room. The room's use is unknown. Burials were found in the next room also, at marker 3.

The kiva behind marker 5 is Mesa Verdean and was built in a square Chacoan room. This type of remodel is typical of Mesa Verdean occupation and is seen in Chaco

Mesa Verdean kiva, marker 6

North interior, tower kiva at top

Canyon great houses and at Aztec Monument. You are now at the western corner of the east wing and can see the plaza and great kiva to the left and the shape of the pueblo to your right. The trail divides at this point. Turn right and then right again into the east wing.

Another kiva at marker 6 is from the Mesa Verdean occupation and has the remains of some original beams. Pictographs of human and abstract figures were found on the walls of the kiva, and some miniature pottery on the floor. The room by marker 7 was used for trash by both the Chacoans and Mesa Verdeans, a common use of lower rooms. This room has been backfilled.

The typically large room at marker 8 is one of seven that ran east–west along the front of the north section and are believed to have been for ceremonial use. The row of narrow rooms in front of these were added later. The trail branches into the narrow front rooms and then there is a kiva added into one of the large square rooms directly behind, again a Mesa Verdean kiva. The narrow front rooms are similar to those at Chetro Ketl behind the square pillars (see page 343). The trail returns to the plaza and then branches right going back into the north section.

East wing, top, north, in the foreground

The evidence points to a third story along the north row of rooms, which is common for these structures. The room at marker 11 showed signs of burning and then reuse as a midden and burial site, indicating the damage was caused by the fire in A.D. 1250 that burned the nearby tower kiva. The row of narrow rooms by marker 12 goes across the north section, abutting against the tower kiva to the left in front of you. The second room from the plaza, to your far left, had a small window for solar observations and an altar in one corner. The large, square room on your left is part of the row spanning the original front, but in this one, the remains of an unbuilt kiva foundation were discovered with the same diameter as the tower kiva just west of it.

The trail returns to the plaza, goes past the tower kiva, and turns right past two large rooms. Both seemed to have been one story, the first having a roof; the back one, an awning of branches. Their use is unknown but the second room may have been used for solar observations. The trail branches to the right past these rooms and goes to the tower kiva.

Tower kivas are rare; there are only four in Chaco Canyon. They are similar to kin kivas but are at least two stories high and bear a resemblance to towers found throughout the Northern San Juan area. However, the tower kiva is always inside the structure and not freestanding or connected to other kivas. It also has the typical features of a kiva, including a ventilation shaft, hearth, and deflector stone. These elements are not found in the more numerous "nonkiva" towers, such as those in Hovenweep (see page 218). Notice the cists on each side of the hearth, an element found in great kivas. A large foundation was built from cobblestones rather than sandstone to support the weight of the 6½-foot-thick (2-meter-thick) walls that were 13 feet (4 m) high. For additional structural support, six stone and wooden buttresses surround the tower. A stone effigy was discovered in this kiva and is on display at the museum. The tower kiva is Chacoan in design.

The trail continues through the north section toward the west, past several narrow rooms that make up the second row from the back that spans the entire length of the pueblo. These rooms were remodeled during the Mesa Verdean occupation and contained large amounts of trash when excavated, as well as several burials. The room on the left had three sets of remains, two adults, and one child, buried with bows and arrows and various types of pottery. The last two rooms along this section were also remodeled and used for corn storage and grinding. A large quantity of corn was destroyed when the pueblo burned.

The trail turns left into the mostly unexcavated west wing. If you have the printed guide from the museum and look at the room numbers, you will notice that they are

Interior, tower kiva

Ramada, Heritage Park

decreasing and go to one at the southern end of the west wing. The reason for this is that the rooms were numbered in sequential order as they were excavated. Thus room 1 is the first discovered and dug out, followed by room 2, and so on. This system only reflects the excavations and has nothing to do with the purpose of, or in what order, the rooms were built.

Only a small portion of the west wing has been excavated but it is probably similar to the east side. At the southern end are two excavated kivas from the reoccupation set in original square rooms. From this point, the trail crosses the plaza to the great kiva. This kiva is not in the center of the plaza but is in a north–south line with the tower kiva. At other great houses, the great kivas are generally not in the center of the plazas. There is an antechamber on the north with steps down into the kiva, a central hearth, low bench around the interior, four bases for roof support posts, and a *sipapu*, an unusual feature in a Chacoan kiva. The great kiva and tower kiva are the only Chacoan kivas discovered here; all the others are Mesa Verdean. The trail goes back to the south side of the east wing where you began. From this point, retrace your steps to the parking lot.

On the other side of the lower parking lot is the restored homestead house of George P. Salmon and beyond this are several examples of various styles of Native American housing from the local region. There are signs for each type of structure. This area is called Heritage Park.

The ramada is a branch-covered wooden structure that was used for shade and was the first kind of aboveground "room" built by the Ancestral Puebloans. The Navajo hogan uses a cribbed roof that is similar to the cribbing over Ancestral Puebloan kivas. There is a possibility that the Navajo learned agriculture and some construction techniques from the Ancestral Puebloans. Originally it was thought that the Navajo came into the Southwest long after the Ancestral Puebloans had left but there is growing evidence they were contemporaries for as many as two or three centuries.

There is an example of the wickiup used by the Jicarilla Apache and others, including the Paiute in southwestern Utah and northwestern Arizona. They also have a partially constructed section of jacal that shows how the posts and mortar were started. And finally there is a pithouse that may be entered, and some underground storage pits behind the pithouse. Depending on the time of year you visit, you may see corn growing in the waffle garden. This is a good illustration of Native American culture and worth walking the short, **easy** path to see.

There are picnic tables beside the lower parking lot, but check for a hornet nest under the awning before sitting down.

This ends the visit to sites near Chaco Canyon.

Example of jacal construction technique, Heritage Park

day 14

Coronado State
Historic Site
New Mexico

■ Established March 7, 1935, as a state
monument to interpret and preserve
the ruins of the pueblo of Kuaua

Nearby Sites

◎ Jemez State Historic Site
◎ Petroglyph
National Monument
◎ Albuquerque

21. Coronado State Historic Site

GETTING THERE: From Bloomfield, follow highway US 550 south toward Albu-querque for around 160 miles (260 km) or 3 hours. The site is located on the edge of Bernalillo, a suburb of Albuquerque. Driving south the ruins are on the left, just past the red light. Watch for the Wendy's restaurant on the right at this intersection. A short road, Kuaua Road, leads to the site, which you cannot see from the highway.

THINGS YOU NEED TO KNOW: Coronado is open daily from 8:30 AM to 5 PM. **NOTE:** The site is closed on Tuesdays, Thanksgiving Day, Christmas Day, New Year's Day, and Easter. There are restrooms and picnic tables at the site and all services are available in Bernalillo, less than a mile (1.6 km) away. There is an entrance fee. For more information, phone 505-867-5351; visit www.nmmonuments.org/coronado; or write to Coronado State Historic Site, 485 Kuaua Rd., Bernalillo, NM 87004.

Kuaua Pueblo was excavated in the 1930s by Edgar Hewett and Gordon Vivian and partially reconstructed. There were some pithouses found nearby dated to A.D. 600, but the ruins are from the P IV period, after A.D. 1300. This was the time when the Ancestral Puebloans were leaving the regions to the west and north and congregat-ing into much larger sites along the Rio Grande. There were over 1,200 rooms exca-vated at Kuaua, built in three connected sections, each with its own plaza. Many more rooms lie unexcavated. The south section is the oldest, having been constructed in

West room block

the early A.D. 1300s but it burned around 1350 and was rebuilt. The pueblo was then abandoned from 1400 to around 1475 after which the north and east sections were added. It was abandoned permanently in the early 1700s.

The construction is different from what is found at most ancient pueblos, as the builders did not use stone—there is very little in the vicinity—but mudbrick. Besides this lack of building stone, there was an abundance of water, as the Rio Grande River is next to the site and mudbrick construction requires a great quantity of water, which is why it was not used in the desert regions of the Colorado Plateau. The Ancestral Puebloans did not use preformed bricks but formed a mixture of water, ashes, charcoal, and clay into balls and flattened them along the top of the walls, allowing one layer to dry before adding another.

The most important find at Kuaua was the discovery of 87 layers of plaster on the inside walls of Kiva III in the south plaza, several containing murals. The walls of kivas had been plastered in earlier periods, and sometimes were painted in solid colors or had figures, but there was nothing like this. These are the best examples of large-scale mural painting in North America and are simply wonderful from an artistic point of view, with vibrant colors and a multitude of figures, both animal and human. The square Kiva III has been reconstructed and copies of some of the murals are painted inside; 19 originals are on display in the museum.

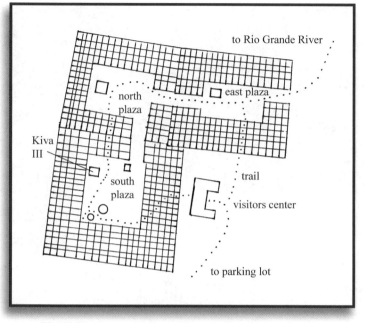

to Rio Grande River

north plaza

east plaza

Kiva III

south plaza

trail

visitors center

to parking lot

PLAN 38: Coronado State Historic Site, Kuaua Pueblo

TOURING CORONADO

The parking lot is next to the site at the end of Kuaua Road, and to the right is the path to the visitors center. You walk along the south section, which has been partially rebuilt, and arrive at the courtyard of the U-shaped visitors center and museum. The room with the murals is to the right, a gift shop and video presentation room is on the left, and the main desk and museum with artifacts from the site and objects from the Spanish period are straight ahead. The doors on the opposite side lead to the ruins along an **easy** trail.

Upon exiting the visitors center, turn left. You are walking along the eastern wing of the south section but there is little that remains. As you look around the site there are pieces of walls that rise above the surface but appear to be melting, and they are. This is the problem with the mudbrick: Once it is no longer protected by the adobe coating on the exterior, the walls erode very quickly, so even though much of the ground floor was reconstructed in the 1940s, most of it is missing. Toward the left is a section that was rebuilt using mortar rather than the original mudbrick and is in good condition, which illustrates the complexity and number of rooms in the pueblo.

The southern plaza is on the right toward the elevated kiva and ends by the north end of the visitors center. There is a large kiva to the right of the path, and a smaller one on the left in front of a reconstructed room in the southwest corner. This room may be entered. There were four kivas in this plaza: the two in this corner; the rebuilt Kiva III on the northwest side, where the murals were found; and another in the northeast corner, almost directly in front of the exit doors from the visitors center.

The path goes along the western rooms to Kiva III, which is square with rounded corners. This kiva may be entered to enable visitors to see the copies of the murals inside, however it is only possible to do so with a park guide. There are no set times; when a few people have gathered, the tour goes into the kiva. Arrangements are made in the visitors center beforehand. It is a wonderful experience to see the paintings where discovered, even if they are copies, and it is the only place in the Southwest where you can see murals such as these. Some of the originals are in the museum but it adds to the viewing pleasure to see them in their original context, plus the copies are vibrant, as the originals must have been when new, whereas the originals in the museum are faded and in some cases difficult to see, though certainly still worth viewing.

The path continues past Kiva III and into the north plaza, where you see sections of wall emerging from the underbrush. Look around carefully; the outlines of the plaza are visible, as well as another square kiva. The square kiva is found mostly in late

Reconstructed room

Kiva III (before being covered with a white tent for repairs)

sites, the P IV period, and only occasionally in earlier pueblos. Some archaeologists see the square kiva as an influence from the Mogollon, who lived in southern New Mexico and were contemporary with the Ancestral Puebloan, but a definite link has not been established at present.

The trail enters the east plaza and many walls are visible in the north room block. There is another square kiva in this plaza, near the northwest corner. From this point you can return to the visitors center or follow the path on the left, which leads down to the river. This section is gravel and steep farther on, but you get some nice views of the Rio Grande without needing to go all the way to the bottom. The picnic tables are located to the right in front of the visitors center.

In the museum, in the north wing, are some of the original paintings found in Kiva III. There are human figures that represent gods, priests, and dancers, as well as animal figures, including rabbits, deer, eagles, and ducks. One common subject is the depiction of rain, which flows from all types of figures and illustrates its importance in the desert climate. Also corn, the main sustenance of the Ancestral Puebloans, is shown. Interpretations vary but some of the figures are still important to modern Pueblo and represent their way of life and how one is to live. These images represent the finest examples of large-scale pre-European painting in North America and should not be missed. **NOTE:** Photographs are not permitted of either the original paintings or the copies in the kiva.

The P IV period, A.D. 1300 to 1540, is characterized by fewer pueblos that were much larger, with some exceeding 3,000 inhabitants. Also the layout of these pueblos changed from the open south-facing unit pueblo design to room blocks completely enclosing the plazas and with limited access, usually via only one narrow entrance that would have been easily defended. Farming continued to be the main way of life, but some archaeologists believe the Ancestral Puebloans were headed toward urbanization in large cities, had their world not been destroyed by the arrival of the Spanish invaders. We will never know what course they would have taken had they continued to live free.

Kuaua Pueblo is the only P IV site on the Grand Circle Tour, but do not expect to see any massive structures as at Chaco Canyon or Mesa Verde, as the building material here makes preservation difficult. There is enough reconstruction to give you a good idea of what the pueblo was originally like, and to see the unique kiva paintings is worth the visit. It is also a beautiful location that affords wonderful views of the Rio Grande and surrounding mountains.

This concludes the tour of Coronado State Historic Site. The timeline for Day 14 of the Grand Circle Tour is: Bloomfield to Coronado State Historic Site, 3 hours; Kuaua Pueblo, 1 to 1½ hours.

This concludes the Grand Circle Tour of the Colorado Plateau archaeological and geological sites. If you have additional time, there are two sites near Coronado that are very interesting and not too difficult to find; Jemez State Historic Site and Petroglyph National Monument. You will also find many sites of interest in Albuquerque, a few of which are listed below.

◎ OTHER SITES NEAR CORONADO

◎ Jemez State Historic Site

was established as a state monument in 1935 to preserve the pueblo of Giusewa and the mission church known as San José de los Jémez. It encompasses 7 acres (2.8 h).

GETTING THERE: From Coronado, go north on US 550 around 24 miles (38.6 km) to the junction with highway 4 and turn right. It is a further 16 miles (25.7 km) to the monument. The site is on the right behind some trees but there is a sign. It is across the road from a large white church. If arriving from Bloomfield, turn left onto NM 4.

The site is open from 8:30 AM to 5 PM Wednesday through Sunday, and is closed Thanksgiving Day, Christmas Day, and New Year's Day. There is a fee. The restrooms are at the back of the museum and there are picnic tables behind the visitors center. For more information phone 575-829-3530; www.nmmonuments.org/jemez; Jemez State Historic Site, PO Box 143, Jemez Springs, NM 87025.

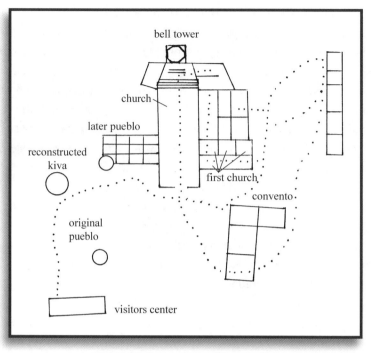

PLAN 39: Jemez State Historic Site

Jemez consisted of seven villages along the Jemez River, with a combined popu-lation of 7,000 to 8,000. It is believed the people were originally from Mesa Verde and migrated to Jemez in the late A.D. 1200s or early 1300s. One of the pueblos was Giusewa, meaning "place of the boiling waters," as there are some hot springs nearby, and was first populated around A.D. 1500. In 1598, the Spanish general Juan de Oñate sent missionaries into the pueblos to convert the Indians but they found it difficult, given the widespread nature of the villages in Jemez. The soldiers then forced the people into larger villages, which made it easier for the priests but increased the spread of diseases that devastated the Pueblo people.

The church was built in 1621, but in 1680, during the Pueblo Revolt, the priest was killed and any other Spanish were driven out. After this, Giusewa was abandoned and the church fell into ruins. The church was 111 feet (33.8 m) long by 34 feet (10.4 m) wide and the bell tower stood 42 feet (912.8 m) high. Excavations took place in 1910, 1920 through 1921, 1935, and 1937. Unfortunately, the findings were never published and for the most part the records have been lost or destroyed. Several frescoes were found on the inside walls of the church.

The first church at the site, on the east side of the San José church, was built be-tween 1598 and 1601 and consisted of only two or three rooms. The large San José de los Jémez was built in 1621 but burned in 1623 and was rebuilt in 1625. Painted designs in floral and geometric patterns lined the interior walls. Several architectural characteristics were built into the building to increase its impressiveness: The nave narrows toward the front, the floor rises, and the windows narrow in width toward the front to lead the eye to the sanctuary, the most holy place, which is raised on the top of several steps. The ceiling was 33 feet (10 m) high.

The buildings east and south of the church were part of the *convento*, the area where the priest, servants, and caretakers lived and worked, and include a kitchen, storage rooms, sleeping quarters, and stables.

Touring the Site

The visitors center and museum are beside a small parking lot next to NM 4. The museum houses both Native American and Spanish artifacts and there are a few books for sale. You enter a small room where you pay your entrance fee; through the door on the right is the museum and the door on the left leads to the site. In the back of the museum are restrooms.

When you exit the visitors center, the mounds in front of you are the remains of Giusewa Pueblo. The **easy** path winds through the village to the plaza in front of a

Pueblo rooms on west side of the church

Church interior looking towards the sanctuary

large kiva, which has been reconstructed by a former park ranger with the help of local Jemez Pueblo individuals. You may enter if it is not being used, but photographs
of the interior are not permitted. To the right are the remains of Spanish buildings
over some original Pueblo rooms, and past these and built against the west side of
the church are some Pueblo room blocks that are dated to the time of the Spanish
occupation, indicating the village was still inhabited, and being expanded, by Native
American contemporaries of the Spanish.

In front of the entrance to the church is a cemetery. The church was built on a
north–south axis and the entrance is on the south end. Notice the large beam over
the doorway. As you step inside it is still impressive, even without the roof, and would
have loomed larger than any other Pueblo buildings in this area. Along the bottom
of the walls are some low pedestals that are thought to have supported the original
wooden floor, which was replaced with stone and adobe after the church burned.
This room is the nave, and at the far end is the sanctuary at the top of the steps. Go

up the steps and turn right, this small room was the priest's private chapel, and to the left were the stairs up to the bell tower. The tower is octagonal in shape, which is rare; it also served as a lookout in times of danger. Return to the nave and as you walk out, imagine the roof on and the walls lined with frescoes, and over the door, a balcony, which held the choir. If you go, or have been, to Acoma, the church there is similar to what this one would have looked like originally.

Once you are outside, turn left and you come to marker 13. This is a square kiva that was built in a Spanish room and indicates that the pueblo was occupied for a time after the 1680 revolt, when the Spanish were driven out of Giusewa, and New Mexico. It is not known when Giusewa was abandoned but it may have been as late as 1692. The next room, marker 14, was the kitchen. The trail branches off to the left and goes along the east wall of the church and through the first church that was built in 1598. The long, narrow room, the two rooms on the right and the square room just after the trail turns right, were part of the original building. This last, square room was the church. The trail continues through here and into the sacristy at marker 16. This room was where the priest's garments and sacred books were kept. Return to the main trail.

The trail crosses the patio to a row of rooms at the far east that acted as a defensive wall to enclose this area from hostile Native Americans and help secure the church and connected buildings, though the pueblo was left exposed. At marker 20, the trail divides; the right returns the way you came, and the left path, which is gravel, continues through the *convento* and rejoins the main trail in front of the church.

Church exterior, east side, bell tower, right

Through this area you will find the remains of a pantry (marker 21), storeroom (marker 22), and corrals. This entire section was enclosed by a wall that went along to the left of the present trail.

This ends the tour of Giusewa. Return to the visitors center by following the same trail. After leaving Jemez State Historic Site, if you go back toward US 550, on the right about 5 miles (8 km) along, there is a museum and visitors center for the modern pueblo of Jemez. There is a nice display in the museum, a bookstore and gift shop, and information about the Pueblo. No entrance fee, only a donation.

The next, and last, site to visit is Petroglyph National Monument on the western edge of Albuquerque.

◎ Petroglyph National Monument

Petroglyph National Monument protects the largest collection of petroglyphs in the Southwest, with over 25,000 images from both the Ancestral Puebloans and the Spanish. In the 1970s the area was made into a state park to preserve the petroglyphs and it became a national monument in 1990. It is jointly administered by the National Park Service and the City of Albuquerque Open Space Division.

GETTING THERE: The easiest way to get to the monument is from I-40. Take exit 154 on the western edge of Albuquerque, go north on Unser Boulevard for about 3 miles (4.8 km) to Western Trail Street, and turn left to the visitors center. There are restrooms, picnic tables, and information, but no petroglyphs.

You can also get to the site from the north without going through the city center but it is a bit tricky. From Bernalillo or Coronado State Historic Site, drive north on US 550 to the intersection with NM 528, Rio Rancho Boulevard, and turn left. Stay on Rio Rancho for about 9 miles (14.5 km), until you come to NM 448, North Coors Road; turn right. Follow North Coors for about 5 miles (8 km) to Western Trail and turn right; this goes straight to the visitors center.

The visitors center is open from 8 AM to 5 PM daily; it is closed Thanksgiving Day, Christmas Day, and New Year's Day. For more information, phone 505-899-0205; visit www.nps.gov/petr; or write to Petroglyph National Monument, 6001 Unser Blvd. NW, Albuquerque, New Mexico, 87120. You may also phone the Open Space visitors center at 505-897-8831; www.cabq.gov/parksandrecreation/open-space/open-space-visitor-center/about. The visitors center is located at 6500 Coors NW.

The petroglyphs are located on the West Mesa, which was formed from a volcanic eruption about 150,000 years ago. This is in the center of a rift valley that extends from Colorado to El Paso, Texas, on a north–south axis. It is known as the Rio Grande Rift and the area has a thin crust in a depression that is being pulled apart by the Colorado

Plateau on the west and the Great Plains to the east. This separating causes fissures in the surface, allowing volcanic lava to erupt to the surface. The West Mesa was formed by six lava flows along a fissure. This lava flow covered the Santa Fe Formation, which consists of sand and gravel sediment over 25,000 feet (7,620 m) thick. As the soft Santa Fe Formation eroded, the harder volcanic surface collapsed, forming an escarpment where the broken pieces of basalt tumbled down. This is where the petroglyphs were created. The basalt is made of iron, manganese, and calcium and it is gray. The dark color you see on the rock is a patina that forms as the iron and manganese rusts when exposed to air. The Native Americans realized that pecking away the dark exterior exposed the lighter interior, creating a nice contrast for the images. The shiny coating on the rocks is desert varnish.

Some of the petroglyphs are believed to be 3,000 years old but around 90 percent were created between A.D. 1300 and 1600. During this time, the population increased greatly as people migrated from the areas to the north and west, searching for reliable sources of water that the Rio Grande, to the east, could provide. Although no habitation sites have been found in the area, the Ancestral Puebloans would have hunted on the West Mesa, and the combination of sandy and volcanic soil was richer than other places for agriculture. There are also Spanish images, such as crosses, sheep, cows and horses, similar to those at El Morro (see page 15).

Touring the Monument

The two main areas where you can see petroglyphs are the Rinconado Canyon and the Boca Negra Canyon. Rinconado is 1 mile (1.6 km) south of the visitors center on the same side of Unser Boulevard. The trail is **moderate** and goes along the bottom of the escarpment, where many images are located. The distance is 2½ miles (4 km) round-trip on a loop trail, but there are no petroglyphs on the section coming back through the middle of the canyon. The trail crosses sand dunes, which can be hard walking at times. **CAUTION:** There are signs warning about break-ins of vehicles in the parking lot, so do not leave any valuables in your car. There are restrooms but no park rangers.

The second section is Boca Negra Canyon, 2 miles north of the visitors center on the right. There is a gate and a ranger on duty and you must pay a fee to get in, but your vehicle is safe. There are three trails: The Mesa Point is **moderate** as it climbs to the top of the mesa; Macaw, **easy**; Cliff Base, **easy** with some elevation change. Watch out for rattlesnakes on all the trails.

After passing through the entrance gate, follow the road around to the right and stop at the first parking lot on the right. The **MESA POINT TRAIL** begins on the left of this parking lot; there are also picnic tables. The trail winds its way up the escarpment past fallen boulders, many of which have petroglyphs on them. Look carefully

Macaw petroglyph

as some are not obvious at first glance. You will see geometric designs, hand prints, animals, humans, masks, and unidentified images along this trail. A short distance up, the trail divides; this is the loop section. You will also see some smooth, shallow basins, which are lighter in color, on a few of the basalt rocks. These are grinding places, which could have been for sharpening tools or grinding grain or pigments or medicines and were possibly for ceremonial use.

At the top of the mesa, if you look to the east, in a counterclockwise direction, you will see the Sandia Mountains, the Sangre de Cristo Mountains, the Jemez Mountains, and sometimes, to the west, Mount Taylor. Significant geographic landmarks such as these are important to Native Americans of all nations and can be found surrounding their home-lands.

After returning to the parking lot, you either can walk along the paved sidewalk to the other trails or drive over to the second parking lot by the building. There are restrooms, a drinking fountain, and places to sit in this building. The **MACAW TRAIL** is on the right of the patio and takes only a few minutes to see. The highlight on this path are two images of macaws, parrots imported from Mexico by the Ancestral Puebloans for their beautiful feathers, which are still used in ceremonies today.

The **CLIFF BASE TRAIL** is on the opposite side of the building and climbs up a bit, but it mostly follows along the lower part of the cliff. This trail has many images, including masks, human figures, and spirals, among others.

This concludes the tour of sites near Coronado.

◎ Albuquerque

There are many interesting sites in Albuquerque, including a few that relate to Native Americans. It is easy to find more information on any of the following places if you are staying in the city for a day or more.

The Indian Pueblo Cultural Center, 2401 12th Street, 1 block north of I-40, is operated by the 19 Pueblos of New Mexico and includes a museum (open 9 AM to 5 PM), an archives and research library (open Tuesday or by appointment, 505-724-3537 or 3546), gift shops specializing in Native arts and crafts (open 9 AM to 5:30 PM), and the Pueblo Harvest Café that serves traditional Pueblo and Southwestern food (open 8 AM to 8:30 PM Monday to Thursday; 8 AM–9 PM Friday and Saturday; 8 AM–4 PM Sunday). There are also Indian dance performances and artist demonstrations. The center is open daily, except on major holidays. There is a fee to enter the museum, but everything else, including the dance performances, is free with paid admission. For information, phone 505-843-7270; visit www.indianpueblo.org; or write to Indian Cultural Center, 2401 12th St. NW, Albuquerque, NM 87104.

Old Town is the heart of the original city and features many restaurants, gift shops selling Native American arts and crafts, street vendors from the various Pueblo, museums, galleries, and several adobe homes and historic buildings. There are also street performances throughout the day. Old Town is located between Central Avenue on the south, Rio Grande Boulevard on the west, Mountain Road on the north, and 19th Street on the east. You will find parking lots on Central and 19th.

The Museum of Natural History and Science is on 1801 Mountain Rd. NW, a couple of blocks east of Old Town. It is open from 9: AM to 5: PM daily, closed Thanksgiving Day, Christmas Day, and New Year's Day, and features a museum of exhibits, planetarium, and Dynatheatre. For more information, visit www.nmnaturalhistory.org.

The Albuquerque Museum of Art and History, 2200 Mountain Rd. NW, is almost across the street from the Natural History Museum and features exhibits of historical and contemporary material. Open 9 AM to 5 PM; closed Monday, Thanksgiving Day, Christmas Day, New Year's Day, and city holidays. For more information, visit: www.cabq.gov/museum.

The Albuquerque Aquarium and Rio Grande Botanic Garden are at 2601 Central Ave. NW, not too far past Old Town to the west. They are open from 9 AM to 5 PM daily; closed Thanksgiving Day, Christmas Day, and New Year's Day. They have wonderful gardens and exhibits, both permanent and seasonal. For more information, phone 505-768-2000 or visit www.cabq.gov/biopark.

The Rio Grande Zoo is at 903 10th St. SW and is open from 9 AM to 5 PM. This 64-acre park has a wide variety of animals. For more information, phone 505-768-2000 or visit www.cabq.gov/biopark/zoo.

These are just a few of the sites in Albuquerque and the surrounding area. For more information, visit www.cabq.gov.

This concludes the Grand Circle Tour of the Colorado Plateau and is the end of Part 1 of this book. Part 2 contains reference material on the Southwest and the Ancestral Puebloans.

Navajo riders in Canyon de Chelly, c. 1904, by Edward S. Curtis

PART 2 ▪ background

TIMELINE FOR THE ANCESTRAL PUEBLOANS (ANASAZI)

The chronology of the Ancestral Puebloans was established in 1927 at the first Pecos Conference in Pecos, New Mexico. Alfred Kidder, who was excavating Pecos Pueblo at the time, invited archaeologists from around the Southwest to gather together and discuss and share their findings with one another, something not done previously. This first meeting, of what has become an annual event, established the Pecos Classification, a chronology still used today, though with some modifications as more information has become available.

One important point to remember about this timeline is that not all changes were occurring at the same time among the different groups of Ancestral Puebloans or, in some cases, even in neighboring pueblos. Developments were not universal throughout the Southwest, so this should be seen as a guideline in which to place the characteristics of the culture. Also, there are separate chronologies for most bands, but I have not included them as they might only serve to confuse. The one exception is for Chaco Canyon, where the timeline accompanies that section. Following the chronology is a brief section on the differences for each classification. (For a more detailed description, see History of Native American Occupation in the Southwest, page 401.)

Paleo-Indian Through Pueblo Culture

Paleo-Indian	ca.10,000–5500 B.C.
Archaic	ca.5500–100 B.C.
BM I	This designation is no longer used and is included in the Archaic.
BM II	ca.100 B.C. to A.D. 500
BM III	ca. A.D. 500–700
P I	ca. A.D. 700–900
P II	ca. A.D. 900–1100
P III	ca. A.D. 1100–1300
P IV	ca. A.D. 1300–1540
P V	A.D. 1540–present

Paleo-Indian. The first identifiable culture in North America is Clovis, discovered in 1932 near Clovis, New Mexico, and now dated to ca. 10,000 to 9000 B.C. These people were hunter-gatherers and lived in widely scattered camps throughout most of the Southwest. They made and used stone and bone tools and the sites are recognized by the spear points they manufactured. They were followed by similar peoples known as

Folsom, again named for their spear points. Very few sites have been found and most of those are kill sites. These peoples relied on the wild plants and animals for survival and did not establish any permanent living sites.

Archaic. The Archaic period is the pivotal time in the Southwest, as this is when agriculture developed, something that would completely change the livelihood of the people in the region. By 6000 B.C. the climate in the Southwest was becoming drier and game scarcer so the people had to rely more on plant material for survival. They began to take care of certain plants to make them more productive. Cultivation also tied these people to the land, as now they could not wander too far at certain times of the year. Corn, which would become the mainstay of the Ancestral Puebloan diet, was introduced as early as 2000 B.C., and possibly earlier, and was in widespread use by 350 B.C. The introduction of corn, which originated in western Mexico, would bring about the rise of the Ancestral Puebloans.

BM II. This Basketmaker period is named for the widespread use of baskets for cooking and carrying goods. There was no pottery. There were some shallow pithouses, located mostly in caves or rock overhangs. Hunting and gathering were still important but were combined with the cultivation of corn and squash. They used a spear, known as an atlatl, for hunting.

BM III. We find the introduction of pottery, the bow and arrow, and beans during this period. Small pithouse villages indicate a move to a more sedentary lifestyle in which agriculture was becoming as important as hunting for survival.

P I. There was a population increase during this time, the first Pueblo period, and some people began to construct aboveground structures, at first from poles and branches held together with adobe, but by the A.D. 800s, some of the buildings were made of stone and mud mortar. The pithouse continued to be used but in some instances they were dug deeper and formed the kiva. The typical unit pueblo developed, consisting of a straight, U-shaped, or L-shaped room block, a kiva, and midden.

P II. Another population increase resulted in many more villages. The kiva was a feature of almost all pueblos and had a standard design. Chaco Canyon reached its peak near the end of the period.

P III. The population continued to increase and the Ancestral Puebloans built larger multiroom, multistoried pueblos, such as those found at Hovenweep and Mesa Verde. There were fewer but much larger sites. The production of pottery, introduced in BM III, and other trade items reached its peak. Overpopulation, drought, and soil depletion put pressure on Pueblo civilization, leading to the abandonment of most sites toward the end of the period.

P IV. This was a time of change, when the Ancestral Puebloans moved south and east into larger pueblos with populations in the thousands. Most were located along the Rio Grande and Little Colorado Rivers and in the Hopi and Zuni regions. Trade continued and there seemed to have been a renewal of sorts in religion, as the Pueblo kivas were decorated with murals in some of the finest examples of large-scale painting in North America.

P V. This was the period of the invasion by the Spanish, followed by the Mexicans and Americans. The Spanish brought horses, cattle, and sheep, which devastated the fragile ecosystem, and diseases that cut through the indigenous populations. The Spanish missionaries beat and enslaved the Pueblo in their zeal to convert "heathens," and they attempted to destroy the Pueblo religion and culture, all of which they failed miserably at, as Native American religion and culture flourishes today. The Americans introduced the reservation system in another attempt to destroy Native American culture and the people themselves, but this also has failed, as today many Pueblo have become, or are in the process of becoming, strong and independent once more.

The Ancestral Puebloan Culture

There are five characteristics used to identify the Ancestral Puebloan culture. While not all of them may be present, at least some must be in evidence to say a site is Ancestral Puebloan rather than one of the other cultures that flourished in the Southwest. These five characteristics are:

The unit pueblo. This formation began when the Puebloans added aboveground structures near their pithouses. The unit pueblo comprises a room block, kiva, plaza, and midden oriented toward the south. The room block can be straight or in the shape of an L or U, crescent-shaped, semicircular, or on rare occasions, square

Pueblos that face south or southeast. Unit pueblos almost always face south or southeast to take advantage of the winter sun for heat, but there can be exceptions. At Mesa Verde, the cliff dwellings are built in the caves and shallow openings that do not all face south, so the builders had no choice in their orientation. But in Chaco Canyon, Pueblo del Arroyo was oriented eastward, even though it could have faced south.

The kiva. This structure comes in many different sizes, depths, and placements within a pueblo and can be round, square, rectangular, oval, or square with rounded corners. Standard features are a ventilator shaft, a hearth, and usually a deflector stone, a banquette around the interior, and support posts. Kivas are commonly built on a north–south axis. A *sipapu* may or may not be present.

Burials. Most remains from burials were found lying on their side in the flexed position: with the legs bent at the knees and close to the chest. The head is usually oriented toward the east, the rising sun.

Gray and white pottery. The gray or white color is from the firing process in the reduced-oxygen environment of a smothered fire. Some of the white vessels were painted with black designs. The Ancestral Puebloans also developed a corrugated style whereby the outside was left rough, exposing the coils of clay used to construct the pot.

The Six Groups

The Ancestral Puebloan consisted of six different groups separated geographically over the Colorado Plateau (see Map 38).

From west to east, the groups were: the **Virgin**, in northwestern Arizona, north of the Grand Canyon and west of the Colorado River, in southwestern Utah, and in southeastern Nevada; the **Kayenta**, in northeastern Arizona north of the Little Colorado River and south of the San Juan River, though there were some settlements north of the river in south central Utah; the **Little Colorado**, in the central eastern section of Arizona along the Little Colorado River; the **Mesa Verde**, in southwestern Colorado and southeastern Utah mostly north of the San Juan River; the **Chaco**, in northwestern New Mexico from the Arizona border to the San Juan River with some pueblos north of the river; and last, the **Rio Grande**, who lived along the Rio Grande River from the Colorado border to south of Albuquerque and west to the Arizona border through Acoma and Zuni lands.

All six groups shared the common traits of the Ancestral Puebloan but there were also differences among them, though in most cases these are slight. These differences are not apparent before A.D. 1000 and only developed in the 1100 and 1200s

Virgin. This group lived in the harshest region and built smaller, scattered pueblos throughout the territory but there were concentrations in a few areas around the Virgin River and Moapa Valley. Some Virgin sites lack kivas. They were farmers but depended on hunting and gathering more than did other branches, and when conditions became drier they returned to a mobile existence. They still grew some corn along the rivers but became dependant on hunting and gathering. They probably were occupying the same lands when the Europeans arrived, only at that time they became known as the Southern Paiute. An example of a Virgin settlement along the Grand Circle Tour is the Red Cliffs Archaeological Site in Utah.

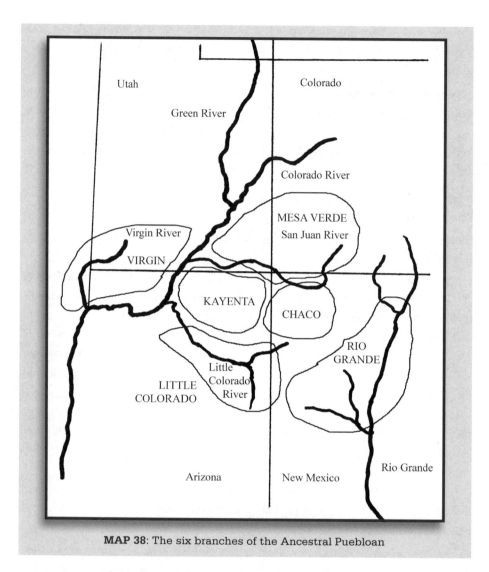

MAP 38: The six branches of the Ancestral Puebloan

Kayenta. The Kayenta made black-on-white painted pottery but some had negative designs; that is the black paint was applied in such a manner as to produce a white image against a black ground. They also made black-on-red and polychrome vessels. In many cases we find square kivas as well as round. Many sites were built for temporary use to watch over fields during the growing season. Examples of Kayenta sites are at Anasazi State Park in Utah, and Tusayan at Grand Canyon.

Little Colorado. This group built round kivas as well as rectangular and square ones that might have been influenced by the Mogollon who lived on their southern border. They also built great kivas. They made a red-slipped glazed pottery. Sites include Atsinna at El Morro and Puerco Indian Ruins in the Petrified Forest.

Mesa Verde. This refers to the territory north of the San Juan River and not just Mesa Verde National Park. This group built stone structures with large blocks pecked into shape by smaller stones, leaving distinct pot marks on the masonry. Their kivas were the "keyhole" design built belowground or in square rooms, and they constructed towers. Many of their pueblos were in caves or overhangs or on the edge of canyons. They produced a black-on-white pottery. Sites include Hovenweep and Mesa Verde.

Chaco. The Chaco built massive structures, using small stones, constructed great kivas, and had a different kiva design, many of which did not have a *sipapu*. Another unique feature of the Chaco is their construction of roads. Sites in Chaco Canyon and outliers, such as Aztec Monument, are examples.

Rio Grande. This group built large pueblos with enclosed plazas that housed thousands of people and had limited access. Some of their kivas were painted with murals. Kuaua at Coronado State Historic Site is an example of a Rio Grande pueblo.

HISTORY OF NATIVE AMERICAN OCCUPATION IN THE SOUTHWEST

If you ask any Native Americans in the Southwest how long their people have lived there, they will give the same answer—*We have always been here*—and, to a certain degree, they have always been here: their ancestry goes back over 10,000 years to the first peoples in the region; so, in fact, Native Americans have lived in the region for as long as there have been people in the Southwest; or, in other words, they *have* always been here.

The "history" of North America is divided into two periods, prehistorical and historical, with the arrival of the Europeans signifying the change to historical. I find this division irrelevant, arrogant, and disrespectful. It is as if there were no people, culture, or events before the Europeans invaded, when people had been living on this continent for over 10,000 years. It also privileges the writings of the invader as the source of our knowledge and debases archaeology and Native American accounts, or at the least trivializes their role in our understanding of the past. The history of the Southwest is the history of Native Americans from the earliest evidence to the present, so I present their history from the beginning divided not between historical and prehistorical but as pre- and postinvasion. I have divided the various periods per the Pecos Chronology, which varies across the region, in some instances by as much as a century (see chart, page 396).

Paleo-Indian. In 1925, a cowboy riding near the town of Folsom, in the northeastern region of New Mexico, discovered some bison bones protruding from the side of a dry wash. Mixed in with the bones were stone points that had been fashioned by human hands. By 1928, after careful excavations, most archaeologists working in the region believed that the deposits were extremely ancient, though precise dates would not be possible until the introduction of radiocarbon dating in the 1950s.

In 1932, near Clovis, New Mexico, on the border with Texas, a similar find would prove to be even older than the one at Folsom. At the time, no one realized that this had been the beginning of human culture in the Southwest.

The Clovis culture has proven to be the oldest yet discovered in North America, dating from ca. 10,000 to 9000 B.C, and ushering in the Paleo-Indian period for the Southwest, which dates from ca.10,000 to 5500 B.C. The Folsom culture succeeded Clovis and dates from ca. 9000 to 8500 B.C.

Both cultures manufactured and used stone and bone tools, including hammer stones, scrapers, and knives, but what distinguishes the two is the type of spear points they produced. Clovis points are generally longer, about the length of a human hand, and narrower than Folsom points, but their flutes are smaller. The flutes, which are very difficult to carve, as one can easily break the point while doing so, were used to secure the point to a wooden shaft: the longer the flute, the more securely it is attached to the shaft. Clovis points are found throughout North America, whereas Folsom points are mostly found in the central and western regions. Both have some variations and differing names that usually refer to the location in which evidence of their presence was discovered.

There are still many questions as to exactly how, and when, humans first arrived in the Americas, but the general consensus is that they crossed a land bridge in the Bering Strait, an area between Alaska and Siberia, probably following migrating herds of animals. During several periods between 23,000 and 8000 B.C., when large amounts of the oceans' waters were frozen into ice, the lower sea levels would have exposed the land bridge, allowing a fairly easy crossing. The most likely times were from 18,000 to 17,000 B.C, and again shortly after 12,000 B.C, with the newly arriving peoples slowly spreading south and east. One problem with this theory is that some sites in the Americas have been discovered with much older dates.

The earliest evidence for pre-Clovis people in North America comes from the Meadowcroft Shelter in Southwestern Pennsylvania, with radiocarbon dates from around 21,000 B.C., and some stone artifacts dating to between 17,000 and 15,000 B.C. From South America, at the Monte Verde site in southern Chile, the dates range from 33,000 to 15,000 B.C. However, there are many critics of these dates and Clovis remains the oldest proven widespread culture, though probably not the first peoples. This view may change in the future as more evidence is discovered.

The Paleo-Indians were hunter-gathers, gaining their livelihood from both plant and animal material. The climate at the time was much wetter and cooler in the Southwest than it is at present, allowing for a more diverse flora and fauna. There were pine and spruce forests and large grasslands on which grew a tall grass ideal for mammoths and large bison. Camels, horses, tapirs, rabbit, muskrat, and bears inhabited the Southwest, as well as species that are present today, including deer and antelope.

Very few Paleo-Indian campsites have been discovered, most of the evidence for their existence comes from kill sites, especially those involving mammoths and bison. Toward the end of the Clovis period, around 9000 B.C., the climate was beginning to dry somewhat, which led to a change in the grasslands from a tall to a predominantly shorter grass that was not well suited for either the mammoths or large bison, causing the extinction of the former and an adaptation of the latter to a smaller size, closer to the modern bison. They are also referred to as buffalo, though the technical term is *bison*.

The change in climate affected the large mammals that were not able to adapt as could the smaller species and humans. Not only did the mammoth die out at the end of the Clovis period, but also the giant beaver, which was the size of a modern bear. Other losses were the 20-foot-long sloth, horses, camels, and musk oxen (though musk oxen did survive, and continue to do so, in the far northern regions of North America). As these species disappeared, the carnivores that fed on them soon followed: the American cheetah and lion, the dire wolf and short-faced bear, which was twice the size of a modern grizzly.

There has been much dispute as to the impact of the Clovis hunters on the extinction of these species but it most likely was minimal. The Clovis population was sparse, and the large mammals, while there is evidence that they were hunted, would have been very difficult, and dangerous, to bring down.

The Folsom culture thus became dependant on the bison as a meat source. At this time, the bison also began to expand onto the great plains, partly due to the extinction of the lion and short-faced bear, two major predators, but the numbers were nowhere near the vast herds that roamed the plains when Europeans arrived.

By 6000 B.C. the climate had changed even more, becoming much dryer and warmer. Many of the animals that had inhabited the Southwest were now extinct, leaving a land similar to that of today and ushering in a great change in the culture of the Southwest.

Archaic. The Archaic period, from ca. 5500 B.C. until 100 B.C., was one of transition from a dependence on hunting and wild plants to one when cultivated species of flora became of equal importance for survival, which occurred partly due to the climate change.

By 6000 B.C. the deserts of the Southwest were spreading, displacing grasslands and forests, and the climate was getting hotter and drier. From ca. 2500 B.C. to about 100 B.C., the climate again changed, with more rainfall and moderate temperatures, and, although never ideal for farming, the conditions did make agriculture feasible, which to some degree produced a more reliable food source.

Peoples' diet became more diversified as the large animals of the Paleo-Indian period disappeared and they were more dependent on seeds, nuts, roots, and small game. Their hunting was on a seasonal basis with rabbits predominant from spring to early fall and then larger game, such as deer, elk and mountain sheep, in the late fall and winter. After ca. 2500 B.C. there was a gradual increase in population. There is clear evidence that the people were grinding grain during this time, as the remains of manos (hand-held grinding stones) and metates (flat stones on which grain was ground) have been discovered.

Agriculture had been well established in Mesoamerica for several millennia before the knowledge and techniques appear in the Southwest. Corn and squash are in evidence from around at least 6500 B.C. in central Mexico; cotton, beans, and gourds were produced by 4800 to 3500 B.C. The earliest date for corn in the Southwest is about 2000 B.C. and it seems to have been in common use by 350 B.C. or earlier, along with bottle gourds. Corn and squash are tropical plants and require much care to grow in the Southwest. People were still dependent on hunting and gathering at this early stage and probably used the crops only to supplement their diet.

A growing dependence on agriculture brought a more sedentary lifestyle, as the people had to stay in a much smaller territory to take care of their crops. Evidence of Late Archaic shallow pithouses, hearths, grinding bins, and sites in caves has been found, as well as of their periodic reuse over a long time. As well, baskets, cradle boards, sandals, and snares have been discovered. The points these peoples manufactured became more diverse. This illustrates, along with the use of local stone, that they were living in many smaller, separate groups rather than in the same cultural group spreading over a larger region as had been the case in the Paleo-Indian period. And we find the first burials at this time, which again shows a connection to a certain territory and a people's claim to that territory by using burials to "mark" what belonged to them.

Two interesting types of finds from this period—rock art and split-twig figurines—also illustrate that a belief system, or religion, was emerging. There are rock art images, possibly from the middle Archaic but certainly from the late Archaic period, and although their meaning is unknown, some seem to be directly related to a system of belief, images that continue through the later periods. The split-twig figurines are small animal figures, meant to represent deer or elk, made from weaving a single willow branch and placed in caves, most likely as an offering for a successful hunt. They probably were also placed in many other locations but would not have survived over time if exposed to the elements.

Two questions that concern the evolution of a hunter-gatherer society to agriculture are: how and why? The "how" probably came through trade. There is evidence of trade routes and the exchange of goods from south to north and vice versa, so it is most likely that both the methods and means traveled north from Mexico. The "why" is probably an increase in population, along with climate change that offered improved conditions for growing crops.

Prior to 2500 B.C. the resources of the Southwest were adequate to supply the people, but the increase in population after this time put pressure on these natural resources, making it necessary for additional means to survive. It would seem that changing to a sedentary, crop-based lifestyle would be beneficial, and easier than surviving as hunter-gatherers. However, research has shown that not only are hunter-gatherers healthier overall, but there is less work involved, and thus more free time, for hunter-gatherers than for farmers. So the reasons for adopting an agricultural way of life generally are either resource degradation, of which there was some, and/or a population increase, as farming can sustain a larger number of people on a smaller territory.

The introduction and spread of agriculture in the Southwest during the Archaic period would provide the means for the first great civilization to emerge in the region during the next period of time, the Ancestral Puebloans.

BM II. Baskets, from which the chronology takes its name, are found in large quantities around the Four Corners region during this period. These extraordinary vessels have survived well in the arid climate of the Southwest and, although created for utilitarian purposes, are, in some cases, true works of art. Some of them were woven so tightly as to be waterproof and remain so 2,000 years later. The Ancestral Puebloans prepared their food in baskets by filling them with water and the ingredients for their meal, and then placing hot rocks into the mixture, continually replacing the cooling stones with hot ones until the water boiled, thus cooking the food. A very effective, though labor intensive, method. There are many examples of these baskets in museums throughout the region.

A few examples exist of a crude brownware pottery that was made at this time, but it was not widespread. It would be a while yet before pottery was in common use throughout the Southwest.

The people lived in shallow caves and rock overhangs, but a few pithouses have been discovered, mostly in caves. The pithouses at this time were round or oval, from 1 to 2 feet (30–40 cm) belowground, lined with upright stone slabs and horizontal beam cribbing forming the walls above ground level. The floors were uneven packed dirt or clay. The roof was low, with a center hole for smoke directly over the hearth, which was also the entrance. They were from 9 to 10 feet (3 m) in diameter. There were also many large storage cists, which were lined with stone slabs and chinked using smaller rocks to protect the supplies from rodents. These cists were located both in the pithouses and outside. The people still depended on hunting and gathering, but growing corn and squash was becoming more important to their livelihood, as the evidence of both larger storage rooms and many manos and metates illustrates.

The atlatl was used instead of the simple spear for hunting. An atlatl is a throwing strap held in the hand with the other end attached to the end of the projectile, thus extending the length of a man's arm, giving the weapon more accuracy and distance. A spear is deadly up to about 75 feet (23 m), whereas the atlatl's range is close to 300 feet (90 m), making it much better for hunting, though it is more difficult to master than a spear. They produced carefully chipped points for their atlatls, as well as knives, drills, sandals, aprons, robes, and bags. The development of the Ancestral Puebloans was not uniform throughout the Southwest, with some areas changing and adapting more quickly than others, a situation which can be seen throughout their entire history.

BM III. The first major development of this period was the introduction of pottery around A.D. 200, although it did not become widespread until A.D. 500. One advantage of pottery was its use as a cooking vessel. Now food could be placed in a vessel that went directly into or over the fire, hastening cooking time and freeing the people from the continuous task of replacing the hot stones to heat the water. This allowed the more thorough cooking of their food, especially corn, whose protein is not digested when raw but becomes almost totally digestible the longer it is cooked. Another benefit of pottery is that it can be used to store dry goods, as it is easily sealed with clay or a large flat stone to prevent rodents and insects from destroying the contents. It is also much easier and faster to produce than a basket, as almost anyone can fashion a vessel of some sort and fire it.

Remains from BM III are found throughout the Southwest and are fairly consistent in their development. The finding of BM III ceramics is common. During this period, the atlatl was replaced by the bow and arrow, a weapon that is easier to use and also better for ambushing animals. The turkey had been domesticated for its feathers, which were used to make blankets, and for limited consumption.

The Ancestral Puebloans were becoming much more sedentary through this period, growing corn, squash, and beans, the latter being easier to cook with the use of pottery. The increased dependency on pottery was also a result of the peoples' becoming less mobile, as pots are heavier to transport than the baskets and considerably more fragile. However, some Native Americans did travel here from outside the region: Trade also increased at this time, with items coming from northern Mexico and the Pacific coast, including such things as pottery, marine shells and turquoise.

The pithouse remained the mainstay of housing but with some changes from BM II. In the A.D. 500s they were shallow, less than 3 feet (0.9 m) deep, and round with an antechamber. By the 600s, the pithouses were deeper, square or rectangular in shape with an average diameter of 20 feet (6 m), and had a wide entrance to the antechamber. In the late 600s, the antechamber was connected by a narrow passage between it and the main structure, and in some cases there was no antechamber, as it had been replaced with a ventilation shaft, a configuration similar to that of the kiva. The antechamber was used for storage and as a ground-level entrance facing south, replacing the ladder over the hearth in the center early in the period, but this would return toward the end of BM III. Four posts supported horizontal beams on which were laid sloping poles covered with brush and mud for the roof. Inside there was a clay-lined fire pit with a deflector stone between the fire and the entrance to stop drafts from blowing directly onto the flames and embers. Low stone slab walls divided the south side of the space, which was used for preparing food. Holes were dug in the floor and filled with sand to hold round-bottomed vessels.

By the end of BM III, the inside storage pits were replaced with aboveground free-standing buildings, and the antechambers had evolved into ventilator shafts, leaving only the center hole in the roof for the entrance. Also found in the pithouses was a small hole filled with clean sand: the *sipapu*, the Hopi name for the entry place into the spiritual world from which the people emerged onto the earth in the beginning. The houses were always on a north–south axis, with the *sipapu* to the north and the ventilator shaft on the south.

The aboveground storage units were constructed with upright poles intertwined with small branches and covered with mud, also known as adobe. These were always located to the north of the pithouses. Along with these storage buildings, the people built roofs on four posts to form an open area of shade in which to work: the ramada. By placing these two types of structures in a straight line, attaching them together and closing in the sides to use as living quarters, they began to form the first ground-level pueblos. They also had pit rooms for storage, shallow spaces 10 to 13 feet (3 to 4 m) in diameter and 20 inches (50 cm) deep with upright stone slab or jacal walls.

Villages began to appear in BM III and ranged in size from 2 or 3 to 25 or more pithouses. The small villages had the pithouses in the center, with storage units to the north and a midden on the south, the same configuration as the later unit pueblo. In a few of the larger villages what appears to be a great kiva is present. It is difficult to estimate the population, or even the number of houses in any given community, as it is not possible to determine whether the houses in a village were all occupied at the same time.

The increased dependency on agriculture and pottery, the congregating into villages, and the changing methods of construction would herald the next stage of the Ancestral Puebloan: stone houses and the pueblo.

P I. From A.D. 700 to 900, in some areas, the change from living in pithouses to the aboveground pueblos was slow and gradual; in others, abrupt; and in a few places, the pithouse continued to be used until the time of abandonment. The reasons for moving into the pueblos are unknown, but a population increase at this time may have been related to the shift.

There were now many more villages spread all across the Southwest. Size varied greatly and was tied to the resources that were available in a particular area, as no village subsisted solely on agriculture but also relied on hunting and gathering of wild plant resources. Not only did the architecture change in the transition from pithouse to pueblo, but the way in which rooms were used also differed. In the pithouse villages, storage was in exterior rooms. Earlier, it was pit rooms and then aboveground rooms, but with the pueblos, all storage was now inside the unit; there were no, or very few, storage rooms away from the main building. And storage capacity increased. If corn is the main food source, the crop will be harvested in a short period of time, requiring much more storage space: enough for an entire year plus the seed to plant next year's crop. In contrast, when there was a major dependence on wild plants, these were harvested throughout most of the year and required much less storage space.

In the pithouse, grinding was first located in the north or northeast part of the house and later south of the partition walls, but in the pueblos, there were specific rooms just for grinding. So the pueblo rooms were divided according to use: living rooms with hearths, grinding rooms with metates, and storage areas.

The early pueblos continued to be made of poles and branches laced together with adobe. However, in the A.D. 800s they began to use stone masonry in the construction. Sandstone blocks, roughly shaped, were placed in a single row, using a large amount of mud mortar that was smoothed both inside and out. Usually only three walls would be made of stone and the other, which contained the door, was still built of branches and mud, possibly because the people had not yet developed the techniques to span the doorway with stone. The roof was made of large poles laid in one direction with smaller ones placed perpendicular, then small branches on top of these, which were covered with mud and were strong enough to support several people, as these were also living areas. This roof was placed directly onto the walls, though in some cases there were additional posts inside the building.

The rooms were small, usually no more than 10 feet (3 m) across, and only had one story, as the thin walls could not support another level. All the rooms were connected together in either a straight line, an L or a U shape, or less often in an arc. The pithouse was much deeper, 6 to 7 feet (2 m) belowground, square with a flat roof and ventilation shaft. The pithouse continued to be used for habitation but was beginning to develop a secondary use as a place for ritual: the kiva (more on this in the next section). This combined with the aboveground room block is known as the unit pueblo: a room block to the north with an open plaza, kiva, and/or pithouse and midden, oriented on a north–south axis. Also the number of great kivas increased during this time.

There was now more reliance on agriculture as the population increased and the Ancestral Puebloans began to develop reservoirs, dams, terracing, and irrigation, though these were not widespread yet. The techniques for irrigation had first been imported from Mexico and developed by the Hohokam in southern Arizona a few centuries before, as this area is much drier than the land of the Puebloans, who had not required it until the pressure of population growth occurred.

The pottery continued to be mostly grayware, including a new form called neck-banded gray. These tall jars had rough coils on the neck while the belly was smooth. They produced mostly black-on-white, but some black-on-red and red-on-orange was also made and traded at this time.

P II. There had been a sharp decrease in population toward the end of P I and early in the P II period, but by A.D. 1000, the numbers were on the rise again and would reach a peak between 1075 and 1100 before beginning the final decrease that would lead to the total abandonment of many regions.

Many of the ruins in the Southwest visible today date from this period, one reason being the change from jacal construction early in the period to stone walls, which survive much better over time. The pueblos were developing into larger, rectangular masonry structures with one or more stories, and the unit pueblo was now standard. Villages consisted of buildings with from 3 to 20 rooms, still small but there were now many more. They were built in canyons and on mesas that had never been occupied before and were spread over the entire Ancestral Puebloan territory.

The kiva originated from the pithouse, which had become a fully subterranean chamber by the P I period. When the people began living in the pueblos, the use of the pithouse changed from habitation to ritual, though some pithouses continued to be used as residences. The construction was standardized with the *sipapu*, hearth, and ventilator shaft on a north–south axis, and the entrance through the roof over the firepit. The kivas, like the room blocks, were built of stone, unlike the pithouses, which had dirt walls. The kiva was used primarily for religious ceremonies, but weaving was also practiced in them by the men, and it most likely served as a place for the men to gather away from the women in what was a matrilineal society. Some were probably used as living spaces, especially in the winter.

Each kiva would have served a family group, which is why there is one kin kiva for every 10 or so rooms, but there were also the great kivas, usually 45 feet (14 m) or more in diameter, which would be used for regional ceremonies involving the surrounding villages. The kiva remains important to Puebloan culture today.

The people were more dependent on agriculture, with corn, beans, and squash still the staples, plus a greater use of turkeys for consumption as well as feathers. This greater dependence left the people more susceptible to climate fluctuations so they increased their use of water control methods, including check dams, irrigation ditches, and terracing. But hunting and gathering still remained an important part of their life.

Bc 59, the remains of 3 kivas. (See page 356, Casa Rinconada, Chaco Canyon.)

While most areas were continuing to expand, Chaco Canyon was hitting its peak toward the end of P II and would soon be abandoned in early P III. This is when the great houses were taking their final shape. Population was at its largest and the Chacoans' influence reached its greatest extent. Walls of the great houses were built with double courses of stone, sometimes with the space in between filled with rubble, and could be much thicker than before: the five- or six-storied wall of Pueblo Bonito is 4 feet (1.2 m) thick at the bottom, tapering to 1 foot (30 cm) on top. Stonework was now more precise and carefully finished on the outside surfaces. While many areas continued to use large stones, especially Mesa Verde, the Chacoan style incorporated many small, finely cut rocks with even smaller stones used as chinking to fill the cracks, while employing very little mortar, producing the finest masonry work in the Southwest. Most of the other bands of Ancestral Puebloans would prosper for another century or more before beginning their own decline.

Corrugated pottery, vessels not smoothed on the outside leaving the ridges from the coils, were in common use, as these were much more efficient for cooking, having a larger surface area allowing them to heat faster.

P III. This is the period of the great centers of population, such as Mesa Verde and Hovenweep. The number of villages was decreasing in early P III but the population was increasing as people moved into the large, multiroom, multistory stone pueblos. Occupancy of some of the largest pueblos exceeded 2,000 people. The architecture began to vary to include cliff dwellings, as found at Mesa Verde, among other sites, the towers of Hovenweep, and tri-wall structures. The number of both kin kivas and great kivas increased.

The larger population required more efficient agricultural production and we now see large-scale water management systems for domestic use as well as irrigation. In Mesa Verde, over 1,000 check dams used to divert or slow streams have been found. The large reservoir, Mummy Lake, near Far View Ruin, is 90 feet (27.5 m) in diameter and nearly 12 feet (3.5 m) deep with outside walls made of stone and mud mortar. A ditch ran along the ridge of the mesa and was fed by several smaller ditches before emptying into the reservoir. This is just one example of many of the engineering capacity of the people.

During this time there is a greater distinction among the various groups of Ancestral Puebloans, especially in pottery and architecture. Prior to A.D. 1,000, all regions remained remarkably similar and were almost indistinguishable from one another, but this began to change during the P II period, becoming more evident into P III, giving us the six different branches of the Ancestral Puebloan.

This is also the time of abandonment. New construction slowed in all regions by the 1270s and completely ceased by the 1290s. By the early 1300s Southern Utah, except for the extreme western section, southern Colorado, northwestern New Mexico, and northeastern Arizona were completely deserted. The inhabitants moved south and east, especially into the Rio Grande, Hopi, and Zuni areas, with some relocating to northern Mexico. There was not a sudden exodus but a slow movement of people over 50 years. Although no one knows the reasons for this change, some possible causes could be: drought, climate change, attacks by outside tribes, warfare among the people, disease, overuse of trees for timber, a shortened growing season, or a combination of some or all of these. There was an extended drought from 1276 to 1299, but they had already sharply curtailed new construction prior to this. But even though many of the villages were deserted at this time, it was not an end to the civilization, or the people; it was another relocation.

Pottery, basketry, weaving, and jewelry reached new heights at this time and trade was expanding at a tremendous rate, even though all movement was by foot as they never had any pack animals. This appears to have been the pinnacle of the Ancestral Puebloan civilization.

P IV. The Rio Grande valley was sparsely populated before A.D. 1000 and continued to have few inhabitants until the early 1200s, when there was a small population increase to be followed by a much greater one in the 1300s. This lack of inhabitants early on seems unusual, considering the fact that the Rio Grande River is one of the few reliable water sources in the Southwest. This was another time of shifting from many smaller villages into fewer larger ones. During this period, the Ancestral Puebloans would construct some of the largest pueblos in their history.

At the end of the A.D. 1200s pueblos had up to 50 rooms, a few close to 100, but in the 1300s we see structures consisting of more than 1,000 rooms and several plazas, but fewer kivas and no great kivas. Some sites grew quickly, were abandoned, reoccupied, and abandoned again, sometimes in less than 20 years. Pueblos were built for defense, with plazas completely surrounded by room blocks that rose to three or four stories toward the exterior, with a single narrow opening to the outside, restricting access. There were no doors on the ground floor as the occupants used ladders to reach the roof and then entered by holes in the roof. The ladders could be pulled up quickly if anyone did enter the plaza; the inhabitants would assault the intruders with arrows and stones from above. Some of the first Spanish accounts of their attack on the Zuni Pueblos in 1540 describe such defenses.

There is much more evidence of violence at this time, as many of the pueblos were burned at some period of their existence, a few several times, and skeletal remains have many injuries and signs of a violent death. Some remains had been scalped. Sites are also much farther apart than during previous periods.

A new religion seems to have arisen during this time, possibly in response to a more stressful life. No one knows the origins of the Katsina (also called Kachina); some speculate it arose in the southwestern part of the Colorado Plateau in the region of Wupatki or south of there, or in the Little Colorado area, but there is no solid evidence. The Katsina are ancestral spirit messengers who communicate between the people and their gods and are responsible for bringing rain. They are only on this level between the winter and summer solstices and reside in the underworld for the other six months. During the Katsina Dances, the dancers become the spirits when they put on the large masks depicting the various Katsina. The dances are performed by large groups in plazas, which could explain the growing importance of plazas in the P IV period.

Kiva murals reach new heights with the large-scale depiction of humans, animals, and gods painted on the interior walls. Never before had there been such colorful, lively depictions in art of the teachings and knowledge of the ancient people. There are also some depictions of warfare, again reflecting the more violent times of this period. The images on pottery changed from almost all geometric to an emphasis on human and bird figures, now painted in the center of bowls instead of around the sides. The color changed from white vessels to yellow, orange, and red painted with red and black designs.

Cotton becomes more prevalent in the late A.D. 1200s and early 1300s with production centered around Homolovi in the Little Colorado region, south of the Hopi mesas. It seems that they became major producers growing their crops along the Little Colorado River in fields that were miles long, but in the 1400s this region was abandoned. Cotton continued to be important to the Pueblos until it was superseded by wool after the introduction of sheep by the Spanish.

Although it is difficult to know the exact number it seems, based on Spanish accounts at first contact, that the population of Pueblos in the early 1500s, pre-invasion, was in excess of 100,000. By 1680, the time of the Pueblo Revolt, the population was only around 17,000. This period ends the pre-invasion history of the Pueblo people, a history which saw many changes over 12,000 years but the people had never encountered anything as devastating as the European invasion that was to come next in their story.

Pueblo V, to the present. It must have been a bizarre site: a tall, muscular black man, a slave, wearing feathers and bells on his ankles, coral and turquoise across his chest, with two greyhounds trotting at his side, several young women following behind, a green ceramic set of plates that only he was allowed to eat from, and the rattle gourd. He was the first European to enter the Southwest. It did not end well for him, or the Native peoples.

The story begins in May 1528, when 300 Spanish explorers were sailing along the west coast of Florida near the panhandle in search of gold. For some reason they abandoned their ship and continued west on foot to the gulf of the Mississippi River, where they fashioned barges from skins to get across. Several were swept out to sea, some drowned when the skin barges sank, while others either starved to death or were killed by hostile Native Americans. In all, only four survived: Alonso del Castillo Maldonado; Álvar Nuñez Cabeza de Vaca; Andrés Dorantes, and his black slave, Estevanico.[1]

These four were soon captured by Native peoples, who believed that they had some mystical healing power, further enhanced when Vaca seems to have miracu-

---

3. There are several different spellings for Estevanico's name.

lously brought one of the Native Americans back to life. The visitors were thought to be the children of the sun.

As they continued their journey west they were given gifts and escorted from one village to the next through what was a very harsh environment where the people lived on the edge of starvation most of the time. Finally they reached Mexico after several months in the desert, but their first encounter with another Spaniard was unfortunately with a slave trader who was interested in their entourage of Native Americans. Vaca, who had become quite fond of the latter by this time, intervened on their behalf and was arrested for his troubles, along with the other three. Taken to a nearby town, they were soon freed by the local mayor and then traveled on to Mexico City, where they received a hero's welcome and told the tale of their unbelievable journey, enhancing considerably the events. It was 1536.

Their stories of large cities made of stone to the north, which they had heard from Native peoples along the way, together with Vaca's belief that the mountains they had passed contained gold, fueled the desires of the Spanish, especially for the gold. The viceroy in Mexico City gave permission for an expedition north, but Vaca declined, as did Dorantes, who either sold or gave Estevanico to the viceroy. Estevanico was considered intelligent, but still a slave, so it was not possible to place him in charge of the expedition. However, he was the only one who knew the route and was familiar with the Native Americans, even speaking several of their languages. So the viceroy engaged a Franciscan priest named Fray Marcos de Niza to lead the party. Estevanico, Niza, another friar named Onarato, and 20 Native American servants departed on March 7, 1539, toward the north, and the unknown.

Niza became disgusted by the antics of Estevanico as he indulged his lust for young women and hunger for power, which grew worse the farther they continued north, so Niza sent the slave on ahead with the following orders: If he (Estevanico) found anything of value, he was to send back a cross the size of a man's hand; if it was exceptional, the cross should be the length of an arm. Estevanico sent a cross the height of a man!

Whenever he approached a village, Estevanico sent in a messenger with a rattle gourd and a demand for women and turquoise. This seemed to work, until he reached Hawikuh, a Zuni pueblo. The Zuni refused, so Estevanico went into the pueblo and told the occupants that a white man from God was following him and there would be dire consequences if they did not do as he ordered. They killed Estevanico, cut his body into pieces, and sent a piece to each Zuni pueblo to prove he was no god. They kept his feathers, bells, turquoise, and green plates, but threw away the rattle, which for some reason had been a grave insult to them.

No one knows how far Niza advanced after hearing the news about Estevanico, but he seems to have reached a small hill a few miles south of Hawikuh, where he observed the pueblo in the distance, planted a cross on the knoll, proclaiming the land for Spain in the name of the king and God, turned around, and returned to Mexico. But he did not return empty-handed, for he brought back tales of the famed Seven Cities of Cibola with streets paved of gold. And Hawikuh was larger than Mexico City. He had seen these with his own eyes!

The governor of the northern Mexican province to whom Niza reported his findings was Don Francisco Vásquez de Coronado. Coronado immediately organized an expedition and marched into New Mexico with an army. This was in 1540. He had arranged for an armada to sail up the Colorado River with supplies for him and his men, in the mistaken belief that the river flowed near their destination, when in fact they would be at least 200 miles (322 km) from the Colorado. That is, if the ships had even been able to navigate upstream on the river, which they could not.

When Coronado arrived at Hawikuh, he saw a small, crowded village of adobe with streets of dirt rather than gold. He soon realized that Niza had not spoken a word of truth. Starving, as the anticipated supplies from the ships had not materialized, Coronado's army attacked the village because they had not been welcomed by the Zuni. This was the first battle of the Southwest. The Zuni surrendered, then abandoned the village to the Spanish, who took their corn, the only thing of value that they found.

Coronado then sent part of his army west to search for the armada. On the way they destroyed a Hopi village, killing most of the inhabitants, and eventually arrived at the South Rim of the Grand Canyon. After spending a week trying to find a route down to the river, they declared that this was a useless piece of land and returned east. Coronado had been moving east, capturing and destroying villages along the way, finally making it to Pecos. He had captured two Plains Indians, one of whom told him of large cities and much gold northeast of Pecos, out on the Great Plains. It appears that the Pueblo had planted the story, which the Spanish completely believed, and the army followed the man onto the prairie. After several weeks they discovered the trick, strangled the man who had led them astray, and returned to Pecos with no gold and barely their lives.

Coronado returned to Mexico in 1542. He had lost his fortune—these early Spanish explorers were self-financing—his reputation, and his health, dying at age 44.

In 1590, the first settlers ventured into the Southwest, attacking Pecos, which was then abandoned by the Pueblo. But their victory was short-lived: They had entered into the territory without the official permission of Spain and were ordered to leave after one year.

In 1598, Don Juan de Oñate took 500 settlers and 7,000 animals, which included sheep, goats, cattle, oxen, pigs, horses, mules, and donkeys, on the first officially sanctioned settlement of the new territory. On July 7, 1598, Oñate received a delegation of Pueblo leaders and informed them "that he had been sent by the most powerful king and ruler in the world, Don Philip, King of Spain, who desired especially to serve God our lord and to bring about the salvation of their souls, but wished also to have them as his subjects and to protect and bring justice to them . . . it was greatly to their advantage that, of their own free will and in their own names . . . they render obedience and submission to the king, and become his subjects and his vassals."[2]

The Spanish, who saw and heard what they wanted to with little regard for the truth or facts, stated that the Indians "replied to this through interpreters, all in agreement and harmony and with great rejoicing. One could easily see and understand they were very pleased with the coming of his lordship."[3] More likely they feared Spanish weapons and cruelty and saw no alternative at the time.

Most pueblos surrendered but Acoma resisted, was attacked and defeated. Seven to eight hundred Native Americans were killed, many after they had surrendered. Over 500 prisoners were taken. Their punishment was appalling: Men over 25 years old were sentenced to have one foot cut off plus 20 years of servitude; boys and women were given 20 years of servitude; and the young girls were given to the friars, possibly the worse fate of all. Two Hopi who were at Acoma and captured each had their hands cut off and were sent back home as a warning.

In 1610, the capitol was established at Santa Fe. Indians were forced to supply food to the settlers, this in an area where they barely had enough for themselves. When homesteaders claimed a piece of land, any Native people found living there became the settlers' property and were used as slave labor. The Franciscans were worse. Some of the food taken by the friars would be returned to its original owners if they converted, which many did if only to survive. Pueblo who did not attend church would be whipped; churches were built with forced labor. The Pueblo were excellent architects, going back to their Ancestral Puebloan ancestors, but they had never constructed large-span buildings, which the friars required for the churches; neither had they worked with mudbrick, another Spanish "innovation." So while the men worked on the large missions, the women would be forced to produce the mudbrick. In 70 years, the population went from 40,000 to 17,000. It would get worse.

At first, many of the Native Americans had embraced the Christian religion, incorporating elements into their own beliefs and ceremonies, which was not a problem

---

2. Paul Robert Walker, *The Southwest* (Washington, DC: National Geographic Society, 2001), 27.
3. Ibid., 27–8.

for the friars, while a few even converted completely of their own free will. But by the mid-17th century the priests were becoming more demanding that the people give up their "heathen" religion and practice only Christian rites. The priests began destroying the religious objects including the Katsina masks and figures, outlawed the dancing and ceremonies, and began filling in the kivas. Punishments were severe if any were caught performing Native American ceremonies. In 1675, 47 men were arrested as sorcerers and several were hanged, but when riots broke out and threatened the safety of Santa Fe, the Spanish were forced to release some of them, including one named Popé who would become a symbol and leader of the rebellion.

The pueblos, of which there were over 100 before the Spanish arrived, had always been more or less independent of one another with no overall leader, something the Spanish never understood. But this also made it difficult for the people to form any organized resistance to the invading Spanish, until 1680. The cruelty and brutality had gone too far.

A series of runners had gone through the territory carrying strings with knots tied in them, leaving one in each village. The people were to untie one knot a day, and when the string was once again smooth, it was time to attack. The plot was leaked to the Spanish, but because of their arrogant belief that the Native peoples would never revolt, they ignored the information. Realizing the plot had been discovered, the people of Tesuque began the revolt by killing a Spanish man who lived with them. The next morning, when their priest arrived for Mass, one of the Pueblo told him that someone wanted to talk to him behind the church. When he returned with bloodied hands, the soldier who had accompanied the priest fled for his life. Priests, settlers, and soldiers were killed along with Native Americans who were seen as collaborators with the Spanish. Churches and all other vestiges of European influence were destroyed.

The Spanish deserted New Mexico after being besieged in Santa Fe by the Pueblo. The governor, soldiers, and settlers, as well as several Native Americans who preferred to remain with the Spanish, were allowed to flee to the south and the safety of Mexico. Unlike the Spanish, the Pueblo did not seek vengeance through cruel acts but only taunted and insulted the captives as they began their march south past the victors. The Europeans were gone from the Southwest, but it would not be for long.

Tentative forays into New Mexico by the Spanish occurred within a few years after the revolts, with some people welcoming them back. One problem was that after their victory, Popé seems to have become a tyrannical leader who some of the Pueblos saw as being worse than the Spanish. The Pueblo had traded for centuries with the Plains tribes to the east and they had always been on good terms with each other, but the Spanish drove a wedge between them, turning the Plains Indians against the Pueblo.

This was fine as long as the Spanish were there with their guns to protect the Pueblo, but after they had left, the Pueblo were exposed to the violence of the Plains Indians, another reason they wanted the Spanish to return. Settlers would not return until 1696, and then they were much more tolerant of the Pueblo peoples.

In the 18th century the Santa Fe Trail was opened, bringing much trade into the Southwest as Santa Fe was the western terminus where the Spanish and Pueblo gathered to buy and exchange goods with the Americans. But the trail was plagued with attacks by the Comanche, Apache, Ute, and Navajo, who were shut out for the most part from the trading and so chose to raid instead.

By 1783, Spain controlled all of the southern United States from the Atlantic to the Pacific. Mostly because of their hatred for the British, the Spanish had supported the Americans in the Revolutionary War but did not like them, describing them as "nomadic like Arabs and . . . distinguished from savages only in their color, language, and the superiority of their depraved cunning and untrustworthiness."[4]

The continued expansion of the Americans into the West was cause for concern to the Spanish but they faced other problems: a weakening presence in the world and increased pressure from Mexico that finally resulted in Mexican independence in 1821. In 1824, a constitution was adopted that made Mexico a republic, but the leadership of General Antonio López de Santa Anna, who presided over Mexican politics for 30 years, revoked the constitution, thus leading to decades of unrest, brought about the loss of Texas in 1836, and finally lead Mexico to defeat in the Mexican-American War from 1846 to 48. Through the Treaty of Guadalupe Hildalgo on February 2, 1848, and the Gadsden Purchase on December 30, 1853, the United States increased its territory by one-third, or more than a million square miles (2,590,000 square km), adding Texas, New Mexico, Arizona, California, Nevada, Utah, half of Colorado, and parts of Wyoming, Kansas, and Oklahoma. This had all been Indian land.

The Native peoples of the Southwest had suffered under the Spanish and then under the Mexicans through repression and loss of territory. Now, under the Americans, it would soon be much worse.

Manifest Destiny. This term represented the belief of Americans in their God-given right to possess the entire continent and everything on it. It meant land that was needed or wanted by settlers from the east but that was occupied by Native Americans had to be freed up. And then there was the problem of Native American attacks on whites and supply lines in the West. The "Indian problem" had to be solved. The solution? Reservations. Place Native Americans on land that no one else wanted,

---

4. Walker, 73.

make them into settled farmers, and they would be "civilized." If not, simply eliminate them.

In 1862, Kit Carson was sent to subdue the Navajo. When the army had tried to remove them, they disappeared into the surrounding rocks like spirits in the wind. General James Henry Carleton had been put in charge of the Southwest and decided that the Navajo should be placed on a reservation in eastern New Mexico at Bosque Redondo. However, they could not be rounded up. Carson approached the problem from a different angle. Rather than try to capture the Navajo, he destroyed their homes, the hogans, drove off their sheep, goats, cattle, and horses, burned the grain, and cut down the fruit trees, starving them into submission. Carleton had estimated there were a few hundred Navajo; in fact, there were 12,000. Starving, they began to surrender in the winter of 1863.

On August 1, 1863, the first group was sent on the march to Bosque Redondo, which is on the Pecos River, a trek of 300 miles (482 km) that would take three weeks and become known as the Trail of Tears. Slave traders snatched children and stragglers, ignored by the soldiers guarding them. Although army records dispute it, Navajo oral tradition tells of the marchers' being killed by soldiers if they fell, stopped to rest, or complained about being sick, or if a woman began in labor.

By March 1865, over 9,000 had surrendered and been sent to Bosque Redondo, joining 400 Mescalero Apache, enemies of the Navajo, already settled there. There was no drinkable water and the alkaline soil would not grow crops; neither were there any trees to cut for houses. It is still a barren region today. In late 1865, the Apache escaped: One morning they had simply vanished. In 1868, with conditions growing worse, and pressure from the east, where news of the living conditions had become known, the Navajo were released and allowed to return to their homeland, Dinétah. Their numbers had been reduced to around 4,000. Today there are over 200,000 living on one of the largest reservations in the United States.

The 20th century has been one of continuing land claims and water rights battles with the US and state governments, as well as a new-found spirit and dignity among the various Pueblo nations. The Pueblo continue to work to better educate their people and preserve their language and culture, and some are glad to share that culture, and their story, with tourists. Today there are 19 pueblos in New Mexico and one in Arizona inhabited by the descendants of the ancient Pueblo people. The foreign invaders of their lands have tried through various methods, some subtle, others blatant, to eliminate their culture, and in some cases, the people, but they have failed. The Native Americans of the Southwest have existed for more than 10,000 years and most likely will survive for another 10,000. The People will always be here.

FURTHER REFERENCE

Agriculture

Corn became the most important crop to the Ancestral Puebloans and was a vital component to their long term success in spreading across the Colorado Plateau. It began as a wild tropical grass with a small seed head somewhere in central Mexico and was first domesticated, that is, planted and cultivated rather than just collected as wild seed, around 5000 B.C. The plant eventually spread into the Southwest by about 2000 B.C. and was fairly widespread by 350 B.C., though it would not become a mainstay of the peoples' diet until after A.D. 900. By A.D. 1000, by means of selective breeding of the plants, the people had developed hardy, drought-resistant varieties with large cobs and grains that were easier to grind. In the 1100s they used a variety that could be planted 1 foot (30 cm) deep to take advantage of the moisture farther down in the soil.

As a hedge against the ever unpredictable climate in the Southwest, several different fields were planted in widely separated areas, as rain can fall in one place while completely missing another nearby. This technique also helped to control insect infestation and lessen the spread of disease. Multiple plantings and different varieties also increased the success of the crops.

Corn does not require too much water when first planted (just enough to germinate) or once it is mature, but it does need a fair amount when growing, which would coincide with the rainy season, if you can call it that, from July through September. But although most of the corn was grown with the method known as dry farming, the Ancestral Puebloans also supplemented the rainfall in other ways. They dug ditches and canals, built check dams and diversion dams, used terracing, and bordered gardens and reservoirs. The ditches and canals were used where they had reliable constant sources of water: either rivers or streams. Check dams were built across arroyos to slow and collect water during a flash flood. Moisture-laden silt would also accumulate behind the check dams, producing a nutrient-rich soil in which to plant. Diversion dams controlled the flow of water by directing it into bordered gardens, gardens with an earth or stone border built around them to hold in the water. Fifteen diversion dams have been located in Chaco Canyon that would have watered massive bordered gardens divided into more than 10,000 small fields. And to control evaporation in these huge plots, a gravel mulch was used that not only held in the moisture but raised the temperature of the soil, increasing the number of frost-free days for the corn to grow, as much of the Colorado Plateau is at the limit of days needed for corn to mature.

Some sites, such as Aztec Monument, were built near reliable streams; others, such as Hovenweep, near the head of a canyon with a spring. Seasonal streams and washes were used at Chaco Canyon and reservoirs at Far View in Mesa Verde. No matter the conditions, the Ancestral Puebloans managed to find a way to utilize the water sources to their advantage.

They faced other problems in growing corn. The wind can be fierce, especially in the spring, when the stalks are small and weak, and can destroy a crop. To prevent this, they would build piles of brush around the field or use broken pieces of pottery to protect the young plants. And animals could be trouble— these tender green plants would be tempting, sprouting in the desert, so we

Squash, foreground left, and corn

find built next to fields many remains of field houses—small buildings used on a temporary basis—in which someone could live close to the crops and protect them. Of course the problem with deer, rabbits, and mice in the fields was also a benefit, as the crops would draw them in where they would be easier to trap and hunt.

Corn was eaten fresh by roasting it in its husk over an open fire, but mostly it was dried either on the cob, the more common method, or the kernels were removed. It would be stored in this condition and then ground as needed on the metates using the hand-held manos. The ground corn would be made into flatbread or cooked in a stew with other ingredients.

An early crop planted with corn was squash, similar to modern pumpkins. Squash was also domesticated in central Mexico at least 1,000 years earlier than corn, though both reached the Southwest at around the same time. As its flesh is difficult to dry, squash was probably grown for its seeds, which could be easily dried. Squash spreads out over the ground and has large leaves that help to hold in moisture, so it would be planted in between the rows of corn and also along the edges as a windbreak.

Humans cannot survive on corn alone. Corn is high in protein but lacks an important amino acid, lysine, and was supplemented with protein from meat to produce a balanced diet. However, meat was an unreliable source, so an important remedy for this lack of protein was the introduction of beans, developed in central Mexico around 2000 B.C. The problem with beans is that, although they are easy to dry, it is difficult to grind them into flour and they must be cooked for a long period of time. When the Ancestral Puebloans were cooking in baskets with hot rocks, the temperature would not rise high enough for long enough to thoroughly cook beans, so it does not seem too much of a coincidence that beans became important to their diet only after the introduction of pottery. A baked clay vessel could be placed in or over the fire and left unattended for long periods of time, thus allowing the ingredients to cook completely. Corn must also be cooked thoroughly to release its nutrients so cooking in clay pots also meant an increase in the nutritional value of staple foods.

Even with corn and beans, the people still lacked protein, especially needed for children and pregnant women. Their diet had to be supplemented with meat, but as the population expanded, game was pushed farther from the settlements, depleting the animals' natural habitat; and with increased hunting, there were more people but less prey. Many Ancestral Puebloan skeletal remains show malnutrition. There was plenty to eat but the nutritional value of their diet was not high enough to meet their needs.

But even with all the problems associated with living in a region that was marginal at best for agriculture, the Ancestral Puebloans were able to sustain themselves and increase their population over several centuries. This is a testament to their ingenuity and abilities as farmers.

Archaeology

Archaeology is the study of past civilizations from the remains that have survived over time. The dry climate of the Southwest is ideal for the preservation of objects, but even with this advantage, only a small percentage of what was made has survived or been found. Certain objects, such as lithics, pottery, and stone buildings, survive extremely well, whereas organic material, cloth, and wood, do not. These disintegrate if exposed to the elements, so the only time they are discovered intact is when found in caves or buried deep in the soil.

Archaeology is based on a simple principle: The deeper you dig, the older it is. This is known as stratigraphy, or the layering of the soil, with the youngest objects closer to the surface and the oldest at the bottom. This idea was adopted from geology in the 19th century and used in the late 19th and early 20th centuries to construct what are known as relative chronologies. Relative dating was the first attempt to date archaeological sites, but is limited in only establishing which objects are older compared to other objects; it cannot tell us how old something is. Relative dating was first developed using pottery in Egypt at the end of the 19th century by Flinders Petrie, one of the pioneers of archaeology.

When archaeology was in its beginning stages in the Southwest at the end of the 19th and into the early 20th centuries, there was no way to date sites, so even though archaeologists knew the material was old, they had no way to determine how old. This would change in the 1920s, when A. E. Douglass, an American astronomer from the Southwest, developed tree-ring dating, also known as dendrochronology, simply written *dendro*. Douglass was interested in using the growth rings of trees to study climate change. A tree adds a new ring of wood each year, and depending on the climate, the ring will be wide if the year was wet and narrow if dry. By overlapping rings of the same width of progressively older trees, a master sequence can be constructed to which samples are compared and placed within the sequence (see Figure 1). This was one of the first absolute chronologies that gave exact, or nearly exact, calendar dates to structures with wooden beams. By using dendro on samples taken from Mesa Verde and Chaco Canyon Douglass was able to give the first precise dates for sites in the Southwest, dates that proved wrong nearly every archaeologist working in the region at that time! The entire chronology had to be rewritten, but no one was complaining as archaeologists finally had a method to date their sites accurately.

The next breakthrough in archaeology would come in 1949, when an American chemist, Willard Libby, introduced radiocarbon dating. Carbon is in the air and absorbed by all living things, but as soon as something dies, the carbon begins to deteriorate at a constant rate that can be measured. If you know the amount of carbon 14, written C14, in the living organism and compare this with what remains in the object to be dated, you will have an approximate age. This technique works on all organic

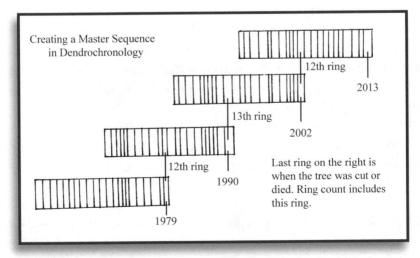

FIGURE 1: How to create a Master Sequence in dendrochronology

material that is less than about 50,000 years old. When we combine dendro and C14, it produces very accurate dates for Southwestern sites.

Archaeological sites are divided into a grid pattern, using small posts and string to provide a specific location when something is found, to enable it to be recorded with precision. The keeping of accurate records is vital in archaeology, as a site will be destroyed during the excavation process; all that remains are these records. When a site has been dug and the results are not published or are lost or destroyed, the site is lost forever; thus the importance of producing the findings for others to share.

Archaeology, like any other profession, has its own terminology. I will explain the most common terms as they are used in this work and other guidebooks. The "things" discovered by archaeologists are placed in specific categories to standardize the field and make the reports easily understandable no matter where the excavations take place. The most common term is *artifact*, which is an object that has been made, used, or altered by humans. *Structures* are the remains of buildings and can be as complete as Pueblo Bonito or as simple as a single row of stones on the ground. *Features* are hearths, storage bins, grinding bins, post holes, or anything that is not a structure or artifact. *Ecofacts* are natural objects found on a site that did not get there naturally but were brought in by humans, such as piñon nuts or animal bones. *Human remains* are the skeletal remains, whether complete or partial, of the people who created the cultural remains from the past. Some archaeologists place human remains under the heading of ecofacts, but I have always preferred to keep them in a separate category.

Today there is a growing interest in *field survey*, which is the examination of the surface for artifacts or the remains of structures over large areas. This requires walking great distances in a grid pattern and recording any sites but does not involve excavation, so it is less intrusive and destructive, and cheaper, as excavation is expensive. Another problem with excavation is acquiring rights to dig. Yet another is the storage of the vast amount of objects found, plus preserving the site if there are intact walls or rooms. There are also political problems, as some groups do not want sites disturbed or excavated, which they consider sacrilege.

Little or no excavation is being done today in any of the national or state parks or monuments, mostly due to pressure from Native American groups. The exception is *rescue archaeology*, which is when a site is in danger of being destroyed by the construction of roads or dams or is exposed by flooding or landslides. As more excavation produces little new knowledge, it makes sense to concentrate on what has already been discovered and find new approaches to study the Ancestral Puebloans. The sites that may be visited provide a wonderful opportunity for even nonarchaeologists to learn and appreciate the people who once lived there. However, some groups have gone as far as attempting to ban visitors from sites and allowing ruins to collapse and disappear. Closing sites or not preserving them, while following the beliefs of some of the descendants of the Ancestral Puebloans, would do nothing to help erase preconceived stereotypes of Native Americans. Such sites as Chaco Canyon and Mesa Verde showcase the skill and intelligence of the Ancestral Puebloan; people should be encouraged to see them, as nothing opens the mind more than knowledge.

Architecture

The Ancestral Puebloans were master architects, building structures on a scale seen nowhere else in North America. They are noted for massive and complex structures, as at Chaco Canyon and Mesa Verde, but also for some of the seemingly inaccessible sites, such as Chimney Rock.

Their architecture begins with the deceptively simple pithouse, a structure found in many parts of North America due to its practicality. The basic pithouse was dug into the ground to varying depths, generally getting deeper as time went on, with an antechamber, a central hearth, and a deflector stone. Four upright posts were placed in a square inside the pit, on top of which four horizontal beams were attached to support the roof. Next, smaller beams were placed at an angle from these to the ground around the edge of the pit, then small branches were added crosswise. Brush was placed on this, and finally adobe to seal it. The upper, flat part of the roof was finished in the same manner, leaving a hole in the center for the smoke to escape. If there was an antechamber, the pithouse it would be constructed in the same way, except a doorway would be left in the southern end. If there was no antechamber, entrance would be through the smoke hole.

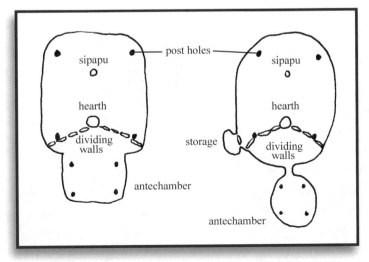

FIGURE 2: Pithouses, early A.D. 600s left, late 600s right

Later pithouses had low divider walls in the south end on each side of the entrance from the antechamber, creating an area for storage and food preparation. Many had a *sipapu* north of the hearth. The pithouse was always built on a north–south axis with the antechamber to the south and the *sipapu* to the north, with the hearth in between. The northeast corner was usually where the metates would be for grinding grain; the west side was for sleeping. The shape of the pithouse could be round, square, rectangular, oval, or square with round corners and the preferred shape changed over time and varies with location. Pithouses have been found nearly everywhere in the Southwest.

The earliest pithouses were very shallow, less than a foot (30 cm) deep, usually round with an antechamber. These are found mostly in caves and under rock overhangs. By the A.D. 500s they were about 3 feet (0.9 m) deep but still the same shape as earlier. In the early 600s they were deeper and could be round, square, or rectangular, averaging 20 feet (6 m) in diameter, with a wide entrance from the antechamber. At the end of the 600s, the entrance from the antechamber was a narrow passage; in some cases it was eliminated and replaced with a ventilation shaft. In the P I period, the pithouses were square with round corners and 6 to 7 feet (2 m) deep. The pithouse would continue to be used up to P IV.

Although the pithouse continued to be used as a living area, it developed another use beginning in P I: the kiva. A kiva is almost exactly the same as a pithouse but does not have the wing walls dividing the space; also, the exterior walls are stone; in fact, in some cases, it is difficult to determine whether a structure was a kiva or pithouse. Kivas are on a north–south axis, with the ventilator shaft on the south, the hearth in the middle, and a *sipapu* on the north. Some kivas had places where looms were set up for weaving. Entrance is always through the roof over the hearth, though occasionally there was a secondary entrance by a tunnel, either from a room block, tower,

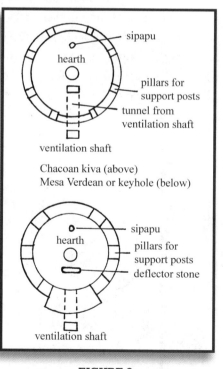

Chacoan kiva (above)
Mesa Verdean or keyhole (below)

FIGURE 3:
The two basic types of kin kivas

or another kiva. The small kivas were for ceremonies within a family group and are called kin kivas. The large ones, over 45 feet (13.7 m) in diameter, are great kivas and were used for the same purpose, except instead of being for just one family, the entire village and surrounding communities would be involved. While mainly religious in nature, they were occasionally used as living space, especially in the winter.

Kivas were mostly round but a few are square or rectangular, though the layout is the same no matter the shape. There are two basic types: the Chacoan, which originated in Chaco Canyon; and the keyhole, also known as Mesa Verdean, originating in the Mesa Verde region north of the San Juan River (see Figure 3). Nearly all kivas are similar to, or some variation on, these two types. The Chacoan is round, has a low banquette around the interior, eight support posts for the roof, and a central hearth. The ventilator shaft is under the floor opening in front of the hearth and does not require a deflector stone, though some have them. A *sipapu* may or may not be present. A keyhole kiva has a higher banquette, six support posts, and a hearth. The ventilator shaft enters the wall in the wide recessed "keyhole," so a deflector stone is needed to protect the fire from sudden drafts. A *sipapu* is nearly always present. Entrance for both types was through a square hole in the roof through which the smoke escaped.

Both types had cribbed roofs, producing a domed ceiling and flat roof. To construct this, cribbing beams would be laid horizontally from the tops of posts set on the six or eight stone pillars around the interior of the kiva. A second row would span these first beams from center to center, a third on the second, and so on, with each succeeding row narrowing toward the center until the entire space was enclosed by a dome, leaving only the square opening over the hearth (see Figures 4 and 5). Smaller sticks and brush covered these beams, then dirt filled the space up to the surface on which adobe finished the flat roof. Kivas are found at almost every Ancestral Puebloan site and continue to be used by Pueblo today.

The great kiva may have originated in Chaco Canyon, as possibly the oldest discovered was excavated in a BM III pithouse village on one of the eastern mesas overlooking the canyon. Most great kivas are round with a minimum diameter of 45 feet (13.7 m). They have a raised stone hearth, foot drums on each side of the hearth, floor cists, and footings for four large pillars to support the roof. The pillars are square and made of stone and wood, sitting on large stone disks set in a pit. Great kivas are dug below the surface but are also partially aboveground. They are oriented north–south, the same as kin kivas. The entrance is from a room on the north rather than through the roof. There was an altar in this north room; a few had tunnels under the floor, leading in from the entrance room. There are also some rectangular great kivas: at Fire Temple on Chapin Mesa and Long House on Wetherill Mesa, both in Mesa Verde.

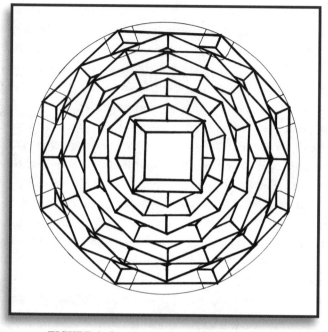

FIGURE 4: Overhead view of a cribbed roof

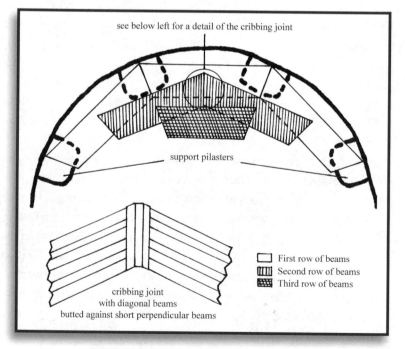

FIGURE 5: Details of the cribbing process

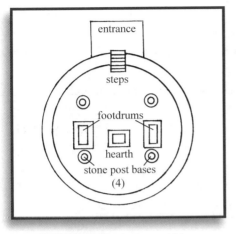

FIGURE 6: Typical great kiva

The earliest aboveground structure the Ancestral Puebloans built was the ramada—four posts stuck in the ground with a brush-covered roof—used as a shaded place to work in during the summer. From these humble beginnings the Ancestral Puebloans added more posts, wove branches through the posts, and filled the spaces with adobe, a technique known as wattle and daub or jacal (pronounced *hacal*). This type of structure was much easier to expand than a pithouse, as rooms could be added at either end as needed. A pithouse is difficult to enlarge and there are few examples of any that were.

Next, the people began to use upright stone slabs around the base of the jacal walls, a technique they had been using for belowground storage bins. Then stone foundations were built and entire walls of sandstone. This material is readily avail-

Sandstone building blocks from a collapsed wall, Pueblo Pintado

able in most regions of the Southwest. It breaks off in thin slabs almost ready made as masonry blocks. Early stone houses had one story but it was not long before they developed the ability to add a second, third, and more stories. Rooms tended to be small, averaging about 10 feet (3 m) across and 5 to 6 feet (1.5 m) high, except in Chacoan construction, where rooms were almost twice this width and height, and in some cases larger.

While the majority of rooms were square or rectangular, the Ancestral Puebloans experimented with other shapes, such as round and oval, especially for their towers. These structures illustrate the great skill in masonry that they developed, as the towers are not only round but the stones are also formed to follow the curve of the structure. Although most of the mesa-top sites were ideal for construction, in many cases the people built on cliff edges and in caves where natural rock formations were impossible to remove, so they had to adapt to the terrain. Some of the most interesting walls wind their way over and around large boulders, becoming an extension of the natural rock. Many examples of this are visible in Mesa Verde and Hovenweep.

The way the Ancestral Puebloans built walls is divided into two types, Chacoan and Mesa Verdean, but there are several variations on these. Chacoan style was used for most structures in Chaco Canyon and the outlier sites. It consisted of numerous small, flat stones placed in a core and veneer wall (see photograph, left) . The stones

Chacoan masonry

are all tied together across the width of the wall. The interior stones are rough, while the exposed surfaces are smooth. This system is very strong; combining this style with tapered walls, wider at the bottom than the top, the Chacoans were able to construct four- and five-story freestanding structures. Some might have been higher.

Mesa Verdean masonry uses large rectangular blocks of sandstone about the size of a loaf of bread. Using harder, smaller stones that leave the characteristic pot marks visible on the exterior, the blocks are pecked square and straight or curved for towers (see photo page 431). Single-course walls—that is, one stone wide—are found in older structures, but later construction used double courses

Mesa Verdean pecked block

to support two- and three-story structures. Some of the room blocks are four stories and a few might have been five, but these tend to have been the cliff dwellings. These were built against the back walls of the caves, which gave added support, as opposed to being freestanding, as in Chaco Canyon.

All the walls were held in place by mud mortar referred to as adobe. In the type I masonry from Chaco Canyon, the Chacoans used large amounts of mortar with fewer stones but this proved to be weak, so subsequent construction has more stones placed closer together with a minimum amount of mortar. The outsides of walls were covered with adobe to help protect the stability, as it is easier to maintain a flat surface of mortar than to try to repair the stone work. Of course, the way these buildings looked when built was vastly different from what we see today. A good example of what the original looked like can be seen at Acoma and the museum at Anasazi State Park.

When the Ancestral Puebloans began living in the surface pueblos, the building placement became standard and is known as the unit pueblo. The unit pueblo consisted of a room block on the north, a plaza and kiva to the south, and a midden on the southern edge. The north–south axis was probably to take advantage of the winter sun for heat, but it also follows the pattern of the pithouse and kiva, so there may have been more significance to it than we understand. This alignment is seen before the development of pueblos in some of the pithouse villages and so was consistent over a long period of time. Even in the largest structures at Chaco Canyon, the unit pueblo arrangement can be found; also in the P IV massive pueblos along the Rio Grande; a few early villages had room blocks arranged in a square.

Ancestral Puebloan architecture is remarkably similar over a vast territory in not only technique but function. The fact that most of the Colorado Plateau is sandstone, a wonderful building material, in part accounts for this, but the architecture also illustrates the strength of the culture. It is interesting to see the connection of their structures to the natural environment: In many cases it is difficult to tell where nature ends and building begins, demonstrating how their culture was part of the natural world; that is, they were able to understand and work with nature. Of course, whether this similarity was intentional or an accident of the easy accessibility of the materials used, we will never know.

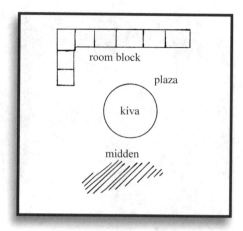

FIGURE 7: The unit pueblo

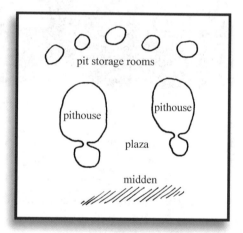

FIGURE 8: Early pithouses in the unit pueblo layout

Geology

The geology of the Southwest is diverse and complex and I offer only a simplified overview of one of the most beautiful and awe-inspiring geologic areas of the world. More detailed description is included with some of the Grand Circle Tour sites.

The region around the Four Corners' area that was inhabited by the Ancestral Puebloans is known geologically as the Colorado Plateau, which in turn consists of several smaller plateaus. These are subdivided into mesas and finally into the smallest formations, buttes, followed by rock spires. The Colorado Plateau contains mostly sedimentary rock that is formed in layers by various materials that produce different types of stone, depending on the original material: Gravel formed conglomerates;

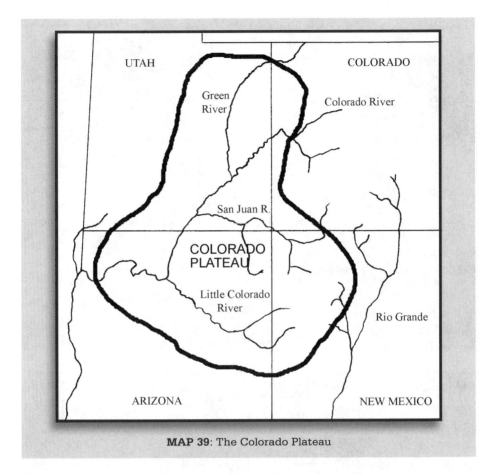

MAP 39: The Colorado Plateau

sand became sandstone, the predominant type of rock on the Plateau; mud turned into shale; and limey ooze formed limestone. They are cemented together with lime silica and iron in varying amounts, which partially determines their respective resistance against erosion. The layers are almost always horizontal and contain other elements, such as the fossilized remains of seashells, fish, trees, snails, bones, tracks, and dinosaurs. The way they were formed created wondrous, abstract formations.

Another type of rock found in the Southwest, but less common, is igneous, which originates from volcanoes. If the lava cooled slowly underground, it formed granite, but if it cooled quickly on or near the surface, it became basalt, the black, porous rock usually associated with volcanic eruptions. This type is found around Sunset Crater and Wupatki and just east of the Colorado Plateau near Albuquerque.

Another force of nature involved in the formation of the Southwest is plate tectonics. The earth's crust is made up of several plates that float over the outer semi-

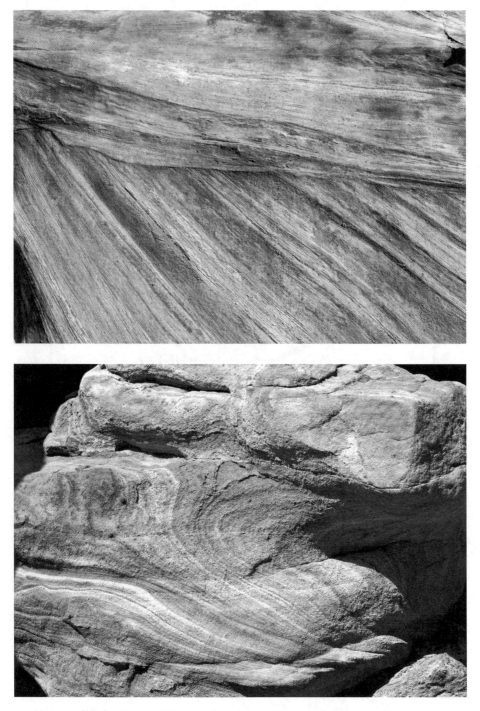

Top: Sandstone; Bottom: Swirls

Top: Sandstone from windblown sand; Bottom: Layers in the sandstone

liquid mantle of the earth. These plates are constantly moving, bumping into one another and building up great pressure that, when released, creates earthquakes. Not only do the plates move sideways relative to one another, but they slide under or over their neighboring plates, causing uplift or sinking.

The formation of the Colorado Plateau began in the Cretaceous period, 100 million years ago, when the Southwest was much farther south than it is today, close to where Mexico City is located, and near the ocean. It was a coastal plain with swamps and marshes, rivers and deltas, tropical vegetation, and dinosaurs. The sea advanced and retracted many times during the Cretaceous period, depositing multiple layers of sediments. Toward the end of the Cretaceous period, around 65 million years ago, was the extinction of the dinosaurs.

There was a westward movement of the North American plate over the Pacific Ocean plate at this time, raising the land and moving it to the west. A new landscape was formed of uplands and shallow basins along with Lake Flagstaff, several thousand square miles (several thousand square km) in size and covering much of the Plateau region. The lake was filled with much rock and debris over time, the heavier near the shore, the lighter farther toward the center, and there was a great amount of expansion and contraction over millions of years. During expansion, limey clays and silts accumulated in the lake bottom; during periods of contraction, rivers brought in sand and gravel. These sediments were cemented together by calcium carbonate of an unknown origin. It was a subtropical environment inhabited by birds, insects, small reptiles, and mammals that had replaced the dinosaurs. Over 2,000 feet (600 m) of sediment accumulated in Lake Flagstaff but the remains today vary from 600 to 1,300 feet (180–400 m).

From 37 to 19 million years ago was the most violent period of volcanism in North America, though most of this volcanic material has now eroded away. By 16 million years ago, there was a great upward movement and the Colorado Plateau was raised over 5,000 feet (1,500 m). Prior to this uplift, the rivers meandered slowly through shallow valleys over a land that was mostly flat, but afterward the rivers became more powerful, causing much erosion, which is responsible for what we see today.

Bedding planes are the horizontal cracks evident in many places throughout the Southwest and the vertical cracks are joints. The freeze/thaw cycle creates many of these cracks, especially on south-facing walls. During the winter months, the sun warms the ice, turning it to water which sinks into the cracks in the rock and then at night refreezes expanding about 10 percent and exerting a force of 2,000 pounds per square inch (140 kg per square cm), forcing the split ever wider. When the sun returns, the cycle repeats itself. Plant roots also work their way into any opening in the rock; as they grow, the cracks are enlarged. Flash floods also contribute to erosion.

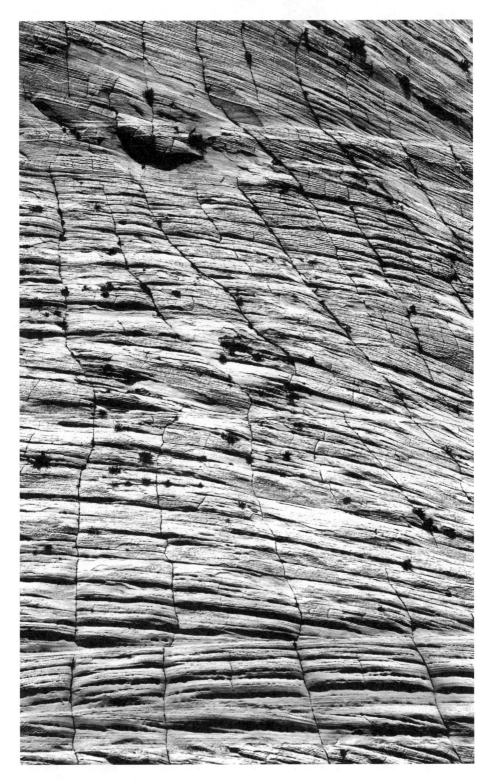

Bedding planes and joints

The difference in hardness of the various rocks results in an uneven rate of wearing, known as differential erosion. This is how the strange shapes are formed in Bryce Canyon, Arches, and other places around the Southwest. The overlying layer of rock erodes more slowly than that which is underneath, eventually leading to the collapse of the upper layers. Another factor that aids differential erosion is the slightly acid nature of water, which dissolves the alkaline "cement" binding the sedimentary rock together. The amount and strength of the cement varies greatly and this also helps to determine the rate and pattern of erosion.

But the wearing away of rock by running water is perhaps the most dramatic and visible form of erosion in the Southwest. There are several rivers in the region but the most important is the Colorado. The Colorado River is 1,450 miles (2,333 km) long and originates in the Rocky Mountains northeast of the Plateau. It drains into the Gulf of California as it is on the west side of the Continental Divide. It drains a watershed of 240,000 square miles (621,600 square km), descends 10,000 feet (3050 m) over its course, and averages 300 feet (90 m) in width. The flow of a river is measured in cubic feet (or liters) per second; that is, how many cubic feet of water pass by a fixed point in one second. The lowest flow on the Colorado was 700 cubic feet (20,000 liters) on December 28, 1924. The most ever recorded was 127,000 cubic feet (3,600,000 liters) on July 2, 1927, but on July 8, 1884, before official records were kept, it is estimated that the flood exceeded 300,000 cubic feet (8,500,000 liters). The flow also has the capacity to move suspended solids, including sand, pebbles, rocks, and large boulders in its waters with a low of 100 tons (90 mt) per day to as much as 27,600,000 tons (25,000,000 mt) during the flood in 1927. The average is around 390,000 tons (354,000 mt) per day. The estimated rate of erosion for the entire drainage area is 6 inches (15 cm) over 1,000 years.

When the Colorado Plateau was pushed up about 13 million years ago, the force was uneven, causing the south to lift higher than the north so the rock layers tilt down toward the north. This uplift was followed by a period favorable for erosion that left behind what is known as the Grand Stairway.

Three great geologic wonders were the result of the creation of the Grand Stairway: Bryce Canyon, Zion, and the Grand Canyon. These are "stacked" one on top of the other with Bryce, the farthest north and the top of the stairway, sitting on top of Zion, the middle step, which rests on the Grand Canyon, the bottom step. But because the land is at an angle, the differences in elevation are small, less than 1,000 feet (300 m) at the respective rims, while the depth exceeds 10,000 feet (3,000 m) from the rim of Bryce to the canyon floor of the Grand Canyon. The age of the rocks in the three varies greatly from about 12 million years on the upper layers of Bryce to two *billion* years in the depths of the Grand Canyon. At one time this land was fairly flat, but not today. The spectacular scenery visible along the Grand Stairway is the result of erosion caused by the rivers and streams that cut through the stairway, a true wonder of nature.

The problem with geologic time is the usually exceedingly slow pace in comparison to human time; we are talking millions and even billions of years, numbers that are difficult to grasp. Due to this slow pace it is not apparent that the forces of erosion are constantly at work. If you visit the region more than once, even only a year later, it will have changed; though these changes are generally not noticeable; you can never see the same Southwest twice! I say the change is usually slow, but occasionally something dramatic happens, such as a landslide in Zion, or a huge chunk of rock that falls from an arch in Arches, or the collapse of thin spire, but these events are rare.

Lithics

Lithics are stone tools or points. These survive well under almost any conditions, so we have a good record of what the Ancestral Puebloans were making and using, though sometimes an object is found that has no identifiable purpose.

Stone points and some tools are made by striking a bigger stone with a smaller, harder one in a process called knapping. While this might seem easy, knapping requires a great deal of skill and precision. A few archaeologists have mastered the technique and in some places you can even take courses in stone knapping. Knapping can produce a large amount of flakes that are not useful; they are called debitage. The debitage is sometimes found in a place where many points were made. It can be reconstructed to understand the methods used, but the process is very time consuming. Not all stone works well to make points and tools and the most common type used in the Southwest is chert, a hard form of silica of various colors, found throughout most of the region. One of the best materials for knapping is obsidian, a hard volcanic glass that produced exceptional, and much sought after, points. There are only a few sources for obsidian in the region.

Projectile points, more commonly known as arrowheads, are found all across the Southwest and were attached to shafts of reed or small straight sticks to make a deadly weapon. Arrowheads

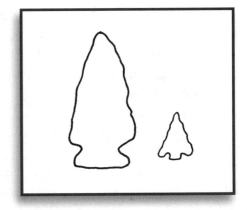

FIGURE 9: Dart, left; arrowhead, right. (not to scale)

are generally smaller than the end of your thumb and have notches at the base to attach them to the shaft, a process called hafting. These notch types varied over time and location helping to identify and date them. Stone points are surprisingly sharp; in fact, the edges are sharper than stainless-steel scalpels used by surgeons today. A variation of the arrowhead is the dart or spearpoint, which is larger than the arrow points and has a different type of notching on the base. A dart would be hafted onto a short, pointed piece of wood that was then inserted into the spear shaft so when the spear struck an animal, the point would break off, releasing the shaft.

A biface is a piece of stone that has been worked on both sides. The most common object of this type is a knife. These are longer than spearpoints and were hafted to a larger piece of wood for a better grip. Knives were generally used to skin and dismember animals.

Drills are less common and were used to pierce such materials as shell and turquoise to make jewelry. The drill was spun back and forth between the hands or turned by using a small bow with the rope twisted once around the shaft of the drill and pulled to and fro like playing a cello. Only one end of a long piece of stone is worked and just the point is sharpened and shows signs of wear.

Cores, or core stones, are the base material for knapping and are usually larger than a fist. They tend to be round or oval. Big flakes would be split from the core and then worked into shape, depending on the tool or point required. Generally, when found, pieces have been broken off.

Hammerstones are small round or oval stones used for knapping, grinding pigments for painting, and shaping building stones. They tend to be of quartzite, a type of hard sandstone.

Ground stone includes metates, manos, and grinding slabs. Metates were used to grind corn. Their surface was pecked with a hammerstone before using to roughen it and make it more abrasive. The deep grooves you will see in metates indicate the wear from repeated use. Manos are either small one-hand types or larger two-hand and were used on the metates to grind the corn. They are usually flattened on one side and have a beveled edge from continued use. Both metates and manos were of sandstone, which wore off during use, depositing grit in the cornmeal, which was very hard on the peoples' teeth. Grinding slabs are flat with a slightly concave surface and were used to sharpen tools.

Polishing stones were used to smooth pots. Ceramic vessels were made by using long ropes of clay that would be placed around a base and then pinched together. The surfaces would have ridges, so both the inside and outside would be smoothed with these stones. After firing, the outside would be further polished to give it some gloss.

Abrading stones were of sandstone and used for sharpening wooden and bone tools and axes, and for shaping building stones.

Ax stones have three notches: one on each side and a third on the top. A wooden handle would be hafted to the ax using the side notches, with another rope over the top to stabilize the implement.

The People

The Ancestral Puebloans were the ancestors of today's Pueblo people, among others, and most likely looked very similar to them, as physical changes take a long time to appear in any particular group. They would have had dark brown skin and black hair and been somewhat stocky and muscular. The men were around 5 foot 4 inches (162 cm) tall, a few were 6 foot (182 cm); the women were about 2 inches (5 cm) shorter. Life expectancy was the early 40s, though some lived into their 80s; there was a high childhood mortality rate. Malnutrition is apparent as a corn diet does not provide enough nutrients on its own and causes problems with the teeth and gums. Tooth wear from the grit of the sandstone metates was common.

The Ancestral Puebloans suffered from osteoporosis and had respiratory problems caused by living in small, smoky rooms. Evidence of tuberculosis and degenerative arthritis is found in many skeletal remains. The men had bad backs from heavy lifting and the women show wear in the knees and elbows from the many hours spent on their knees, grinding corn. Many people had fractures, especially among the cliff dwellers, and some of these had been set, while others were not. Overall, the skeletal remains tell a story of a hard existence filled with manual labor, pain, and the constant threat of the lack of food.

During the warmer months the people wore very little clothing, if any, but they always wore sandals, which were woven from yucca thread and leaves. For the winter they made robes of rabbit fur wrapped around strings and woven together but later these robes were made from turkey feathers, which were easier to work with. Deer skin was used for coats but rabbit fur and turkey feathers were preferred. Dog and human hair woven into sashes and cotton garments appeared after A.D. 750. Their legs would be covered with woven grass.

For adornment, bone, shell, and turquoise necklaces and pendants were worn by both sexes, but the men seem to have had many more. The men also had long hair fashioned into various styles, while the women tended to cut theirs to use to make string.

The society was matrilineal, with property passing from mother to eldest daughter. When a man married he left his family and village to live with his wife's. She could divorce him at any time by exiling him from her clan. The village chief was usually male

Footprints possibly representing a migration

but a woman could hold the position, and both men and women had an equal say in the decisions concerning the village and/or family. Men did the weaving and the women made pottery. In many tribes across North America, women were in charge of building the home, as this was seen as a living being that was born from Mother Earth and was too important a task for men. There is no evidence among the Ancestral Puebloans as to who built the pueblos but very likely the women played a crucial role.

Origin and migration myths were important to their belief system. The origin stories tell of the people living on various levels underground and moving up through the underworld until they reached the final level after emerging from the *sipapu* onto the surface. The migration stories concern the spirit guides' leading and teaching the people as they moved to different locations. Ancestral Puebloan history is one of occupation, abandonment, and reoccupation around the Four Corners and it is possible they would have relocated again had their world not changed abruptly with the invasion of the Spanish. These stories are told and retold in the rock art but unfortunately we can only catch glimpses of them, as interpreting the images is very difficult. A few signs are indicative of migrations, including the footprints of humans and animals, as well as a spiral.

The Ancestral Puebloans practiced animism, whereby all people, animals, and objects posses a spirit or soul and none is more important than another, so all must be respected equally. Certain ceremonies would ask for the spirit of an animal to give itself to the hunter so that he, the hunter, and his family might survive. This was very important because if you killed something improperly, other spirits would not co-operate in the future and you might starve. There are many scenes of hunting and animals among the rock art images.

They believed that life was a journey in a circle and that we emerged from the underworld, lived on the surface, and would then return to the earth and reemerge in the future, completing the circle. The position of the body in death was important and the head was placed either toward the east-northeast or east-southeast for the rising sun at either the summer or winter solstice. Food, tools, pottery, clothes, and jewelry were placed in the graves for the afterlife and the journey to continue the circle.

Pueblos were divided between north and south for the summer and winter peo-ple. Summer people were responsible for summer rituals and ceremonies, and the winter people for the winter events. This is reflected in the burial positions: summer people were faced toward the summer solstice sunrise, northeast; winter people, toward the winter solstice sunrise, southeast. Rituals were important to ensure the circle continued, with an emphasis on rain, corn, and fertility. These were also con-nected to the celestial observations, which have been noted in many locations across the Southwest. It is vital to perform ceremonies at the correct time of year and this could be determined by the sunrise, sunset, and/or position of the sun during the day, which required careful and diligent observations by the sun watchers.

From the earliest times, the people traded over a vast territory but most likely not through specific "traders" who traveled from one place to another. Rather, goods and ideas would move slowly from village to village, with limited opportunities or means for travel. This would have been the way corn and other crops moved north over time, as well as irrigation techniques. Innovations would not only have migrated into the Southwest but would have changed and been adapted to local conditions as they passed through various territories. Cotton originated in Mexico and was first grown by the Hohokam in Southern Arizona, who traded it with the Ancestral Puebloans before they in turn began growing it themselves. And you must remember that in the case of corn, for example, it was between 2,000 and 3,000 years from its point of first domes-tication in central Mexico until its arrival in the Southwest, a very long period of time.

Other objects traveled faster but we are not able to tell by which route or in what way they got from point A to point B. What we do know is that the Ancestral Puebloans had trade goods in their possession from south, west, and east of their region including seashells from the coast of California, parrots and copper bells from western Mexico, and buffalo hides from the Plains tribes to the east. They probably were trading in turn turquoise and pottery.

Pottery

The earliest pottery produced by the Ancestral Puebloans was brownware dating between A.D. 200 and 500 and made from iron-rich clay with a natural temper. This clay produced a rough, coarse vessel that was not particularly durable. In the A.D. 500s the pottery was gray-brown, made from better clays and with temper added to the mix to produce a higher-quality vessel. The 600s saw the introduction of grayware, which would continue to be the standard for pottery production for several centuries. Tempers included iron, sand, silt, volcanic material, crushed rock, and ground-up pot sherds.

Pottery breaks easily and must be replaced on a regular basis, meaning that great quantities were produced. The quantity combined with its being virtually indestructible under most environmental conditions makes it one of the best objects for archaeologists to study. Even the broken pieces, known as sherds, are useful in estimating the number of whole vessels and for the study of painting styles. Pottery can be dated by style, as the designs changed over time and with location, but there is also an absolute dating method, known as thermoluminescence, abbreviated as TL. This method uses radioactive particles to date pottery in a way similar to C14, but C14 works only with organic material. When a vessel is fired, all radiation is freed from the clay, but once the vessel is buried in the soil, the clay begins to absorb radiation again, as there are radioactive minerals in all soil. After a vessel or sherd is excavated, the surrounding soil must be tested for its radioactive levels. Next, the sample is heated and the amount of radiation released is measured. This amount is compared to the soil radiation that has been absorbed at a constant known rate, resulting in an age for the pottery. It is not an easy method and proper collection methods must be employed to ensure correct dates.

There is much clay in the Southwest but not all of it can be used to make pottery, so a good source must first be found through trial and error. Once collected, the clay is cleaned of debris and impurities and then dried and ground on a metate into powder. Water and the temper are added. Clay does not bind to itself well when heated, so a hard material, such as sand or crushed stone, must be mixed in; this is the temper. Starting with a round base, coils of clay are pressed onto the flat base in the shape the pot will take. These are pinched together and then smoothed with a polishing stone or wooden paddle. If a vessel is going to be painted, a slip, a thin mixture of water and clay, is painted over the entire area and then the design is painted on the slip. The next step is to slowly dry the vessel as much as possible by placing it in the shade for several days or longer to prevent cracking when fired. Finished vessels were placed in a pit among the coals and ashes of a smoldering fire and buried for the firing process.

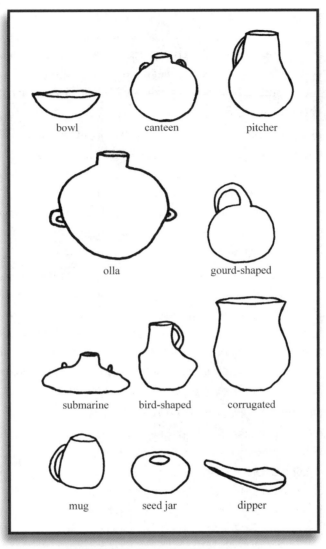

FIGURE 10: Typical pottery shapes

Some slab-lined pits have been found that are believed to have been kilns, but these are only from the P III period. One was 4 feet (1.2 m) wide by 10 feet (3 m) long and 1 foot (30 cm) deep. Sometimes abandoned pithouses were used.

It is possible the Ancestral Puebloans discovered the techniques for making pottery on their own, as they did line some baskets with clay for cooking. It is more likely that the knowledge was passed north from the Mogollon, who had a much earlier tradition with pottery. The Ancestral Puebloans had many different shapes of pots with new ones being added, while other shapes were discontinued over time. These shapes usually reflect their use but it is possible for one vessel to have had many and various uses. Painted designs also changed in both execution and subject matter. Following are listed some of the types of vessels made through the different periods and their changes in design, both of which are used in dating vessels and determining their place of manufacture.

BM II–III. During this time, brownware evolved to grayware, which would spread across the Southwest but with some differences: In the west they used organic-based paints and sand temper, while in the east, the paint was made from minerals and the temper was crushed stone. Late in BM III, the Ancestral Puebloans began painting designs on vessels, using geometric patterns in a rough, almost sloppy manner. It was mostly black paint on a white slipped vessel. Typical shapes included bowls, canteens, split gourd–shaped dippers, bird-shaped vessels, and odd figurines.

P I. Neck-banded pots were introduced by smoothing the entire vessel, except the wide neck, where the bands remained rough, creating ridges. The painted designs were still geometric but much more accurate and carefully drawn, with repetitive and bold patterns. Bowls, canteens, dippers, and bird-shaped vessels continued to be made, but several new shapes appeared: large water containers called ollas; tall pitchers with handles; seed jars that look like two bowls one on top of the other, with a small hole in the center of the top one; and gourd-shaped containers.

P II. Corrugated pots for cooking were introduced, on which the entire exterior was left rough, exposing the coils. This form gave a greater surface area to the pot and allowed the interior to heat faster than did those with a smooth surface. Corrugated pots were not painted. On smooth pots, the geometric patterns now covered most of the vessel and had bold striking lines, triangles, dots, and hatching, which drew attention to them. The surfaces were now polished with stones making them shiny and enhancing the painted patterns. Black on white is still the favored color combination, but in the northern Kayenta area the potters were painting black on red and making some with several colors, known as polychrome. Bowls, pitchers, canteens, ollas, bird-shaped pots, seed jars, and dippers continued with some new shapes: double and triple attached bowls, and long, narrow vessels with a small spout on the top that are referred to as submarines; their use is unknown.

P III. Effigy vessels in the shape of deer, elk, toads, and skunks, among others, became prominent, as well as pitchers with animal-shaped handles. Bowls, canteens, ollas, bird-shaped pots, seed jars, and dippers remain the same, but mugs first appeared, especially in the Mesa Verde region, as did tall cylindrical pitchers that seem unique to Chaco Canyon. The geometric designs were larger with bold complex patterns, and in the Kayenta region, the design became negative, with most of the vessel painted black, leaving only the lines in white. Corrugated was less popular and most of the rough coils were at least partially smoothed.

P IV. The pots had thicker walls by this time, which is an indicator of less-skilled potters, as it is more difficult to produce thin-walled vessels. Cooking pots were more carelessly made, pitchers were shorter, and the bowls were smaller and lower. Black on white continued but black on yellow became popular along with polychrome. The designs were made with large areas of paint and fewer lines and patterns. Swirling shapes and bird figures became prominent, as well as some mythical and human figures. Shallow and conical bowls, pitchers, seed jars, dippers, canteens, ollas, bird-shaped pots, and mugs were the prominent shapes.

P V. It is most likely that women were the ancient potters as this tradition has continued down through time to the present. Many of the designs seen on modern Pueblo pottery have a connection to the Ancestral Puebloan paintings—they are not necessarily copies, but a strong influence can be seen in some artists' work. Many of the Pueblo produce pottery that is readily available for sale in the region and there are a few artists whose work is internationally known.

Rock Art

The rock art of the Ancestral Puebloans is one of the most fascinating, and least understood, of the various cultural remains from the ancient Southwest. There are two types of rock art: petroglyphs and pictographs. Pictographs were made by painting images onto the rock surface with organic and/or mineral paints, usually in caves or rock overhangs, as paintings were more likely to be washed away over time if exposed to the elements. Petroglyphs were pecked into the rock surface exposing the lighter colored rock underneath the dark surface and were virtually permanent. Both types are very difficult to interpret.

The images are aesthetically pleasing, though this was probably not their intended purpose, or at least not their sole purpose. Some interpretations suggest the images were used to mark a shrine, record visions, rituals, dreams or battles, or ensure rain, good harvests, and fertility. They are not believed to be a form of writing, though there are stories and messages in the images.

They are found in many locations throughout the Southwest that are considered sacred. A few seem to have been used for astronomical observations, especially of the sun at the solstices and equinoxes and as calendrical markers. The most common

Sun markers, Hovenweep

symbol for these is the spiral, examples of which are found at Hovenweep and Chaco, among other places.

There are problems with dating the images as no direct method exists at this time. Estimates of lichen growth or mineral deposits on the images, repatination of desert varnish,[5] and the differing styles are some of the ways that have been used. Known subjects, such as horses or guns, can give a date after which these were introduced into the area. Also, comparisons to dated ceramics, murals, baskets, weavings, figurines, or jewelry incorporating similar images can give a fairly accurate date for the rock art.

Rock art is divided into two general categories: geometrical and representational. The earliest images are geometrical and were produced by hunter-gatherers, though this type does continue into later periods. There are no images from the Paleo-Indian period. From the Archaic we find zigzags, circles, triangles, wavy lines and snakelike designs, which filled large spaces. Into the Basketmaker period, representations appeared of birds and snakes, a symbol of rebirth, masks, horns on figures, and anthropomorphic figures with spirit helpers. Some scholars believe these early images could have been produced by shamans (spiritual leaders) under the influence of hallucino-

5. Desert varnish is the streaking that is seen on many canyon walls throughout the Southwest and is caused by a combination of water, minerals, and bacteria. Repatination is the recoating of a petroglyph with desert varnish.

gens, though this is speculative as no tradition of shamanism or the use of hallucinogens exists among the Pueblo people.

The Ancestral Puebloans produced images of flute players, hand- and footprints, hunting scenes, mountain sheep, bears, spirals, concentric circles and many other designs. Rock art continued into the postinvasion period, with the Paiute, Ute and Navajo producing images, in many cases in the same places as the ancients did, drawing horses, hunting scenes, and battles, among others.

Many of the rock art sites are easily accessible, with some next to highways. One unfortunate aspect of this easy accessibility is the fact that many sites have been damaged by vandals. Bullet holes and graffiti scar some images and in a few places people have tried to remove the art by chipping off a slab of the underlying rock, which usually ends in the destruction of the image when the panel breaks into pieces.

There are tens of thousands of these images throughout the Southwest and, whether one regards them as works of art, spiritual symbols, or a form of communication, there is much to admire about them and their creators.

Riders and horses, probably Ute

Glossary

abut: When two walls touch but are not attached to each other.

adobe: Mud mortar.

Anasazi: A group of people that inhabited the Colorado Plateau region and shared several cultural similarities, now mostly refered to as Ancestral Puebloans.

Ancestral Puebloans: Another name for the Anasazi.

antechamber: A small entrance and storage room attached to the south side of a pithouse.

archaeological site: An area that had been used by humans at some point in the past.

archaeo-astronomy: The study of ancient astronomy.

arroyo: A small gully with steep sides that is usually dry.

atlatl: A short stick or strap attached to the end of a spear and used to extend the length of the arm when throwing the spear.

backfill: To refill an excavation site when finished digging or to protect the site.

banquette: A low shelf or bench around the interior of a kiva or pithouse. Not used to sit on.

bedrock: Solid rock at or near the surface which continues deep below the ground.

butte: A hill with sheer sides topped with a hard capstone.

CCC: The Civilian Conservation Corps, which was set up during the Depression to create jobs. The people working for the CCC built roads and buildings and made improvements to the national and state parks, among many other projects.

cairn: A pile of stones used to mark a trail.

check dams: Dams built across gullies to slow the flow of water during heavy rains.

chert: One type of a hard silica used to make points and tools

chinking: Small stones chucked between larger building stones in a wall for added stability and strength.

cist: A stone-lined covered pit usually for storage.

core and veneer: A wall of interlaced flat stones that has a smooth exterior.

cradle board: A wooden frame that was used to carry infants, who were tied to it by cords. In the late BM III period, the baby's head was secured to a hard board, causing flattening of the back of the head.

cribbing: Wooden beams laid from center to center to form a hexagonal or octagonal dome.

deflector: An upright stone placed between the hearth and draft from the ventilator shaft.

dendrochronology: The method of archaeological dating using the relative width and number of growth rings from trees and wooden beams.

desert varnish: A thin glossy brown, blue, or black coloring caused by iron and manganese in combination with water and bacteria, appearing as streaks down cliff faces.

differential erosion: Differing rates of erosion due to the differences in hardness of two or more overlaying types of rock.

double course: A wall built two stone thicknesses wide.

dry wash: see *arroyo*.

drywall: Stones laid in a wall without mortar.

foot drums: Stone cists covered with animal skins and danced or pounded on with the feet.

Four Corners: The region surrounding the common intersection of four states: New Mexico, Arizona, Utah, and Colorado.

freeze/thaw cycle: The freezing of water in cracks of stone expands, thus enlarging the fissures. It then thaws during the warmth of the day, allowing the water to soak further into the rock before refreezing at night.

great house: A large D-shaped structure with many rooms and stories found mostly in Chaco Canyon.

great kiva: A kiva larger than 45 feet (13.7 m) in diameter set partially below and above ground level with a stone hearth, four interior support posts, foot drums, and a northern entrance.

hafting: The method of attaching a stone point, knife, or axe to a wooden shaft with cord.

hearth: A firepit. Can be both inside or outside structures.

Hohokam: A cultural group contemporary with the Ancestral Puebloans and living in southern Arizona between ca. 300 B.C. and A.D. 1450.

hoodoo: Rock spire eroded into a bizarre shape.

jacal: Wall construction using vertical poles interlaced with brush and covered with adobe. Also known as wattle-and-daub.

Kachina: See Katsina.

Katsina: Spirits of ancestors living on this level for half of the year and in the lower level the other half. They assist in ceremonies, bringing rain and ensuring good crops among other things.

kiva: An underground room for ceremonial and secular use. Kivas are either round, square, oval, or rectangular, with a hearth, ventilator, and, most of the time, a *sipapu*. Entrance is through the smoke hole in the flat roof.

lithics: Objects made of stone.

Macaw: A large red and green parrot imported into the Southwest from western Mexico for its feathers.

mano: A hand-held stone used for grinding grain into flour.

mesa: A large flat geographical area with steep sides and resistant cap rock, similar to a butte but much bigger.

metate: A grinding stone on which a mano is used to grind grain.

midden: A trash dump.

Mogollon: A cultural group contemporary with the Ancestral Puebloans who lived in southern New Mexico and east-central Arizona.

multicourse: A wall that is several stones thick. These walls allow higher multistoried room blocks.

outliers: Pueblos sharing building characteristics of the Chacoan great houses but located outside Chaco Canyon.

petrified: Organic material that has turned to stone as minerals slowly replaced the the original cells.

petroglyph: A symbol or picture pecked into rock. The dark surface layer is removed, revealing the lighter-colored stone underneath.

pictograph: A symbol or picture painted on rock.

pilaster: A square support post attached to a wall.

pillar: A square freestanding support post.

pithouse: A semi- or subterranean dwelling with a central hearth and sometimes an antechamber.

point: A stone arrowhead or spearhead.

pueblo: Spanish for "town."

Pueblo: Refers to a specific town for either the Ancestral Puebloans or their descendants. Also indicates the descendants of the Ancestral Puebloans.

ramada: Four wooden vertical poles with a roof of branches built for shade.

reconstruction: Rebuilding a collapsed section of an ancient room or building based on what someone believes it originally looked like.

rock art: See *petroglyph* and *pictograph*.

seep: Water that soaks vertically through permeable rock until it strikes hard rock, such as shale, and exits horizontally. Similar to a spring but with less water flow.

shard: A broken piece of glass. May also refer to a broken piece of pottery.

sherd: A broken piece of pottery.

Sinagua: A cultural group contemporary with the Ancestral Puebloans that lived around and south of the Flagstaff area and central Arizona.

single course: A wall that is only one stone thick.

sipapu: The Hopi word for "the place of emergence from, and return to, the underworld."

slick rock: Exposed sandstone bedrock, also referred to as slip rock.

spire: A tall, narrow upright piece of stone which can be straight or in contorted formations.

stabilized: Walls that have been reinforced in some way to prevent collapse but without changes or additions.

stone knapping: The art of producing stone points and tools from a core stone by splitting off flakes and forming them into the desired shape.

switchback: Where the road or trail goes back and forth around 180 degree curves. Usually found when climbing or descending a steep hill or mountain.

talus slope: The accumulation of rock debris at the bottom of a cliff.

temper: A hard binding material, such as sand or ground-up pot sherds, added to the clay used to make pottery.

tower kiva: A kiva two or more stories high that has all the standard features of a regular kiva (see *kiva*).

tree-ring dating: see *dendrochronology*.

turquoise: A bluish-green gemstone used for jewelry.

unit pueblo: A standard configuration consisting of room blocks on the north with a midden to the south and a kiva/plaza in between.

ventilation shaft: A shaft descending into a pithouse or kiva to bring in fresh air.

wash: A dry streambed that only occasionally has any water flowing in it.

Bibliography

Amber, J. Richard. *The Anasazi*. Flagstaff, AZ: Museum of Northern Arizona, 1989.

Baars, Donald L. *The Colorado Plateau*. Albuquerque: University of New Mexico Press, 2000.

Ballantine, Betty, and Ian Ballantine, ed. *The Native Americans*. Atlanta, GA: Turner Publishing Inc, 1993.

Beal, Merrill D. *Grand Canyon*. Las Vegas, NV: KC Publishing, Inc., 1978.

Bezy, John. *Bryce Canyon*. Las Vegas, NV: KC Publications Inc., 1980.

Chronic, Halka. *Pages of Stone*. Seattle: The Mountaineers, 1998.

———. *Roadside Geology of Utah*. Missoula, MT: Mountain Press Pub. Co., 1990.

Cordell, Linda S. *Prehistory of the Southwest*. San Diego, CA: Academic Press, Inc., 1984.

Dale, Bruck, and Jake Page. *The American Southwest, Land of Challenge and Promise*. Washington, DC: National Geographic Society, 1998.

Eardley, A. J., and James W. Schaack. *Zion*. Las Vegas, NV: KC Publications Inc., 1971.

Elliot, Melinda. *Great Excavations*. Santa Fe, NM: School of American Research Press, 1995.

Fairchild, Gary, and Glenn Raby. *Chimney Rock Archaeological Area*. Pagosa Springs, CO: Chimney Rock Interpretive Association Inc., 2005.

Ferguson, William M., and Arthur H. Rohn. *Anasazi Ruins of the Southwest in Color*. Albuquerque: University of New Mexico Press, 1986.

Johnson, David W. *Arches: The Story Behind the Scenery*. Las Vegas, NV: KC Publications, Inc., 1985.

Kidder, Alfred Vincent. *Southwestern Archaeology*. New Haven, CT & London: Yale University Press, 2000.

Knack, Martha C. *Boundaries Between: The Southern Paiutes, 1775–1995*. Lincoln and London: University of Nebraska Press, 2001.

Lavender, David. *The Southwest*. Albuquerque: University of New Mexico Press, 1980.

Lister, Florence C. *In the Shadow of the Rock*. Durango, CO: Herald Press, 1997.

Lister, Robert H., and Florence C. Lister. 1993 *Those Who Came Before*. Tucson, AZ: Western National Parks Association 1993.

_____. *Anasazi Pottery*. 1978, Albuquerque, NM: Maxwell Museum of Anthropology and Albuquerque: University of New Mexico Press, 1978.

Malville, J. McKim, and Claudia Putnam. *Prehistoric Astronomy in the Southwest*. Boulder, CO: Johnson Printing Co. 1998,.

Marriott, Alice. *Indians of the Four Corners*. Santa Fe, NM: Ancient City Press, 1952.

Martineau, LaVan. *Southern Paiutes; Legends, Lore, Language and Lineage*. Las Vegas, NV: KC Publications, 1992.

Minge, Ward Alan. *Acoma, Pueblo in the Sky*. Albuquerque: University of New Mexico Press, 1991.

Morrow, Baker H., and V. B. Price. *Anasazi Architecture and American Design*. Albuquerque: University of New Mexico Press, 1997.

Murphy, Dan. *El Morro National Monument*. Tucson, AZ: Western National Parks Association, 2003.

Nabokov, Peter, and Robert Easton. *Native American Architecture*. New York and Oxford: Oxford University Press, 1989.

Neitzel, Jill E., ed. *Pueblo Bonito, Center of the Chacoan World*. Washington, DC, and London Smithsonian Books, 2003.

Noble, David Grant. *Ancient Ruins of the Southwest*. Flagstaff, AZ: Northland Publishing, 2000.

_____., ed., *New Light on Chaco Canyon*. Santa Fe, NM: School of American Research Press, 1984.

Nordby, Larry V. *Prelude to Tapestries in Stone: Understanding Cliff Palace Architecture*. Denver, CO: Colorado Historical Society and Mesa Verde: CO: Mesa Verde National Park, 2001.

Plog, Stephen. *Ancient Peoples of the American Southwest*. London: Thames and Hudson, 2008.

Reed, Paul F., ed. *Foundations of Anasazi Culture: The Basketmaker-Pueblo Transition*. Salt Lake City: University of Utah Press, 2000.

Reid, Jefferson, and Stephanie Whittlesey. *The Archaeology of Ancient Arizona*. Tucson: University of Arizona Press, 1997.

Sando, Joe S. *Pueblo Nations*. Santa Fe, NM: Clear Light Pub. 1992.

Sebastian, Lynne. *The Chaco Anasazi: Sociopolitical Evolution in the Prehistoric Southwest*. Cambridge: Cambridge University Press, 1992.

Slifer, Dennis. *Guide to Rock Art of the Utah Region*. Santa Fe: Ancient City Press, 2000.

Snead, James E. *Ruins and Rivals*. Tucson: University of Arizona Press, 2001.

Stokes, William Lee. *Geology of Utah*. Salt Lake City, UT: Utah Museum of Natural History, 1986.

Stuart, David E. *Anasazi America*. Albuquerque: University of New Mexico Press, 2000.

Thompson, Ian. *The Towers of Hovenweep*. Moab, UT: Canyonlands Natural History Association, 2004.

Vivian, R. Gwinn, and Bruce Hilpert. *The Chaco Handbook*. Salt Lake City: University of Utah Press, 2002.

The Penguins, Arches National Park

Walker, Paul Robert. *The Southwest, Gold, God, and Grandeur*. Washington, DC: National Geographic Society, 2001.

Walling, Barbara A., Richard A. Thompson, Gardiner F. Dalley, and Dennis G. Weder. *Excavations at Quail Creek*. Salt Lake City, UT: Bureau of Land Management, 1986.

Wenger, Gilbert R. *The Story of Mesa Verde National Park*. Denver, CO: Good Stuff Publishing, 1980.

Index

Site Bc 50, Casa Rinconada, Chaco Canyon

Pueblo Bonito from the rubble of Threatening Rock, Chaco Canyon

Mummy Lake and entrance canal, Far View Community, Mesa Verde National Park

Great kiva, Salmon Ruins, New Mexico

Monument Valley, Utah

Mountain lion petroglyph

West section looking south, Pueblo del Arroyo, Chaco Canyon

Fire Temple (stop 9), Ruins Road, Mesa Verde National Park

Speaker Chief Complex (looking north), in Mesa Verde National Park